The Postmodern Urban Condition

To Jennifer,
Who made possible this enterprise.

The Postmodern Urban Condition

Michael J. Dear

University of Southern California

This publication was supported by Southern California Studies Centee
of the University of Southern California

First published 2000

2 4 6 8 10 9 7 5 3 1

Blackwell Publishers Ltd
108 Cowley Road
Oxford OX4 1JF
UK

Blackwell Publishers Inc.
350 Main Street
Malden, Massachusetts 02148
USA

British Library Cataloguing in Publication Data

A CIP catalogue record for this book is available from the Biritish Library.

Library of Congress Cataloging-in-Publication Data

Dear, M. J. (Michael J.)
     The postmodern urban condition / Michael J. Dear.
          p.   cm.
     Includes bibliographical references and index.
     ISBN 0–631–20987–5 (alk. paper)—ISBN 0–631–20988–3 (pbk.: alk. paper)
          1. Urbanization—California—Los Angeles. 2. Urbanization—Mexico—Tijuana (Baja California) 3. Urbanization—Nevada—Las Vegas. 4. Postmodernism—Social aspects—California—Los Angeles. 5. Postmodernism—Social aspects—Mexico—Tijuana (Baja California)
6. Postmodernism—Social aspects—Nevada—Las Vegas. 7. Human geography—California—Los Angeles. 8. Human geography—Mexico—Tijuana (Baja California) 9. Human geography—Nevada—Las Vegas. I. Title.

HT384.U52 L674 1999
307.76'09794'94 21—dc21

                                                                            99–043567

Typeset in 10 on 12pt Sabon by Kolam Information Services Pvt Ltd., Pondicherry, India

Printed in Great Britain by TJ International, Padstow, Cornwall

This book is printed on acid-free paper.

Contents

List of Figures

List of Tables

Preface

The tenets of modernist thought have been undermined, discredited; in their place, a multiplicity of new ways of knowing have been substituted.

Analogously, in postmodern cities, the logics of previous urbanisms have evaporated; absent a single new imperative, multiple forms of irrationality clamor to fill the vacuum.

The localization (sometimes literally the concretization) of these multiple effects is creating the emerging time–space fabric of what may be called a postmodern society.

Traditional concepts of urban form imagine the city organized around a central core; in postmodern urbanism, the urban peripheries are organizing the center.

There is no longer a conventional center in philosophy or in urbanism; what you see depends upon where you are seeing it from. In science, as in all human affairs, knowledge is inseparable from the people and places employed in producing it.

Acknowledgments

No one who writes from or about Los Angeles can avoid the influence of Mike Davis. Mike has done more than any other individual to focus serious critical attention on contemporary LA. For this, he has enjoyed acclaim, but also some of the most vitriolic personal criticisms. I will use this occasion to publicly thank Mike for making it possible for others to make a sustained scholarly case for Los Angeles.

I am especially grateful to Steven Flusty and Gustavo Leclerc, both of whom have graciously permitted me to use portions of previously published work co-authored with them.

Next, I must emphasize how fortunate I have been to live and work in Southern California for the past decade or more. The region is home to a remarkable collection of scholars, who together form what some call the "LA School." Inevitably, many of its members are colleagues at my home institution, the University of Southern California (USC). I especially thank those who have read pieces of this work at various stages, including Phil Ethington, Greg Hise, H. Eric Schockman, David Sloane, and Marita Sturken. Virtually the entire faculty of the Critical Studies department of the USC School of Cinema and Television has (at one time or another) contributed to my education, including Todd Boyd, Elizabeth Daley, David James, Marsha Kinder, Michael Renov, and Lynn Spiegel. At the USC School of Fine Arts, Selma Holo and Robbert Flick have also been extremely generous in sharing their time and wisdom; so has Abe Lowenthal of the School of International Relations. I have been fortunate in the quality of graduate and undergraduate students who have suffered through my sometimes-tortured disquisitions on postmodernism. There are too many to recall, but the current crop includes Aandrea Stang, Robert Wilton and Harmony Wu, all of whom continued conversations with me long after the course work was a distant memory. At USC's Southern California Studies Center (SC2), I have been greatly assisted by Lana Krtolica, Hector Lucero, Jaime Pacheco-Orozco, Richard Parks, Heidi Sommer, and Clare Walker. Dallas Dishman, Steven Flusty, and Lawrence Mull helped to pull this manuscript together.

Needless to say, the LA School is not limited to the faculty and students of USC. Across town at UCLA (*el otro lado*), Allen Scott, Ed Soja, and Michael Storper have been a constant inspiration. So have Dana Cuff, Kevin Daly, and (now at Yale) Dolores Hayden and Peter Marris. From Occidental College, Raúl Villa has taught me about the *pocho* experience, as well as Ulises Diaz and Gustavo Leclerc of ADOBE LA. From outside the academy, John Levy and Carol Levy allowed me to see cities with different eyes, as has film-maker Jesse Lerner. Beyond Los Angeles, I have been influenced and helped by many friends and colleagues, even though they might have difficulty in recognizing their influence on this book! They include Stuart Aitken, Richard Candida-Smith, Ed Dimendberg, Steve Erie, Bill Fulton, Larry Herzog, Harvey Molotch, and Manuel Pastor. From that minor metropolis in northern California, Allan Pred, Mike Teitz, Dick Walker, and Michael Watts. In Vancouver, David Ley and Gerry Pratt. In Berlin, Margit Mayer and Bruce Spear. In Toronto, Ute Lehrer and Roger Keil. In Melbourne, Ruth Fincher and Michael Webber, Kim Dovey, Jane Jacobs, and Ross King. In Amsterdam, Ad Goethals, Eric Hoffman, and friends at the Amsterdam Patients and Consumers Platform. In England, Gordon Clark, Doreen Massey, Kevin Robins, and Nigel Thrift.

Special thanks to those who read and commented on the entire manuscript: Bob Beauregard, Steven Flusty, Derek Gregory, and Jennifer Wolch. Their criticisms have immeasurably improved this work.

At various stages of this project, I have received numerous fellowships, and enjoyed other forms of institutional support. I wish to acknowledge the Solomon R. Guggenheim Foundation, as well as the Center for Advanced Studies in the Behavioral Sciences at Stanford where my year-long fellowship was supported by the US National Science Foundation (SES-9022192). Neil Smelser, Bob Scott, and the entire class of CASBS 1995–6 was an inspiration. During a relatively brief fellowship at SISWO (the Netherlands Universities Institute for Coordination of Research in the Social Sciences), I managed to make crucial progress with the manuscript. And I have benefited more than I can say from the supportive research environment at USC. My colleagues at the Department of Geography have been generously accommodating (though not always uncomplaining!) of my work schedule: sincere thanks to Bernie Bauer, Rod McKenzie, Laura Pulido, Curt Roseman, Doug Sherman, John Wilson and Jennifer Wolch. USC granted me a vital sabbatical leave and, by appointing me as director of its Southern California Studies Center, allowed me access to a wonderfully insightful faculty. I am grateful to USC's President Steven B. Sample, Provost Lloyd Armstrong, Jr, and Dean of the College of Letters, Arts and Sciences, Morty Schapiro for creating an exceptional research environment at USC. When you are in such an environment, it's too easy to overlook how much hard work goes into creating it.

At Blackwell, I thank my editor Jill Landeryou for her support, patience and perseverance. Sarah Falkus, Brian Johnson, and Joanna Pyke were a pleasure to work with.

Many friends and colleagues have allowed me to use their artwork and other materials, for which I am deeply grateful. Thanks to the Los Angeles County Museum of Art, especially Stephanie Barron and Paul Holdengräber, for permission to reproduce some important images; and to Dallas Dishman, who was responsible for preparing most of the artwork in this book.

Finally, I am grateful to the editors and publishers of the following journals for permission to reprint portions of previously-published materials:

Dear, M. and Leclerc, G. "Tijuana Desenmascarada," *Wide Angle*, 8, 20(3), 210–21, © 1999 Ohio University: Athens Center for Film and Video. Reprinted by permission of the Johns Hopkins University Press.

Dear, M. and Flusty, S. "Postmodern Urbanism," Annals of Association of American Geographers 1998, 88(1), 1998.

Dear, M. "Postmodern Bloodlines," from G. Benko and U. Strohmayer (eds.) *Space and Social Theory: Geographic Interpretations of Postmodernity*, 49–71 (Blackwell Publishers, Oxford, 1997. Copyright © The Royal Geographical Society with The Institute of British Geographers 1997).

Dear, M. "Identity, Authenticity, and Memory in Place-Time," from S. Pile and M. Keith (eds.) *Geographies of Resistance*, 219–35 (Routledge, London, 1997).

Dear, M. "In the City, Time Becomes Visible," from Allen J. Scott and Edward W. Soja (eds.) *Los Angeles and Urban Theory at the End of the Twentieth Century*, 76–105 (Copyright © 1996 The Regents of the University of California reprinted by permission of University of California Press, Berkeley).

Dear, M. *Postmodern Human Geography: a preliminary appraisal*, 48(1), 2–13 (Erdkunde, 1994).

Dear, M. "Taking Los Angeles Seriously: Time and Space in the Postmodern City," *Architecture California*, 13(2), 36–42, 1991.

Dear, M. "The Premature Demise of Postmodern Urbanism," *Cultural Anthropology*, 538–52, 6(4), 1991.

Dear, M. "Privatization and the Rhetoric of Planning Practice", *Society and Space*, 449–62, 7(4), 1989, Pion.

Dear, M. "The Postmodern Challenge: Reconstructing Human Geography", *Transactions of the Institute of British Geographers*, 1988, NS 13(3), 262–74. Copyright © The Royal Geographical Society with The Institute of British Geographers.

Dear, M. "Postmodernism and Planning," *Society and Space*, 4, 367–84, 1986, Pion.

This work was supported by the University of Southern California's Southern California Studies Center, and by the James Irvine Foundation.

Introduction

This book is about learning to live with postmodernism, especially the moral, theoretical and political consequences of an intellectual movement that continues to profoundly influence the conduct of Western thought. It is also about cities, and the significant forms of urbanism emerging in the twenty-first-century global village. My purpose is to engage these two discourses under the rubric of what I shall term a 'postmodern urbanism.'

There are two arguments why a focus on postmodern urbanism is timely. First, it is by now obvious that the global political economy has shifted into a period of intense restructuring and associated instability. Old spaces are being defiled, and new spaces are being defined, including those associated with deindustrialization, environmentalism, reinvigorated nationalisms, diminished democracies, cyberspace, NIMBYism and minority-led social movements. Paralleling these shifts is the creation of different kinds of urbanism, characterized by edge cities, gated communities, and a global hierarchy of new 'world cities' that is a key to understanding the burgeoning geopolitical order. Like many others, I am concerned to make sense of this restructuring. Secondly, as these geographies of the twenty-first century are being born, the rise of postmodern thought has encouraged, even insisted on new ways of seeing. Founded on a sensitivity to difference and a radical undecidability, postmodernism has brought into question the ways we read, represent, and make choices. As a consequence, previously disenfranchised groups have established critical voices, and existing authority – from whatever source – has been subjected to a penetrating scrutiny.

Needless to say, postmodernism's assault has met with a stiff resistance, especially from those who are threatened by its seductive inclusiveness. Critics from the Right have identified a stultifying political correctness in postmodernism; and from the Left, a crippling, antiprogressive pluralism. It is neither a rhetorical feint nor alarmist attention-seeking on my part to claim that the gains made by postmodernism are being threatened by the forces of established authority. And I firmly believe that the demise of postmodern thought would signal the triumph of obsolete verities, a victory by entrenched hegemonies. To embrace postmodernism remains a transgressive act, despite its several decades of intellectual currency. One risks being regarded as hopelessly faddish, already obsolete, or terminally indecisive. Such criticisms are usually the product of hostile or lazy minds; either way, the project assailed in this book will be a provocation.

The theme of city life is the theme of difference.

Richard Rodriguez

I have never understood why history succeeds in its instant appeal to the popular imagination, whereas geography does not. Everyone understands and reveres the search for roots, but the same cannot be said about spatial origins (due, in part, to the appalling levels of geographical illiteracy throughout most of the world). It is as though the world is now completely explored, everything in its place; and consequently, there is no longer any need for a Geographical Imagination. Yet a child's curiosity about place (the highest mountain, longest river, etc.) is a valid precursor to the profoundest questions of spatial structure and being.

Geographers have taken postmodernism seriously because of its emphasis on space. Indeed, postmodern thought represents a long overdue reassertion of the significance of space in social thought. Some analysts have suggested that we may be witnessing the birth of a postmodern hyperspace – a stretching and reorganization of society's time–space fabric into dimensions we can so far only dimly perceive. One of my principal concerns in these essays will be to unlock this putative hyperspace. My emphases will be on space, place, and locality in uncovering the complex archeologies of past, present and future urbanisms. For many centuries, cities have been the dominant physical expression of the global order. If anything, the pace and magnitude of global restructuring have accelerated during the latter half of the twentieth century. The wide currency granted terms like post-Fordism, flexible accumulation and disorganized capitalism is symptomatic of attempts to grapple with the emerging political–economic forms of the contemporary global political economy. The role of the government is also being renegotiated. Debates about privatization are emblematic of a fundamental distrust of the merits of public enterprise, as well as a reordering of the rights and obligations of democratic citizenship. At the same time, latent and renascent nationalisms call into question the boundaries of nation-states, which are being elided by multinational capital and deeply compromised by the collapse of the Cold War political equilibrium. Socio-economic polarization, at the international and intranational scales, is mirrored in the ubiquitous presence of crime and corruption in all walks of life. And the real prospect of the demise of our planet's natural ecosystems is finally being taken seriously, measured, and fumblingly acted upon.

In order to make sense of this complex global dynamic, my focus in many subsequent chapters will predominantly be on Los Angeles, or the broader region of Southern California. As an urbanist, I can imagine no better place to live and work. During the mid-1970s, I paid my first visit to the region (Orange County, during a blisteringly hot December!), and could make no sense of the place whatsoever. By 1986, having become increasingly enamoured of the city and its physical setting, I happily accepted an appointment at the University of Southern California. To complete a book with Jennifer Wolch, I launched myself into research and policy work on homelessness. We got to know LA from the sidewalk, from street encampments, from freeway underpasses, all the places where homeless people struggled to survive. Then, as now, I love the fact that USC is in South-Central LA; every day, the drive to work is a vivid reminder of what matters most in the city. I would not wish this university to be anywhere else. Even in 1992, when the worst urban civil unrest of the century scorched its way up the streets adjacent to USC, my reaction was to intensify my involvement with the city and its peoples. In 1995, I was honored to become founding director of USC's Southern California Studies Center, which is dedicated to collective dialogue about the region's future.

The current pre-eminence of Southern California's urban dynamic is well-captured by Joel Garreau in the (syntactically-challenged) opening sentence of his study on edge cities: "Every American city that is growing, is growing in the fashion of Los Angeles." This is certainly true of many cities in the US sunbelt, including Phoenix and Atlanta; even long-established centers such as Seattle and Chicago now betray signs of 'Los-Angelization' – a trend regarded with equal measures of alarm and disdain by many of their residents. Garreau might have added that many other world cities (such as Mexico City and São Paulo) resemble Los Angeles more than they do the conventional industrial metropolises of earlier times. Yet until very recently, Los Angeles was not taken seriously by most urbanists. The least-studied major city in the United States, LA has consistently been portrayed as an exception to the rules governing US urban dynamics, a *sui generis* invention on an isolated continental margin. This attitude, characteristic of insiders and outsiders alike, has been reinforced by the emphatically aberrant images of LA perpetrated on the world by the purveyors of art, literature, movies and television. But if we can set aside, even for one moment, the fantasy-tinted spectacles of Hollywood, what would a more careful, clear-eyed analysis reveal? What is Southern California trying to tell us?

Los Angeles is a polycentric, polycultural, polyglot metropolis regarded by many as the prototype of contemporary urbanization. It is a burgeoning capital of the Pacific Rim, undergoing a simultaneous deindustrialization and reindustrialization. It is an ungovernable city of intense socio-economic polarization, where (it is said) a glittering 'First World' sits atop an impoverished 'Third World' substructure. Los Angeles is a collection of theme parks where privatized, partitioned spaces exist for all tastes – communities of industry, leisure, sexual preference, and so on. The residents of such packaged dreamscapes evince some of the most fantastic consumptions patterns in the world. But equally importantly, they have produced a multicultural mosaic in which the existing social contract is under stress. Acute socioeconomic polarization, crises in political representation, racism, and community fragmentation produced in 1992 the worst civil unrest experienced in twentieth-century urban America. It is a city that has cannibalistically devoured its greatest asset – its natural environment.

In what follows, I place special emphasis on intentionality in the creation of the city, i.e. how and why certain key players came together at a particular place and time to create the urban places. The apparatus of land-use planning is especially indicative of these past (and future) urban processes. My focus on city planning is analogous to Fredric Jameson's claim that the architecture of the built environment is the privileged aesthetic of postmodern culture, because it represented (in his view) a virtually unmediated relationship with the production processes of multinational capitalism. For the past two centuries, the urbanization process in the Western world has been powered by the insistent demands of capitalist industrialism, and by the state's response to the contradictions and crises invoked by capitalism's inherent inequalities. This civil society/state dialectic is a crucial process in the creation and growth of cities. On one hand, capitalist civil society is characterized

by the myriad decisions of private firms and households; on the other, the state's
interventions are constantly invoked – though oftentimes simultaneously resisted – to
protect the broader fabric of social relations threatened by the unbridled pursuit of
wealth. Born out of a need to correct the inefficiencies and inequalities of capitalist
land and property development, modern urban planning became simultaneously a
practical search for healthy cities and a discourse on utopian social order.
Both traditions found spectacular realizations in the plans of late-nineteenth-and
twentieth-century cities (for instance, in Vienna's Ringstrasse and in the plan for
Brasília).

Government has always been an imperfect and contested modality, and in the
present state–civil society dialectic, the pendulum has swung decisively against the
state. In a pinched world of scarcity and recession, governments at all levels actively
court entrepreneurs and developers, and visions of urban rationality dissolve into a
plethora of fragmentary, privatized enclaves that increasingly punctuate the landscape. The utopian in urban discourse has been smothered by an instrumentalism
that has reduced city planning ideals to technical subservience in the land and
property development markets. Cast adrift from its ideological and spiritual moorings, public planning may already be an anachronism, and the term
'postmodern planning' an oxymoron. If these conditions hold, if public intentionality
is indeed being erased from urban landscapes, then the cities of the next millennium
may yet become dystopian, unsustainable frontiers where ignorant armies clash by
night.

> Theory is good, but it doesn't prevent things from existing.
>
> Charcot to Freud

Social theory is fundamentally an attempt to make sense of everyday life. Many
contemporary social theories can be traced to Enlightenment traditions, including
those theories that define their identity in opposition to such traditions. The principal
legacy of the Enlightenment impulse can be found in the search for rationality,
foundations, and universal truths. Whether applied to large-scale social systems or
to small-scale individual behaviors, a faith in the existence of some form of generic
laws has characterized most Enlightenment enterprises. And it is precisely this belief
that postmodernism has challenged.

Postmodernism is a difficult word. The task of understanding is complicated by
the multiplicity of shiny carapaces that encase the term. It has been used to refer to
underwear, ice cream, and philosophy. Its meanings and applications have multiplied
during recent decades, a fact gleefully (and mindlessly) seized upon by critics. But
there is nevertheless a transparent genealogy for those who are prepared to recognize
it; an unambiguous heritage links the neo-Marxism and structuralism of the 1960s
with the subsequent rise of post-structuralism, and later to the invention of postmodernism. Three principal references are discernable in postmodern thought:

(a) a series of *distinctive cultural and stylistic practices*, that are in and of them-
     selves intrinsically interesting;
(b) the totality of such practices, viewed as a *cultural ensemble characteristic of the
     contemporary epoch of capitalism*; and

(c) a *philosophical and methodological discourse antagonistic to the precepts of Enlightenment thought*, most particularly the hegemony of any single intellectual persuasion.

Implicit in all three approaches is the notion of a 'radical break,' that is, a discontinuity between past and future trends (whether cultural, political-economic, or philosophical). Thus, somewhere close to the veiled heart of postmodernism is the problem of *theorizing contemporaneity*, of making sense of the swirling maelstrom of contemporary life.

In this book, I shall be dealing with all three dimensions of postmodern thought: specifically, the cultural artifacts of cities; the rise of an era of postmodernity; and the revolution in the way we think. My emphasis throughout is on the negotiated, contingent nature of knowing; i.e. the conviction that getting at the 'truth' is inseparable from the processes and peoples involved in determining it. I could paraphrase Voltaire and say that theory is simply the lie that intellectuals have agreed upon. But I will be less inflammatory, and state simply that I prefer to remain skeptical in the face of the supreme fictions of all 'metanarratives,' recognizing instead the radical incommensurabilities that separate competing theoretical perspectives as well as the identifiable limits to even the best-framed theories. In this respect, I concur with Isaiah Berlin, who spent much of his life arguing that legitimate human values and ideals cannot necessarily be ranked or reconciled.

I shall also engage the crisis of representation, i.e. the inescapably imprecise ways in which we observe and describe the world around us. Deconstructionists have drawn attention to the nature of authority in all textual statements, whatever the medium (written, filmed, oral, etc.). They reveal that absences are just as important as presences in any text, and that a text's impact cannot be controlled once it departs a creator's hand. Instead, a radical indeterminacy arises once a reader confronts the text; the relationship among author, text, and reader produces an interpretive tension that may never be adequately resolved.

How one responds to the challenges of postmodernism is a matter of personal persuasion. All too often, debates on varying perspectives tend to dissolve into belligerent assertions about the wisdom of one's own bias, or burlesque misrepresentations of opponents' frailties. I am by now convinced that many scholars are simply unwilling to seek the common ground between competing perspectives, largely because this would involve compromising, even sacrificing their own intellectual authority. This does not, however, excuse the rest of us. We can begin by conceding that different ways of seeing inevitably produce different representations of the object of analysis. This is not to say that people will be unable to come to agreement about what they are observing. For example, postcolonial and feminist eyes may see things differently, but come to similar conclusions about a patriarchy-driven discrimination. It follows that the deliberate attempt to engage multiple ways of seeing should result in a richer envisioning and representation of the world. I understand that this is not a simple task. But, at a minimum, the incorporation of diverse ways of seeing will radically and productively undermine the unavoidable positionality of my understanding. In these pages, I shall deliberately strive for new ways of seeing, to create a demonstrably superior practice of postmodernism.

The pedagogical implications of a postmodern stance are enormous. Mapping the postmodern entails a commitment to teaching difference. The teaching of a unified canon of agreed-upon principles thus becomes an act of crass dishonesty; the very presumption of a canon is simply an intellectual conceit, a chimera. Yet such conceits can have powerful and tangible real-world consequences, as when political and intellectual leaders use traditional values as sticks to punish opponents. And in one heavily-publicized conflict at Stanford University in 1998, the department of anthropology split into two distinct administrative units as a result of the faculty's inability to reconcile conflicting versions of the discipline: one unit was called 'anthropological science;' the other, 'social and cultural anthropology'. (It was the latter, needless to say, that was tarred with the 'postmodern' epithet!) Many critics tend to view postmodernism's relativism as a dangerous, directionless anarchy – a pluralist, amoral, 'anything-goes' wasteland. They insist on the continuing viability of the modernist project. But even the most articulate defenders of modernity provide little guidance on how their modernist edicts intersect with a society that has long since passed them by, or how their demonstrably obsolete moralities can address the present drift. Their general assumption seems to be that norms once existed, are needed, and can therefore somehow be willed back into existence. But such a defense seems to me to be mired in a miasma of nostalgia and political irrelevance. Nothing could be more comforting to an established political order than the insistence that everything can be assigned a clearly-defined meaning based upon established transcendental precepts.

In political terms, postmodernism is about a loss of innocence. We can no longer make choices oblivious to a broader matrix of difference, even though many would prefer it that way. There is no doubt in my mind that the advent of postmodernism has had a liberating effect on previously silent voices, including those of feminists, disabled and disadvantaged people, gays and lesbians, and people of color (granting that their political activism preceded the postmodern era). Such groups have benefitted from the new legitimacies accorded to difference, even though some have subsequently abandoned postmodernism in favor of a more defiantly particularistic political agenda, as reflected in the rise of standpoint theory and identity politics. These shifts have in turn called attention to the personal ideologies that are pervasive in all scholarly agendas. In recent years, the intellectual vision of many scholars has been questioned as a consequence of revelations about their personal lives, e.g. Martin Heidegger's Nazism. That such preferences exist should surprise no-one; the more pertinent issues are to what extent is an intellectual project constrained by such preferences, and with what consequences?

The politics of postmodernity do not stop at the personal. In 1998, Pope John Paul issued an encyclical, entitled 'Faith and Reason,' condemning the nihilism implicit in an undifferentiated pluralism which assumes that all positions are equally valid, and promising salvation in a reasoned approach to matters of faith (and nicely eliding the two oppositions at the same time). It is also no coincidence that postmodernism should emerge at the time when the world political map is undergoing a traumatic upheaval. The end of the Cold War and the rise of a multipolar geopolitical world heralds an indefinite period of global instability and insecurity. The resulting power vacuum is occurring at a time when multinationals are rendering nation-state boundaries increasingly irrelevant, and when new nationalisms threaten to tear apart existing polities. Into this vacuum, unrestrained by legal conventions, rush forces of corruption and lawlessness that are defining new ways for nations and cities to conduct their business, and that may yet render obsolete conventional notions of democracy and citizenship.

Postmodern thought is not going away, even though no-one can be sure of its ultimate legacy. In the meantime, I believe that there is an acute intellectual imperative to meet its challenge. Whether one decides ultimately to be for or against postmodernism may be less important than the obligation to engage its discourse. In discussing of our "theory-drenched" age, Charles Taylor argued persuasively that the ultimate judge of any theory is the changed quality of practice that it permits. Such an imprecation applies equally to the political and the scholarly worlds: by our theories you will know us; by our actions you may judge us. So be it.

> Los Angeles threatens ... because it breaks the rules.
>
> Reyner Banham

Cities – large and small, global and local, north and south – have become (for better or worse) the principal material expressions of contemporary human civilization. Yet theories of city development and structure are rare. We have far too little to say about the work that cities do: as mechanisms for individual growth; as institutions for care of the disadvantaged and disabled; as crucibles of democracy and citizenship. In recent years, many have come to regard Los Angeles as emblematic of our collective urban future. In Chapter 1, I begin to sketch the outlines of a new urban theory, based on the lessons from Southern California. A fresh perspective on the urban will likely require an orginal theoretical perpective; accordingly Chapter 2 assesses the postmodern turn in social theory. This most profound challenge to centuries of Western thought has drawn attention to the significance of space in the construction of human existence. In Chapter 3, I map the genealogy of postmodern geographies through the work of Henri Lefebvre and Fredric Jameson. Their legacies are prominent in two influential texts by Ed Soja and David Harvey; my personal odyssey through postmodernism has been profoundly at odds with their visions. So, in Chapter 4, I examine the ways in which the Soja/Harvey texts are contrary to the spirit of postmodernism, and employ Derek Gregory's geographical imagination to lay the foundations for my own exegesis.

I launch my construction of a postmodern urbanism by considering the specificities of LA's urban experiences. Chapter 5 takes a highly abbreviated excursion through the particularities of two centuries of history to reveal the passage from a modernist to a postmodern urbanism. Crucial in this 'radical break' are the altered intentionalities that have created the urban landscapes of Southern California; in Chapter 6, I outline the twentieth-century shift in urban planning from (broadly speaking) a public civic will to a more privatized intentionality. Contemporary evidence from Southern California is assembled in Chapter 7, where I describe a framework for a distinctly postmodern urbanism. This is the pivotal moment in the book's narrative, and the remainder of the volume begins to examine its extensive ramifications.

Las Vegas (Nevada) and Tijuana (Baja California) are two of the fastest-growing cities in the USA and Mexico respectively. Both are characterized by extraordinary, larger-than-life cityscapes and politics, which I read as representative of a 'youthful' postmodern cityscape. (LA is a 'mature' postmodern landscape.) In Chapters 8 and 10, I reveal representations of Tijuana and Las Vegas in film, and use these two essays to bracket a more formal inquiry into film, architecture and a theory of filmspace (Chapter 9). As the boundaries between fantasy and reality become ever more blurred, the form of postmodern cities is increasingly determined by the demands of spectacle and consumption. And as this blurring accelerates and intensifies, postmodern urbanism spirals out of real life into virtual reality. Chapter 11 considers what happens when the representational cities of cyberspace displace everyday urban reality. Yet virtual realities perforce remain grounded. Whatever its features, postmodern urbanism is firmly situated in a real world of acute environmental crisis. So, inevitably, Chapter 11 returns to earth, to consider how postmodern urbanism is axiomatically an environmental issue.

In a postmodern world, conventional political categories and practices have been destabilized. De-centered individuals are obliged to invent their own radically subjective politics, and the production of identity (and place) becomes fragmentary, deeply conflicted, and frequently contradictory (Chapter 12). The practice of collective politics is inevitably a product of (urban) places and personal identities (Chapter 13). Democratic politics is mired in deep wells of mistrust and apathy, which have caused an acute legitimacy crisis for the nation -state. At a global level, the demise of the Cold War has left another vacuum – this time at the center of world geopolitics – which is being taken up by anarchic forms of a free-market *zeitgeist* characterized by the emphatic rise of crime and corruption as normal political/business practice. In a postmodern world, city–states may soon overtake nation-states, and competition between city–states may determine the new world geopolitical order (Chapter 14).

Another kind of politics is epistemological, embracing the politics of the academy. In Chapter 15, I examine the case against postmodernism, and show how human geography was significantly reconstituted through its encounter with postmodernism, and why the theory and practice of urban planning remains largely untouched. The yawning antipathy that has greeted postmodernism in some intellectual circles has surprised me. But I am appalled that so many others, sincerely devoted to scholarship, should so acrimoniously dismiss postmodernism. And with such small grace.

[We are witnessing] part of a slowly emerging cultural transformation in Western societies, a change in sensibility for which the term postmodern is...at least for now, wholly adequate.

Andreas Huyssen

I am under no illusions about the possible reception that might greet this book. Many years ago, in Canada, after I had delivered one of my earliest presentations on Los Angeles and postmodern urbanism, a respected senior colleague at my host institution rose to break the silence. "I liked your earlier work," he remarked, and then sat down. On another occasion, one of the central essays in this volume was described by an anonymous referee as setting the discipline of geography back several decades. You be the judge!

My text is a meditation on cities and postmodern thought. Through engagement with its narrative, I hope that readers will discover an original way of understanding cities, an appreciation of the value of postmodern thought, and insight into the practical politics of everyday life. While I have not compromised on complexity, I have done all I can to make the text engaging and accessible. I anticipate that the book will be of interest to anyone who is curious about cities. It will be of particular relevance to students in architecture, city planning, cultural studies, film, geography, social theory, and urban studies. It should interest those in any academic field with an urban emphasis, including economics, international relations, political science, and sociology. And it will be relevant in several professional fields, such as communications theory, public administration, public policy, social work, and urban planning (despite my criticism of the planning profession in this book, I remain a practicing city planner).

Cities are the vital engines of human life on this planet. My efforts in this book have brought together the philosophical core of postmodern thought with the practicalities of contemporary urban life. The conjoining of these two is the *sine qua non* for understanding the production of knowledge about the production of cities. On neither issue would I claim the last word. This entire text is but a fragment of the project I foresee, and that I hope others will now engage. It is but an opening; highly personal, even idiosyncratic, in no way complete. Yet although my task is unfinished, the very existence of this text is testimony to my judgement regarding the utility of the transgressive idioms of postmodernism. It must be left to others to reveal what a postmodern urbanism is capable of.

1

Taking Los Angeles Seriously

The state of theory, now and from now on, isn't it California? And even Southern California?[1]

Jacques Derrida

Los Angeles Exceptionalism

The first and perhaps most likely response to the title of this chapter is: Why? Why take Los Angeles seriously? The most straightforward answer is: because for most of the twentieth century, the Southern California region has witnessed an irresistible population expansion, and is likely soon to become the nation's largest metropolitan area. Yet, for most of its history, Los Angeles has typically been viewed as an exception to the trajectories of US metropolitan development. Located on the continent's southwest frontier, the city tends to conjure up visions of infinite suburban sprawl, inconsequential architecture, freeways, sun, surf and smog. These images have been encouraged and exaggerated by the movies and television that Hollywood has sold to the world. Of course, in many ways Los Angeles is different from other cities. For instance, it stands in stark contrast to Chicago, the city that has universally been regarded as the prototypical industrial metropolis. For many decades, urbanists have analyzed the cities of the world according to precepts of the "Chicago School."

There is, however, a deep problem with these exceptionalist narratives. They render much of what happens in LA as merely illustrative, a series of quirky, even staged set-pieces. Fortunately, during the past two decades, increasing scholarly attention has been directed toward the five-county region that comprises Southern California. As the volume of evidence accumulates, new challenges are being offered to our assumptions and predictions concerning future urban growth. The dominance of the Chicago model is being challenged by what may be an emergent "Los Angeles School," emphasizing multi-centered, dispersed patterns of low-density growth. Ed Soja makes a case for the prototypical nature of Los Angeles:

Ignored for so long as aberrant, idiosyncratic, or bizarrely exceptional, Los Angeles … has, more than any other place, become *the paradigmatic window through which to see the last half of the twentieth century*. I do not mean to suggest that the experience of Los Angeles will be duplicated elsewhere. But just the reverse may indeed be true, that the particular experiences of urban development and change occurring elsewhere in the world are being duplicated in Los Angeles, the place where it all seems to "come together."[2]

Figure 1.1 La Virgén de Guadalupe mural (ADOBE, LA, photo by Julie Easton)

I shall leave on one side, for the moment, whether or not it is feasible or desirable to establish a "postmodern archetype." But the sheer scale and significance of LA in the regional, national, and global political economies are reasons enough to correct the long-established analytical amnesia regarding Southern California. In terms of population size, Los Angeles is already the second largest metropolitan region in the United States, and eleventh in the world. It is expected to have more than 20 million people by the year 2000. The five-county region (Los Angeles, Ventura, San Bernardino, Riverside and Orange counties), encompassing approximately a 60-mile circle centered on downtown LA, comprises only 5 percent of California's total land area. Yet by the early 1990s, this circle has more than half the state's population and personal income. The gross product per person in the 60-mile circle ranks it as fourth in the world. The region is also known for its extraordinary consumption patterns. In Los Angeles alone, over 2,000 cars are sold daily, including 20 percent of all US Rolls Royce registrations, and 70 percent of all California registrations.

Understanding Los Angeles

Most world cities have an instantly-identifiable signature: think of the boulevards of Paris; the skyscrapers of New York; or the churches of Rome. But Los Angeles appears to be a city without a common narrative, except perhaps an iconography of the bizarre. If pressed, most observers would single out the freeways as the key to LA, but the tenacity of this symbol seems to rest more with picture-postcard makers than in the minds of residents. Other more media-conscious observers take their lead from the cinematic and televisual, invoking images of LA as the labyrinth of *film noir*, a warren of half-truth and deception.[3]

Figure 1.2 WattsTowers, Simon Rodia 1921–45 (Michael Dear)

Table 1.1 Population Growth in the Five-County Region of Los Angeles

Census Year	Los Angeles	Orange	San Bernardino	Riverside	Ventura	Five-County Region	LA County as % of Region
1870	15	–	4	–	–	19	79
1880	33	–	8	–	5	46	72
1890	101	14	25	–	10	151	67
1900	170	20	28	18	14	250	68
1910	504	34	57	35	18	648	78
1920	936	61	73	50	28	1,150	81
1930	2,209	119	134	81	55	2,597	85
1940	2,786	131	161	106	70	3,253	86
1950	4,152	216	282	170	115	4,934	84
1960	6,011	709	501	303	199	7,724	78
1970	7,042	1,421	682	457	378	9,981	71
1980	7,478	1,932	893	664	530	11,496	65
1990	8,863	2,411	1,418	1,170	669	14,531	61

Source: Soja and Scott, *The City*, p. 3.

In 1973, Rayner Banham provided a enduring map of the Los Angeles landscape. To this day, it remains powerful, evocative, and instantly recognizable. He identified four basic "ecologies:" surfurbia (the beach cities); the foothills (the privileged enclaves of Beverly Hills, Bel Air, etc.); the plains of Id (the endless central flatlands); and autopia (the freeways).[4] Banham provided thumbnail sketches of the four basic ecologies:

Surfurbia: "The beaches are what other metropolises should envy in Los Angeles ... Los Angeles is the greatest City-on-the-shore in the world;"[5]

the foothills: "where the financial and topographical contours correspond almost exactly – "the foothill ecology is all about ... narrow, tortuous residential roads serving precipitous house plots that often back up directly on unimproved wilderness even now; and air of deeply buried privacy ... ;"[6]

the plains of Id: "An endless plain endlessly gridded with endless streets, peppered endlessly with ticky-tacky houses clustered in indistinguishable neighborhoods, slashed across by endless freeways that have destroyed any community spirit that may have once existed, and so on ... endlessly;"[7] and

autopia: "As the car in front turned down the off-ramp of the San Diego freeway, the girl beside the driver pulled down the sun-visor and used the mirror on the back of it to tidy her hair. Only when I had seen a couple more incidents of this kind did I catch their import: that coming off the freeway is coming in from outdoors. A domestic or sociable journey in Los Angeles does not end so much at the door of one's destination as at the off-ramp of the freeway, the mile or two of ground-level streets counts as no more that the front drive of the house.... [The] freeway system in its totality is now a single comprehensible place, a coherent state of mind, a complete way of life."[8]

For Douglas Suisman, it is not the freeways but the LA boulevards that determine the city's overall physical structure. A boulevard is a surface street that "(1) makes arterial connections on a metropolitan scale; (2) provides a framework for civic and commercial destination; and (3) acts as a filter to adjacent residential neighborhoods." Suisman argues that boulevards do more than establish an organizational pattern; they constitute "the irreducible armature of the city's *public space*," and are charged with social and political significance that cannot be ignored. These vertebral connectors today form an integral link among the region's municipalities.[9]

For Ed Soja, Los Angeles is a decentered, decentralized metropolis powered by the insistent fragmentation of post-Fordism, i.e. an increasingly flexible, disorganized regime of capitalist accumulation. Accompanying this shift is a postmodern consciousness, a cultural and ideological reconfiguration altering how we experience social being. The center holds, however, because of its function as the urban panopticon: the strategic surveillance point for the state's exercise of social control. Out from the center extend a melange of "wedges" and "citadels," interspersed between corridors formed by the boulevards. The consequent urban structure is a complex quilt, enormously fragmented, yet bound to an underlying economic rationality: "With exquisite irony, contemporary Los Angeles has come to resemble more than ever before a gigantic agglomeration of theme parks, a lifespace composed of Disney-worlds."[10]

These three sketches provide differing insights into LA's landscapes. Banham considers the city's overall torso, and recognizes three basic components (surfurbia, plains and foothills), as well as connecting arteries (freeways). Suisman shifts our

Figure 1.3   Girl Gang Members, East Los Angeles (ADOBE, LA, photo by Ulises Diaz)

gaze away from the principal arteries to the veins that channel everyday life (the boulevards). Soja considers the body-in-context, articulating the links betweenpolitical economy and postmodern culture to explain fragmentation and social differentiation in Los Angeles. All three writers maintain a studied detachment from the city, as though a voyeuristic, top-down perspective is needed to discover the rationality inherent in the cityscape. Yet a postmodern sensibility would be willing (even eager) to relinquish the modernism inherent in these "objective" representations of the urban text. What would a postmodernism from below reveal?

Postmodernism is, in this context, about complication, which is manifest in Los Angeles as an intense localization and fragmentation of social process. LA's micro-geography is extremely finely grained and variegated. In the manner of Michel de Certeau, the key to its social life lies at the street level, where human beings may be observed in their myriad daily practices.[11] One way to understand LA, then, is as an accretion of the local. There is never a single reality to the city (although there have been singular myths in the minds of its many observers).

The social heterogenity and spatial extensiveness of the metropolis have encouraged intense and effective local autonomies. These appear in all walks of life, including politics, work, family, culture, and environment. One important consequence of physical sprawl is that Los Angeles may yet prove to be the harbinger of a new style of decentered politics. The region is split into many separate fiefdoms, with their leaders in constant battle. (Los Angeles County, for instance, has close to one hundred separate municipal governments of one kind or another – including the City of Los Angeles – plus many more special district overlays.) The problems of political representation include on-going disputes between county and city governments, the resurgence of the slow-growth/no-growth movements, and the difficulties

Table 1.2   Los Angeles County: Ethnic Composition, 1960 and 1990

Group (1960)	Number of Persons	% of tot. pop.	Group (1990)	Number of Persons	% of tot. pop.
Total Population	6,038,771	100.0	Total Population	8,863,164	100.0
White (non-Spanish surname)	4,877,850	80.8	White (non-Hispanic)	3,618,850	40.8
Spanish-surname White	576,716	9.6	Hispanic origin	3,351,242	37.8
Black	461,546	7.6	Black (African-American)	992,974	11.2
American Indian	8,109	0.1	American Indian	45,508	0.5
Asian and other non-White	115,250	1.9	Asian and Pacific Islander	954,485	10.8

Source: Allen & Turner, 1996, p. 3.

associated with political participation by ethnic and racial minorities. As a consequence, formal and informal, legal and illegal alliances have risen to press the
claims of gays, gangs, feminists, racial and ethnic minorities, and other interest
groups. These alliances reside within the interstices of the formal power structures,
which then become increasingly redundant in the everyday lives of alliance members.
Left to their own devices, and encouraged by the rules of politics, elected
officials exercise power within their fiefdoms in an increasingly autocratic and
often corrupt manner. And so the bifurcation of formal and informal politics is
intensified.

In an apparent paradox, the rising pre-eminence of the local in the postmodern city
has been facilitated by the appearance of a global capitalism. The emergence of post-
Fordism has resulted in an accelerated flow of global capital, and an endless search
for cheap labor supplies on an international scale.[12] These trends have connected the
local ever more effectively to the world-wide developments of post-Fordism; what
happens in downtown LA tomorrow may result from yesterday's fluctuations in local
labor markets in East Asia.[13] At home, the consequences have been a rapid deindustrialization especially in the snowbelt, and (re)industrialization in the sunbelt. Los
Angeles, in perhaps a typically postmodern way, is experiencing both simultaneously.
Within its limits, the city has vestiges of a major automobile manufacturing
industry, as well as the glittering towers of corporate high-techdom. LA is an
"informational city" with, at the same time, a proliferation of minimum-wage,
part-time service industry jobs (e.g. fast food outlets) and a massive informal sector
(street vendors on freeway off-ramps; can recycling efforts from the backs of trucks;
etc.). In social terms, the postmodern metropolis is increasingly minoritized and
polarized along class, income, racial and ethnic lines. The disadvantaged classes
are overwhelmingly people of color. Their family lives are increasingly disrupted
by the demands of a flexible, disorganized workplace (for example, the pressure on
both parents to work, or the need for families to crowd together to be able to afford
housing). These trends have been aggravated by the strong dose of privatism, as well
as the practical effects of privatization, that emerged during the Reagan era and show
few signs of abating.[14]

The region's acute openness to world trends would probably have been cushioned if it were not for erosion of the linkages, horizontal and vertical, between branches of the state apparatus. At home, the rhetoric of less government was reflected in government's aversion to dealing with social, economic, and political problems, as well as in the rise of "fiscal federalism" (federal transfers to California cities in the 1990s had declined by two-thirds from their 1980 levels). Issues of social reproduction, community, and the public interest have consequently taken a back seat. In effect, governments and populace have colluded in the decline of the commonwealth.

In many ways, I have to say that LA's urban political economy is no different from that of many other cities in North America and Europe, except perhaps that by its very scale and diversity, it throws certain trends into particularly high relief. What is special about LA, however, is that most countries of the world get to observe pieces of the city's good and bad fortune on an almost daily basis, and in excruciating detail, via the movies and television. The apocalyptic images of Ridley Scott's *Blade Runner* (1982), Kathryn Bigelow's *Strange Days* (1996), and a deluge of TV trivia, have by now congealed in the memory-banks of ordinary people around the world.[15] For those of us who live in LA, these fictions often seem uncomfortably close to reality. For example, air quality in the city, in spite of major improvements, remains the worst in the country. The physical expansion of the urbanized area has generated other acute, human-induced environmental crises, especially those connected with urban services such as water supply, toxic waste disposal, and sewage. These problems, together with LA's especially hazardous natural environment (earthquakes, floods, landslides, fires), are proving increasingly intractable as Southern California continues to act as a magnet for development. Although lip service is paid to environmental issues, the survival of nature (in all its forms) is typically a low priority.

Images of doom and gloom are, however, relentlessly offset by the ubiquitous presence of an industry devoted to fantasy, glamour and wealth. Known universally as "The Industry" (always capitalized), film and television maintain a steady flow of quirky, celebratory versions of the city. In Steve Martin's *LA Story*, for instance, earthquakes do not disturb the ritual of ordering the exactly correct kind of coffee with lunch. Or we casually encounter homeless people who are represented as handsome, healthy, free-wheeling *idiots savants* capable of enriching our lives (*Down & Out in Beverly Hills*). Angelenos are encouraged by nightly TV news to take a perverse pride in the climate of Southern California, or in having made it through another day, even if their biggest personal challenge has taken the form of a gridlocked freeway.

And yet, people love to live in Southern California. And the city works. The intense localizations, and the presence of one of the nation's most extensive public transportation networks, make decentralization possible and even necessary to everyday life. Angelenos daily re-invent their city. Thus, there is no need to go "downtown" to enjoy entertainment and cultural events in the postmodern city. There are major theater districts also in downtown Pasadena, Hollywood, Long Beach, and in Orange County. Art flourishes in Santa Monica, along Wilshire Boulevard, and on a mountain-top (cropped for the purpose!) in Brentwood. Indeed, downtown LA is not the downtown for the vast majority of the region's population; many Angelenos have never even been there. Periodic attempts have been made to create a regional hub at the intersection of four major freeways, but a large part of downtown LA's agglomeration of commercial and residential highrises is, as Mike Davis points out, "a perverse monument to US losses in the global trade war" which permitted a massive inflow of international capital for speculative real estate investment.[16]

From Chicago to LA

It has been a traditional axiom of classical writing about the city that urban structures are the domain of reason.

Jonathan Raban[17]

As the rock-and-roll classic reminds us, *Route 66* winds from Chicago to LA, more than two thousand miles all the way. Although the physical distances may be large, the intellectual distance between the two cities might be insurmountable. How shall we shift from a view of urban evolution that has dominated discourse for most of the twentieth century (based on the Chicago example) to a new vision based upon the florid hyperbole of Southern California? And how shall we know that such a shift, even if possible, is in any way desirable?

General theories of urban structure are a scarce commodity. One of the most persistent and popular models of urban structure is associated with a group of sociologists who flourished in Chicago in the 1920s and 1930s. According to Morris Janowitz, the "Chicago School" was motivated to regard the city "as an object of detached sociological analysis," worthy of distinctive scientific attention:

> The city is not an artifact or a residual arrangement. On the contrary, the city embodies the real nature of human nature. It is an expression of mankind in general and specifically of the social relations generated by territoriality.[18]

The most enduring of the Chicago School models was the zonal or concentric ring theory, an account of the evolution of differentiated urban social areas by E. W. Burgess.[19] Based on assumptions that included a uniform land surface, universal access to a single-centered city, free competition for space, and the notion that development would take place outward from a central core, Burgess concluded that the city would tend to form a series of concentric zones. (These are the same assumptions that were later to form the basis of the land rent models of Alonso, Muth et al.) The main ecological metaphors invoked to describe this dynamic were invasion, succession, and segregation, by which populations gradually filtered outwards from the center as their status and level of assimilation progressed. The model was predicated on continuing high levels of immigration to the city.

At the core of Burgess' schema was the Central Business District (CBD), which was surrounded by a transitional zone, where older private houses were being converted to offices and light industry, or subdivided to form smaller dwelling units. This was the principal area to which new immigrants were attracted; and it included areas of "vice" and generally unstable or mobile social groups. The transitional zone was succeeded by a zone of working-men's homes, which included some of the city's oldest residential buildings inhabited by stable social groups. Beyond

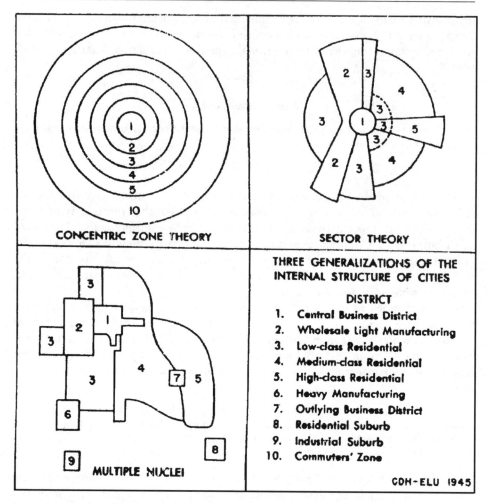

Figure 1.4 Generalizations of Internal Structure of Cities (reproduced by permission of The American Academy of Political Social Science, Philadelphia)

this, newer and larger dwellings were to be found, occupied by the middle classes. Finally, the commuters' zone was to be found separate from the continuous built-up area of the city, where much of the zone's population was employed. Burgess' model was a broad generalization, and not intended to be taken too literally. He expected, for instance, that his schema would apply only in the absence of "opposing factors" such as local topography (in the case of Chicago, Lake Michigan). He also anticipated considerable variation within the different zones.

Other urbanists noted the tendency for cities to grow in star-shaped rather than concentric form, along highways that radiate from a center with contrasting land uses in the interstices. This observation gave rise to a sector theory of urban structure, an idea advanced in the late 1930s by Homer Hoyt,[20] who observed that once variations arose in land uses near the city center, they tended to persist as the city expanded. Distinctive sectors thus grew out from the CBD, often organized along major highways. Hoyt emphasized that "non-rational" factors could alter urban form, as when skillful promotion influenced the direction of speculative development. He also understood that the age of buildings could still reflect a concentric ring structure, and that sectors may not be internally homogeneous at one point in time.

The complexities of real-world urbanism were further taken up in the multiple nuclei theory of C. D. Harris and E. Ullman.[21] They proposed that cities have a cellular structure in which land-uses develop around multiple growth-nuclei within the metropolis – a consequence of accessibility-induced variations in the land-rent surface and agglomeration (dis)economies. Harris and Ullman also allow that real-world urban structure is determined by broader social and economic forces, the influence of history, and international influences. But whatever the precise reasons for their origin, once nuclei have been established, general growth forces reinforce their pre-existing patterns.

Much of the urban research agenda of the twentieth century has been predicated on the precepts of the concentric zone, sector, and multiple nuclei theories of urban structure. Their influences can be seen directly in factorial ecologies of intra-urban structure, land-rent models, studies of urban economies and diseconomies of scale, and designs for ideal cities and neighborhoods. The specific and persistent popularity of the Chicago concentric ring model is harder to explain, however, given the proliferation of evidence in support of alternative theories. The most likely reasons for its endurance are probably related to its beguiling simplicity, and the enormous volume of publications produced by adherents of the Chicago School. Even as late as 1992, Mike Davis' vision of an "ecology of fear" in Los Angeles managed to produce a sketch based on the now-familiar concentric rings.[22]

During the 1980s, a group of loosely-associated scholars, professionals, and advocates based in Southern California became aware that what was happening in the Los Angeles region was somehow symptomatic of a broader socio-geographic transformation taking place within the United States as a whole. Their common, but then unarticulated, project was based on certain shared theoretical assumptions, and on the view that LA was emblematic of some more general urban dynamic. One of the earliest expressions of an emergent "LA School" was the appearance in 1986 of a special issue of the journal *Society and Space*, which was entirely devoted to understanding Los Angeles. In their prefatory remarks to that issue, Allen Scott and Ed Soja referred to Los Angeles as the "capital of the twentieth century," deliberately invoking Walter Benjamin's reference to Paris as capital of the nineteenth century.[23] They predicted that the volume of scholarly work on Los Angeles would quickly overtake that on Chicago, and drew particular attention to current research on industrial growth and change, geographical decentralization, and the internationalization of capital and labor.

The burgeoning outlines of an LA self-consciousness were given crude form by a series of meetings and publications that occurred during the late 1980s. A pivotal meeting, at Lake Arrowhead, was attended by myself, Dana Cuff, Mike Davis, Allen Scott, Ed Soja, Michael Storper, and Jennifer Wolch, plus a few others. The discussions were hilariously inconclusive – too many intellects on too rich a scholarly diet! – demonstrating that this group would never become reconciled (subordinated?) under a single, coherent rubric. To some extent, the School's explosive fragmentation was a precise microcosm of everyday political life in LA! Even so, by 1990, in his

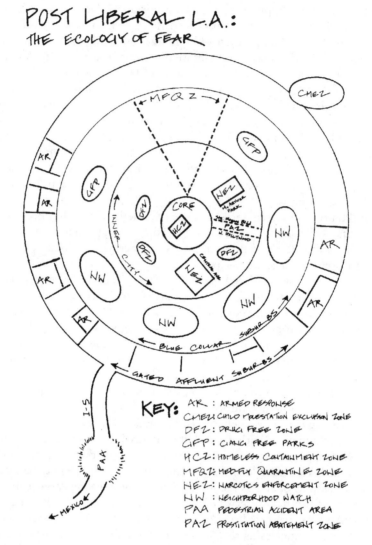

Figure 1.5   Post-Liberal LA: The Ecology of Fear (reproduced by permission of Los AngelesTimes December 13, 1992, p. 60)

penetrating critique of Southern California urbanism (*City of Quartz*), Mike Davis was able to make specific reference to the School's expanding presence. He commented that its practitioners were undecided whether to model themselves after the Chicago School (named principally for the city that was its object of inquiry), orthe Frankfurt School (a philosophical alliance named only coincidentally after its place of operations).[24] Then, in 1993, Marco Cenzatti published a short pamphlet that was, I believe, the first to explicitly examine the focus and potential of an LA School. Responding to Davis, he claimed that the School's practitioners combine precepts of both the Chicago and Frankfurt Schools (i.e. a place focus, plus a common project):

> Thus Los Angeles comes...into the picture not just as a blueprint or a finished para-
> digm of the new dynamics, but as a laboratory which is itself an integral component of
> the production of new modes of analysis of the urban. [25]

Just as the Chicago School emerged at a time when that city was reaching new national prominence, Los Angeles is now making its impression on the minds of urbanists worldwide. And, like the Chicago School, their theoretical inquiries focus not only on a specific city, but also on more general questions concerning urban process. Cenzatti identifies one theme common to all adherents of the LA School, and that is a focus on restructuring, which includes deindustrialization and reindustrialization, the birth of the information economy, the decline of nation-states, the emergence of new nationalisms, and the rise of the Pacific Rim. Such proliferating logics often involve multiple theoretical frameworks that overlap and coexist in their explanations of the burgeoning global/local order. This heterodoxy is consistent with the project of postmodernism, and it is no accident that Los Angeles has come to be regarded as the prototypical postmodern metropolis.

Los Angeles undoubtedly is a special place. But adherents of the Los Angeles School do not argue that the city is unique, nor necessarily a harbinger of the future, even though both viewpoints are at some level demonstrably true. Instead at a minimum they assert that Southern California is a suggestive archetype – a polyglot, polycentric, polycultural pastiche that is somehow engaged in the rewriting of the American social contract.[26] The peculiar conditions that have led now to the emergence of a Los Angeles School may be coincidental: (a) that an especially powerful intersection of empirical and theoretical research projects have come together in this particular place and time; (b) that these trends are occurring in what has historically been the most understudied major city in the United States, and are thus accompanied by bursts of energy and excitement; (c) that these projects have attracted the attention of an assemblage of increasingly self-conscious scholars and practitioners; and (d) that the world is facing the prospect of a Pacific century, in which Southern California is likely to become a global capital. The validity and potential of the Los Angeles School derive principally from the intersection of these events, and the promise they hold for a re-creation of urban theory.

Los Angeles and Postmodern Urbanism

Is Los Angeles the model of twenty-first century urban development? Should an avowedly postmodern inquiry even engage in the search for a new prototype? I cannot answer these questions definitively at this point. Besides, even as I write, the Los Angeles School may have already been superseded by a burgeoning "Orange County School." Mark Gottdiener and George Kephart wrote, in *Postsuburban California* (1991), that Orange County is the paradigmatic window on late-twentieth century urbanism:

> We have focused on what we consider to be a new form of settlement space – the fully
> urbanized, multinucleated, and independent county...formally separated from but
> adjacent to large well-known metropolitan regions.... As a new form of settlement
> space, they are the first such occurrence in five thousand years of urban history.[27]

Figure 1.6   Los Angeles Civil Unrest, 1992 (Alejandro Alonso)

Postsuburban districts "possess relatively large populations; they are polynu-cleated, with no single center that dominates development as it does in the traditional urban model; and they possess relatively robust employment bases and also serve as residential areas, especially for the white middle class." [28] Such districts appear to be identifiable by four characteristics "postsuburban spatial organization, information capitalism, consumerism, and cosmopolitanism." [29]

The claims of Orange County are probably premature (if not a trifle grandiose), since there has been a flurry of recent attention to the remaking of the urban land-scape. Joel Garreau's 1990 work on edge cities was one important stimulus in this renaissance. [30] It may have been instrumental (although unreferenced) in Chauncy Harris' reworking of his multiple-sector theory model into a peripheral model of urban development. [31] But equally important has been the steady, painstaking work of other urbanists who over the years have built up a detailed catalogue of the texts of contemporary cities. An unprecedented amount of attention is now being paid to "middle-tier" cities, in search of understanding how globalization is impacting various localities. For instance, in 1998, Greg Hise, David Sloane and Bill Deverell collaborated on an "Orange Empires" conference which compared LA with Miami. Other comparative urban studies have been reported in special issues of *Urban Geography* (1996), and of the *Annals of the American Academy of Political and Social Science* (1997), guest-edited respectively by Barney Warf and Rodney Erick-son, and by David Wilson.

Whatever happens next, the Chicago model is manifestly no longer suitable for describing contemporary metropolitan evolution. And LA can no more be regarded as an exception to the rule. Exactly what all this adds up to is, at least for the moment, teasingly veiled. I may have pushed LA's prophetic aura beyond decent limits. Even so, few cities are so well-equipped to direct us to the proper questions regarding contemporary urbanism.

Notes

1. Quoted in Carrol, D., (ed.), 1990: *The States of Theory*, New York: Columbia University Press, p. 63.
2. Soja, E., 1989: *Postmodern Geographies*. New York: Verso, p. 221, emphasis added.
3. Arthur, P., 1996: "Los Angeles as Scene of the Crime," *Film Comment*, 32, 4 (July/August), pp. 21–26.
4. Banham, R., 1973: *Los Angeles: Architecture of the Four Ecologies*, Harmondsworth: Penguin Books.
5. Ibid., p. 37.
6. Ibid., p. 99.
7. Ibid., p. 161.
8. Ibid., p. 213.
9. Suisman, D. R., 1989: *Los Angeles Boulevard*, Los Angeles: Los Angeles Forum for Architecture and Urban Design.
10. Soja, E.: *Postmodern Geographies*, p. 246.
11. de Certeau, M., 1984: *The Practice of Everyday Life*, Berkeley: University of California Press.
12. In one of the clearest discussions of the rise of "flexible production," Michael Storper and Allen Scott identify the shift from a Fordist to a post-Fordist industrial organization as a pivotal moment in an emerging global capitalism. This shift was in fact composed of four separate moments: (1) the central sectors of industrial society became less focused on manufacturing consumer durables and more directed toward high-tech industries, a revitalized craft sector, and producer and financial services; (2) the emergence of flexible production methods, as distinct from Fordist mass production; (3) a shift in the geographical foundations of production which resulted in a new set of core industrial regions; and (4) associated forms of new collective and institutional arrangements, including especially the dismantling of the Keynesian welfare state. At the theoretical core of the shift to post-Fordism, Storper and Scott place the emergent regime of accumulation and mode of social regulation. Fordist rationality was based in assembly-line mass production, and geared to economies of scale, standardized outputs, routinization of process, and dedicated capital equipment. This led to the development of large-scale oligopolistic corporations and industry-wide labor unions, associated with a Keynesian welfare state whose purpose was to offset the effects of recession and maintain social and industrial harmony. In contrast, a post-Fordist flexible production regime prized the abilities to shift promptly from one process/product configuration to another, and to adjust output quantities quickly. This form of industrial organization encouraged the proliferation of small units and inter-unit competition; it also ushered in the dismantling of the welfare state and the rise of a new conservatism. Storper and Scott argue that the rise of post-Fordism has given birth to a set of "new industrial spaces," away from the older (especially urban) foci of Fordist production. A concomitant new politics of place has also been identified, different from the rigid politics of Fordist rationality. Post-Fordists have sought alternative sites and arrangements. In the United States, for instance, suburban industrial expansion has been facilitated by a neo-conservative, non-unionized labor force; older inner cities have adopted an entrepreneurial mantle and entered the competitive national and international marketplace for "selling places;" and emergent growth, no-growth, slow-growth coalitions dominated local politics, having only the most tenuous connection (if any) to conventional class-based politics. (See Storper, Michael and Scott, A. J. , "The geographical foundations and social regulation of flexible production complexes," in Dear, M. and Wolch, J., (eds.) 1989: *The Power of*

Geography: How Territory Shapes Social Life, Boston: Unwin Hyman, p. 21.)

Similar features were described by Scott Lash and John Urry who noted the rise of a "disorganized capitalism." Broadening their focus beyond the economic sphere, Lash and Urry stress the importance of the decline in the core working class and union membership; increased independence of corporations from the nation-state and the decline of traditional class-based politics; and a decline in the size and domination of industrial cities plus a new spatial division of labor. They also foreshadow the rise of cultural pluralism, and the appearance of a new, postmodern mass culture and ideology. (See Lash, S. and Urry, J., 1987: *The End of Organized Capitalism*, Cambridge: Polity Press.)

13. Davis, M., 1990: *City of Quartz: Excavating the Future in Los Angeles*, New York: Verso.

14. Wolch, J., 1990: *The Shadow State: Government and Voluntary Sector in Transition*, New York: The Foundation Center.

15. But Roman Polanski's *Chinatown* and Stephen Frears's *The Grifters* capture the essence of LA more accurately: a surficial gloss of striking beauty, glowing light, and pastel hues which together conspire to conceal a hideous subculture of malice, mistrust and mutiny.

16. Davis, M., *City of Quartz: Excavating the Future in Los Angeles*, p. 138.

17. Raban, J., 1974: *Soft City*, New York: E. P. Dutton, p. 157.

18. Janowitz, 1967 in Park, Robert E., Burgess, E. W., and McKenzie, R., 1925 (Midway reprint 1984): *The City: Suggestions for Investigation of Human Behavior in the Urban Environment*, Chicago: University of Chicago Press, p. ix.

19. Burgess, E. W., in Park, Robert E., Burgess, E. W., and McKenzie, R., 1925: "The Growth of the City," in *The City: Suggestions of Investigation of Human Behavior in the Urban Environment*, Chicago: University of Chicago Press, pp. 47–62.

20. Hoyt, H., 1939: *The Structure and Growth of Residential Neighborhoods in American Cities*, Washington: US Federal Housing Administration; Hoyt, H., 1933: *One Hundred Years of Land Values in Chicago*, Chicago: University of Chicago Press.

21. Harris, C. D., 1997: "The Nature of Cities," *Urban Geography*, 18, pp. 15–35; and Harris, C. D. and Ullman, E. L., 1945: "The Nature of Cities," *Annals of the American Academy of Political and Social Science*, 242, pp. 7–17.

22. M. Davis, 1992: "Think Green," in "Remaking LA," by Aaron Betsky. Los Angeles Times Magazine, December 13.

23. Scott, A., and Soja, E., 1986: "Los Angeles: Capital of the Late Twentieth Century" *Environment and Planning D: Society and Space*, 4, pp. 249–254.

24. Davis, M., *City of Quartz: Excavating the Future in Los Angeles*, p. 84.

25. Cenzatti, M., 1993: *Los Angeles and the LA School: Postmodernism and Urban Studies*, Los Angeles: Los Angeles Forum for Architecture and Urban Design.

26. Dear, M., et al., 1996: *Rethinking Los Angeles*, Thousand Oaks, CA: Sage Publications; Scott, A, J., and Soja, E., *The City: Los Angeles, Urban Theory at the End of the Twentieth Century*; Steinberg, J. B., et al., 1992: *Urban America: Policy Choices for Los Angeles and the Nation*, Santa Monica, CA: RAND Corp.

27. Gottdiener, M., and Kephart, G., 1991: "The Multinucleated Metropolitan Region: a comparative analysis," in Kling, Rob, Olin, Spencer, and Poster, Mark, *Postsuburban California*, Berkeley: University of California Press, p. 51.

28. Ibid.

29. Ibid., p. 4.

30. Garreau, J., 1991: *Edge City: Life on the New Frontier*, New York: Doubleday.

31. Harris, C. D., "The Nature of Cities," pp. 15–35.

2

Mapping the Postmodern

A Mix-in, for those who have not yet followed aerobic eating into its postmodern era, may be butterscotch chips and walnuts, pulverized Reese's peanut butter cups, crushed Oreos, M&Ms or – in some temples of ascetism – granola.

notice on carton of Steve's Ice Cream

The Origins of Postmodernism

The term *postmodern* is akin to a tease. Its seductive surfaces seem to promise much, but when you succumb, it appears insubstantial, unsatisfying. Simply stated, it's hard to know what postmodernism is. Let me confess right away that I am unclear about what postmodern ice cream is, except that it seems to promise an outrageous combination of flavors that may be analogous to the promiscuous pastiches of postmodern architecture. Another flaky notion is postmodern television, whose singular quality is that it seems to require the attention-span of a nervous flea. There is even postmodern underwear. Perhaps one thing that many of these post-modern conceits share is the notion of *fragmentation* of traditions, fashions and trends.

Transition is another common element in the postmodern repertoire. In architecture, for instance, Charles Jencks observed that:

> Defining our world today as Post-Modern . . . doesn't tell us very much, either flattering or predictive. All it says is what we have left – the Modern world, which is paradoxically doomed, like an obsolete futurist, to extinction.[1]

In his introduction to postmodern literary studies, Charles Newman is simultaneously peripatetic and directionless, thus combining the fragmentation and transition metaphors:

> The 'Post-Modern' is neither a canon of writers nor a body of criticism, though it is often applied to literature of, roughly, the last twenty years. The very term signifies a simultaneous continuity and renunciation, a generation strong enough to dissolve the old order, but too weak to marshal the centrifugal forces it has released. This new literature founders in its own hard won heterogeneity, and tends to lose the sense of itself as a human institution. My account is accordingly a survey of attitudes and tendencies, gestures and drifts, alibis and advertisements, cliches and obfuscation, which comprise an institution without a theory.[2]

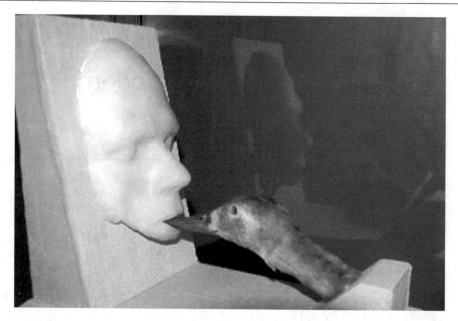

Figure 2.1/a Museum of Jurassic Technology (photo by Michael Dear)
Duck's Breath: Children affected with thrush and other fungous mouth or throat disorders can be cured by placing the bill of a duck or goose in the mouth of the afflicted child for a period of time. The cold breath of the fowl will be inhaled by the child and the complaint will disappear.

For his part, Umberto Eco advises that postmodernism should not be regarded as a chronologically-defined trend, but as an "ideal category;" since every period must inevitably have its own postmodernism.[3] He observes that a moment arises when the "modern," meaning any avant-garde, can go no further.[4] The "postmodern" response is to recognize that the past (since it cannot be destroyed, because its destruction would lead to silence) must be revisited. But it is revisited with irony, self-consciously, and not with innocence. In order to be understood, postmodernism requires not the negation of the past, but its ironic rethinking.[5] Eco warns, however, that such an exercise can rapidly become self-defeating, because according to his characterization the label "postmodern" can be extended back to include Homer!

All this can be very confusing. What sets out as a radical transition, as a profound fragmentation (even a breakdown) of the existing order, is followed by an exasperating silence about what comes next. In such an ambiguous landscape, absent cartographic signposts, Christopher Norris declares: "texts and interpretative strategies compete for domination in a field staked out by no single order or validating method."[6] To help us through this morass, I shall focus on a simplified intellectual history in this chapter, including an etymology of the term "postmodern." Let me warn the reader that many other interpretations are possible (a guide to some of the most useful is included at the end of this book). Also, I regard any attempt to reconcile these various archeologies as beside the point; ultimately, I am more persuaded by Stanley Fish, who asks not what postmodernism means, but instead focuses on what it does.[7]

Figure 2.1/b   Museum of Jurassic Technology (photo by Michael Dear)
Mouse Cures: Bed wetting or general incontinence of urine can be controlled by eating mice on toast, fur and all. Mouse Pie, when eaten with regularity, serves as a remedy for children who stammer.

A flayne Mouse, or made in powder and drunk at one tyme, doeth perfectly helpe such as cannot holde or keepe their water: especially, if it be used three days in this order. This is verie trye and often puruved.

1579 Lupton
Thousand NotableThings 1/40

Origins

It is a general weakness of men delivering ideas that they are able to convince themselves their words represent a break with the past and a new beginning. . . . If ours is the advanced civilization we pretend it is, there should be no need to act as if all decisions were designed to establish certainties.

John Ralston Saul[8]

According to Stephen Toulmin, if any historical era is ending, it is the era of Modernity itself: "The very project of Modernity...seems to have lost momentum, and we need to fashion a successor program."[9] With commendable clarity and wit, Toulmin determines that the modern world began in the 1630s; that its problems were caused by the lust for certainty and stability that obsessed those who had suffered through the earlier war-torn eras.[10] Before that, in the late Renaissance, the generations of Erasmus, Rabelais and Montaigne had fostered an intellectual openness, a tolerance of diversity, and an uneasiness with assertions of definitive truth. Montaigne, for example, regarded attempts to reach theoretical consensus as presumptuous and self-deceptive.

The mid-seventeenth century's economic depression brought prosperity to a skidding halt. It was also a time when printing opened up the classical traditions to lay readers, and the emergence of nationstates permitted new loyalties. Religious fanaticism and war had driven Europe to the edge of chaos, and as a consequence, certainty and stability came to be prized above skepticism and tolerance. Following 1600, the indeterminate gave way in a few quick decades as "scholars condemned as irrational *con*fusion what others welcomed as intellectual *pro*fusion."[11] For the next three centuries, the "modernity" represented by Descartes, Galileo and Newton dominated scholarship and encased our intellects in bonds that we are only now beginning to unravel.

Instead of expanding the scope for rational debate, seventeenth-century scientists narrowed it. Instead of grounding their debates in the real world, seventeenth-century philosophers sought to render their questions independent of context. In Toulmin's felicitous phrases, the consequent intellectual narrowing may be understood as a shift:

> *from oral to written* (formal logic and proof were approved; rhetoric and argument were rejected);

> *from particular to universal* (general principles were favored over particular cases);

> *from local to general* (concrete diversity was rejected, abstract axioms preferred); and

> *from timely to timeless* (the permanent was foregrounded at the expense of the ephemeral or transitory).[12]

In sum, theirs was a move from a practical philosophy toward a theoretical philosophy.[13]

Charlene Spretnak notes how the development of what we now understand as modernist precepts relied on four historical moments: the Renaissance, the Reformation, the Scientific Revolution, and the Enlightenment. Each was a well-intentioned reaction against the church–state monopoly on power and knowledge in the medieval world, yet all had internal contradictions that ultimately would lead to the crisis of modernity. The *Renaissance* represented a rebirth of classical learning that eventually led to the establishment of secular education based on humanist values; it contrasted a Christian view of humans as weak and prone to sin with a neo-classical sense of Rational Man's unbounded potential.[14] The *Reformation* was a rationalization of religious belief and practice that shifted the emphasis from sacramental experiences to study of the word and text. The Protestant rebellion also advanced private judgement and autonomy against monolithic institutional authority, and established a focus on internal subjectivity which was to become a core feature of modern thought. Spretnak argues that the Reformation doctrine of God's absolute sovereignty precluded revelation through contemplation of the natural world, and thus prepared the ground for the idea of the passivity of nature that was central to the *Scientific Revolution*.[15] As church authority declined, a growing uncertainty about truth, valid knowledge, and reality was ultimately replaced by the precepts of the Scientific Revolution which located truth in that which could be measured (e.g. quantitative data, mathematical formulation, and the laws of physics). Finally, the last of four movements that created the modern worldview, the *Enlightenment*, extended the search for laws and truth to all aspects of human behavior. The task of the Age of Reason was to affect radical 'social engineering' by designing institutions and practices to reflect natural laws. The Enlightenment was a scientific reforming of society as a whole.[16]

But, as many have observed, modernist thought over-reached itself, becoming as rigid and intolerant as that which it was intended to replace. In the name of order and stability, Enlightenment thought went on to condone social injustice, and punish claims that cast doubt on its veracity. The science that was so extravagantly admired as pure and impartial was actually place- and time-bound, although its advocates chose to forget that it was only one epistemological variant among many. They were so effective in their advocacy that the subsequent centuries have effectively been held hostage by a desire for order that stemmed from the conflicts of the sixteenth and seventeenth centuries. As a result, the open-mindedness and adaptability of (for instance) the generation of Montaigne were erased from collective memory. Only now have postmodernists begun to reclaim this heritage. In Toulmin's acid wit: "The surgery imposed on European thought by the 17th-century zealots and perfectionists was so drastic that convalescence was unavoidably slow."[17]

Legacies

Despite John Ralston Saul's presumption that we are presiding over the "dotage of the Age of Reason", we perforce live with the legacies of modernism.[18] These ubiquitous axioms are so taken for granted that we tend to forget them. Charlene Spretnak spells them out for us:[19]

1. Humans are considered essentially as economic beings, so the proper arrangement of economic endeavors will bring contentment in all other spheres of life. In the search for material well-being, evolution is assumed to be unidirectional, i.e. the human condition progresses toward increasingly better states as the past is continuously improved upon.
2. Ontological and epistemological world views are dominated by:
   - *objectivism*, the belief that there is a rational structure to reality, and that through reason, these structures can be uncovered;
   - *rationalism*, a commitment to reason as the sole basis for knowledge and action, especially 'pure reason,' untainted by emotions, senses, or social constructs;

- *a mechanistic worldview* of the physical world as a composite of matter and energy, subject to laws of cause and effect;
- *reductionism*, a bias toward understanding the smallest unit of composition in a given system; and
- *scientism*, the belief that all fields of inquiry can obtain objective knowledge by following the investigative practices of the scientific method.
3. The design and organization of work in an industrial society are based on principles of standardization, bureaucratization, and centralization/hierarchization.
4. Modern interactions with nature are anthropocentric (in the sense that the human species is viewed as the central phenomenon of the natural world), and guided by instrumental reasoning (i.e. directed toward ends or "successful" actions). Most especially, modern culture defines itself in opposition to nature, through its ability to control/dominate natural forces; it is contemptuous of non-modern cultures that do not share these dispositions.
5. Modern life is compartmentalized to such an extent that family life, work, spiritual life (and so on) are considered as discrete spheres. A social Darwinist view of life as a competitive struggle establishes antagonist relations among these spheres, and such relationships are often characterized as 'hypermasculine' (for their emphasis on rationality, dominance, etc.) as distinct from more feminine traits such as empathy.

Modernity persists as a pervasive ideology. Spretnak still uses it to describe the era in which we live. It has been institutionalized as a normative belief system in our society, despite the fact that many of its central tenets (including the perfectibility of human existence through rational thought) has been repeatedly refuted. Ironically, today the very realization of the modern condition has itself caused the greatest disillusionment with modernity.

Archeology of the Postmodern

There is no unified postmodern theory, no consensus regarding its history, and no coherent set of positions. The term itself is often under-theorized and haphazardly applied. In one of the clearest efforts to shed light, Best and Kellner begin by distinguishing between modernity, conceptualized as the modern age, and post-modernity, understood as an epochal term describing the period following modernity.[20] There are, of course, many discourses of modernity, referring to a variety of economic, political, and socio-cultural transformations. Thus, for Karl Marx and Max Weber, modernity is the historical epoch following Feudalism; for others, "modernity" is used generically to refer to any shift from more traditional societies. The ways in which modernity produced a newly-industrialized world are described by Best and Kellner as "modernization", a term denoting those processes of "individualization, secularization, industrialization, cultural differentiation, commodification, urbanization, bureaucratization, and rationalization which together have constituted the modern world."[21] The era of postmodernity constitutes a novel stage of history and cultural formations that require a revamping of our concepts and theories, principally because the theoretical discourses of modernity championed reason as the source of progress and the privileged locus of truth and systematic knowledge.

In their etymological detective-work, Best and Kellner discovered that an English painter, John Watkins Chapman, used the phrase "postmodern painting"around 1870 in order to designate artwork that was more modern and avant-garde than French Impressionism. After 1945, the notion of a "postmodern" break appeared in D. C. Sommervell's account of Arnold Toynbee's *A Study of History*. Toynbee himself adopted the term, claiming that Western Civilization entered a transitional period about 1875 which he termed a "postmodern age," characterized by anarchy and relativism. In the mid-1950s, US economist Peter Drucker described a postmodern society as roughly equivalent to what came to be called post-industrial society. More ominous overtones of a postmodern age emerged in C. Wright Mills' *The Sociological Imagination* (1959). According to Mills:

> We are at the ending of what is called The Modern Age. Just as Antiquity was followed by several centuries of Oriental ascendancy, which Westerners provincially call the Dark Ages, so now The Modern Age has been succeeded by a post-modern period.[22]

He advocated that we begin to conceptualize the changes taking place in order to "grasp the outline of a new epoch we suppose ourselves to be entering."[23]

In the cultural sphere, Best and Kellner noticed that the term "postmodern" became current during the 1960s and 1970s, although it had been used before then in poetry and architecture. Cultural and social theorists picked up on both the ideas of an epochal break and an emergence of new artistic forms. Against modernist seriousness, purity, and individuality, postmodern art counterposed a new playfulness and eclecticism characterized by pastiche, irony, even nihilism. By the mid-1970s, the idea of postmodernism as a new historical era had picked up some momentum. For instance, Daniel Bell regarded postmodern culture as a radical assault on the bureaucratic, technocratic, and organizational imperatives of capitalist democracy.

The most important public events that provided an intellectual impetus to postmodern thought occurred in France during the 1960s. There, rapid changes in the political economy were paralleled by dramatic changes in a scholarly world that had previously been dominated by structuralist theory and philosophy. Until then, structuralists had focused on the underlying rules that organized the social system. They aimed at objectivity, coherence, rigor, and truth; they claimed scientific status for their theories. In the inevitable dialectic of response and counter-response, post-structuralists began to attack the scientific pretensions of structuralism, which they regarded as based in the standard modernist ideals of foundation, truth, and objectivity. Instead, post-structuralism stressed the history and politics of everyday life that had been suppressed by the abstractions of the structuralist project. Many post-structuralists were later to follow Jacques Derrida in the search for a radically new philosophical practice. Precursors of such a critique are Nietzsche, Heidegger, and Wittgenstein. For example, Nietzsche argued for a perspectivist orientation in which there are no facts only interpretations, and no objective truths only social constructs of various individuals or groups.

These shifts in French intellectual life were given a sharper edge by contemporaneous political upheavals that questioned broader social conventions. The street demonstrations of May 1968 taught many (including Michel Foucault) about the intimate connection between power and knowledge, and that power saturates all aspects of social and personal life. These new social movements posed strong challenges to Marxian political conceptions based on the primacy of labor, calling forth a politics that addressed multiple sources of oppression that were irreducible to the exploitation of labor. Marx's emphasis on the primacy of economic relations of power was replaced with the Nietzschean focus on multiple forms of domination, and decentered political alliances anticipated postmodern principles of decentering and difference.

Best and Kellner interpret post-structuralism (correctly, I believe) as a subset of a broader range of theoretical tendencies that constitute postmodern discourse. Post-structuralism, understood as a critique of structuralist theory and a desire for new modes of thought, writing, and subjectivity, was appropriated by postmodernism, radicalized, and extended into new theoretical fields. The prefix "post" signified a rupture with what had gone before; it has been regarded positively as a liberation from old constraints, or negatively as a loss of traditional or still-valuable elements of modernity. Yet the prefix also signifies a continuity with past trends, leading some to regard postmodernism as merely an intensification of the modern, a hyper-modernity, or a super-modernity.[24]

For their part, Best and Kellner do not interpret postmodernism as a radical break, requiring totally new theories and modes of thought. But they concede that vast changes in society and culture, sometimes justifying the term "postmodern," do warrant a reconstruction of social and cultural theory.[25] Likewise, while accepting parts of the postmodern critique of modernity, they are unwilling to completely renounce modernity.

The Meanings of Postmodernism

For me, the radical opening made possible by postmodernism is both invigorating and sometimes exasperating. On one hand, it has liberated our theoretical discourse and legitimized a wide variety of different voices. We no longer need to rely on implausible doctrines of objectivity to defend our contributions to knowledge, and we can treat truth claims as arguments rather than as unassailable findings.[26] The echoes of Nietzsche are once again loud: whatever the "facts" are, it is we who do the talking. On the other hand, the Babel of different, newly-enfranchised voices can also be profoundly disorienting. In a relativistic world, where intellectual pretensions of any kind are often treated with disdain, how can we begin to make sense of the pluralistic pastiche of plausible alternative theoretical visions?

In order to move beyond a sense of pleasurable yet directionless exhilaration, I need to review in more detail the most important meanings of postmodernism: as style, method, and epoch. Needless to say, other mental taxonomies are possible, but this one has proven to be quite durable since I first used it in the mid-1980s. At the very minimum, it will help to clear some common ground.

Postmodernism as style

The contemporary explosion of interest in postmodern thought may be traced to the emergence of new styles of literature and literary criticism in the 1960s and 1970s.[27] A particular vision of "affirmative" modernism in the late 1960s gave rise to a series of mixed-media productions and performances which aimed to break down the boundaries of artistic specializations. The aim of these "postmodernists" was to open up "the immense variety and richness of things, materials and ideas that the modern world inexhaustibly brought forth. They breathed fresh air and playfulness into a cultural ambience which in the 1950s had become unbearably solemn, rigid and closed."[28]

Postmodern cultural sensitivities quickly spread to other artistic endeavors including design, painting and photography. The example of architecture is particularly revealing.[29] Most cities have, by now, been tainted or blessed by postmodern architecture. The term was used to mark an architectural departure from the modern style. The search for the new was associated with a revolt against the formalism and austerity of the modern style, epitomized by the unadorned office tower. No destination was specified for the departure, but this central ambiguity was part of the seductiveness of postmodernism. Some advocates of the postmodern no doubt had the intention of creating a new building style for popular consumption. But postmodern architecture never gained widespread popular appeal. Instead, it was hailed because it provided architects with the opportunity to comment on previous stylist genres, often caustically and with wit.[30] Postmodernism thus became an internal dialogue for the initiated. Buildings assumed an iconography (or signification) directed both at previous architectural styles and at anticipated critics of the new buildings itself. The postmodern building became a self-referential symbol and commentary. In many cities, revamped design traditions of every era embellished with witty devices began to appear; it mattered little that few people understood the points of reference in these pastiches.

Needless to say, advocates of postmodern architecture will not necessarily share this skeptical view. Inveterate chronicler Charles Jencks takes the trend very seriously (to his credit), placing much emphasis on the demands by public and client for a new building style:

> Post Modern Architecture is doubly-coded, half-Modern and half-conventional, in its attempt to communicate with both the public and a concerned minority, usually architects.[31]

Jencks argues that the way to avoid degenerate pastiche is through participatory design, in which clients subject the designer to "codes not necessarily his own in a way he can respect them."[32] He recognizes that it is difficult to adopt a plural coding without degenerating into compromise and unintended pastiche. This is unwittingly revealed in his periodization of the postmodern architectural movement that includes such terms as historicism, straight revivalism, neo-vernacular, ad hoc urbanism, metaphor and metaphysics, and postmodern space.[33] Several other themes were added to these (for example, radical eclecticism) as his book proceeded through successive editions.

To a critical but uninitiated outsider, postmodern architecture seems on occasion to be fun, sometimes clever, and even attractive. It apparently rejuvenated a somewhat jaded, directionless profession. (Architecture has not been immune from contemporary economic and political vagaries.) However, beyond its origins as a stylistic device, postmodern architecture has remained a singularly superficial philosophy. As it has done before in its history, architecture seemed once again to have established a rhetorical code solely for the benefit of practitioners. It was disparagingly referred to as "memory architecture" by its detractors, for its grafting of historical references onto contemporary design; and its obituary appeared very early in architectural magazines. The disembodied version of postmodern architectural style does great disservice to the spirit behind the movement. Postmodernism is not solely a matter of aesthetics. To their credit, a small coterie of architects and critics have managed to resuscitate the broader meanings of postmodernism in architectural thought. And postmodernism continues to flourish in other fields of artistic endeavor.

Postmodernism as epoch

Perhaps the grandest dimension of postmodernism is its claim to represent an epochal transition. In some sense or other, as Eco warned, most proponents of ideas or movements wish to appear "modern."[34] This desire may take a relatively innocuous form, as in the wish to appear fashionable or to represent a break with precedent. More particularly, an intellectual movement might experience a period of reflection during which it becomes self-conscious of its collective identity.[35] The sum of self-awareness, of a shared culture, of a niche in time–space might then be adopted to ascribe an historical limit to the movement. This is one sense in which we may speak of postmodernism as an epoch of transition, as some kind of "radical break" with past ideas.[36] Many use the term "postmodernity" to refer specifically to this epochal emphasis in postmodern discourse.

Another common concept of radical break applies to the material world. Fredric Jameson is the author of an audacious claim that postmodernism is:

> A periodizing concept whose function is to correlate the emergence of new formal features in culture with the emergence of a new type of social life and a new economic order.[37]

Needless to say, it is not easy to recognize the emergent order. This may be because radical breaks between periods

> do not generally involve complete changes of content but rather the restructuration of a certain number of elements already given; features that in an earlier period or system were subordinate now became dominant, and features that had been dominant again became secondary.[38]

Despite the problems of identification, Jameson asserts that the total ensemble of presences and differences has accumulated into a postmodern "cultural dominant." It has been generated by the "late capitalist" era of commodity production, which has imposed its own peculiar cultural stamp on society. The imprint that remains is characterized by a new depthlessness, in which reality is visible only through a multitude of superficial reflections; by a dominant mode of pastiche, a "stupendous proliferation of social codes" including the random cannibalization of architectural styles; and by a consequent loss of historical coordinates.[39]

Assessing postmodernity as an intellectual and/or material epoch is an exercise in theorizing contemporaneity.[40] How can we begin to interpret the overall significance of an infinity of overlapping realities? Obviously, the simultaneous appearance of two objects at the same chronological spatial moment need not imply a causal relation. The time–space landscape is more likely to consist of a melange of the obsolete, current, and newborn artifacts commingling anachronistically in each place. How do we make sense of this variety? Space and time take on a new significance in assessing the postmodern era. According to Jameson, old systems of organization and perception have been destroyed, and replaced by a postmodern hyperspace.[41] Space and time have been stretched to accommodate the multinational global space of advanced capitalism. Because we are currently unable to grasp the coordinates of this space, Jameson calls for a new "global cognitive mapping, on a social as well as spatial scale."[42] One key to this new map is architecture, a "privileged aesthetic language"[43] that best illuminates the virtually unmediated relationship between culture and commodity production.[44]

Jameson's project simultaneously liberates the concept of postmodernism to imply something much more than architectural filigree, but also imposes a tremendous burden of proof on those who would use the concept in any historical sense. Especially challenging are his appeal to time–space relations in understanding postmodern hyperspace, and his focus on the built environment as the text for decoding this hyperspace. Mike Davis is profoundly critical of Jameson's view of the radical break implied by postmodernity.[45] He argues that it is unreasonable to read too much into postmodern architecture, which

> has little organic or expressive relationship to industrial production or emerging technology; it is not raising "cathedrals of the microchip" ... [Whereas] the "classical" skyscraper romanticized the hegemony of corporate bureaucracy and mass production, the postmodern tower is merely a package of standardized space to be gift-wrapped to the clients' taste.[46]

He also warns of the methodological dangers in subsuming "under a master concept too many contradictory phenomena which, though undoubtedly visible in the same chronological moment, are nonetheless separated in their true temporalities."[47] Instead, Davis deliberately adopts the notion of late capitalism to emphasize postmodernity as (if anything) a decadent *fin-de-siècle frisson*, a culmination more than beginning.[48]

Postmodernism as method

Postmodernism is, in Lyotard's words, frankly "incredulous toward metanarratives."[49] It holds out for a philosophical culture free from the search for the ultimate foundations of everything. Such a philosophy would be a "conversation" from which no-one is excluded and in which no-one holds a privileged position. The philosopher's sole purpose is to keep the conversation going. In practical terms, postmodernism has taken the form of a revolt against the too-rigid conventions of existing method and language. It has attacked the intellectual conditions that allow for and tolerate the dominance of one discourse over another. It has therefore worked against the potentially repressive power of theoretical metalanguages that act to marginalize nonconforming discourse.

Postmodern philosophy has been powered by a simple but penetrating question: On what basis can a claim be made for a privileged status of one theoretical view-point over another? The answer given is that all such claims are ultimately undecid-able. The impact of this response has been immense.[50] The central issue in most subsequent debates is authority; i.e. on what basis is a privileged position being claimed? One specific focus in these debates is on how language is used to maintain the hegemony of the privileged discourse, and how it may be reclaimed to permit an open dialogue. The effects of these questions have been profoundly destabilizing and potentially anarchic. Why? Well, because all paradigms, theoretical frameworks, and discourses are obliged to surrender their privileged status. They are, in principle at least, all equally important or unimportant. Moreover, there is no clear consensus on the criteria by which claims to privilege will be judged; and, as importantly, hard-line postmodernists hold that all attempts to forge such a consensus should be resisted, since its effect will ultimately be to re-establish the hegemony of some metanarrative.

Postmodern philosophy rose to prominence partly because of its association with the "linguistic turn." This refers to the realization/belief that language lies at the heart of knowledge. Our conceptual orderings, it is claimed, do not exist in the nature of things, but instead reflect our mental architectures. These, in turn, contain conscious and unconscious strategies of exclusion, and are rife with internal contra-diction and suppressed paradox. The task of deconstruction is to expose these contradictions and paradoxes. Deconstruction shows how language imposes limits on our thinking. The stress on what has been spoken or written becomes only as important as what is hidden or unsayable (i.e. beyond the conventions of language). According to Derrida, this kind of paradox can never be entirely avoided. We can never control the effects of the language we use; they will always go beyond what we intend or anticipate. Hence, we inevitably fail in the exercise of representation, and the interpretive task is complicated by the essential undecidability of textual mean-ing. Since no textual system can be complete and fully self-validating, deconstruction focuses on showing us how to read for absences in a text, particularly the way in which archetypes of linguistic convention can lull us into a false sense of security about the "truth" of a text.

Taken together, postmodernism and deconstruction represent a profound intellec-tual challenge. Irrespective of how one feels about these trends, it must be recognized that their effects have already been felt in even the most parched corners of intellec-tual life. The impacted disciplines now face the task of making sense of a post-modern-induced anarchy. There is no simple method for the task of reconstruction. Postmodernists reject the very notion of constructing metanarratives. They have been accused of promoting the end of philosophy because they have transformed the discipline into an infinity of incommensurable language games – no more than an extended sequence of conversations (an idea most notoriously associated with philo-sopher Richard Rorty).[51] Critics have attempted to recover rationality in discourse: some plead for a return to old verities; others defend the traditions of Modernism or the Enlightenment even as they begin the search for a transformation in philosophy. I examine some of these alternatives later in this chapter.

Postmodern pedagogy and politics

Many difficulties in postmodernism derive from the problem of knowing the present. As Steven Connor put it: "knowledge arrives too late on the scene of experience."[52] Indeed, one of the principal reasons for postmodernism's obsession with culture is the need to understand the current. For Connor, postmodernism negotiates the space between cultural and critical activity.[53] He appeals to the Foucauldian notion of "heterotopia" (the multiplication of centers of power and the dissolution of totalizing narratives) to underscore that the current ambiguity and uncertainty have intensified the issue of political legitimacy. The consequent crises of legitimacy are experienced everywhere, including academia, where practitioners deal daily with structures of radical incommensurability of many types and sources. Such conditions, Connor asserts,[54] present the academy with a crisis of self-definition in which it "may no longer be possible to deny that postmodernism exists."[55]

Connor makes clear that he is not against Modernism, but against its institution-alization within the academy.[56] This is an important distinction. It understands postmodernism as a discursive function that attempts "to see knowledge produced in and alongside critical and academic institutions in terms of power-interests and relations that sustain them." [57] The pedagogic challenge is accepted by literary theorist Gerald Graff, who (echoing Toulmin) welcomes the intellectual profusion which others condemn as the irrational confusions of postmodernism. The conse-quence may well be, according to Graff, a "disabling incoherence,"[58] but there is no purpose to be served by restoring some artificial consensus – going back to "basics," or reasserting "the canon." Indeed, Graff insists that from the outset there never was agreement about what constituted the canon. Instead, we dwelt blithely among a series of unacknowledged and unresolved conflicts which were assumed to be outside the realm of (literary) studies.[59] Intellectual battles were thus fought in private, according to principles of "professionalization" and "academization" that were far from neutral.

When academic hegemonies are left unexamined or unchallenged, the result is inertia, even decline. Graff points out that, in practice, dissent is most usually dealt with through the "field-coverage" model. The curriculum is assumed to be a self-regulating Grid of (in Graff's case) "periods, genres, and themes." Innovations are accounted for by adding a new piece to the curriculum, thereby removing the necessity for confrontation. It is assumed that the subject teaches itself, since ex-posure to the Grid is all that is needed to provide students with the tools to make up their own minds.

Graff identifies the essential dishonesties in this approach,[60] pointing out that:

(a)   Grids and disciplinary boundaries constitute the fields they organize and thereby control the process of learning;
(b)   students are not provided with the tools to distinguish between legitimate and illegitimate forms of institutional power; and

(c)   what does not go into the curriculum cannot be manifest in a student's thinking
      (e.g. if you don't teach feminist theory, you cannot expect it to feature in a
      student's intellectual tool-kit).

There is no alternative, in Graff's mind, but to teach difference, i.e. to deliberately
confront the contradictions and ambiguities inherent in any structure of knowledge.

Let it be said immediately that Graff's conclusion is not popular. Conservative
critics have attacked vehemently what they perceive to be the political correctness
lurking behind efforts to insist on diversity in curricula. In one of her many broad-
sides during (and after) her tenure as George Bush's chair of the US National
Endowment for the Humanities, Lynne V. Cheney accused "liberal" scholars of
using classrooms to advance their political agendas and indoctrinate students. In
apocalyptic terms she claimed: "The aim of education, as many on our campuses
how see it, is no longer truth, but political transformation – of students and
society."[61] This is but one skirmish in what has become known as the "Culture
Wars" of the 1990s in the United States. Broadly speaking, these wars flared up when
conservatives attempted to counter what they perceived as the erosion of traditional
values of family, country, and religion. In one instance, a 1995 exhibition at the
Smithsonian Institution in Washington DC, to commemorate the fiftieth anniversary
of the end of World War II, was canceled after protests that its perspective on the
atom-bombing of Japan was politically correct and thoroughly anti-American. Then
presidential candidate Bob Dole attacked the exhibition even after its cancellation,
blaming

> "the arbitrators of political correctness," "government and intellectual elites who seem
> embarrassed by America." and "educators and professors" engaged in "a shocking
> campaign...to disparage America" and destroy the "keys" to American unity, its
> "language, history, and values."[62]

Evidently, the decision for or against postmodernism is peppered with politics.
According to Hal Foster postmodernism is a "strategy of interference;"[63] the purpose
of deconstructing modernism is "to open its closed system...to challenge its master
narratives with the 'discourse of others'."[64] Foster zeroes in on just how radical the
postmodern project can be:

- it involves a critique of what he terms the "supreme fictions" of grand theories
- a sensitivity to difference
- a skepticism toward experts and disciplinary boundaries
- a commitment to tracing the social affiliations of truth claims and those who
  make them.[65]

The reconstructive agenda thus implied distinguishes between what Foster calls a
postmodernism of reaction and a postmodernism of resistance.[66] The first repudiates
deconstruction to celebrate the status quo; it is conceived essentially as therapeutic or
cosmetic, a retreat to the lost verities of tradition. The second mode of resistance
seeks to use deconstruction to resist the status quo. It desires to change the object and
its social context. The distinction between reaction and resistance is crucial in

understanding the potential futures of the postmodern agenda. It highlights the political nature of the reconstructive choices, opposing a rhetoric of the status quo (reaction) against an agenda for political change (resistance). Foster advocates the second "oppositional" or "resistant" postmodernism. For him, "postmodernism is best conceived as a conflict of new and old modes... and of the interests vested therein."[67] His oppositional postmodernism is

> concerned with a critical deconstruction of tradition, not an instrumental pastiche of pop- or pseudo-historical forms, with a critique of origins, not a return to them. In short, it seeks to question rather than exploit cultural codes, to explore rather than conceal social and political affiliation.[68]

What next?

"To every human problem, there is a solution that is simple, neat, and wrong."[69]
                                                                                    Walter Lippman

What will happen after postmodernism? I would like to gesture toward some of the next steps without foreclosing on any of the major issues.

The hype surrounding the rhetoric of postmodern architectural style masks a more profound question: that is, how does the spatial form of the built environment reflect, and condition, social relations over time and space? This is not solely an architectural issue, although architecture is part of socio-spatial structuring. My view of the urban question is that the built environment is both the product of and mediator between social relations. Because of the inertia inherent in physical structures, obsolescent and newly-forming structures will exist side-by-side in the text of the city, adding to the complexity of textual interpretation. The city is an exceedingly complex ensemble of signs and signatures: architectural decoration is one key to decoding; so is the structure of city systems over time and space. So we shall need to retain the stylistic/textual emphasis in our study of postmodern urbanism.

The question of contemporaneity seems, at first glance, to be a sterile concern. What does it matter if we can (or cannot) say that we have entered a new epoch? How many material or intellectual artifacts do we have to accumulate before we can speak authoritatively of the existence of a cultural dominant? Postmodernism could ultimately prove to be an aberration in the evolutionary cycle, or the foreshock to some more catastrophic change. And yet it is difficult to deny the cumulative weight and speed of current social change: the nuclear age, the emergence of the "Third World," the collapse of Cold War geopolitics, globalization, space travel, deindustrialization, etc. The sense of a radical break (in material terms at least) somehow seems justifiable. And it would, to put it kindly, be humbling if we overlooked this transition in an unseemly haste to categorize objects and trends according to established tenets.

The methodological innovations of postmodernism are potentially far-reaching. The postmodern turn has spawned an extraordinarily rich series of projects in the social sciences and humanities, shattering conventional disciplinary boundaries. The plurality of discourse released by such work has severely undermined and strained traditional academic communities. In political terms, an oppositional postmodernism has called for a critique of existing master narratives, a refusal to privilege any particular discourse, a restoration of the constructive tension between different theories, and a willingness to trace the social origins of intellectual bias.[70] This is anything but the easygoing pluralism that some see as characteristic of postmodernism. Jameson regards a plurality of discourse as part of postmodernism, but its purpose is to turn reason against itself and uncover the tacit dependence on other repressed or unrecognized levels of meaning.[71] It seeks to undo the given order of intellectual priorities and the conceptual system that makes this ordering possible.[72]

How, then, shall we begin to discriminate amongst the cacophony of competing claims for theoretical preeminence? At the moment, we can only glimpse the structure of that emergent discourse; we remain "awash in a sea of private languages."[73] Some authors provide signposts for what could happen after postmodernism. For example, Jürgen Habermas argues for a recovery of the modernist project; Sandra Harding for a political way out of postmodernism's relativism; Stephen Toulmin for a compromise among postmodern, modern, and pre-modern thought; and Charlene Spretnak for a holistic reinvention of intellectual attitudes and practices. Let me briefly indicate what each of these positions is about.

Jürgen Habermas was fifteen years old when World War II ended. He had known no other society other than that of the Nazis, and had been a member of the Hitler Youth. Following the Nuremberg trials, he realized that he had been living in a "politically criminal" regime, and (to greatly oversimplify) much of his subsequent philosophy has been concerned with how we reason about human behavior. Prompted by the horrors of unreason represented by Nazism, Habermas believes that better communication will permit people to live together with respect and equality. The enduring morality and values of the Enlightenment are at the heart of his defense of what he terms the "project of modernity." And, importantly for us, Habermas readily concedes the strongly personal impetus to his philosophical concerns.[74]

Others are less sanguine about the prospect of recovering Enlightenment verities. Sandra Harding reveals the political dilemmas facing feminist thinkers. Once empowered by the advent of postmodernism, some feminists became less enamoured by what they perceived as postmodernism's apolitical ambivalence. For instance, Harding observes that Irigary denounced postmodernism as a patriarchal ruse; di Stefano observed that white men who have had their Enlightenment may now be prepared to subject it to critical scrutiny, but postmodernism makes a feminist politics impossible; and Hartsock faulted postmodernism because it gives little guidance to feminist politics. Harding herself leans towards what she terms a "principled ambivalence," a striving to combine those elements of science that can be harnessed to the feminist project. [75] Yet she cannot prevent her feminist "standpoint theory" from slipping toward Enlightenment essentialisms. There is a powerful undercurrent in her work that better theory and empirical work can lead to progressive improvement in the material conditions of women. In addition, though she claims that standpoint theory is against a unitary consciousness and is therefore anti-Enlightenment in its vision,[76] others have insisted on the unitary subject inherent in feminist thought (based on gender differences and the experience of otherness). In the final analysis, Harding asserts that feminists need both the Enlightenment and the postmodern agendas if they are to escape the damaging limitations of male-dominated social relations and conceptual schemes.[77]

Stephen Toulmin is more explicit about the need for intellectual reconciliation. Following Wittgenstein, he rejects the universal, timeless questions as unanswerable, as having no determinate meanings. He prefers not to build new, comprehensive theories but "to limit the scope of even the best framed theories."[78] In short, he recommends humanizing modernity by refusing to choose between humanism and science, and insisting on preserving the positive achievements of both. Above all, his recipe for the future is based on a revival of the lost Montaignian outlook, with its humanistic acceptance of diversity, concern for local circumstance, skepticism toward authority, rejection of hierarchy, refusal to make universal claims, and willingness to find particular solutions to difficult problems of values and ethics.

Charlene Spretnak makes a stunning claim that the replacement of modernity's outdated paradigm by a "postmodern ecological vision" is crucial to humanity's survival:

> Thanks to modern advances, traditional concerns stemming from the human condition have been largely conquered, managed, or replaced altogether: Modern life promised freedom from the vagaries of the body, the limits of nature, and the provincial ties to place. The body came to be seen as a biological machine, the natural world as a mere externality in modern economies, and the sense of place as a primitive precursor to cosmopolitan sophistication.[79]

The present challenges to modernity, she claims, are coming from precisely those areas that were marginalized by the modern age. The resurgence of body, nature, and place represents a rejection of the deep structure of modernity, with its view of the body as nothing but a biological machine, the biosphere as clockwork mechanism, and place as mere receptacle for human endeavors. In Spretnak's terms: "The real is poking its true nature through the modern abstractions that have denied it for several centuries."[80] She describes our age is hypermodern, not because the tarnished ideologies of the modern worldview are still cherished, but because modernity is now driven by the dynamics of the "technosphere and the globalized economy."[81] A truly "postmodern alternative" she claims, would counter the ideological flight from body, nature, and place; it would be a grounded, deeply ecological, and spiritual postmodernism, or, an ecological postmodernism: "To be truly postmodern is to reject that discontinuity by opening the box to connect anew with our larger context: The Earth, the cosmos, the sacred whole."[82]

Spretnak's holistic ecological postmodernism, Toulmin's vision of a humanized modernity, Harding's of a principled ambivalence, and Habermas' of a rebuilt modernity represent a far from complete account of the range of *post*-postmodern alternatives. I include them here to demonstrate that there has been much gnashing of teeth over resolving the perceived impasse of postmodernism's relativism (noting *en passant* how personalized the responses to postmodernism inevitably become). I should also warn that other writers will reject the postmodernism problematic I have presented in this chapter. It would take a separate volume to digress into these myriad perspectives. I will simply let Bruno Latour stand in for them all. He dismisses postmodernism as "a symptom, not a fresh solution," because "No one has ever been modern. Modernity has never begun. There has never been a modern world."[83] Well, perhaps. But readers will understand and forgive me if I do not pick up Latour's gauntlet at this time.

Instead, permit me to draw together some threads that will assist in what follows. Philosophy and social theory are best regarded as conversations about the way we know things. The conversation is a constant ebb and flow, of proposition and counter-proposition, with no prospect of final resolution. Certain conditions surround the conversation, including:

(a)   that social theory has never been composed of a single, coherent body of thought, and it likely never will;
(b)   that, inevitably, each theory is only a partial vision of the whole;
(c)   that theories possess a range of applicability, or "home domain," over which particular insight may be possible;
(d)   that all theories are not created equal, different theories do different things; and
(e)   that the various frameworks that comprise social theory all have some merit.

Fragmentation is thus an inevitable condition of the corpus of theory, and the totalizing tendency in many theories (much admired by adherents of "grand theory") is a misleading, reductionist exercise.

A pivotal skill in theory-building is the ability to identify the range of applicability (or home domain) of any given theory. This is not to suggest that we can decide which theory is right or wrong, but we may be able to identify the particular circumstances under which a theory best applies. However, this task is complicated by the lack of consensus on what criteria to employ when adjudicating between theories; in addition, different criteria may be appropriate on different occasions. We may, for instance, prefer a theory because it specifies the causal connections among a set of variables; because it has the capacity for prediction and empirical verifiability; because it possesses a strong internal consistency; or because of its elegance and parsimony. The very existence of a smorgasbord of evaluative criteria is testimony to the lack of general consensus, the elusive nature of truth.

The indeterminate conditions of knowing place an enormous premium on interpretation. Our knowledge of the world alters as we (the observers) change, and as the world itself (the observed) evolves. The practice of science is never still; it is, in a phrase, infinitely hermeneutic. "Truth" and "fact" are very elusive constructions, determined by the evolving states of the observer and the observed. There are no absolute truths about which there can be a common and permanent consensus; there are only degrees of freedom about an interpretation, which even then should be understood as being time- and place-contingent. In some sciences there may be relatively few degrees of freedom around an interpretation, leading us to speak of "laws;" the practices that lend themselves to this degree of certainty are often fondly referred to as the "hard" sciences. Other approaches (not "soft," and certainly not "easy") are beset by greater degrees of persistent ambiguity; in this sense, they are actually harder, in the sense of providing insurmountable interpretive problems, than are the "hard" sciences. In any event, ambiguity is a condition that besets all knowing. It therefore makes little sense to talk about facts, truth, the fidelity of a theory, or science itself without further qualification. These qualifiers should elucidate the conditions under which knowledge claims have been constructed. Understand that it is fully feasible to construct such conditional claims; what becomes damaging is when advocates assume the unconditional status of their statements, or when they institutionalize their conditions of knowing. Analysts/advocates should expect to specify and defend the criteria through which their claims of privilege are sought; and they should anticipate that such claims may then be systematically analyzed, and counter-positions advanced. The development of such a mode of comparative discourse is, unsurprisingly, one of the most difficult tasks in philosophy and theory – both technically and politically.

The diverse perspectives identified in this chapter all represent various ways of explaining the world. They are different ways of knowing, and the study of epistemology is concerned with such differences in perspective. When we begin to ask how we know things, to make judgements about the conditions of existence (or being) surrounding these diverse epistemologies, then we move into the realm of ontology. Postmodernism is best understood as an ontological stance. It is not a metanarrative in any conventional sense; that is, it is not simply one more epistemological variant, another kind of grand theory. In its purest form, postmodernism is a deliberately relativist stance with respect to all ways of knowing, and is profoundly anti-hegemonic in its vision. Most fundamentally, in postmodernism the conditions of knowing become an integral part of the problematic. The hegemony of any single theory is axiomatically rejected because the construction of theory is itself a key element of definition and understanding.

I realize that this is not the end of the story; rather it is the beginning of a whole host of new difficulties that must be confronted everywhere in this book. In a fractured world of knowing, the question of discriminating between different theories will always be with us, and the problems of personal and collective choice are in no way alleviated. But in a very preliminary way, I have begun in this chapter to set down the ramifications of the postmodern turn.

Figure 2.2   Calvin and Hobbes © 1990 Watterson. Reprinted with permission of Universal Press Syndicate. All rights reserved

Notes

1. Jencks, C., 1984: *The Language of Post-Modern Architecture*, New York: Rizzoli, p. 5.
2. Newman, C. H., 1985: *The Post-Modern Aura: The Act of Fiction in an Age of Inflation*, Evanston: Northwestern University Press, p. 1.
3. Eco, U., 1984: *Postscript to the Name of the Rose*, translated from the Italian by William Weaver, San Diego: Harcourt Brace Jovanovich, p. 66.
4. Ibid., pp. 66–68.
5. Berman quotes Kierkegaard to the effect that the deepest modern seriousness must express itself through irony. (Berman, M., 1982: *All That is Solid Melts into Air: The Experience of Modernity*, New York: Penguin Books, p. 14).
6. Norris, C., 1982: *Deconstruction: Theory and Practice*, London: Methuen, p. 87.
7. Quoted in Connor, S., 1989: *Postmodernist Culture : An Introduction to Theories of the Contemporary*, Cambridge, Mass: Blackwell, p. 6.
8. Saul, J. R., 1993. *Voltaire's Bastards: The Dictatorship of Reason in the West*, London: Penguin, pp. 38 and 585.
9. Toulmin, S., 1990: *Cosmopolis: The Hidden Agenda of Modernity*, New York: The Free Press, p. 3.
10. Ibid., p. 9.
11. Ibid., p. 27.
12. Ibid., pp. 30–5.
13. Ibid., p. 34.
14. Spretnak, C., 1997: *The Resurgence of the Real: Body, Nature and Place in the Hypermodern World*, Reading, MA: Addison-Wesley, p. 45.
15. Ibid., p. 50–2.
16. Ibid., p. 56–7, and 85.
17. Toulmin, S., *Cosmopolis: The Hidden Agenda of Modernity*, p. xxx.
18. Saul, J. R., *Voltaire's Bastards: The Dictatorship of Reason in the West*, p. 9.
19. Spretnak, C., *The Resurgence of the Real: Body, Nature and Place in the Hypermodern World*, pp. 40–1, and 219–21.
20. Best, S. and Kellner, D., 1991: *Postmodern Theory: Critical Interrogations*, New York, Guilford Press.
21. Ibid., p. 3.
22. Mills, C. W., 1959: *The Sociological Imagination*, New York: Oxford University Press, pp. 165–6.
23. Ibid., p. 166.
24. Augé, M., 1995. *Non-Places: Introduction to An Anthropology of Super-Modernity*, New York: Verso.
25. Best, S. and Kellner, *Postmodern Theory: Critical Interrogations*, p. 32.
26. Nelson, J. S., Megill, A. and McCloskey, D. N. (eds.), 1987: *The Rhetoric of the Human Sciences: Language and Argument in Scholarship and Public Affairs*, Madison: University of Wisconsin Press, p. 4.
27. Best, S. and Kellner, D., *Postmodern Theory: Critical Interrogations*; Huyssen, A., 1984: "Mapping the Postmodern," *New German Critique*, 33, pp. 5–52.
28. Berman, M., 1982: *All That is Solid Melts into Air: The Experience of Modernity*, New York: Penguin Books, p. 32.
29. Jencks, C. (ed.), 1992: *The Postmodern Reader*, London: Academy Editions, New York: St. Martin's Press.
30. Jencks, C., *The Language of Post-Modern Architecture*.
31. Ibid., p. 6.

32. Ibid., p. 88.

33. Ibid., p. 80.

34. Compare Eco, U., 1984: *Postscript to the Name of the Rose*, translated from the Italian by William Weaver, San Diego: Harcourt Brace Jovanovich.

35. Foster, H., 1985: *Postmodern Culture*, London: Pluto Press.

36. Jameson, F., 1984: "Postmodernism, or the Cultural Logic of Late Capitalism," *New Left Review*, 146, p. 53.

37. Jameson, F., 1985: "Postmodernism and Consumer Society," in Foster, H. *Postmodern Culture*, London, Pluto Press, p. 113.

38. Ibid., p. 123.

39. Jameson, F., "Postmodernism, or the Cultural Logic of Late Capitalism," p. 55–65.

40. Davis, M., 1985: "Urban Renaissance and the Spirit of Post-Modernism," *New Left Review*, 151, p. 107.

41. Jameson, F. "Postmodernism, or the Cultural Logic of Late Capitalism," pp. 83–4.

42. Ibid., p. 92.

43. Ibid., p. 79.

44. Ibid., p. 56.

45. Davis, M., "Urban Renaissance and the Spirit of Post-Modernism."

46. Ibid., pp. 108–9.

47. Ibid., p. 107.

48. Ibid., p. 108.

49. Lyotard, F., 1984: *The Postmodern Condition: A Report on Knowledge*, translation from the French by Geoff Bennington and Brian Massumi, Minneapolis: University of Minnesota Press.

50. See, for example, Rorty, R., 1982: *Consequences of Pragmatism: Essays, 1972–1980*, Minneapolis: University of Minnesota Press; Unger, 1986: *The Critical Legal Studies Movement*, Cambridge: Harvard University Press; Jencks, C., *The Language of Post-Modern Architecture*.

51. Rorty, R., *Consequences of Pragmatism: Essays, 1972–1980*.

52. Connor, S., 1989: *Postmodernist Culture: An Introduction to Theories of the Contemporary*, Cambridge, Mass: Blackwell, p. 3.

53. Ibid., p. 7.

54. Ibid., p. 19.

55. Ibid., p. 20.

56. Ibid., p. 12.

57. Ibid., p. 11.

58. Graff, G., 1987: *Professing Literature, An Institutional History*, Chicago: University of Chicago Press.

59. Ibid.

60. Ibid., pp. 11–13.

61. Cheney, L. 1992, quoted in Burd, Stephen: "Humanities Chief Assails Politicization of Classrooms," *The Chronicle of Higher Education*, September 30, p. A22. Cheney, L. 1995: *Telling the Truth: Why Our Culture and Our Country Have Stopped Making Sense, and What We Can Do About It*, New York: Simon & Schuster, p. A21.

62. Quoted in Linenthal, E. T. and Engelhardt, T. (eds.) 1996: *History Wars: The Enola Gay and Other Battles for the American Past*, New York: Metropolitan Books, p. 2.

63. Foster, H. *Postmodern Culture*; Said, E., "Opponents, Audiences, Constituencies, and Communities," in Foster, H. (ed), *Postmodern Culture*.

64. Foster, H. *Postmodern Culture*, p. xi.

65. Ibid., p. xv.

66. Ibid., p. xii.

67. Ibid., p. xi.
68. Ibid., p. xii, emphases added.
69. Ibid., p. 201.
70. Foster, H. *Postmodern Culture*, p. xv; Jameson, F., "Postmodernism, or the Cultural Logic of Late Capitalism," pp. 55–65, pp. 74–8; Owens, C., 1985: "The Discourse of Others: Feminism and Postmodernism" in Foster, H. *Postmodern Culture*, p. 63–4; and Said, E., "Opponents, Audiences, Constituencies, and Communities," in Foster, H. (ed) *Postmodern Culture*.
71. Jameson, F., "Postmodernism and Consumer Society," in Foster, H. *Postmodern Culture*, p. 112.
72. Norris, C., *Deconstruction: Theory and Practice*, pp. 31 and 64.
73. Foster, H., *Postmodern Culture*, p. xiv.
74. Stephens, M., 1994: "The Theologian of Talk," *Los Angeles Times Magazine*, October 23, p. 44.
75. Harding, S., 1990: "Feminism, Science and the Anti-Enlightenment Critiques," in Nicholson, L. J., *Feminism/Postmodernism*. New York, London: Routledge, p. 80.
76. Ibid., p. 98.
77. Toulmin, S., *Cosmopolis: The Hidden Agenda of Modernity*, p. 101.
78. Ibid., p. 193.
79. Spretnak, C., *The Resurgence of the Real: Body, Nature and Place in the Hypermodern World*, p. 2.
80. Ibid., p. 13.
81. Ibid., p. 222.
82. Ibid., p. 66.
83. Latour, B., 1993: *We Have Never Been Modern*, Cambridge: Harvard University Press, pp. 46–7.

3

Postmodern Bloodlines:
From Lefebvre to Jameson

Space, one might say, is nature's way of preventing everything from happening in the same place. Much of Henri Lefebvre's work is essentially a fugue on this simple proposition. Richly embellishing the theme in *The Production of Space*, he identifies the following kinds of space: absolute, abstract, appropriated, capitalist, concrete, contradictory, cultural, differentiated, dominated, dramatized, epistemological, familial, instrumental, leisure, lived, masculine, mental, natural, neutral, organic, original, physical, plural, political, pure, real, repressive, sensory, social, socialist, socialized, state, transparent, true, and women's space. At the end of all this, there can be little doubt that " . . . space is never empty: it always embodies a meaning."[1] Most social theorists are by now aware that Lefebvre's project is aimed at a reorientation of human inquiry away from its traditional obsession with time and toward a reconstituted focus on space. There is scarcely a project in theoretical human geography, architecture, and urban planning within the past two decades that has remained untouched (consciously or otherwise) by Lefebvre's problematic.[2]

The emergence of postmodern thought has provided an important impetus for reconsideration of the role of space in social theory and in the construction of everyday life. The significance of space is widely conceded, yet programmatic statements on postmodern spatiality remain rare. Fredric Jameson's 1984 essay "Postmodernism, or the cultural logic of late capitalism" provided a touchstone for a postmodern spatiality, asserting that space is the "supremely mediatory function" in the construction of a postmodern society.[3] In this chapter, I shall focus on continuities and departures in postmodern thinking about space in order to demonstrate the enduring significance of the issues it raises. I shall concentrate on these two principal texts: Henri Lefebvre's 1974 masterwork *La Production de l'Espace*, available since 1991 in a translation by Donald Nicholson-Smith; and Fredric Jameson's *Postmodernism, or the Cultural Logic of Late Capitalism* (1991).[4] The former will serve as an exemplar of modernist traditions in spatial analysis, the latter provides a perspective on postmodernity (although I shall adjust this over-simple dichotomy later). I hope to show that postmodern thought is clearly traceable from modernist "bloodlines"; that it signals equally transparent departures from that heritage; and, hence, that it cannot be dismissed or subsumed without considerable loss. In what follows, I shall touch on matters of spatial ontologies, epistemology and method, spatiality and the production of space, and social action. The essay concludes with some reflections on the conformities and departures represented by the two texts, and how they inform the analysis in the remainder of this book.

Ontologies of Space

Where there is space, there is being[5]

Lefebvre goes back to the beginning in his search for the meaning of space. He is highly critical of previous ontologies that describe space strictly in geometrical terms, as an "empty space." This construct, he asserts, enabled modern epistemologists to adopt the notion of space as a mental thing, capable of absorbing a myriad meanings according to the analyst's whim. Subsequent work in the science of space:

> has produced either mere descriptions which never achieve analytical, much less theoretical, status, or else fragments and cross-sections of space. There are plenty of reasons for thinking that descriptions and cross-sections of this kind, though they may well supply inventories of what *exists in* space, or even generate a *discourse on* space, cannot ever give rise to a *knowledge of* space.[6]

Instead, what we have is an indefinite multitude of spaces, piled one upon the other, each pored over and dissected by analysts from respective disciplines.

Against this, Lefebvre posits the need to uncover the theoretical unity among three fields that are usually apprehended separately: the physical (nature); the mental (logical and formal abstractions); and the social. The loss of an appropriate unitary theory is blamed upon Hegel, whom Lefebvre describes unforgettably as a "sort of [intellectual] Place de l'Etoile."[7] But others, including Heidegger, have contributed to the devaluation of place. Lefebvre turns to Nietzsche as the principal voice asserting the primordality of space; time may be distinguished from space, but the two cannot be separated:

> Time *per se* is an absurdity; likewise space *per se*. The relative and the absolute are reflections of one another: each always refers back to the other, and the same is true of space and time.[8]

Lefebvre is quick to point out that his unitary theory does not imply a privileged language, nor even a metalanguage. Instead, it stresses the dialectical character of spatial decoding:

> The project I am outlining . . . does not aim to produce a (or the) discourse on space, but rather to expose the actual production of space by bringing the various kinds of space and the modalities of their genesis together within a single theory.[9]

Lefebvre organizes his understanding around separate concepts of space:[10] *absolute space*, which is essentially natural until colonized, when it becomes relativized and historical; *abstract space*, associated with the space of accumulation, in which production and reproduction processes are separated and space takes on an instrumental function; *contradictory space*, where disintegration of the old and generation of the new occurs in response to the contradictions inherent in abstract space; and *differential space*, the consequent mosaic of different places. At the core of the

Lefebvrian project are the concepts of *production* and the *act of producing* space; i.e. "(social) space is a (social) product."[11] Four precepts are constitutive of this project:[12]

(1) *Physical (natural) space is disappearing*, which is not to say it is of diminishing importance.[13]

(2) *Every society, every mode of production, produces its own space*.[14] Social space contains, and assigns appropriate places to, the relations of production and of reproduction (including biological reproduction and the reproduction of labor power and social relations). The process of creation requires the availability of specialized sites associated with production, prohibition, and repression. As a consequence of this process, dominant spaces are able to mold the subordinate spaces of the periphery.

(3) *Theory reproduces the generative process*.[15] If space is a product, our knowledge of it will reproduce and expound the process of production. In order to move from a concern with things in space to the production of space, additional explanations will be required. Lefebvre emphasizes the dialectical nature of this understanding. He distinguishes among spatial practices (our perceptions); representations of space (our conceptions); and representational spaces (the lived space). Each contributes differentially to the production of space, varying according to local conditions.

(4) *The passage from one mode of production to another is of the highest theoretical importance*.[16] Since each mode of production is assumed to have its own particular space, the shift from one mode to another necessarily entails the production of a new space. If this is so, the key issues – greatly exercising students of the putative shift to postmodernity – are exactly how does one identify the emergent spaces, and at what point do they add up to a new mode of production? These determinations are partly a task of determining the appropriate spatial codes (which are often ambiguous), and the proper periodization.[17]

In sum, the Lefebvrian ontology assumes that space is present and implicit in the very act of creation and being, and that the process of life is inextricably linked with the production of different spaces. The production of space is inherently a political project, the consequences of which Lefebvre does not shy from, as we shall see later.

The essence of Jameson's postmodernity is, I believe, a way of seeing. Jameson regards society as a text, and postmodernism as a periodizing hypothesis.[18] He is fascinated by the glittering surfaces in the strange landscapes of late-twentieth-century capitalism, and willing to assume that a new social order is in the making. At the same time, he is appalled by the contradictions in this society, which juxtapose corporate monoliths with homelessness, and the "increasing immiseration of American society" with the "self-congratulatory rhetoric of contemporary political pluralism".[19] He grabs onto the surficial threads and follows them, expecting to find not a labyrinth, but maybe a gulag or a shopping mall. Since we lack an adequate road-map to guide our exploration, Jameson concludes that the challenge lies in making sense of these surfaces – a task that I have characterized as the "geographical puzzle" of unravelling obsolescent modernisms from emergent postmodernisms.[20]

Jameson argues that we needed the term postmodernism without knowing it. Now we cannot *not* use the term. The "motley crew of strange bedfellows" who embraced the term have coalesced into a new discursive genre – less a "theory," and more a diverse "theoretical discourse."[21] Such a discourse is necessarily imperfect and impure; it is driven to abandon the metaphysical baggage surrounding truth, foundationalism and essentialism. Hence, postmodernism is not something that can be settled once and for all, then used in a noncontroversial manner. Each time it is invoked, Jameson insists:

> we are under the obligation to rehearse those inner contradictions and to stage those representational inconsistencies and dilemmas; we have to work all that through every time around.[22]

This is an awesome task, but Jameson suggests that what has happened to culture provides important clues for tracking the postmodern. He is quick to point out that social change is not purely a cultural affair, although postmodernism is properly regarded as the "cultural dominant" of late capitalism. By so contextualizing his analysis, Jameson insists on a concept of postmodernity that is essentially historical rather than merely a disembodied stylistic or aesthetic. This leads him, in turn, to the core of his problematic: that the emergence of a postmodern cultural dominant signals a "radical break" from previous cultures (cf. Lefebvre's emphasis on transitions in the mode of production). Jameson situates this rupture at the end of the 1950s, and associates it with the waning of the 100–year old modern movement. He concedes that granting historical originality to a putative postmodern culture is a risky business, and that self-awareness usually comes later, and then only gradually. But an even greater worry is that:

> period concepts [may] finally correspond to no realities whatsoever, and that whether they are formulated in terms of generational logic, or by the names of reigning monarchs, or according to some other category or topological and classificatory system, the collective reality of the multitudinous lives encompassed by such terms is unthinkable (or nontotalizable . . .) and can never be described, characterized, labeled, or conceptualized.[23]

Jameson escapes this dilemma by situating his inquiry firmly within a Marxian historical materialism. He adheres to Mandel's now-familiar periodization: classical/market capitalism; monopoly capitalism; and multinational/late capitalism. (The term "late capitalism" is not his preferred slogan, since it carries so much ideological and political baggage; he prefers "multinational capitalism" to refer to capitalism's third phase.) And, despite his apparent eagerness to kick over the intellectual traces, he is frequently drawn back to what he calls "old friends" in the Marxian grid. For example:

> if modernization is something that happens to the base, and modernism the form the superstructure takes in reaction to that ambivalent development, then perhaps modernity characterizes the attempt to make something coherent out of their relationship.[24]

Most of Jameson's attention is focused on the third phase of capitalist development. He argues that older cities and nation states become obsolete as capital leaps prodigiously beyond them. In the emergent spaces of multinational capital, the suppression of conventional distance and the saturation of remaining voids or empty spaces create a "perceptual barrier of immediacy from which all sheltering layers and intervening mediation have been removed."[25] Everything in this global space becomes cultural, though not solely in its intent and origins. The subsequent saturated space has become dominated by the USA, giving rise to the "first specifically North American [sic] global style".[26] In so forcefully admitting cultural complexity into the analysis, Jameson undermines the notion of the mode of production as a "total system", in the sense of an all-encompassing explanation for everything.

It is to surfaces that Jameson is irresistibly drawn. In this, he once again reveals his Lefebvrian genealogy.[27] For Jameson, postmodern society is characterized by a flatness, or depthlessness, a "new kind of superficiality in the most literal sense"[28] a waning of affect, the diminution of feeling, emotion, and subjectivity in postmodern images (Warhol is his archetype);[29] and a decentering of the formerly-centered subject or psyche.[30] The consequent eclipse of the norm[31] is due to the staggering proliferation of private styles and linguistic fragmentation, marked by the rise of pastiche[32] – a neutral, blank parody devoid of parody's satiric impulse. This emptied culture reaches its apex in the simulacrum, the identical copy for which no original ever existed, and brought vitally to life in a society where the "the image has become the final form of commodity reification".[33] Postmodern culture is characterized by fragmentation.[34] In the final analysis, Jameson attributes these trends to the "universalization of capitalism".[35]

Epistemologies of Space

Things lie... in order to conceal their origins[36]

Lefebvre's method in analyzing the production of space is firmly grounded in Marxist thought, and is nourished by the conviction that a proper treatment of space will inevitably revitalize Marxism. What is for me most intriguing about these epistemological voyages is the extent to which Lefebvre travels toward a postmodern consciousness.[37]

Lefebvre wears his Marxism lightly, with no trace of dogma.[38] When he turns to *Capital* for inspiration, it is not "in the sense of sifting it for quotations nor in the sense of subjecting it to the 'ultimate exegesis.'"[39] He avoids the quicksand of reductionism, and is wary of overemphasizing the economic sphere. His epistemoligical openness is expressed straightforwardly, in a way that theoretical dogmatists of all persuasions could usefully take to heart: "Marxism should be treated as one moment in the development of theory, and not, dogmatically, as a definitive theory."[40] This anti-hegemonic stance is a principal instance of Lefebvre's postmodernism *avant la lettre* (notwithstanding his avowed search for a unitary theory). But in addition, he is extremely critical of the fragmentation brought about by disciplinary fiefdoms, with their predilection for partial representations and occasional arbitrary totalizations.[41] He is particularly hard on traditional philosophy, which "in its decline, stripped now of any dialectical dimension, serves as a bulwark as much for illegitimate separations as for illegitimate confusions."[42]

Lefebvre also betrays a postmodern sensitivity in the matters of language and reading the text (of cities, etc.) All the same, he is categorically against the priority-of-language thesis, insisting that Western culture has overemphasized speech and the written word.[43] For him, every language is located in space, and he offers a timely warning to all those who would raise language onto some new epistemological pedestal:

> To underestimate, ignore and diminish space amounts to the overestimation of texts, written matter, and writing systems, along with the readable and the visible, to the point of assigning to these a monopoly on intelligibility.[44]

Lefebvre insists that space is lived before it is perceived, and produced before it can be read, which raises the question of what the virtue of readability actually is, especially since the "spaces made (produced) to be read are the most deceptive and tricked-up imaginable".[45] He quotes the example of fascist monumentality, which claims to express the collective will yet masks the will to power and the arbitrariness of its exercise. He concludes that the principal purpose of reading, the decoding of the spatial text, is to help us understand the transition from representational (i.e. lived) spaces to representations (conceptions) of space.

Tolerant of different voices, critical of disciplinary fragmentation, suspicious of hegemonies, and sensitive to language, Lefebvre in these ways reveals himself as a latent postmodernist.[46] Yet he still abides by certain normal codes of scientific inquiry, seeking to have his theory confirmed by application to other societies, other modes of production.[47] He also concedes that what he seeks could be described by traditional philosophers as a metaphilosophy.[48]

Jameson is quick to emphasize that postmodernism requires new methods. He rejects the modernist mind-set that has "blocked the creative mind with awkward self-consciousness,"[49] and portrayed modernism as "a time of giants and legendary powers no longer available to us."[50] He recognizes multiple, though not infinite, possibilities of explanation (while rejecting the term "undecidability"), and leaves open the question of whether or not it is possible to create an internally self-coherent theory of the postmodern, i.e. an antifoundationalism that truly eschews all founda-tions, a nonessentialism without the least shred of essence. This fundamental para-dox – the desire to break free from Modernity's strictures, and yet make sense out of postmodernity's theoretical plenitude – is at the heart of Jameson's (and postmoder-nism's) epistemological dilemma. Previously, Jameson has argued for a "doctrine of levels" (i.e. different levels of abstraction), whereby incompatible codes and models may be differentiated.[51] In *Postmodernism*, this essentially dialectical approach takes the form of transcoding. Jameson abandons "beliefs" about philosophical or political world visions in favor of specific "ideolects" or "ideological codes" which are demonstrably partial languages for understanding the world. Transcoding is about:

> measuring what is sayable and "thinkable" in each of these codes or ideolects and compar[[ing]] that to the conceptual possibilities of its competitors: this is, in my opinion, the most productive and responsible activity for students and theoretical or philosophical critics to pursue today....[52]

In order to be truly free from past traditions, he calls for the production of a theoretical discourse dedicated to generating new codes.

Several important consequences follow from this position. First, no ideology or theory (in the sense of a code or discursive system) is particularly determinant. Second, closure in theoretical debate in unlikely, indeed is better avoided. Third, we can never go far back enough to make primary statements, so that there are no conceptual (but only representational) beginnings, and that the doctrine of foundations is simply a testimony to the inadequacies of the human mind. The consequent theoretical aesthetic excludes philosophical propositions as well as statements about being and truth, since our language is no longer able to "frame utterances in such a way that these categories might be appropriate."[53]

Jameson's theoretical aesthetic is obviously highly demanding. The theorist walks a tightrope, threatened constantly by lapses into obsolete determinisms or stark opinion. Yet the potential gains are enormous. Jameson quotes Rorty, for example:

> It is a mistake to think that Derrida, or anybody else, 'recognized' problems about the nature of textuality or writing which had been ignored by the [previous] tradition. What he did was to *make the old ways of speaking optional*, and thus more or less dubious.[54]

There are risks associated with this aesthetic. These arise especially when the custodians of existing codes (hitherto presented as non-optional) take umbrage, and embark on "search-and-destroy" missions on any linguistic misconceptions in their enemy's camp, meanwhile hoping against hope that they will not themselves become the target of such linguistic demystification. What we have then is a discursive struggle of Hobbesian dimensions, a *bellum omnium contra omnes*. In order to avoid a Babel of incommensurable narratives, Jameson (like Lefebvre) discounts the notion that a theoretical code organized around language could have ontological primacy. Such a separation would, he insists, simply create another "named theory" in a world already replete with them.[55]

The Production of Space

What exactly is the mode of existence of social relationships?[56]

The production of social space, according to Lefebvre, begins with "the study of natural rhythms, and of the modification of those rhythms and their inscription in space by means of human actions, especially work-related actions. It begins, then, with the spatio-temporal rhythms of nature as transformed by a social practice."[57] In other words, while social space is a product to be used or consumed, it is also a means of production.[58]

The shift from former habits of analyzing things in space to a new gaze on the actual production of space is fraught with difficulties:

> (Social) space is not a thing among other things, nor a product among other products: rather it subsumes things produced, and encompasses their interrelationships in their coexistence and simultaneity – their (relative) order and/or (relative) disorder. It is the outcome of a sequence and set of operations, and thus cannot be reduced to the rank of a simple object. At the same time there is nothing imagined, unreal or 'ideal' about it as

compared, for example, with science, representations, ideas or dreams. Itself the outcome of past actions, social space is what permits fresh actions to occur, while suggesting others and prohibiting yet others.[59]

Social relations exist to the extent that they possess a spatial expression: they project
themselves into space, becoming inscribed there, and in the process producing that
space itself. Thus, social space is both a field of action and a basis for action.[60]

The consequent layers of spatial texture interpenetrate and superimpose upon one
another, linking the global and the local despite the persistent tendency to fragmentation in socio-economic and intellectual processes. Nothing can be taken for granted
in analyzing these spaces: spaces that are meant to be read are in reality often the
most opaque; some spaces are overinscribed; others deliberately conceal. Above all,
space is multi-faceted and multiply-coded; hence, Lefebvre warns, transparently
clear representations of space must be disavowed precisely because they offer an
already clarified picture.[61]

In attempting to subordinate space and its contradictions, the capitalist mode of
production thereby produces difference. The resulting uneven geographical development consists of dominated spaces (i.e. those transformed by technology) instead of
appropriated spaces (i.e. natural space modified to serve the needs and possibilities of
a group). Thus, in the spatial logic of capitalism:

> the capitalist 'trinity' is established in space – that trinity of land–labor–capital which
> cannot remain abstract and which is assembled only within an equally tri-faceted
> institutional space: a space that is first of all *global*...; a space, secondly, that is
> *fragmented*, separating, disjunctive, a space that locates specificities, places or localities,
> both in order to control them and in order to make them negotiable; and a space, finally,
> that is *hierarchical*, ranging from the lowliest places to the noblest, from the tattooed to
> the sovereign.[62]

Deeply embedded at the core of the production of space is the capitalist state. The
political apparatuses, while loudly proclaiming themselves to be readable and transparent, are in fact the epitome of opacity. Lefebvre emphasizes the historical importance of state-sanctioned violence and the nation state. Although he is curiously silent
about Max Weber's contribution to these themes, he suggests that misapprehension
of the role of space may have led Hegel and Marx to downplay the theory of the
state.[63]

Lefebvre uses the city and urbanism as constant touchstones in his analysis, viewing the built environment as a "brutal condensation of social relationships."[64] There
is nothing more contradictory than 'urbanness,' especially the role of planners in
effective support of capitalism and the capitalist state.[65] Planners, Lefebvre contends,
are perfectly at home in dominated space, sorting and classifying space in service to a
class. They deal only with "an empty space, a space that is primordial, a container to
receive fragmentary contents, a neutral medium into which disjointed things, people
and habitats might be introduced."[66] He refers to Haussmann's Paris and Niemeyer's
Brasília as evidence of the consequences of planners' fractured spaces and partial
logic. In the production of urban space, state political power dominates at all scales.
Power plays a pivotal role in maintaining the dominance of the core over the
periphery – Lefebvre's centrality thesis – and in connecting the punctual to the global.

Today, centrality aspires to total control despite the prevailing anarchy of fragmenta-tion which inhibits the appearance of a new mode of production by the selling of space parcel "by parcel, by a mere travesty of a new space."[67]

Concepts of space are central to the production of Jameson's postmodernism. He offers the following crucial distinction in what he describes as "so spatialized a culture as the postmodern:"[68]

> A certain spatial turn has often seemed to me to offer one of the more productive ways of distinguishing postmodernism from modernism proper, whose experience of tempor-ality – existential time, along with deep memory – is henceforth conventional to see as a dominant of the high modern.[69]

In short, categories of space and spatial logic dominate the postmodern in the way time dominated the world of modernism. At the core of Jameson's geography is the assertion that we are experiencing a mutation in built space, i.e. the production of a postmodern "hyperspace." We currently lack the perceptual apparatus to assess this hyperspace, experiencing for the moment little more than a "bewildering immersion" in the new medium.[70] The postmodern hyperspace, Jameson observes:

> has finally succeeded in transcending the capacities of the individual human body to locate itself, to organize its surroundings perceptually, and cognitively to map its posi-tion in a mappable external world. It may now be suggested that this alarming disjunc-tion point between the body and its built environment...can itself stand as the symbol...of that even sharper dilemma which is the incapacity of our minds, at least at present, to map the great global multinational and decentered communicational network in which we find ourselves caught as individual subjects.[71]

The altered spaces of postmodernity are evident in many sectors. For instance, in the saturated space of multinational capitalism, place no longer exists except at a "much feebler level," drowned by other more powerful abstract spaces such as communications networks. The truth of an experience "no longer coincides with the place in which it takes place,"[72] meaning that the structural coordinates of the lived experience are no longer accessible to, or even conceptualizable for most people. In particular, Nature has been erased from the postmodern by the "essential homogenization of a social space and experience now uniformly modernized and mechanized."[73] At the same time, however, postmodernity includes space for various forms of oppositional culture. According to Jameson, the very term "cultural domin-ant" implies co-existence with other resistant forces, including utopian socialists, feminists, and minorities.

In attempting to decode the postmodern hyperspace, Jameson relies greatly upon architecture – the "privileged aesthetic language"[74] – because it possesses a virtually unmediated relationship with the economic. Echoing Jane Jacobs, Jameson credits high modernism with the destruction of the physical fabric of the traditional city and its neighborhood culture, together with an elitism and authoritarianism in contem-porary buildings. In contrast, postmodernism is a kind of "aesthetic populism," associated with the emergence of the new texts of mass/commercial culture (includ-ing the "degraded" landscapes of schlock and kitsch). The architecture of post-modernism has, in particular, embraced an historicism which "randomly and

Figure 3.1   Bonaventure Hotel, Los Angeles John Portman Associates, 1974–6 (Michael Dear)

without principle but with gusto cannibalizes all the architectural styles of the past and combines them in overstimulating ensembles."[75]

Jameson spent a lot of time in Los Angeles – which he seems to regard as the ultimate effacement of place – trying to make sense of postmodern architecture. From his examination of John Portman's Bonaventure Hotel and Frank Gehry's Santa Monica house, he concludes that postmodernism has abolished the distinction between inside and outside, as well as a great many other elements of conventional architectural syntax and grammar. The Bonaventure he describes as a "total space," a "complete world" that does not wish to be part of the city that surrounds it.[76] Revealing his textual strategy, Jameson the place-reader observes:

> the words of built space, or at least its substantives, would seem to be rooms, categories which are . . . related and articulated by the various spatial verbs and adverbs – corridors, doorways, and staircases, for example – modified in turn by adjectives in the form of

paint and furnishings, decoration, and ornament . . . Meanwhile, these "sentences" – if that indeed is what a building can be said to "be" – are read by readers whose bodies fill the various shifter-slots and subject-positions; while the larger text into which such units are inserted can be assigned to the text-grammar of the urban as such (or perhaps, in a world system, to ever vaster geographies and their syntactic laws).[77]

Figure 3.2   Frank Gehry House, Santa Monica, 1978 (Michael Dear)

Figure 3.2 *cont.*   Frank Gehry House, Santa Monica, 1978 (Michael Dear)

He offers Kevin Lynch's cognitive mapping as a broadly-applicable method for attaching the "situational representation ... of the individual subject to that vaster and properly unrepresentable totality ... of society's structures as a whole."[78] (Jameson draws an analogy with the Althusserian/Lacanian redefinition of ideology as the representation of the subject's Imaginary relationship to his or her Real conditions of existence.) A global cognitive mapping on a social and a spatial scale would, he claims, endow the individual with a heightened sense of place in the global system, as well as clarifying the linkage between the global and the local.

Jameson's spatial dialectic is not confined to architecture. Directly acknowledging his debt to Lefebvre, he examines the distinctive modes of production in space.

Lefebvre's reassertion of space did more than correct the modernist imbalance toward time; it also underscored the increasing importance, in daily life and multinational capitalism, of the urban and the new globality of the system. Following Lefebvre, Jameson calls for a revitalized "spatial imagination capable of confronting the past...and reading its less tangible secrets off the template of its spatial structures."[79] Most interestingly, he incorporates the notion of the "market" into the problematic of postmodernism. For Jameson, the rhetoric of the market has been a fundamental tool in the conservatives' largely successful ideological struggle to delegitimize the political claims of the left. Moreover, the concrete reality of the market is as much about "real markets" as it is about "metaphysics, psychology, advertising, culture, representations, and libidinal apparatuses."[80] Most ominously, he asks whether "the practice of consumption has not replaced the resolute taking of a stand and the full-throated endorsement of a political opinion."[81]

The geographical expression of cultural difference is apparently being homogenized by culture's link to global communications and its consequent ability to overcome distance and penetrate into all places. Jameson argues that a new euphoria or intensity accompanies the postmodern cultural experience, especially as a consequence of video – postmodernism's "most distinctive new medium,"[82] and the "most likely candidate for cultural hegemony" in the future.[83] Such developments do not prevent local differences in culture; however, they are strongly implicated in the creation of postmodernity's "saturated space."[84]

From Social Theory to Social Action

To change life...we must first change space[85]

Within the creative anarchy of capitalist spaces, Lefebvre uncovers his political project, in an immensely skillful and prescient way. Urban conditions tend to uphold a measure of democracy, largely because spatial contradictions allow for a measure of local autonomy. However, these same contradictions pose a continuous threat to the social order. So, Lefebvre asks, with a crucial insight that foreshadows the political fragmentation of the postmodern era: "Might not the spatial chaos engendered by capitalism, despite the power and rationality of the state, turn out to be the system's Achilles' heel?"[86]

Under conditions of modernity, the role of the state has grown to encompass an absolute political space. While few have recognized the extent of this encroachment, fewer still are able to influence it, thus accounting for the silence or passivity of the users of space. Nevertheless, even the powerful experience difficulties in mastering what is "at once their product and the tool of their mastery, namely space."[87] And it is here, in the crucial interstices between locus of power and its reach, that Lefebvre glimpses the emergence of a new politics.

New forms of political struggle involving minorities, women, and community-based coalitions are truly threatening to existing power blocs since they go beyond manipulable tests of ideological purity, and propose counter-spaces. To be successful, the counter-spaces of politics would need to overcome the domination of masculinist principles, and make "the reappropriation of the body, in association with the reappropriation of space, a non-negotiable part of its agenda."[88] Lefebvre, incidentally, has no patience for what he terms the asininity of claims that community-based politics obscure class consciousness.

The political project of postmodernity has been under attack since its inception. The left has tended to view postmodernism as the collapse of any progressive politics; the right (which rejects diversity and favors the restoration of modernist traditions) sees it as the source of all that is evil in the current malaise of "political correctness." Even some of those who initially gained from postmodernism's assault on the authority of existing hegemonies have since retreated from postmodernism's perceived threat to their political projects. Jameson, however, is in no doubt that postmodernism is about politics:

> every position on postmodernism in culture – whether apologia or stigmatization – is also at one and the same time, and *necessarily*, an implicitly or explicitly political stance on the nature of multinational capitalism today.[89]

He holds to the pivotal role of class-based politics, but concedes that class is confounded by issues of status (referring here to Bourdieu, not to Weber), and that postmodern theorists have yet to provide an account of current class formations. Jameson's steps in this direction are often wonderfully evocative, but hampered by a strange blend of resignation and unfettered optimism. For instance, he speaks of what remains of a residual, unacknowledged "party of Utopia:"

> an underground party whose numbers are difficult to determine, whose program remains unannounced and perhaps even unformulated, whose existence is unknown to the citizenry at large and to the authorities, but whose members seem to recognize one another by means of secret Masonic signals.[90]

Yet he looks ahead optimistically:

> That a new international proletariat (taking forms we cannot yet imagine) will reemerge from this convulsive upheaval it needs no prophet to predict: we ourselves are still in the trough, however, and no one can say how long we still [sic] stay there.[91]

One of Jameson's most telling political insights arises in connection with his treatment of the claustrophobic modernism described in Kafka's *The Trial*. Here, he identifies the crucial nonconformity between the emergence of a "modern (or at least modernizing) economy" and the backdrop of an "old-fashioned political structure."[92] The peculiar overlap between past and future, the resistance of archaic structures to irresistible modernizations, "is the condition of possibility for high modernism." Postmodernism is, then, the situation in which the relict and the archaic have finally been swept away without a trace. If this is indeed so, what does the new postmodern politics look like?

Jameson draws on Laclau and Mouffe's "overtly postmodern" post-Marxist politics,[93] which emphasizes the proliferation of new social movements based in what Foucault would term a burgeoning micro-politics.[94] Postmodernism includes space for such oppositional cultures, which flourish in the presence of "discursive heterogeneity without a norm."[95] Jameson cites the role of feminism, virtually alone in maintaining a Utopian imagination. Yet for all his admiration of diversity in the new politics, Jameson rejects the claim that such groups have arisen from the void left by the disappearance of social classes. He dismisses social movements as the basis for a new class politics, because fractured groups are unable to combine in collective action. Ultimately, he joins other Marxist critics in devaluing difference, because it smacks of the "offensive complacencies" of a lugubrious "liberal tolerance."[96]

At the core of Jameson's current political project is the need to overcome the discourse and ideology of the market. This, he claims, is the "most crucial terrain of ideological struggle in our time," because the "surrender to the various forms of market ideology...has been imperceptible but alarmingly universal." As a consequence, politics has been reduced to the "care and feeding of the economic apparatus."[97] Consensus now dominates representative democracy, through ballots and opinion polls. Conscious ideologies and political opinions have "ceased to be functional in perpetuating and reproducing the system;" consumption has replaced politics.[98] This explains how we can celebrate capitalism at the same time as human misery engulfs us. Jameson again points to cognitive mapping as a way of more fully sketching the lineaments of an emergent postmodern politics, enabling "the coordination of existential data (the empirical position of the subject) with unlived, abstract conceptions of geographic totality."[99] The pedagogical political culture derived from such a mapping should aim to fuse the global with the local, on a social and spatial scale, because:

> the incapacity to map spatially is as crippling to political experience as the analogous incapacity to map spatially is for urban experience.[100]

From Lefebvre to Jameson: The Necessity for Postmodernism

It is impossible...to avoid the conclusion that space is assuming an increasingly important role in supposedly 'modern' societies[101]

Let me now summarize the two problematics and then proceed to emphasize the connections between Lefebvre's ostensible modernism and Jameson's postmodernism. In so doing, I shall hope to convey the utter centrality of the postmodern project in contemporary spatial theory and practice.

The project encompassed by Lefebvre in *The Production of Space* runs counter to many long-entrenched habits of thought.[102] Lefebvre notes that the illusion of transparent/neutral/pure space is slow to dissolve, even though the promise of the new philosophy is great:

> The more carefully one examines space, considering it not only with the eyes, not only with the intellect, but also with the senses, with the total body, the more clearly one becomes aware of the conflicts at work within it, conflicts which foster the explosion of abstract space and the production of a space that is *other*.[103]

Lefebvre the postmodernist calls for a retreat from the errors and lies of the modernist trio of readability, visibility, and intelligibility. We are, he asserts, teetering on the edge of a science of social space, which

> in no way aspires to the status of a completed 'totality', and even less to that of a 'system' or 'synthesis'.... [T]his approach aims both to reconnect elements that have

been separated and replace confusion by clear distinctions; to rejoin the severed and reanalyze the commingled.[104]

Lefebvre calls his approach "spatio-analysis" or "spatiology" in order to distinguish it from the baggage associated with existing disciplinary terminology. The conceptual grid that he offers is founded in the connectivity between various levels, or scales of analysis: "it discriminates – without sundering them – between a 'micro' level (architecture...), a 'medium' level (the city...), and finally a 'macro' level (...land considered in national, global or worldwide terms)."[105] In the final analysis, Lefebvre's science of space is a science of use. It runs counter to the dominant (and dominating) tendency by according appropriation a special practical and theoretical status: for appropriation and use, and against exchange and domination. He suggests that such a science would imply real knowledge about the production of space, but warns against the inevitable counter-challenges of disciplinary chauvinists and reductionists. Lefebvre argues some absolutely fundamental propositions, which extend way beyond the confines of geography, ancient and postmodern: in particular, that the absence of space in human inquiry has led to overemphasis on other dimensions of thought; and that the re-introduction of space will require a recasting of the entire fabric of social theory.

The spatial problematic I have distilled in turn from Jameson's postmodernity is remarkably rich, even though he himself makes no claim to provide such a thing. (The closest he gets is in a call for a theory of "separation.")[106] But there is little doubt in my mind that Jameson has encouraged a new way of seeing socio-spatial relations. He portrays society as a text, and postmodernism as a periodizing hypothesis. Culture is the key to tracking postmodernity, and to determining whether or not there has been a radical break. Theory, in his scheme, is composed of a broad discourse on diverse ideologies. Contradicting modernist traditions, Jameson eschews foundationalism, theoretical closure, and the notion of a determinant ideology; instead, he identifies transcoding (comparative analysis between theories) as a principal epistemological goal. Space and spatial logic dominate postmodernity, just as time permeated modernity. One urgent task is to discover the coordinates of the new postmodern hyperspace, by exploring the spaces of the built environment, the mode of production, and culture. The techniques of cognitive mapping will assist in this task, as well as in formulating future progams of social action. Social action in postmodernity is confounded by the nonconformity between the emergent economy and an obsolete politics. Localized social movements may be emblematic of a decentered politics, but Jameson argues they do not constitute a new form of class politics. Until we can decipher these politics, he advocates attacking the ideology and practices of the market. In the final analysis, Jameson attributes the fluxes of postmodernity to the universalization of capitalism. He portrays himself as a "relatively enthusiastic consumer of postmodernism,"[107] despite the unresolved ambiguities engendered as he pulls the cloak of Marxism about him:

> I occasionally get just as tired of the slogan "postmodernism" as anyone else, but when I am tempted to regret my complicity with it, to deplore its misuses and its notoriety, and to conclude with some reluctance that it raises more problems than it solves, I find myself pausing to wonder whether any other concept can dramatize the issues in quite so effective and economical a fashion.[108]

Taken together, both Lefebvre and Jameson privilege space as central in their problematics. Lefebvre, perhaps more than any other contemporary philosopher, outlines a basic ontological framework for the study of the production of space. In this, he emphasizes the connectedness of an integrated hierarchy of global and local spaces, which are highly fragmented and multiply-coded. Jameson acknowledges his debt to Lefebvre, but places his primary emphasis on the transition between modes of production. He is also able to address the spatial turn in postmodernity, suggesting that modernism's obsession with time has been usurped by the reassertion of space in postmodern theory.

From an epistemological viewpoint, the continuities between Lefebvre and Jameson are transparent. Both are founded in Marx. Lefebvre is more than prescient in his characterization of Marxism as simply one moment in the development of theory. Yet he remains motivated by the search for science, a unitary theory that he concedes some would regard as a metaphilosophy. Jameson, writing in an era of greater theoretical diversity, concedes the importance of different voices and the need for a comparative theoretical discourse. But he doubts (along with many others) the possibility of an internally coherent theory of the postmodern, and ultimately seeks refuge among old friends in the Marxist canon. Although both writers are unwilling or unable to sacrifice their broader allegiance to Marxism, Jameson takes us a step further in realizing the necessity of diversity in theoretical discourse.

The gains made by Jameson are also evident in their respective treatments of the production of space. Once again, Lefebvre seems remarkably contemporary in his analysis of the concrete materialization of social relations. And although Jameson advances the specific concept of a postmodern hyperspace consequent upon the cultural logic of late capitalism, it is clear that his emphasis on culture is (to some extent at least) a reaction against the privileging of the economic sphere that characterizes most previous Marxisms.[109] Here is one case in which intellectual bloodlines are clear, but the dialectic has thrown up an entirely original hypothesis.

The case of politics in Lefebvre and Jameson is very revealing. Both insist (not surprisingly given their points of departure in Marxism) on the primacy of class-based politics, but they also recognize the significance of the political heterogeneity implied in the emergence of locally-autonomous micro-powers. Lefebvre uncovers how the spatial contradictions of capitalism allow for a measure of local autonomy in what he terms the counter-spaces. These produce new forms of political struggle which (he suggests) do not obfuscate the potential for a burgeoning class consciousness. Jameson dissents from this view. In drawing particular attention to archaic institutions and the oppositional cultures associated with proliferating social movements, Jameson categorically dismisses such movements as a basis for a new class-based politics. At the same time, he manages to assess the potential for a postmodern politics without once incorporating the state into his analysis. This is in stark contrast to Lefebvre, who has elsewhere developed notions of (for instance) a state mode of production.

In sum, the conformities between what we can now only loosely characterize as Lefebvre's modernism and Jameson's postmodernism are quite transparent. They have to do with the common heritage in Marx, an obsession with a problematic that emphasizes space and transitions in the mode of production, a focus on surfaces and the quotidian, and commitment to social change through a class-based politics.

At the same time, the bridges between the modern and the postmodern are also clear, especially because of the remarkably forward-looking nature of Lefebvre's analysis. We can witness this in several dimensions: the sensitivity to difference, the importance of local autonomies in the spatial chaos of capitalism, and the emphasis on the interelatedness between global and local in the world order.

And yet? And yet, Jameson has categorically identified at least three new emphases that should guide any inquiry into a putatively postmodern society. These are: *hyperspace*, or a radical break in the time/space coordinates of the contemporary world; *culture*, a necessary counter-emphasis to previous obsessions which privileged the sphere of production over the sphere of reproduction; and *transcoding*, which despite Jameson's own retreat to Marxism imposes an unavoidable imperative for dealing with the implications of epistemological diversity. To this list, I must append the need to return to the question of *postmodern politics*, because neither Lefebvre nor Jameson deal adequately with this issue from behind the mask of Marxism.

Jameson emphasizes space as the key to mapping postmodernity, via a cognitive mapping of the glittering surfaces of postmodern culture. In this, he would probably concur with Berger that: "Prophesy now involves a geographical rather than historical projection; it is space not time that hides consequences from us"[110]; and with Soja that we need a new ontology, i.e. a "meta-theoretical discourse which seeks to discover what the world must be like in order for knowledge and human action to be possible, what it means to *be*."[111] Soja has taken us further than Jameson toward an ontology based on space, time and being. He writes:

> spatiality, temporality, and social being can be seen as the abstract dimensions which together comprise all facets of human existence... Thus the spatial order of human existence arises from the (social) production of space... Similarly, the temporal order is concretized in the making of history... [And] the social order of being-in-the-world can be seen as revolving around the constitution of society, the production and reproduction of social relations, institutions and practices.[112]

A large challenge persists with the notion of postmodernity as an epoch, representing a radical break with previous cultures. This invigorating hypothesis emphasizes culture, text, spatiality, theoretical discourse, and the problem of periodization. Like Derrida, Jameson asserts that the way to understand differences and discontinuities is to continually rehearse the conditions that lead to change. He ultimately elects an explanation based in the universalization of capital, even though this choice remains unmotivated in his text. His analysis of periodization, for example, has none of the subtlety and lucidity that characterized Nigel Thrift's or Michael Webber's investigations of post-Fordist periodizations.[113] In the final analysis, it may matter little that there has been a radical break; what is much more important will be that a new way of seeing has been opened up, and with it, the potential for transcendental social change.

Jameson invokes the homogenized, saturated hyperspace of postmodernity, where place is enfeebled and our cognitive maps so weak that the link between the global and the local is almost entirely obscured. The articulation of these linkages must be regarded as the principal challenge for any postmodern spatiality.[114] Of special concern is exactly how difference becomes localized in particular places. Soja again offers some important insights, drawing attention to our "existential spatiality," an "original spatialization" implicit in the birth of human consciousness.[115] Subsequently, our being in the world occurs through a distancing (detachment, objectification) that allows us to assume a point-of-view on our surroundings. Difference in and between places thus becomes a consequence of personal psychology and experience of the lifeworld, and is manifest in many various ways (e.g. stigma and residential differentiation, or via land-use planning). Another way of saying this is that culture and human agency are crucial factors in the production and reproduction of spatial relationships. Despite awareness that his work has been criticized for its absence of agency, Jameson makes little headway with the problem, beyond identifying "multinational capital" as a "higher" kind of agency. He nowhere broaches, for example, the structure–institution–agency triptych of Anthony Giddens, and fails to observe how the generic crises of capitalism become spatialized as crises of the locale (as, for example, in the place-specific process of deindustrialization, or in the ghettoization of the homeless).[116] Part of Jameson's (and our) problem lies in the ambiguities and overdetermination associated with the texts of place. The built environment, for example, is much more than an unmediated outcome of the capitalist mode of production; it contains representations of many other authentic human interactions, including the socio-cultural and the political.

In the epistemological realm, Jameson opts for transcoding – an impassioned plea for comparative theoretical analysis. Yet, somewhere along the way, he makes an unannounced retreat into a (Marxian) modernism. Given his political commitments, this is obviously a deliberate decision, although it may also be fuelled by a desire to avoid some of the extremes of postmodern relativism. However, it is achieved only at some cost, most notably a revitalized defense of totalizing discourse, and a repression of difference. Jameson's retreat ironically sacrifices one of postmodernism's greatest gains, i.e. the focus on comparative merits of different theories. The challenge posed by transcoding remains; the voices of the Other (e.g. feminist, multicultural, and postcolonial theorists) are muted, if not totally silenced.

Finally, it is impossible to overemphasize the central political lesson of postmodernity, which has taught us that Rationality is not an innocent category upon which to base a political program. Our twentieth-century history of technological industrialization, wars, death camps, and the nuclear threat has put paid to such naivety. Scholars such as Horkheimer and Adorno revealed that behind Enlightenment rationality lay a logic of domination and repression (as well as academic hegemony). Postmodernism offers a reconstituted vision of the politics of the local, founded in the distribution of micropowers and situated in the fragmented interstices between formal power structures; this vision must necessarily be incorporated with a politics of the global, including revitalized nationalisms, nation state disintegration, and so on.[117] The frequently-heard complaints that postmodernism represents an anti-progressive pluralism or that it imposes a crippling political correctness, amount to little more than nostalgia for past verities; the world has shifted, whether or not we appreciate or approve of its mutations. Equally obviously, the need for moral and political judgements is an inevitable concomitant of being in the world. Postmodernism has not removed the necessity for such judgements; what it has done is to question the status of these judgements. Postmodernism itself has not disenfranchised any political organization or social movement; it uncovered the need for a reconstituted political practice.

The consistencies and nonconformities in the conjoined projects of Lefebvre and Jameson offer profoundly important insights into the ways of place-making of the late-twentieth century. More than most, Lefebvre allows us to understand the process of place-making; and Jameson shows us the ways of postmodern place-making.

Notes

1. Lefebvre, H. 1991: *The Production of Space*, translated by Donald Nicholson-Smith, Oxford (UK), Cambridge, Mass: Blackwell, p. 154.
2. A brief overview of Lefebvre's work is available in Soja (Soja, E. 1989: *Postmodern Geographies*, New York: Verso, especially Chapter 2). See also Gregory, D. 1994: *Geographical Imaginations*, Cambridge, Mass: Blackwell; and Koffman, E. and Lebas, E. 1996: *Writings on Cities / Henri Lefebvre*, Oxford, UK; Cambridge, Mass: Blackwell.
3. Jameson, F. 1991: *Postmodernism, or the Cultural Logic of Late Capitalism*, Durham, NC: Duke University Press, p. 104, emphasis added.
4. Jameson, F. 1991: *Postmodernism, or the Cultural Logic of Late Capitalism*, Durham: Duke University Press; Lefebvre, H. 1991: *The Production of Space*, translated by Donald Nicholson-Smith. Oxford (UK), Cambridge, Mass: Blackwell.
5. Lefebvre, H., *The Production of Space*, p. 22
6. Ibid., p. 7.
7. Ibid., p. 21.
8. Ibid., p. 181.
9. Ibid., p. 16.
10. Ibid., p. 48–52.
11. Ibid., p. 26.
12. Ibid., p. 30–64.
13. Ibid., p. 30.
14. Ibid., p. 31.
15. Ibid., p. 37.
16. Ibid., p. 46.
17. See also Lefebvre, H. 1976: *The Survival of Capitalism: Reproduction of the Relations of Production*, translated by Frank Bryant. London: Allison & Busby.
18. Jameson, F., *Postmodernism*, p. 3.
19. Ibid., p. 320.
20. Dear, M. 1988: "The Postmodern Challenge: Reconstructing Human Geography," *Transactions of the Institute of British Geographers*, NS 13(3), pp. 262–74.
21. Jameson, F., *Postmodernism, or the Cultural Logic of Late Capitalism* , p. xvi.
22. Ibid., p. xxii.
23. Ibid., p. 282.
24. Ibid., p. 310.
25. Ibid., p. 413.
26. Ibid., p. xx.
27. "The everyday is covered by a surface: that of modernity. . . . Modernity and everydayness constitute a deep structure that a critical analysis can work to uncover." (Lefebvre, H. 1992: *Critique of Everyday Life*, vol. 1, translated by John Moore, London; New York: Verso, pp. 10–11).
28. Ibid., p. 9.
29. Ibid., p. 10.
30. Ibid., p. 15.
31. Ibid., p. 17.

32. Ibid.
33. Ibid., p. 18; the phrase is Guy Debord's.
34. Ibid., p. 372.
35. Ibid., p. 405.
36. Lefebvre, H. *The Production of Space*, p. 81.
37. Kofman, E. and Lebas, E. *Writings on Cities / Henri Lefebvre*, p. 45. In their useful overview of Lefebvre's oeuvre, assert that Lefebvre rejected postmodernism. They themselves go further by suggesting that: "Postmodernizing Lefebvre thus imposes an undifferentiated and homogenizing thought" (p. 51). Leaving aside the notion of exactly what it means to postmodernize a person, neither Lefebvre's own rejection nor his editors' personal predilections can erase Lefebvre's complicity in the evolution of postmodern thought.
38. A fact undoubtedly related to his persistent search for a critical Marxism (Lefebvre, H. *Critique of Everyday Life*).
39. Lefebvre, H. *The Production of Space*, p. 99.
40. Ibid., p. 321.
41. Ibid., p. 89–91.
42. Ibid., p. 418.
43. Ibid., p. 16, p. 36.
44. Ibid., p. 62.
45. Ibid., p. 143.
46. This latency is also betrayed by Lefebvre's emphasis on the quotidian (see Lefebvre, H. *Critique of Everyday Life*).
47. Lefebvre, H. *The Production of Space*, p. 41; See also Lefebvre, H. 1972: *Le Droit a la Ville suivi de Espace et Politique*, Paris: Editions Anthropos; Lefebvre, H. 'The right to the city,' in Ockman, J (ed.) 1993: *Architecture Culture 1943–1968: A Documentary Anthology*, New York: Columbia Books of Architecture and Rizzoli International Publications.
48. Lefebvre, H. *The Production of Space*, p. 405.
49. Jameson, F., *Postmodernism*,p. 317.
50. Ibid., p. 305.
51. Cf. Sayer, A. R. 1992: *Method in Social Science: A Realist Approach*, London: Routledge.
52. Ibid., p. 394.
53. Ibid., p. 392.
54. Ibid., p. 397, my emphasis.
55. Ibid., p. 184.
56. Lefebvre, H. *The Production of Space*, p. 129.
57. Ibid., p. 117.
58. Ibid., p. 85.
59. Ibid., p. 73.
60. Ibid., p. 182–3, 190–1.
61. Ibid., p. 189.
62. Ibid., p. 282.
63. Ibid., p. 279.
64. Ibid., p. 227.
65. Lefebvre, H. 1976. "Reflections on the politics of space," *Antipode* 8(2), pp. 30–7.
66. Ibid., p. 308.
67. Ibid., p. 358, p. 410.
68. Jameson, F., *Postmodernism*, p. xvi.
69. Ibid., p. 154.

70. Jameson, F., *Postmodernism*, p. 43.
71. Ibid., p. 44.
72. Ibid., p. 411.
73. Ibid., p. 366.
74. Ibid., p. 37.
75. Ibid., p. 19.
76. Ibid., p. 40.
77. Ibid., p. 105.
78. Ibid., p. 51.
79. Ibid., pp. 364–5.
80. Ibid., p. 264.
81. Ibid., p. 398.
82. Ibid., p. xv.
83. Ibid., p. 69.
84. Ibid., p. 413.
85. Lefebvre, H. 1991: *The Production of Space*, p. 190.
86. Ibid., p. 63.
87. Ibid.
88. Ibid., p. 166–7.
89. Jameson, F., *Postmodernism, p. 3.*
90. Ibid., p. 180.
91. Ibid., p. 417.
92. Ibid., p. 308–9.
93. Laclau, E. and Mouffe, C., 1985: *Hegemony and Socialist Strategy*, New York: Verso.
94. Jameson, F., *Postmodernism*, p. 318.
95. Ibid., p. 17.
96. Ibid., p. 341. For further development of Jameson's politics, see Dowling, W. C. 1984: *Jameson, Althusser, Marx: An Introduction to the Political Unconscious*, Ithaca: Cornell University Press; Jameson, F. 1981: *The Political Unconscious: Narrative as a Socially Symbolic Act*, Ithaca: Cornell University Press; and Kellner, D. 1989: *Critical Theory, Marxism, and Modernity*, Baltimore: Johns Hopkins University Press.
97. Jameson, F., *Postmodernism*, pp. 263–5.
98. Ibid., p. 398.
99. Ibid., p. 53.
100. Ibid., p. 416.
101. Lefebvre, H. *The Production of Space*, p. 412.
102. For an extended consideration of Lefebvre's oeuvre in the context of French Marxist thought, see Gregory, D., *Geographical Imaginations*.
103. Ibid., p. 391.
104. Ibid., p. 413.
105. Ibid., p. 388.
106. Jameson, F., *Postmodernism*,p. 399.
107. Ibid., p. 298.
108. Ibid., p. 418.
109. Lefebvre himself, with his consistent emphasis on the sphere of social reproduction, is a noteworthy exception to this general observation. See, for instance, Lefebvre, H. 1976: "Reflections on the politics of space," *Antipode* 8(2), pp. 30–7.
110. Quoted in Soja, E., *Postmodern Geographies*, p. 22
111. Ibid., p. 131.
112. Ibid., p. 25.

113. Webber, M. 1991: "The Contemporary Transition," *Environment and Planning D: Society and Space*, 9, pp. 165–82. Also Thrift's editorials (Thrift, N.J. 1990: "For a New Regional Geography 1." *Progress in Human Geography* 14(2); Thrift, N.J. 1991: "For a New Regional Geography 2." *Progress in Human Geography* 15(4); Thrift, N. J. 1993: "For a New Regional Geography 3." *Progress in Human Geography* 17(1)).

114. See, for example, Gregory, D. "Areal Differentiation and Post-Modern Human Geography," in Gregory, D. and Wolford, R. (eds) 1989: *Horizons in Human Geography*, Basingstoke: Macmillan; and Cooke, P. 1990: *Back to the Future: Modernity, Postmodernity and Locality*, London: Unwin Hyman.

115. Ibid., p. 132.

116. The process of localization in the homelessness crisis is examined in Wolch, J. R. and Dear, M. 1993: *Malign Neglect: Homelessness in an American City*, San Francisco: Jossey-Bass.

117. Some of the new forms of government, in the form of a "shadow state," are discussed in Wolch, J. R. 1990: *The Shadow State*, New York: Foundation Center.

4

The Premature Demise of Postmodern Urbanism

Theory is no longer theoretical when it loses sight of its conditional nature, takes no risk in speculation, and circulates as a form of administrative inquisition.

Trinh Minh-ha[1]

Postmodernism has not been universally popular. In this chapter, I want to engage two books that have strongly influenced the development of postmodern urbanism: Edward Soja's *Postmodern Geographies: the reassertion of space in critical social theory*, and David Harvey's *The Condition of Postmodernity: an enquiry into the origins of cultural change*.[2] Both books were published in 1989, and proceed from a structuralist/post-structuralist grounding. But whereas Soja contrives to celebrate the intersection between the Marxian and postmodern realms, Harvey labors mightily with a sustained, hostile attack on postmodernism (in effect, to write its obituary). Both authors ultimately devise a thoroughly modernist (Marxian) reconstruction of urban theory; and it is this outcome that I want to refute before we go further.

Soja's deep immersion in postmodern thought and his energetic focus on Los Angeles as a postmodern archetype lift his text out of the singularities of the Marxian framework, as well as providing important extension to the Lefebvrian-inspired revision of the role of space in critical social theory.[3] Harvey's text is routinely cited by critics of postmodernism, but also surprisingly by analysts of all persuasions who simply wish to reference a general overview of postmodern thought (they are often seemingly oblivious to the fact that Harvey's purpose is to eradicate it). Both texts have tended to obscure other sympathetic sorties into postmodern urbanism – most importantly Philip Cooke's 1990 text, *Back to the Future* – and both have attracted extensive criticism, especially from feminists.[4] In 1990 and 1991, I published critical reviews of *Postmodern Geographies* and *The Condition of Postmodernity* which, taken together, form the basis of the critique offered in this chapter. These arguments are being recast here because I believe that, in different ways, both books have fundamentally derailed the project of postmodern urbanism. Even though the authors have gone on to publish later volumes (Soja's representing a significant extension of his earlier work), their 1989 texts remain influential and are indicative of a wrong turn in the development of postmodern urbanism. This is a legacy that I wish to correct in this book.

Before I begin, let me make it perfectly clear that my critique is not an attack on the continuing validity of Marxian social theory, nor on the more broadly-based

Figure 4.1   House Warning Sign, Marina Del Rey (Michael Dear)

projects undertaken by Soja and Harvey. Indeed, I have occasion to draw construct-ively on their work and the Marxian heritage everywhere in this book. What interests me in this chapter are the ramifications of their particular responses to the post-modern turn. How were their modernist reconstructions achieved? What emascula-tions of postmodern thought were necessary to enable the authors to rescue the modernist project? And what are the principal consequences of Soja and Harvey's encounters with the postmodern? I shall attempt to answer these questions through a constructive engagement with the authors' readings of postmodernity; their representations of contemporary urban process; and their reconstructions of a mod-ernist urbanism via Marxian social theory. I conclude that Soja and Harvey obtained their coherent visions of urban theory by adopting Enlightenment strategies that foreclose on the promise of postmodern urbanism.[5] Finally, I employ Derek Gre-gory's geographical imagination to bring Lefebvre and Jameson, Harvey and Soja together in the same discursive space, as an essential prelude to my subsequent formulations.

Reading Postmodernity

In *Postmodern Geographies*, Soja seeks to re-establish "a critical spatial perspective in contemporary social theory and analysis." He hopes thereby to redress the scho-larly imbalance that has privileged time and the "making of history" over space and the "making of geography." The correction of this imbalance is, according to Soja, the "insistent premise and promise of postmodern geographies."[6]

Soja's postmodernism is complex. Several versions are offered during the course of the book. Above all, he views postmodernism as a periodizing concept that attempts to make "theoretical and practical sense of [the] contemporary restructuring of capitalist spatiality."[7] His postmodernism applies equally to the epochal transitions in critical thought and material life. In coming to grips with these upheavals, Soja argues that Modern Geography requires a "radical deconstruction and reconstitution."[8] A postmodern geography would involve:

> a resistance to paradigmatic closure and rigidly categorical thinking; the capacity to combine creatively what in the past was considered to be antithetical/uncombinable; the rejection of totalizing "deep logics" that blinker our way of seeing; the search for new ways to interpret the empirical world and tear away its layers of ideological mystification.[9]

This is a laudable ambition. At the core of Soja's reconstituted geography is a new way of seeing, enabling us to envisage and to describe the simultaneity inherent in all landscapes. The problem, in his opinion, is that language and description tend to be linear, sequential, and necessarily stuck in "the prevailing grain of time."[10] It is here, in the discontinuity separating/linking time and space, that Soja locates his post-modern proclamation. He quotes Berger as one source:

> Prophesy now involves a geographical rather than historical projection; it is space not time that hides consequences from us.[11]

To oversimplify, Soja's modernism consists of four dimensions, each of which would find some precedent in the burgeoning literature on postmodernity (compare Chapters 2 and 3 above): an epochal transition in material life; an analogous transition in critical thinking; a rejection of totalizing discourse; and a search for a new language of representation.

Soja proceeds to sketch a new ontology derived from the intersection between Western Marxism and Marxist Geography. He identifies the pioneers of postmodern geographies as Michel Foucault, John Berger, Ernest Mandel, Fredric Jameson, Marshall Berman, Nicos Poulantzas, Anthony Giddens, David Harvey, and especially Henri Lefebvre. He also draws directly on Marx, Heidegger and Sartre. According to Soja's historiography, the period 1880–1920 was dominated by two great Modernisms, positivism and Marxism. These traditions caused the "virtual annihilation of space by time in critical social thought," and "squeezed [geography] out of the competitive battleground of theory construction."[12] Exactly why this happened remains unclear from the text, but its consequences have been enormous. Most importantly, the devaluation of place hid the profound "spatial fix" which was occurring as capitalist social relations were being restructured through recurrent periods of crisis. But equally important was geography's subsequent involution – its evolving, internalized obsession with areal description and its self-imposed isolation from contemporary social thought. By 1960, according to Soja's account, the discipline of geography was "theoretically asleep."[13]

A rebirth of interest in space occurred during the 1970s, associated with the rise of Marxist Geography and the "spatializing voices" influencing Western Marxism. Soja concedes that other pressures were building outside Marxist Geography, but pays them little heed. (This may be the principal reason for the many striking omissions in his text, as noted below.) The effect of the burgeoning spatial awareness was to reveal the need for a new ontology, i.e. a "meta-theoretical discourse which seeks to discover what the world must be like in order for knowledge and human action to be possible, what it means to be."[14] Drawing on Berman, Soja focuses on the onto-logical issues of space, time and being:

> Just as space, time, and matter delineate and encompass the essential qualities of the physical world, spatiality, temporality, and social being can be seen as the abstract dimensions which together comprise all facets of human existence... How this ontolo-gical nexus of space–time–being is conceptually specified and given particular meaning in the explanation of concrete events... is the generative source of all social theory.[15]

In the boldest claim in the book, space is accorded the same ontological priority as time and being. Soja makes some provocative headway toward this reconstructed ontology. He begins with Martin Buber's existential spatiality, which draws attention to the "original spatialization" implicit in the birth of human consciousness. Our being in the world occurs through a distancing (detachment, objectification) that allows us to assume a point of view on the world. From this beginning, Soja passes to Sartre, Heidegger and Husserl to examine the separation of the world-as-lived and the transcendental ego, emphasizing the fundamental spatiality in Heidegger's and Sartre's philosophies. Finally, he leaps to Giddens who "provides, for the first time, a systematic social ontology capable of sustaining the reassertion of space in critical social theory."[16] Giddens is only a beginning, however, and the task of creating the new ontology awaits further attention.

Eschewing Soja's exuberant embrace of the postmodern, Harvey, in the opening sentences of *The Condition of Postmodernity*, reveals his hostility:

> I cannot remember when I first encountered the term postmodernism. I probably reacted to it in much the same way as I did to various other 'isms' that have come and gone over the past couple of decades, hoping it would disappear under the weight of its own incoherence or simply lose its allure as a fashionable set of 'new ideas.'[17]

But it didn't, so Harvey stirs himself to battle. For him, postmodernism is principally about the death of metanarratives. Its roots lie in the collapse of the Enlightenment (later the modernist) project, which was "to develop objective science, universal morality and law, and autonomous art according to their inner logic."[18] At the same time, Harvey concedes that our twentieth-century history of wars, death camps, and the nuclear threat has put an end to a naive rationality.

Despite the warnings of history, Harvey swiftly distances himself from those who would abandon the Enlightenment project:

> there are those – and this is... the core of postmodernist philosophical thought – who insist that we should, in the name of human emancipation, abandon the Enlightenment project entirely. Which position we take depends upon how we explain the "dark side" of our recent history and the degree to which we attribute it to the defects of Enlight-enment reason rather than to a *lack of its proper application*.[19]

Harvey launches stinging attacks on Foucault and Lyotard – postmodernists who swim, even wallow, in the "fragmentary and chaotic currents of change as if that is all there is."[20] He thoroughly repudiates their perspective on both scholarly and political grounds. Hence:

> How can we build, represent, and attend to these surfaces [of everyday life] with the requisite sympathy and seriousness in order to get behind them and *identify essential meanings*? Postmodernism, with its resignation to bottomless fragmentation and ephemerality, generally refuses to contemplate that question.[21] But if, as the postmodernists insist, we cannot aspire to any unified representation of the world, or picture it as a totality full of connections and differentiations rather than as perpetually shifting fragments, then how can we possibly *aspire to act coherently* with respect to the world? [22]

For Harvey, postmodernism simply "takes matters too far."[23] He defends the project of modernity against what he characterizes as the "relativism and defeatism" of postmodernism.[24] Asserting that "metatheory cannot be dispensed with,"[25] Harvey advances Marx's account of capitalism as a "very solid basis" for thinking about modernism and postmodernism.[26]

Representing Postmodern Urbanism

Soja uses his postmodernism to make sense of past, present, and emergent patterns of social being that exist simultaneously in the city. This is what I earlier described as the problematic of theorizing contemporaneity, particularly the difficulties of periodizing time and space, and of identifying and explaining the specific spatializations of societal evolution. According to Soja, modernization refers to "a continuous process of societal restructuring that is periodically accelerated to produce a recomposition of space–time–being in their concrete forms . . . that arises primarily from the historical and geographical dynamics of modes of production."[27] He locates the passage to postmodernity in the late 1960s. Its accompanying geographical restructuring has taken three different paths of spatialization:

- *posthistoricism*, the reassertion of space in the ontological struggle;
- *post-Fordism*, an increasingly flexible, disorganized regime of capitalist accumulation; and
- *postmodernism*, an accompanying cultural and ideological reconfiguration changing how we experience social being.

All three spatializations are simultaneously needed to unravel the geographical puzzle. Soja appeals to Fredric Jameson to evoke the postmodern landscape, but returns to Giddens for a systematic account of the spatiality of social life, viewing the intelligible lifeworld as a "multilayered system of socially created nodal regions, a configuration of differentiated and hierarchically organized locales."[28] Such a lifeworld encompasses many different scales, from the human body, through the urban and the nation state, to the social whole; it is everywhere permeated with Foucauldian notions of power and authority.

From such principles, Soja analyzes contemporary urban and regional restructuring and spatialization. At the regional level, he focuses on geographically uneven development, the spatial division of labor, and flexible specialization under post-Fordism, as they combine to produce a new (and as yet unstable) regionalization of national economies. At the urban level, he examines four prototypes of the North American city (mercantile, competitive industrial, corporate monopoly and state-managed Fordist), as well as an emergent fifth form – the postmodern city, with Los Angeles as its archetype. Soja takes the reader on a whirlwind tour of the LA region, from the flanking ramparts (the amazing assemblage of military bases on the metropolitan periphery), to the panopticon-like center of surveillance surrounding the downtown City Hall. Postmodern Los Angeles resembles "a giant agglomeration of theme parks, a lifespace comprised of Disneyworlds,"[29] which at the same time is one of the most fascinating and revealing of late-twentieth century world cities:

> Ignored for so long as aberrant, idiosyncratic, or bizarrely exceptional, Los Angeles … has, more than any other place, become the paradigmatic window through which to see the last half of the twentieth century. I do not mean to suggest that the experience of Los Angeles will be duplicated elsewhere. But just the reverse may indeed be true, that the particular experiences of urban development and change occuring elsewhere in the world are being duplicated in Los Angeles, the place where it all seems to "come together."[30]

Exactly what Soja intends by this evocation of the postmodern is not entirely clear. He seems to allow that Los Angeles is a world leader, but also a mere Petri dish with peculiar powers to distill external global forces. His postmodern urbanism seems to be about local territorial fragmentation in the face of globalizing capitalism.

Harvey's postmodernism is placed categorically within the global political–economic transformation of late-twentieth century capitalism. His position is summarized in a brief prefatory remark, entitled *The argument*, which is worth quoting in its entirety:

> There has been a sea-change in cultural as well as in political–economic practices since around 1972.

> This sea-change is bound up with the emergence of new dominant ways in which we experience space and time.

> While simultaneity in the shifting dimensions of time and space is no proof of necessary or causal connection, strong a priori grounds can be adduced for the proposition that there is some kind of necessary relation between the rise of postmodern cultural forms, the emergence of more flexible modes of capitalist accumulation, and a new round of "time-space compression" in the organization of capitalism.

> But these changes, when set against the basic rules of capitalistic accumulation, appear more as shifts in surface appearance rather than as signs of the emergence of some entirely new post-capitalist or even post-industrial society.[31]

Harvey's monumental work on urban political economy is by now reasonably familiar. It posits that emergent crises of capitalist accumulation will be associated with new spatial and temporal adjustments, or fixes. He explores the contemporary shift from the rigid structures of Fordism to a new system of "flexible accumula-tion,"[32] arguing that "the changing experience of time and space underlies...the impulsive turn to postmodern cultural practices and philosophical discourses."[33] He shows how individual experiences of "time-space compression" have mutated since Renaissance times in ways reflective of the transition from modernity to postmoder-nity. The Renaissance, for instance, laid the conceptual foundations for a scientific sense of time and space, separate from more fluid concepts that might arise experi-entially; worldwide economic depression in 1846–8 caused a radical realignment of time-space conceptions toward more modernist themes. Between 1850 and 1914, a new internationalism, fueled by innovations in transport and communications, redrew the map of the world's spaces. These multiple representations of relative spaces were ripped apart by World War I. In the ensuing half-century, according to Harvey, "the real tragedy of modernism begins," when its precepts "were absorbed for purposes that were not, by and large, its own." For instance, "the insights of the Bauhaus were mobilized for the design of the death camps."[34] Time-space compres-sion advanced as postmodernity took hold. The mobilization of mass markets and the emergence of a service economy gave rise to "another fierce round in that process of annihilation of space through time that has always lain at the center of capitalism's dynamic."[35] Paradoxically, in a regime of flexible accumulation, "the less important the spatial barriers, the greater the sensitivity of capital to varieties of place within space."[36]

At the core of Harvey's urban political economy lies the ontological triad: "space, time and money."[37] The staggering reductionism inherent in this conceptualization (cf. Soja's more conventional "space, time, being") is echoed in yet another enormous conceptual leap, when he claims that the fragmentation of flexible accumulation is replicated in the dispersal of politics, philosophy and social thought.[38] Despite this emphasis on fragmentation, Harvey's urbanism remains resolutely at the level of the global. When he does descend to urban specificities (e.g. the case of Baltimore), he focuses almost exclusively on issues of architecture and urban design, particularly the conspicuous consumption palaces and staged spectacles associated with the malling of America.

Reconstructing Modernity

Although the projects of Soja and Harvey are similar, a quite different ethos pervades the two books.[39] Thus, it is doubly ironic that both authors should end up with such a profoundly modernist reconstruction of urban theory. Several interrelated themes account for this closure: the absence of any sustained engagement with the con-sequences of difference; the lack of critical self-reflection about the authors' own epistemological stances; and misunderstandings/misrepresentations concerning the politics of postmodernity. Let's look at each of these criticisms in detail.

Soja's project is deeply flawed by his commitment to a single theoretical agenda – an action that is fundamentally antithetical to the postmodern project. Post-modernism celebrates difference and undecidability; it categorically rejects the hege-mony of any single perspective. (The fact that Soja's view is Marxist is irrelevant to this point.) The notion of a postmodern geography (in the singular) is oxymoronic; a postmodernist would axiomatically write postmodern geographies. This is perhaps what Soja intended to convey by the book's title; but he has in fact written a postmodern geography.

Soja's commitment leaves the ontological project intact. This is because Marxism, at least in the way he uses it, is about epistemology (i.e. knowledge, as distinct from being); and the space/time/being ontological triad remains insulated from the problematics of epistemology, empirical analysis, and social action. However, if we assume the need to teach or to practice postmodernism, how does a committed theorist (of any persuasion) teach differences? Those infused with a postmodernist sensibility will routinely alert students to the discontinuities between different theoretical perspectives, and encourage an openness to diversity.[40] This should not be regarded as an invitation to a bland pluralism, in which anything goes. A critical openness is advisable, based on an understanding that all theories are not created equal. To put it crudely, when it comes to theory, postmodernists are fence-sitters – by definition. Soja has jumped down from the fence. From what perspective will he now teach difference? How can he persuade students of the value of fence-sitting when his position is so firmly grounded? And how are his ontological excursions blinkered by Marxism?

At the level of epistemology, much greater damage has been done. In the theoretical realm, Soja has embraced a fairly conventional historical materialism that privileges the economic over the political and socio-cultural spheres. Predictably, those factors not directly linked to the production nexus play only a minor role in Soja's subsequent explanation. Lost (in the superstructural clouds?) are most of the elements of social reproduction (race, gender, family, education, etc.), and – most surprisingly for an avowedly postmodern text – the whole question of culture. There is, for example, no Habermas or Frankfurt School in Soja's postmodernism. Feminist thought, the insights of ethnography, and social history all get short shrift in this book.[41] In methodology, too, there are surprising hiatuses. For one so concerned with text, the almost complete absence of attention to language and rhetoric is hard to explain.[42] Derrida is mentioned once, in passing; Gunnar Olsson's geography is all but ignored. And the question of discourse between meta-narratives (i.e. Jameson's transcoding) never arises, presumably because the author's prior choice of a preferred metanarrative renders this unnecessary.

Finally, Soja forecloses on the question of social action. Politics rarely surface in his book. To be fair, the author avows that this is not part of his project. Nevertheless, along the way, he manages to identify with Jameson's "postmodernism of resistance"[43] warns of the possibilities for neo-conservatism implicit in postmodernism;[44] and calls for a "politicized spatial consciousness and a radical spatial praxis."[45] But this is all too glib. Postmodernism has emphasized that rationality is no longer an innocent category upon which to base social action. Yet what is available to put in its place? Soja's suppression of this dilemma (and its consequences) is made all the more remarkable by his frequent reference to the role of planning and the state in capitalist urbanization. Yet these issues, along with the political sphere in general, remain silent echoes in his text.

In the event, Soja has written a peculiarly Modern account of postmodern geography. The postmodern challenge has been named; therefore it has been tamed. Its brilliant potential has been tempered by the discipline of Marxist thought. The consequent closure is totally antithetical to my reading of the postmodern challenge. Soja's biggest failing is that he has elected not to analyze the consequences of this closure.

Harvey creates analogous lacunae regarding difference, theory and politics. In thinking critically about *The Condition of Postmodernity*, it is impossible to escape from his unrelieved antipathy toward postmodern thought, postmodern politics, postmodern architecture, postmodernists in general. Even though his treatment of geography and political economy remains as perceptive as ever, Harvey seems incapable of accommodating differences. (Meaghan Morris also makes this distinction, between what she calls "the good Harvey (the Marxist geographer) and the bad Harvey (the cultural critic)." [46] The theme of otherness is taken up very early in his book, where it is grudgingly identified as "the most liberative and therefore most appealing aspect of postmodern thought."[47] However, it is promptly dropped from serious consideration until it appears again (very late in the book) as part of a rallying call for a new historical materialism.

The catalogue of different voices that is consequently denied relevance in Harvey's urbanism is long and depressing. First, there is the specific problem of otherness, i.e. the meaning and significance of alternative human subjectivities and experience. In particular, Harvey's treatment of gender and feminism is noticeable by its almost complete absence.[48] Women figure most prominently in Chapter 3, a treatment of art history; they are also mentioned as a source of low-cost wage-labor. On the rare occasions that women appear in the text, it is usually as objects never the subjects of representation. A second kind of difference relates to relevant postmodern discourse in ancillary disciplines. Different voices from non-Marxian social theory are usually ignored by the author. He omits other relevant work in ethnography and political science, as well as ignoring a burgeoning contemporary literature on postmodern human geography. Thus, for all his emphasis on culture, Harvey never seriously engages the spectacular renaissance of cultural geography or the new cultural history. Like Soja, he ignores the strictures of text and language, although if deconstruction has taught us nothing else, it has emphasized (following Wittgenstein) how language acts as a prison to our thought, speech and action. Thirdly, Harvey gives short shrift to different voices on nature and the environment. When these topics are mentioned, the author appears to sanction an obsolete paradigm based in the domination of nature, [49] without apparent concern that this is the logic that has brought us to the brink of planetary disaster. (Soja is equally silent on this topic. Harvey himself corrected this imbalance in his 1996 book.)

Harvey drives inexorably through the maze of postmodernity primarily to dissolve differences. But why on earth would anyone want to do that? Why should we sacrifice our hard-won openness to thick description in favor of some new/old closure? Why pillory those who reject totalizing discourse? Just because one dislikes fragmentation doesn't mean that it can be wished away; nor can one concede to difference on the condition that it stays in its proper place.

While taking an axe to postmodernism, Harvey leaves his own historical materialism almost totally unexamined. His mental constructs remain untainted by the spirit and currents of postmodernity. In stark contrast to Lefebvre's openness (cf. Chapter 4), he brings to the text an extraordinarily confining range of assumptions, among them the following:

(1) that all aspects of social process can be unproblematically encompassed within fundamental historical materialist categories. (for example "There are in fact no serious difficulties in extending Marx's theory of commodity production to cope with it.")[50]

(2) that, as long as the real world can be subsumed within Marxian categories, then no further proof of a proposition is needed. (for example "A careful reading of Marx's *Capital* sustains the point.")[51]

(3) that historical materialism is the only way to approach social analysis. (for example "Flexible accumulation appears at least, to be a new configuration and, as such, it requires that we scrutinize its manifestations with the requisite care and seriousness, using, nevertheless, the theoretical tools that Marx devised.")[52]

(4) that there is no need for theory beyond historical materialism. (for example "If there is a meta-theory with which to embrace all these gyrations of postmodern thinking and cultural production, then why should we not deploy it?")[53]

Harvey's metatheoretical deployment leads him to dissolve the "sharp categorical distinction" between modernism and postmodernism, and between the global and the local, replacing them with the "flux of internal relations within capitalism as a whole."[54] He insists on the existence of "laws of process at work under capitalism,"[55] and their utility in explaining where "real change" comes from.[56] His modernist mindset manufactures "laws of capitalism," searches for "essential meanings," and valorizes only "real change." He is unable to concede that far from refusing to contemplate questions of meaning and rationality,[57] postmodernists have arrived at their position precisely because they have thought deeply about such issues. They have concluded that there is no unambiguous basis for accepting laws, truths, essences as if they possessed an unassailable authority or could guarantee prescriptions for social choices. Postmodernists further assert that it is exactly because of the exercise of ill-founded, unquestioned authority that we have created a world of war, political domination and repression, and (need I say) of academic hegemony.

It would have been far truer to the postmodern challenge if Harvey had examined his own theoretical choices, in what Laclau and Mouffe[58] term the "post-Marxist" era. For instance, on one occasion he belittles Foucault because the localized struggles he encouraged do not have the effect of "challenging capitalism."[59] Now, the gay liberation and feminist movements may or may not have significantly challenged capitalism, but few would question the achievements of these local struggles against homophobia and patriarchy! [60] Are such gains any less important in the scheme of things? In this, and countless other cases, Harvey's conceptual juggernaut does not stop to consider the exclusionary nature of his theorizing. Instead, he is all silence and closure, losing himself in the text and language of *Capital*.

Harvey has emphasized that his bias in favor of Marxism is based in its prescriptive capacity, i.e. its ability to link social thought with progressive political action. Yet at the core of his book is a political paradox so devastating that it totally undermines the credibility of his attack on postmodern politics. To show this, let me recall his defense of the Enlightenment: that rationality and ethics were plausible bases of social action; that Enlightenment ideas were, however, absorbed for evil purposes or improper applications; but that a renewal of the Enlightenment project is possible. We are left to take on faith that the New Enlightenment will avoid the pitfalls that compromised the Old. In a less forgiving mood, Harvey characterizes postmodern politics as beset by "relativism and defeatism,"[61] and taking things "beyond the point where any coherent politics are left [sic]."[62] Yet strangely, in the penultimate chapter, he concedes:

> A mode of thought that is anti-authoritarian and iconoclastic, that insists on the authenticity of other voices, that celebrates difference, decentralization, and democratization of taste, as well as the power of imagination over materiality, has to have a radical cutting edge even when indiscriminately used. *In the hands of its more responsible practitioners*, the whole baggage of ideas associated with postmodernism could be deployed to radical ends, and thereby be seen as part of a fundamental drive toward a more liberatory politics.[63]

This apparent breakthrough has already been canceled, however, by an earlier proclamation. Harvey avers that, while postmodernism recognizes the authenticity of other voices, "postmodernist thinking immediately shuts off these other voices from access to more universal sources of power by ghettoizing them within an opaque otherness."[64]

This is double-speak. The acknowledged emancipatory potential of postmodern politics is dismissed (a) because irresponsible practitioners may have co-opted its potential for their own ends; and (b) because by recognizing their otherness, minorities automatically consign themselves to impotence, beyond the "more universal" sources of power (i.e. class-based politics). But if a perverted Enlightenment thought could be re-harnessed for progressive political purposes, as Harvey claims, why couldn't a postmodern politics? How has this double standard arisen? Why should non-class-based politics be trashed in this way? [65]

Whether or not Harvey is willing to concede this, any contemporary reconstruction of urbanism, politics, and social theory will have to take account of the postmodern condition. Laclau and Mouffe, writing in 1985 and echoing Lefebvre in 1976, observed:

> Just as the era of normative epistemologies has come to an end, so too has the era of universal discourses. . . . For this very reason, Marxism is *one* of the traditions through which it becomes possible to formulate this new conception of politics.[66]

A revamped historical materialism is certainly needed, Harvey concedes. It will require:

> The treatment of difference and "otherness" not as something to be added on to more fundamental Marxist categories (like class and production forces), but as something that should be omnipresent from the very beginning in any attempt to grasp the dialectics of social change. The importance of recuperating such aspects of social organization as race, gender, religion, within the overall frame of historical materialist inquiry (with its emphasis upon the unity of the emancipatory struggle) cannot be overestimated.[67]

These words appear too late in the book to have any tangible effect on their author. And I find it hard to be optimistic about the future, since the same paragraph warns that any further analysis of politics, difference, and social theory must be contained within the "more fundamental" categories of historical materialist inquiry before it can be sanctioned.

Anticipating the demise of the postmodern, Harvey looks forward to a "renewal of historical materialism and of the Enlightenment project."[68] This program again appears rather late in the book; supportive argument is scarce and questionable. We never learn what the revamped Enlightenment will look like, nor how it will avoid the pitfalls that beset the previous Enlightenment (its cooptation by the powerful, and its inner logic of domination and repression). As the book ends, it is clear that Harvey has emerged unscathed from his encounter with postmodernism. Despite its ethos of collectivism and progressiveness, Harvey's solipsism has made *The Condition of Postmodernity* very much a book of the eighties – inward-looking, private, and nostalgic.

Coherence Through Exclusion

While both books have been enormously influential, in their different ways *Postmodern Geographies* and *The Condition of Postmodernity* both presaged the death of a postmodern urbanism. The vibrant complications of postmodernity were subsumed by Soja, and summarily dismissed by Harvey. In the final analysis, both books were undemocratic and profoundly monological. As Rosalyn Deutsche succinctly states, they regain the high ground of total knowledge only by "violently relegating others to positions of invisibility."[69] By insisting on totalizing and reductionist visions, Soja and Harvey squander the insights from different voices and alternative subjectivities. Difference is relegated to the status of an obstacle hindering a coherent theoretical and political praxis. In particular, Harvey's characterization of postmodern fragmentation as something negative strays uncomfortably close to conservative tenets that emphasize "our" common heritage and culture.[70] Moreover, for two so overtly committed to progressive politics, it is surprising that neither recognizes that the left, by insisting on unity and ignoring divisions in the past, has itself contributed to a diminished political efficacy.[71]

The hegemonic belligerence manifest in both texts derives from their authors' use of standard Enlightenment strategies, principally (a) an unproblematized reassertion of the coherence, objectivity, and adequacy of a single (in this case, Marxian) social theory; (b) a suppression of alternative epistemologies and subjectivities that do not conform to their metanarrative; and (c) a calculated unwillingness to valorize emergent, non-class-based forms of politics that have successfully challenged existing authority. Through these tactics, Soja and Harvey once again expose the palimpsest of Enlightenment authoritarianism that originally motivated the postmodern turn. It is their authority which defines adequacy and completeness. Coherence and fidelity lie in their images and representations of the world (i.e. their theory), and less in the patterns of everyday life. Beyond their syntheses lie incompleteness and inadequacy.

Time will tell if Soja and Harvey have succeeded only in reconstructing an anachronistic Marxian ghetto.[72] Since 1989, Harvey has published some answers to his critics, but moved on to matters of justice and environment.[73] His latest book (*Justice, Nature and the Geography of Difference*, 1996) rarely engages the postmodern; the word appears with some frequency, but often within quotation marks.

Figure 4.2   Gated Community, Calabasas (Michael Dear)

Soja's answer to his critics is found in *Thirdspace*[74] which is a significant extension and elaboration of *Postmodern Geographies*; I shall return below to this important text. In the meantime, let me urge that the promise of a postmodern urban theory is far richer than the versions promulgated in either the hostile hothouse of *The Condition of Postmodernity* or the heady heights of *Postmodern Geographies*.

Demise Deferred

Postmodernism lives. Legions of detractors and years of intellectual debate have done nothing to arrest its expansion or reduce its impact, and scores of usurpers have failed miserably in stultifying its scope...

[P]ostmodernism is the only possible contemporary answer to a century worn out by the rise and fall of modern ideologies, the pervasion of capitalism, and an unprecedented sense of personal responsibility and individual impotence.

Whether one likes it or not, postmodernism is a state of things...What is at stake is the very constitution of our being – the ways we perceive ourselves and others, the modes of experience that are available to us, the women and men whose sensibilities are shaped by urban exposure.

Celeste Olalquiaga[75]

I have presented this extended critique of Soja and Harvey's important works so as not to allow their significant distortions of the postmodern perspective to remain uncorrected. As a bridge between this critique and my own excursions into post-modern urbanism, it will be helpful if I insert two connections: the first summarizes efforts by Soja to correct and extend his *Postmodern Geographies*; and the second joins Derek Gregory in an imaginative discursive space that he opened up to include Lefebvre and Jameson, Soja and Harvey.

With Soja Into Thirdspace

With commendable forthrightness, Soja, in his *Thirdspace: Journeys to Los Angeles and Other Real-and-Imagined Places,*[76] confronted many of the criticisms that were leveled at *Postmodern Geographies.*[77] Large portions of what is projected to be a two-volume work are directed toward encounters with race and ethnicity, cultural studies, feminism, and postcolonialism, i.e., that which was largely absent from the 1989 volume. Soja has clearly gleaned great insights from these encounters, and now he attempts to convince the reader (successfully, I believe) of their validity. Soja's purpose in *Thirdspace* is "to encourage you to think differently about the meanings and significance of space…,"[78] especially those "most interesting and insightful new ways of thinking about space and spatiality" that derive from a "radical postmodern perspective." [79]

At the core of Soja's revisions is his notion of "Thirdspace," which is related to but not the same as Homi Bhaba's "third space," (i.e. the liminal margins of otherness where hybridity flourishes).[80] Soja's Thirdspace, by contrast, is a "purposefully tentative and flexible term that attempts to capture what is actually a constantly shifting and changing milieu of ideas, events, appearances, and meanings."[81] He envisages Thirdspace as a "space of extraordinary openness, a place of critical exchange," where no vision or persuasion holds sway over any other.[82] Drawing as always on Lefebvre, Soja situates a trialectical thinking at the heart of his new work. This is composed of an "ontological trialectic" which understands our being in the world as a relationship of spatiality, historicality, and sociality.[83] From this, he moves to a more specific "epistemology of space," related to practical knowledge of our

Figure 4.3 Informal street encampment for homeless people, Towne Avenue, Los Angeles (Michael Dear)

existential spatiality, and understood as another trialectic convergence involving
lived, perceived, and conceived spatialities. Their three associated "mentalities"
are:[84] *Firstspace epistemologies*, emphasizing the accumulation of analytical,
objective knowledge, and tending toward a formal science of space; *Secondspace
epistemologies*, involving conceived or imagined geographies that are typically the
interpretive locale of creative artists, philosophers, utopianists and the like; and
Thirdspace epistemologies, describing the flexible spaces that arise from "the
sympathetic deconstruction and heuristic reconstitution of the Firstspace–
Secondspace duality,"[85] i.e. a strategic re-opening and rethinking of new possibilities.

Part II of *Thirdspace* begins Soja's reconstruction of the postmodern urban (via
consideration of Los Angeles, Paris, Orange County, and Amsterdam). His synthesis
proper, however, awaits the second volume in this work, entitled *Postmetropolis*,
which promises to uncover (a) how new urbanization processes have "reshaped the
metropolitan cityscape and everyday life over the past thirty years"; and (b) the "new
modes of urban analysis that have been developing in the wake of this profound
metropolitan restructuring and postmodernization."[86] Thus, in a real and important
sense, I must perforce remain unclear about the exact and detailed intent of his
promised synthesis. In some ways, I prefer this impasse, since it leaves me less
encumbered for the journey I must undertake in the rest of this book.

Epistemic membranes: Gregory's Geographical Imaginations

In an act of intellectual daring and bravado, Derek Gregory's *Geographical Imaginations* has brought together Lefebvre and Jameson, Soja and Harvey in the same
discursive space. Gregory's own positionality owes a great deal to postcolonialism,[87]
although his densely-woven epistemic membrane also encompasses feminism, postmodernism, and historical materialism.[88] Insisting that postmodernism, poststructuralism and postcolonialism cannot be folded "directly and indiscriminately into
one another,"[89] he claims that postcolonialism's "urgent sense of historicity" sets it
apart from postmodernists who prioritize space over time.[90] And, following Homi
Bhabha, he identifies "a particularly creative and intimately political form of com-
munality" in postcolonialism, precisely because it lacks a single paradigm or text.[91]
However, both postcolonialism and postmodernism in different ways remind us of
our own "otherness," and make us attentive to "difference."[92]

In several extended chapters, Gregory parses the texts of *Postmodern Geographies* and *The Condition of Postmodernity*. I cannot do justice to the nuances and
depth of his exegeses in this chapter, but (at the risk of being presumptuous) I will
assert that Gregory arrives at judgements on these texts that broadly equate with
mine: both remain resolutely modernist projects. The way in which Soja employs
spatiality to differentiate modernism from postmodernism is, in Gregory's view, his
most forceful and original contribution.[93] Nevertheless, Soja's "unrelieved anti-
historicism" and his "authoritarian" univocality drown out a truly postmodern
openness.[94] As for Harvey, Gregory's main complaint centers on his failure to deal
with difference – that vital heart of a postcolonial vision.[95] He quotes Meaghan
Morris approvingly, though seemingly ruefully, that Harvey prefers to adhere to the
"mythic space of meta-theory."[96]

Then quickly, with surgical precision, Gregory brings Soja and Harvey together with Jameson in a few short paragraphs.[97] Jameson's project, Gregory observes, constantly invokes a totalizing Marxism as the meta-narrative that makes everything work. Jameson's engagement with postmodernism is intended not to celebrate but to subvert it. In introducing his 1994 collection of essays on the postmodern, *The Seeds of Time*, Jameson berates some of his own earlier writings for having forgotten a "fundamental structuralist lesson." [98] He also reiterates his basic Marxian vision:

> Postmodernism as an ideology. . .is better grasped as a symptom of the deeper structural changes in our society as a whole – in other words in the mode of production.[99]

Gregory observes that Harvey's distaste for postmodernism is of a piece with Jameson, so it makes perfect sense for Harvey to yoke his critique to Jameson's. But, when Soja enlists Jameson to his cause, the results are somewhat messier. This is because Soja, while asserting that he continued to draw inspiration from western Marxism, was equally tart in his insistence that his project could no longer be contained within its boundaries.[100] And it is precisely this tension that has led to many of the problems in Soja's text that I described earlier in this chapter.

But the mystery has even greater depth. It is intriguing and somewhat perplexing that Jameson, Soja and Harvey all claim their inspiration in Henri Lefebvre! (To a large extent, Gregory does, too.) Perhaps Lefebvre's iconoclasm lends itself to many interpretations? Or perhaps his life-long insistence on the important of space has a claim on many contemporary attentions, including that of postmodernists? As Gregory reminds us, Lefebvre was an implacable foe of structuralism and structural Marxism, but was also sharply critical of Derrida, Foucault and others.[101] The contradictions and incommensurabilities that inhere to these flirtations are mind-boggling, but I must set them aside for a separate occasion. What I prefer for the moment is to follow Gregory's lead and bring Lefebvre back into the discursive space, not to uncover yet more connections, but to recover Lefebvre's focus on the urban, plus the notion of changing rationalities in contemporary society. In this task, I have been helped by the enormous amount of ground-clearing that Gregory has already undertaken.[102]

In his history of space, Lefebvre glimpsed the immanent production in modernity of a supremely abstract, hyper-rationalized space.[103] Two aspects of this process are of special interest here: the developing "urban society," and the "de-corporealization" of space.[104] Urban society is a consequence of the destruction of "nature," and its replacement by a "second nature," i.e. the town and the urban, a future world of the "generalized urban."[105] To the extent that this occurs, the conflicts and contradictions of capitalism are likely to be found within the urban itself – a point that Gregory identifies as a "mainspring" for Harvey's project.[106] The de-corporealization of space ("one of the central achievements of Lefebvre's problematic," according to Gregory) [107] establishes an essential connection between the history of the body and the history of space. In examining Lefebvre's concept of nature, Neil Smith has written critically about his treatment of nature as a "corpse at the behest of abstract space."[108] Instead, Smith argues, the "production of space is integral to the production of nature and fashioned within it." [109] "First" nature is thus not a residual of Lefebvre's "second nature," but is "produced and reproduced from within this generalized second nature and as an adjunct to it." [110] Steve Pile has been equally critical of Lefebvre in his valuable examination of psychoanalysis, space and subjectivity.[111]

The burgeoning hyper-rationality of the modern world is described by Lefebvre as a progressive invasion of the concrete space of everyday life by the abstract spaces of the economy and state. This process is facilitated by the spatial practices, representation of spaces, and spaces of representation I described in Chapter 3.[112] Lefebvre attaches special importance to the discourses of the spatial sciences (including architecture and planning) in the rationalization of space.[113] His notion of time–space colonization is regarded by Gregory as an "outward" movement (an invasion, occupation, spreading); Gregory contrasts this with Harvey's notion of time–space compression which Gregory describes as an "inward" movement, a view of the world collapsing in on itself.[114] Harvey insists that it is "the intensity of the experience of time–space compression that distinguishes the conditions of postmodernity"[115] – all local economies have been incorporated into a global pattern of commodity exchange, and local systems of meanings subsumed within global information networks, with the result that multiple and compound geographies tend to be erased.[116] Such statements are best regarded as provocations and hypotheses, rather than statements of theoretical or empirical truth. Many statements about "globalization" have been regarded with a profound suspicion, especially by feminists.[117]

Out of Gregory's long and erudite synthesis of these synergistic spaces, which I have only glossed over here, we may take a myriad concerns: the global and the local, the urban and nature, a geopolitical imperative and the body as resistance, a modernist hyper-rationalization plus an postmodern intentionality, epistemological nuance plus representational hybrids. This is a rich diet on which to begin our journey into postmodern urbanism.

Notes

1. Minh-ha, Trinh, T. 1989: *Woman, native, other*, Bloomington: Indiana University Press, p. 42.
2. Soja, E., 1989: *Postmodern Geographies: the reassertion of space in critical social theory*, Verso: London; and Harvey, D., 1989: *The Condition of Postmodernity: an enquiry into the origins of cultural change*, Oxford: Blackwell.

    Soja had previously published an extended book review essay on the "postmodernization" of human geography (Soja, E., 1987: "The Postmodernization of Human Geography: A Review Essay," *Annals, Association of American Geographers*, 77, pp. 289–96), and Harvey had also written on the subject (Harvey, D., 1987: "Flexible Accumulation Through Urbanization: Reflections on 'Post-Modernism' in the American City," *Antipode*, 19, pp. 260–86). Despite its title, Harvey's article cannot be construed as a critical engagement with postmodernism, being largely concerned to appropriate Bourdieu's vision of habitus and Debord's "society of spectacle" into a conventional political economy.
3. Soja's own recasting of the socio-spatial dialectic was most memorably announced in his 1980 paper (Soja, E., 1980: "The Socio-spatial Dialectic," *Annals, Association of American Geographers*, 70, pp. 207–25).
4. Among the best are essays by Rosalyn Deutsche, Doreen Massey, and Meaghan Morris. For a broader perspective, see also Bondi, L., 1990: "Feminism, Postmodernism, and Geography: a space for women?," *Antipode*, 22, 2, pp. 156–67.

5. Issues of place, time, representation, alternate subjectivities, and polyvocality are equally prominent in postmodern anthropology. Indeed, it is no accident that the interface between the disciplines is the site of a highly fertile interchange. Good examples of such interdisciplinary work include the penetrating analysis of the modernist city, by Holston, J., 1989: *The Modernist City: An Anthropological Critique of Brasília*, Chicago: University of Chicago Press; the ethnographies of homeless women by Rowe, S. and Wolch, J., 1990: "Social Networks in Time and Space: Homeless Women in Skid Row, Los Angeles," *Annals, Association of American Geographers*, 80, pp. 184–204; as well as specific consideration of spatialization in anthropology (for example, de Certeau, M., 1984: *The Practice of Everyday Life*, Berkeley: University of California Press; and Marcus, G., 1989: "Imagining the Whole: Ethnography's Contemporary Efforts to Situate Itself," *Critique of Anthropology*, 9, pp. 7–30, on multiplace ethnographies).
6. Soja, E., 1989: *Postmodern Geographies*. London and New York: Verso, p. 1.
7. Ibid., p. 159.
8. Ibid., p. 45.
9. Ibid., p. 73.
10. Ibid., p. 2.
11. Ibid., p. 22.
12. Ibid., p. 31.
13. Ibid., p. 38.
14. Ibid., p. 131.
15. Ibid., p. 25.
16. Ibid., p. 155.
17. Harvey, 1989: *The Condition of Postmodernity*, Oxford: Blackwell, p. vii.
18. Ibid., p. 12.
19. Ibid., p. 14, emphasis added.
20. Ibid., p. 44.
21. Ibid., p. 59, emphasis added.
22. Ibid., p. 52, emphasis added.
23. Ibid., p. 116.
24. Ibid., p. 52.
25. Ibid., p. 117.
26. Ibid., p. 112.
27. Soja, E., *Postmodern Geographies*, p. 27.
28. Ibid., p. 148.
29. Ibid., p. 246.
30. Ibid., p. 221.
31. Harvey, *The Condition of Postmodernity*, p. vii.
32. Although he makes clear his distaste for the ephemeral and fashionable, Harvey is nevertheless quick to embrace the concept of "flexible specialization," which he promptly and uncritically converts into a regime of flexible accumulation.
33. Harvey, *The Condition of Postmodernity*, p. 197.
34. Ibid., p. 282.
35. Ibid., p. 293.
36. Ibid., pp. 295–6.
37. Ibid., p. 299.
38. Ibid., p. 302.
39. I shall leave it to others to speculate on what led Soja to identify Harvey as one of the "pioneers" of postmodern geography.
40. Graff, G., 1987: *Professing Literature: an Institutional History*, Chicago: University of Chicago Press.

41. See, respectively, Nicholson, L. J. (ed.), 1990: *Feminism/Postmoderism*, New York: Routledge; Connolly, W.E., 1987: *Politics and Ambiguity*, Madison: University of Wisconsin Press; Clifford, J., 1988: *The Predicament of Culture: 20th Century Ethnography, Literature and Art*, Cambridge, Massachusetts: Harvard University Press; and Hunt, L. (ed.), 1989: *The New Cultural History*, Berkeley: University of California Press, for exemplary treatments of these topics.

42. C. f. Nelson, J. S., Megill, A., McCloskey, D. N. (eds)., 1987: *The Rhetoric of the Human Sciences*, Madison: University of Wisconsin Press.

43. Soja, E., *Postmodern Geographies*, p. 63.

44. Ibid., pp. 173, 246.

45. Ibid., p. 75.

46. Meaghan Morris, p. 273.

47. Harvey, *The Condition of Postmodernity*, p. 47.

48. Meahgan Morris is especially critical of what she describes as Harvey's "profoundly reductive impulse" in his "massive exclusion of feminism" (pp. 255–6).

49. Harvey, *The Condition of Postmodernity*, e.g., p. 109.

50. Ibid., p. 287.

51. Ibid., p. 191.

52. Ibid., p. 188.

53. Ibid., p. 337.

54. Ibid., p. 342.

55. Ibid., p. 343.

56. Ibid., p. 345.

57. As Harvey claims on p. 59.

58. Laclau, E., and Mouffe, C., 1985: *Hegemony and Socialist Strategy*, New York: Verso Books.

59. Harvey, *The Condition of Postmodernity*, p. 46.

60. Both Deutsche (personal communication) and Massey, D., 1991: "Flexible Sexism," *Environment and Planning D: Society & Space*, 9, pp. 31–57, emphasize that Harvey never makes clear his precise rationale for characterizing feminism as a "local" struggle.

61. Harvey, *The Condition of Postmodernity*, p. 52.

62. Ibid., p. 116.

63. Ibid., p. 353, emphasis added.

64. Ibid., p. 117.

65. Morris provides a deliciously witty critique of Harvey's judgement on feminist politics (see especially p. 253).

66. Laclau, E. and Mouffe, C., 1985: *Hegemony and Socialist Strategy*, New York: Verso Books, p. 3, emphasis in original.

67. Harvey, *The Condition of Postmodernity*, p. 355.

68. Ibid., p. 359.

69. Deutsche, R., 1990: Men in Space, *Artforum*, 28, p. 22.

70. Ibid. p.22.

71. Massey, D., 1991: Flexible Sexism, Environment & Planning D: Society & Space, 9, p. 43.

72. Let me re-iterate that this statement is not meant, nor should it be read, as a condemnation of Marxian social theory.

73. The most direct and sustained of these engagements is Harvey, D., 1991: "Postmodern Morality Plays," *Antipode*, 24, 4, pp. 300–26, which deals at length with the criticisms by Deutsche and Massey. Harvey concedes that he was stung by their criticisms ("unnecessarily personalized, hurtful and sometimes abusive," p. 308), but on this and other occasions, he too is quite ungracious in his ripostes.

74. Soja, E., 1996: *Thirdspace: Journeys to Los Angeles and Other Real-and-Imagined Places*, Cambridge, Mass: Blackwell Publishers, Inc.

75. Olalquiaga, C., 1992: *Megalopolis*, Minneapolis: University of Minnesota Press, p. xi), quoted in Soja, E., 1996: *Thirdspace: Journeys to Los Angeles and Other Real-and-Imagined Places*, Cambridge, Mass: Blackwell Publishers, Inc., p. 92.

76. Soja, E., *Thirdspace*.

77. Soja, E., *Postmodern Geographies*.

78. Soja, E., *Thirdspace*, p. 1.

79. Ibid., p. 3.

80. Ibid., p. 140.

81. Ibid., p. 2.

82. Ibid., p. 5.

83. Ibid., pp. 70–1.

84. Ibid., pp. 74–82.

85. Ibid., p. 81.

86. Ibid., p. 84.

87. Gregory, D., 1994: *Geographical Imaginations*, Cambridge, Mass: Blackwell Publishers, Inc., pp. 168–205.

88. Elsewhere (Gregory, D. 1998. Explorations in Critical Human Geography: Hettner-Lecture 1997, Heidelberg, Germany: University of Heidelberg) Gregory explains that he is "careful not to use" the term "postmodernism" because of (a) its emphases on a "sharp discontinuous" break in human history, which is a "fundamentally wrong" conception of history and temporality; and (b) the "lack of historical depth" in so many discussions of the late twentieth century (p. 91).

89. Gregory, D., *Geographical Imaginations*, p. 182.

90. Ibid., p. 174.

91. Ibid., p. 167.

92. Ibid., pp. 409, 414.

93. Ibid., p. 262.

94. Ibid., Chapter 4, especially p. 312.

95. Ibid., Chapters 5 and 6.

96. Ibid., p. 415.

97. Ibid., pp. 279–81.

98. Jameson, F., 1994: *Seeds of Time*, New York: Columbia University Press, pp. xiv–xv.

99. Ibid, xii. See also Jameson, F., 1998: *The Cultural Turn: Selected Writings on the Postmodern: 1983–1998*, New York: Verso.

100. Kofman and Lebas, 1996: *Henri Lefebvre: Writing on Cities*, Oxford: Blackwell, p. 45 insist that Lefebvre also rejected postmodernism.

101. Gregory, D. *Geographical Imaginations*, p. 326.

102. Ibid., Chapter 6.

103. Ibid., pp. 157–8.

104. Ibid., p. 368.

105. Ibid., pp. 371–2.

106. Ibid., p. 377.

107. Ibid., p. 383.

108. Smith, N., 1998: "Antinomies of Space and Nature in Henri Lefebvre's The Production of Space," in *Philosophy and Geography II: The Production of Public Space*, Lanham, Maryland: Rowman & Littlefield Publishers, Inc., p. 59.

109. Ibid., p. 61.

110. Ibid., p. 62.

111. Pile, S., 1996: *The Body in the City*, London: Routledge, esp. pp. 145–69, 211–17. See also Gregory, D., 1995: "Lefebvre, Lacan and the production of space," in G. Benko and U. Strohmeyer (eds.) *Geography, History and Social Science*, Dordrecht: Kluwer; Blum, V. and Nast, H., 1996: "Where's the Difference? The Heterosexualization of Alterity in Henri Lefebvre and Jacques Lacan," *Environmental and Planning D: Society and Space*, 4, pp. 559–80.

112. See Gregory, D. *Geographical Imaginations*, Figure 30, p. 401.

113. Ibid., p. 404.

114. Ibid., p. 414.

115. Ibid., p. 412.

116. Ibid., p. 413

117. For example, Massey points to the inherent diversities of differentially produced global senses of place; also see Gibson-Graham, J. K., 1996: *The End of Capitalism (as we knew it): A Feminist Critique of Political Economy*, Cambridge, Mass: Blackwell Publishers, Inc.

5

Reading the Modern City: A Colonial History of Los Angeles, 1781–1991

In the city, time becomes visible.

Lewis Mumford

Los Angeles landscapes are a direct consequence of the interplay between the intentionalities of the private realm and those of the public sphere. For example, although LA appears as an intensely private, anarchic vision of urban growth, the city also has a long history of formal urban planning (including the nation's earliest experiments with zoning and regional planning). Since the earliest colonial times, urban outcomes have been the product of a public–private dialectic in which the hegemony of either sector has periodically shifted according to specificities of time and place. Yet although patterns of dominance have shifted, there has through it all been a consistently identifiable "civic will," a series of broad alliances that has guided the city through its many phases of urban growth; very explicit forms of intentionality underlay LA's urbanism for most of its two centuries of existence. This inherent rationality has created a "landscape of modernity" in Los Angeles, albeit a unlike the more monumental modernities associated with (for instance) New York City.[1] Now, Los Angeles is no different from other US cities in that it is the product of the public–private dialectic that characterizes urbanization in a capitalist society.[2] But LA provides a special opportunity to analyze the emergence of a postmodern condition, in which past traditions and intentionalities have collapsed, and previous verities suspended.[3] Certainly, residual modernities persist in the built environment and the land-use planning apparatus; but the rest of the city – its socio-cultural, political and economic fabric – has shifted irrevocably. Today, postmodern Los Angeles finds itself saddled with a relict planning apparatus characteristic of a period of high modernism, unable to mobilize the civic will necessary to legitimize formal urban development schemes. Postmodern Los Angeles challenges us to consider the origins and ramifications of a potentially radical break: that land-use planning, as it has been practiced for most of this century, is now defunct, irretrievable; and that new legitimacies and intentionalities must be sought if LA's urban development is to be channeled away from a dystopian future.

In order to examine these propositions, I have divided this chapter into two broad themes: the first explores the theoretical dimensions of a putative shift from modernist to a postmodern urbanism; the second offers an interpretation of some pivotal periods in the history of intentionality and land-use planning in Los Angeles.

I conclude with some preliminary reflections on the nature of the shift to a postmodern urbanism.

From Modern to Postmodern

The phrase "In the city, time becomes visible" is, of course, Lewis Mumford's. It suggests *avant la lettre* the possibility of examining the text of the city for insights into existing and emergent urban rationalities. My focus in this essay is upon the texts of land-use planning as evidence of intentionality in the production and reproduction of the built environment. This is, as I shall hope to show, a matter of considerable theoretical and practical consequence.

The essence of the problematic of postmodern urbanism can be captured, in an entirely serious way, by placing Babar the Elephant alongside Mickey Mouse. These two cartoon figures provide provocative exemplars of past and future urbanisms. In her study of the politics of design in French colonial urbanism, architectural historian Gwendolyn Wright shows how powerful were the myths of colonial order by examining Babar's 1931 design for the construction of Célesteville, a city of elephants in Africa.[4] Behind a harbor, standardized shuttered huts for native peoples were arranged in neat rows below a hillside dominated by two monumental buildings: the *Palais du Travail* and the *Palais des Fêtes*. The vision of Babar's creator (Jean de Brunhoff) was one of "social hierarchy, orderly growth, a thriving economy, and effective political authority." All this was to be accomplished by the colonial masters (needless to say) without effacing the indigenous African social fabric.

Contrast Babar's world with that of Mickey Mouse: a vision of the city as a collage of theme parks, best exemplified by the various Disneylands, and in particular by the postmodern archetype, Los Angeles. The emergent reorientations invoked by the postmodern city are nowhere more evident than in Michael Sorkin's edited collection *Variations on a Theme Park*. In his introductory remarks, Sorkin observes that:

> the city has historically mapped social relations with profound clarity, imprinting in its shapes and places vast information about status and power.[5]

However, in Sorkin's "recombinant" city, this earlier modernist legibility has been obscured, and dramatically manipulated: the phone and the modem have rendered the street irrelevant; social hierarchies, once fixed, have become "despatialized"; and space itself is "departicularized."[6]

Let us, for the moment, grant that this is so (even though I later dissent from Sorkin's view). That between the rigidities of modernist planning (in Babar's colonial guise) and the departicularized places of postmodernity (in Disney's theme parks), there is a world of difference. My question is: how? How are modernist legibilities being transformed and the peculiar spatialities of postmodernity being created? I can best respond to these questions by successively examining the origins of land-use planning in the United States, the principles of modernist city planning (as exemplified by Brasília), and the particularities of the shift to a postmodern urbanism (following the arguments of Marshall Berman).

The origins of rationality in American urbanism

According to Christine Boyer, the rationalities of American urban land-use planning were established somewhere between the end of the nineteenth and the beginning of the twentieth centuries. The end of the nineteenth century was a period when people searched for "an instinct for improvement."[7] The key reformist language of this era referred to such notions as uplift, harmony, and instinct. By the beginning of the twentiethth century, a few decades later, an emergent land-use planning discourse had appeared, emphasizing unity, control, and expert skills.[8] According to Boyer, this new disciplinary order had as its goal the use of surplus capital for civilizing and socializing purposes. It required state intervention, a revised municipal politics, and the production of a category of experts.

The emergent social rationality grew out of the post-Civil War turmoil, when reformers worried how to discipline and regulate the urban masses, and how to control and arrange the spatial growth of cities.[9] A host of urban ills were attributed

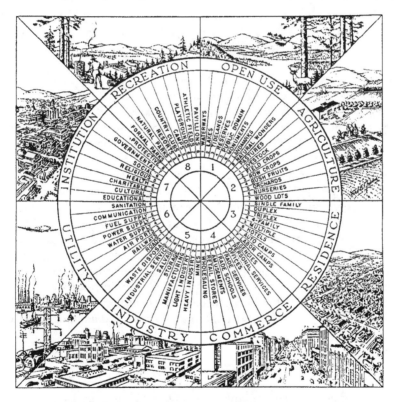

CLASSIFICATION OF LAND USES

Figure 5.1 Rational Land Use Planning (Regional Planning Commission, Los Angeles County, in public domain)
A lust for rationality and order is expressed in this logo, which decorated many land-use planning documents in the 1920s.

to indusltrialization and urbanization, and an intense anti-urbanism was re-invented. A new relationship between the urban public and social science knowledge was forged, which by the end of the nineteeth century had called forth a process of city planning. Capitalists joined Reformers to address social and economic needs: environmental reform was promoted as a remedy for the social pathologies of urban areas; and public health legislation was closely followed by the design of model tenements intended to improve the quality of life in urban areas. There was also a need for centralized, supervised operations by some form of institutional authority, especially in order to contain what some perceived as ill-distributed relief.[10] Around this time, for example, Charles Mulford Robinson, a journalist who identified himself as a "city improver," remarked upon the strange evil of excessive urban generosity.[11]

The new "totalization of poverty" required an expanded chain of information. A concept of the "curative whole" emerged, reflecting the linkage between pathologies of the individual and pathologies of family, neighborhood, and city.[12] As a consequence, attention shifted to new spatial categories and to new environmental causes. The search for spatial order was principally directed through nature and classical architecture. Robinson was an important figure in the search for municipal art, reflecting the influence of Haussmann when he wrote:

> it has been found that often there is no better way to redeem a slum district than by cutting into it a great highway that will be filled with through travel of a city's industry. Like a stream of pure water cleansing what it touches, this tide of traffic pulsing with the joyousness of the city's life of toil and purpose, when flowing through an idle or suffering district, wakes it to larger interests and higher purposes.[13]

The birth of a planning mentality meant a new spatial order in American cities, but planning documents quickly zeroed in on the minutiae of the built environment. A concern with physical detail became increasingly abstracted from the motives and conflicts that led to the production of the urban landscape, and civic improvements were recommended without consideration of those vested interests that led to the production of city form. In short, the process of capitalist urbanization was overlooked while an idealized/utopian planning theory developed and a bureaucratic maze regulated the practice of development control. Planning practice thus created its own totalization; for detailed plans to be constructed, an extensive fact file was needed to organize the physical, social, economic and legal/administrative fabric of the city.[14]

Building the modernist city

The verities of modernist land-use planning and the consequences of separating the capitalist process from planning theory and practice are succinctly revealed in anthropologist James Holston's account of the construction of the city of Brasília.[15] Holston notes that the city's modernist plan was founded on the principles of the Athens charter and the philosophy of the Congrès Internationaux d'Architecture Moderne (CIAM). The CIAM philosophy concentrated on four functions of the city: housing, work, recreation and traffic; it later added the administrative function to this list. Most importantly, Holston reveals how the modernist city managed to harness mutually antagonistic social and political programs to a single architectural program:

> Brasília was planned by a left–center liberal, designed by a communist, constructed by a developmentalist regime and consolidated by a bureaucratic authoritarian dictatorship each claiming an elective affinity with the city. Precisely because the CIAM model manages to unite such dissident interest, its brand of modernism has come to dominate development projects worldwide.[16]

The CIAM city was a city of salvation. It was intended to solve the urban and social crises attributed to maladies caused by unfettered private interests. The most important exponent of CIAM principles was the architect Le Corbusier. (His seminal text, entitled *The Radiant City*, includes the following epigraph: "This work is dedicated to authority.") The rationalist metropolis that resulted was a city that dehistoricized the particular; it was a city distilled into an universal model. The plan was sketched initially by Costa and executed by Neimeyer. Their view was one of the harmony of the whole.[17] Brasil's totalitarian President Kubiteschek was committed both to modernism and modernization; he was also a utopianist, who envisaged the architecture of Brasília as a prescription for social change. But how could capitalists and communists simultaneously find their visions signified by the same set of symbols? The answer according to Holston lies in the polysemous nature of architecture – each group could identify with the break with a colonial past and the leap into the future implied in the plan.[18] Moreover, no priority could be established among the competing ideological claims represented in the plan.

There is, however, another condition beyond architectural ambiguity that explains how a single representation could absorb the multiple significations implied by its communist and totalitarian supporters. The peculiar genius of the modernist city plan lies in its "empty vessel" quality; anyone can pour identity or signification into that vessel. The abstract ahistoricism and aspatiality of modernist thought allowed a split to occur between the material side of modernism and its spiritual side. It is this division that has given modernist thought its remarkable resilience – a chameleon-like ability to satisfy all persuasions at once. At the same time, however, the qualities of ahistoricity and aspatiality betray modernity's greatest flaw, i.e. its separation of the political economy of modernization from the culture and spirit of modernity. Thus the rationalities of production and reproduction in capitalist urbanization have been divorced from the utopian ideals of planning thought as well as from the minutiae of planning practice. This is a recipe for impotence. And somewhat predictably, the particular dynamism of Brasilian society conspired to destroy the plan's utopian dreams.[19] Even as the physical design persisted, albeit in a mutated form, the practices of everyday life (the accretion of the local) preempted the modernist logics that underlay it.[20]

From modernity to postmodernity

In his well-known examination of the culture of modernity, Marshall Berman captures the essence of the separation I have just described.[21] Let me use some of

Berman's definitions to clarify his terminology. Modernity is the experience of contemporary life that has been fed by numerous movements including science, industrialization, demographic change, urban growth, mass communication, nation states, social movements, and the rise of a worldwide capitalism. Modernization refers to a state of perpetual becoming, a process which brought modernity into being. Modernism is a discussion about a changing visions and values that accompany modernization.[22] According to Berman, the essence of the twentieth century is the dialectic between modernization and modernism. The process of modernization has engorged the world, and the developing global culture of modernism has achieved much in art and social thought; but as the modern public expanded, it shattered into a multitude of fragments speaking incommensurable private languages. Thus fragmented, modernity loses much of its capacity to organize and give meaning to people's lives. As a result, we find ourselves today in the midst of a modern age that has lost touch with its roots. As Berman puts it:

> To be modern . . . is to experience personal and social life as a maelstrom, to find one's world and oneself in perpetual disintegration and renewal, trouble and anguish, ambiguity and contradiction: to be part of universe in which all that is solid melts into air. To be a modernist is to make oneself somehow at home in the maelstrom, to make its rhythms one's own, to move within its currents in search for the forms of reality, of beauty, of freedom, of justice, that its fervid and perilous flow allows.[23]

The consequences for a disoriented, decentered society are profound. According to Berman a dynamic new landscape has been created through which we experience modernity. A radical flattening of perspective has occurred, accompanied by a shrinking of the imaginative range. The twentieth century has lurched towards rigid polarizations and flat totalizations; open visions have been supplanted by closed visions (for example "both/and" is replaced by "either/or"). The iron cage of a capitalistic, legalistic, and bureaucratic framework has closed around us, giving rise to a state of "total administration." And finally, the kind of person constructed by the new modernity is Marcuse's "one-dimensional man" – people who recognize themselves solely through their consumption of commodities.[24]

Using the examples of Charles Baudelaire, Le Corbusier, Robert Moses and Jane Jacobs, Berman reveals how the burgeoning dualism between modernization and modernism diminishes our understanding of the ways materialism and spiritualism invade each other.[25] The early Baudelaire portrayed a pastoral vision of modernity, celebrating modern life as a fashion show, a carnival. The later Baudelaire constructed a counter pastoral vision which poured scorn on the notion of progress and modern life, suggesting that the concept of indefinite progress must be the most cruel and ingenious torture ever invented. (Until I rediscovered Bandelaire in later life, I must confess that my only recollection of his work – encountered in sixth-form grammar school French classes – was an extreme sensuality which was catnip to an overheated teenager. All those calm, voluptuous, luxuriant settings!) It is important that the historical context for Baudelaire's work was the modernization of Paris by Haussmann on behalf of Napoleon III. Through Haussmann, Paris became a different kind of unified physical and human space, especially via the construction of the boulevards. Baudelaire's description of life on the boulevard shows how new private and public worlds came into being through the re-creation of the cityscape. Berman quotes Baudelaire's primal modern scene:

> I was crossing the boulevard, in a great hurry, in the midst of a moving chaos, with death galloping at me from every side.[26]

The archetypal modernist is a (male) pedestrian thrown into the maelstrom of modern city traffic, contending against an agglomeration of mass and energy that is heavy, fast, and lethal. The street and traffic know no spatial or temporal bounds; they spill into every urban place and impose their tempo on everybody's time, transforming the entire environment into a moving chaos. The boulevard thus becomes a perfect symbol of capitalism's inner contradictions: rationality exists in each individual unit, but an anarchic irrationality in the social system results when all these units are brought together.[27]

Berman argues that the creation of modernist urban space required that collisions and confrontations do not occur. He extends Baudelaire's example to Le Corbusier's discovery of traffic. After fighting his way through the congestion, Le Corbusier makes a sudden daring leap, identifying totally with the forces that have just been bearing down on him:

> On that first of October 1924, I was assisting in a titanic rebirth of a new phenomenon: traffic. Cars, cars, fast, fast! One is seized, filled with enthusiasm, with joy... the joy of power. The simple and naive pleasure of being in the midst of power, of strength. One participates in it, one takes part in the society that is just dawning. One has confidence in this new society: it will find a magnificent expression of its power. One believes in it.[28]

From being the familiar man in the street dodging the snarling traffic, in the next moment Le Corbusier's viewpoint has radically shifted, so that now he lives and moves from within. He has gone from fighting traffic to joining it. His is the perspective of "the new man" in the automobile – what was to become the paradigm for twentieth-century modernist urban planning. Such a paradigmatic shift implies the death of the street.

In his search of a revitalized modernism, Berman draws a distinction between Robert Moses and Jane Jacobs. The Moses myth was founded on a conflation of progress and people's rights. He was able to orchestrate the release millions of federal dollars following the initiation of several important New Deal agencies, in particular the Federal Housing Administration and the Federal Highway Program. Subsequently, he constructed new and sometimes imaginative public places, parkways, and bridges within the New York City area. But Berman suggests that just as the construction of Moses' cross-Bronx Expressway was completed, "the real ruin" of the Bronx began; the fundamental results of his intervention were suburbanization of the metropolitan fringe and abandonment of the inner city. For her part, Jane Jacobs recognized that everyday street life nourished modern experiences and values. She brought the opinions and perceptions of women into the discourse of modernist urbanism, recognized that streets are places of twenty-fourhour detail, and drew attention to the ecology and phenomenology of the sidewalk. Jacobs argued that for the sake of the modern, we must preserve the old and resist the new, and her writings were instrumental in provoking a wave of community activism to protect neighborhoods from further destruction by expressways and other forms of urban redevelopment.

The difference between a Moses megaproject and Jacobs' focus on the quotidian raise a host of issues pertaining (for instance) to the gendering of modernist space, including the question of a modernist, masculinist morality. Returning to the Bronx to recover what was good about his old neighborhood, Berman discovered a contradiction. One resident asserted that the moral imperative of the Bronx was to get out of the neighborhood in order to achieve advancement. Berman generalizes this sentiment, recognizing that the American way to overcome contradictions has generally been to drive away from them.[29] The important change that occurred sometime in the 1970s was that economic recession meant that modern societies lost much of their ability to blow away their past; they were forced to remain, to confront their modernism by remembering instead of forgetting:

> at a moment when modern society seemed to lose the capacity to create a brave new future, modernism was under intense pressure to discover new sources of life through imaginative encounters with the past.[30]

Those who are awaiting the end of modernity can be assured of steady work, according to Berman. However,

> if modernism ever managed to throw off its scraps and tatters and the uneasy joints that bind it to the past, it would lose all its weight and depth, and the maelstrom of modern life would carry it helplessly away. It is only by keeping alive the bonds that tie it to the modernities of the past – bonds at once intimate and antagonistic – that it can help the moderns of the present and the future to be free.[31]

But, I must add, the loosening of fetters feared by Berman has already occurred; modernism has floated away, loose, weightless, and depthless. This has already happened; this is what postmodernity is.

Unravelling the postmodern time–space fabric

By now, it is commonplace that postmodern sensitivities require new ways of seeing.[32] Questions of difference and representation are uppermost in the minds of those who would rehearse the break with modernity. It is certainly evident that urbanists seeking to understand the postmodern metropolis have increasingly turned away from traditional manufacturing cities and the conventions of the Chicago School in their search for explanations of Los Angeles, São Paulo, and Mexico City, or Atlanta, Seattle and Phoenix (cf. Chapter 1).[33] Understanding the intentionality of postmodern urbanism requires a different kind of geographical imagination, one that not only allows Sorkin's departicularization of space, but also focuses on the particularization of place. There is every reason to assume that postmodern society is just as profoundly imprinted in its urban places; it is simply that the manner of inscription, and the consequent urban forms, will likely differ from that of modernist conventions.

The social construction of space is at the core of the geographer's agenda, and uneven spatial development has long been understood as capital's way of overcoming the contradictions inherent in its "progress." Berman recognized that the American way to overcome contradictions is to leave them behind, to continually create new places representative of the unfolding American dream. And as we saw in Chapter 3, Fredric Jameson goes further, identifying a new postmodern "hyperspace" characteristic of our era but so vast and complex that no-one can as yet imagine its time–space coordinates.[34]

In what follows, I shall begin to engage the proposition that Los Angeles is the archetype of an emergent postmodern urbanism, as evidenced in the texts of past built environments. My historical analysis should reveal a progressive erosion of the intentionalities of unity, control, and expert skills which characterized the new-born planning profession at the turn of this century. It should portray the pre-eminence of a totalizing discourse that facilitated the production of a modernist landscape, favoring urban abstractions (plans as empty vessels) that were capable of accommodating multiple ideologies, but ill-suited to the exigencies of socio-economic and political change. My analysis should also uncover a constant renegotiation of the public/private dialectic in the city, and the emergence of a fragmented metropolis characterized at once by centralizing administrative tendencies and by intensely developed local autonomies. Postmodern Los Angeles should be a city that has lost contact with the heritage of its past modernisms, and (free-floating) betrays a new depthlessness. The intentionalities guiding previous urbanisms will either be discarded or renegotiated; at a dysfunctional extreme, outmoded and obsolescent intentionalities may still remain to impede an urban process that has long since superseded them.

Before I begin, let me underscore the obvious: that what follows in no way purports to be a comprehensive urban history. I simply identify six pivotal moments from two centuries of urban growth in order to examine the proposition that LA provides significant insights into the transition toward a postmodern urban society. Each of these six periods (broadly chronological but also overlapping) provides examples of strikingly different rationalities in the creation of the built environment – intentionalities sometimes dominated by private interests, at other times by the public interest, most usually an alliance between public resources and private profiteering. But on every occasion, the deliberate intentionality that (re)creates the urban environment is backed by a clearly demonstrable collective civic will (even though, on occasion, the collective spirit turns out to be kinder to some groups than to others). In conclusion, I shall consider the consequences of the atrophy of civic will implied by the emergence of the postmodern city.

There is another obvious difficulty in writing colonial history: it usually leaves little or no space for a non-colonial agency or voice. The rationalities and intentionalities that I reconstruct in this case are those of the Spanish, Mexican and American occupations of "Alta California." Even this naming implies a dispossession, the imposition of an external intelligibility on the landscape. Derek Gregory[35]

Figure 5.2/a–d   Chávez Ravine (Don Normark)
In 1948, Swedish immigrant Don Normark took hundreds of photographs of Chávez Ravine, a multiracial/multiethnic community that was later bulldozed to make way for the Dodgers' baseball stadium.

illuminates the difficulties in an excellent discussion of the work of Paul Carter and Edward Said, inter alia, concluding that while deconstruction of imperialist histories is vital, it is still not clear how the histories of aboriginal cultures are to be effectively portrayed, since the adoption of (say) a postmodern experimentation might do little beside co-opt (post)colonial experiences within yet one more discourse of the West. There is a double jeopardy here, since colonial/colonized and post-colonial spaces are also profoundly gendered spaces (as the work of Mary Louise Pratt and others has shown); so the depth of these silences are even more profound. There is no simple way out of this conundrum. In this sense, all our knowledges are situated knowledges.[36] Colonizers will inevitably see things differently from the colonized, and consequently their historical accounts will differ. My approach in this chapter is squarely to focus on the colonizers' story, with only rare sidelong glances explicitly at the colonized, because this is the story I need to tell at this point. Inevitably, this renders the fleeting, impressionistic account that follows even less satisfactory. However, I think it is methodologically defensible even as a cartoon, since it facilitates the more inclusive parsing that succeeds it.

The Making of Los Angeles

Colonial "beginnings," 1781–1846

Look carefully at the places and ports where it might be possible to build Spanish settlements without damage to the Indian population.[37]

On August 2, 1769, a Spanish land expedition was making its way from San Diego to Monterey under the command of Gaspar de Portolá. It stopped at the site where, twelve years later, the pueblo of Los Angeles was to be founded. In a contemporary diary, Father Crespi noted the advantages of the site: it had "all the requisites for a large settlement," including "a large vineyard of wild grapes," "an infinity of rose bushes in full bloom," and soil "capable of producing every kind of grain and fruit."[38] He recorded that a number of the Indians who "live in this delightful place among the trees on the river" brought the visitors gifts, while some old men "puffed at us three mouthfuls of smoke."[39] The Indians who met the Spanish army were the Yang-na (or Yabit); they were Shoshonean in speech, and had settled an area close to the present day City Hall. The Portolá party named the local river "Nuestra Señora la Reina de Los Angeles de Porciúncula."[40]

In April 1781, Felipe de Neve, governor of Spanish California, arrived at the mission of San Gabriel to prepare for the settlement of a pueblo on the river.[41] De Neve had in mind to establish a new kind of settlement, located at an inland river site, to be primarily agricultural rather than military or missionary. In this way, he hoped to make the *presidios* less dependent on Mexico for food supplies.[42] As part of his colonial armory, de Neve had at his disposal a set of city planning ordinances – the so-called "Laws of the Indies" – that had been issued by the Spanish King Philip II in 1573 (themselves a compilation of previous land-use planning edicts issued since the beginning of the Conquest).[43] Based on Roman city planning principles, the 148 ordinances dealt exhaustively with every aspect of site selection, city planning and political organization. The ordinances effectively:

> reinforced the unilateral objectives of conquest, emphasized the urban character of Spanish colonization, and specified clearly the physical and organizational arrangements that were to be developed in the new cities of America. Above all, the ordinances stressed a Christian ideology and a cultural imperialism . . . .[44]

Following a royal request to update settlement legislation in California, de Neve used his new-found autonomy to significantly modify the existing ordinances. His detailed regulations – the *Reglamento* – received royal assent in 1781. Among other things, they shifted power from the church to the state, paid settlers a salary, and encouraged Indians to continue living in villages apart from the missions.[45] Fifty years later, this shift in authority would ultimately culminate in the secularization of the missions.[46]

On the evening of September 4, 1781, 44 settlers arrived at the site chosen by de Neve, accompanied by four soldiers who had escorted them from the Mission San Gabriel.[47] The new settlement was called El Pueblo de Nuestra Señora la Reina de Los Angeles de Porciúncula; it was situated not far from the present-day Olvera Street in downtown Los Angeles. The site was systematically surveyed according to regulations:

> The original pueblo consisted of four square leagues or 28 square miles, the center of which was a plaza 275 ft. by 180 ft. Building lots 55 ft. by 111 ft. were plotted around this plaza and assigned to the eleven families that constituted the settlement, a population of 44 persons. There were 12 of these building lots, 4 on the northwesterly side, 4 on southeasterly side, 2 on the northeasterly side and one each on the northerly corner and the easterly corner. The southwesterly side was reserved half for public buildings and half for open space. Two streets $27\frac{1}{2}$ ft. in width extended through the building lots on each of the long sides of the plaza and three on the short side. A short distance away 36 fields, each containing about 7 acres, were laid out and each settler was allowed two cultivation. Beginning in 1875 the governor granted ranches of large tracts of land outside the pueblo, some of which are owned today by the descendants of the original grantees.

The pueblo prospered beyond expectations and, by the 1830s, it ranked first in size among California settlements. But the Spanish army and Christian religion were to prove disastrous for the aboriginal inhabitants of the pueblo and California as a whole. As Fogelson observed: "For the aborigines, slavery in this world was a prerequisite for salvation in the next." [48] By the time of the Mexican–American War (1846–48), a sizeable Indian population lived "in misery and squalor" at the pueblo.[49] When California came under American control, the city council was prompted to take action against Indian squatters. Council required all individuals with Indian servants to keep them inside "to check their excesses;" and those Indians without employment were to be granted lots at the edge of the city.[50] Between 1770 and 1832, the aboriginal population in California declined from 130,000 to 90,000.[51]

American rationality, 1846–1853

> After 1860, with surveys complete, land parcels could be bought and sold in the normal American manner.[52]

Under Spanish rule, some 25 concessions permitted settlement and the use of a specified tract of land, even though title remained with the Spanish Crown. In practice, such concessions amounted to little more than grazing rights. But in 1822, control of California passed from Spain to Mexico, and the subsequent extensive system of Mexican land grants became one of the most important influences on California history. The system of *ranches* facilitated the later concentration of the state's land ownership in relatively few hands.

Once California had been ceded by Mexico to the United States, the logic of the former Spanish–Mexican system of land tenure did not long survive. The conquerors promptly imposed their own values and institutional arrangements, including political structures, taxation, and land ownership.[53] These replaced more traditional methods of trading agricultural products and land titles (including the subdivision of *ranchos*) that characterized Mexican Alta California. Long-standing problems associated with the absence of a competent land survey were resolved when Lt. Edward O.C. Ord was dispatched in 1846 to survey Los Angeles. The imposition of "American order" was one of the primary tasks of the new authorities, and it was understood that "the permanent prosperity of any new country is identified with the perfect security of its land titles."[54] Ord mapped all the lands then under cultivation, thus enabling city authorities to understand what they were governing, and to sell land parcels to benefit the city treasury.

In 1848, gold was discovered in California, and triggered the first of many spectacular development booms in Southern California (this time based in beef production for the gold town markets in the north).[55] In 1853, pueblo lands beyond Ord's original survey were extensively mapped by Henry Hancock. Local business interests sought to incorporate as much land as possible into the survey so that it could be sold at city prices.[56] In 1785, the Northwest Ordinance established a system of principal meridians and base lines in California (and the rest of the USA) to ensure the orderly sale of public lands.

Emergence of the entrepreneurial state, 1880–1932

And so came into being *a* great American city destined to become *the* great American city.[57]

Between 1880 and 1932, Los Angeles grew from a town of 10,000 people covering roughly 29 square miles to become the country's principal western metropolis with 1.2 million people and a territory of 442 square miles. During this period, so well described by Steve Erie, LA transformed itself from a small entrepreneurial growth regime to a state-centered growth regime in which public infrastructure projects (most notably in water, power, and harbor development) and influential local bureaucracies shaped the region's development.[58]

LA's early entrepreneurial regime, from 1880 to 1906, was composed of an hegemony of business interests with primary emphases on boosterism and real estate speculation to produce growth.[59] The business community, dominated by the Southern Pacific (SP) Railroad, created and controlled what was essentially a small caretaker local state.[60] SP treated Southern California as a colony, and effectively constrained local economic development. But as the century drew to a close, Southern Pacific's stranglehold was increasingly challenged by a locally-based commercial, financial and real-estate elite, who did not share the vision of a railroad-dominated LA.[61] For Harrison Gray Otis (of the *Los Angeles Times*) and his partners in the newly-formed LA Chamber of Commerce, the 1888 collapse in the land boom had revealed the weakness of a regional economy founded on real estate. They firmly believed that industrialization was the key to the region's growth.[62] Otis and the Chamber envisioned LA as the commercial and manufacturing center of the west coast, and they challenged Southern Pacific over the matter of LA's harbor.[63] While Southern Pacific was promoting Santa Monica Bay as the preferred site for harbor investment, LA's broad business coalition countered with a proposal for a municipally-owned harbor at San Pedro (which would also bring in the Santa Fe Railroad to challenge the SP's monopoly). The eventual selection of San Pedro as the site for massive federal investment in harbor development signaled the beginning of the shift in balance of power to local business and away from outside corporate influence over the region's political economy.

But it was potable water, not a harbor, that fundamentally limited Southern California's regional growth. At the turn of the century, the Los Angeles River and nearby artesian wells could sustain a population of only 300,000. Fresh from its harbor victory, the *Times* and its business allies brought the privately-owned Los Angeles City Water Company under public control by organizing a special election enabling voters to approve the city's 1899 bond issue to purchase the existing private waterworks.[64] A political reform movement followed, and the railroad's hegemony was squashed. By 1906, an activist, progressive city council had replaced the caretakers, and began the task of building the public infrastructure deemed necessary for the region's growth. Two actions by the growth-oriented local state were harbingers of things to come: territorial expansion to link the city with the new harbor; and a $23 million Los Angeles Aqueduct bond issue (which in turn paved the way for public provision of cheap power).[65]

In 1906, voters approved the so-called "Shoestring Addition", a narrow 16–mile long strip of annexed land linking Los Angeles with San Pedro and Wilmington. The land thus acquired expanded the city's area by almost 50 percent, and became the prototype for LA's subsequent campaign of infrastructure-based territorial expansion.[66] Though the newly-formed LA Board of Harbor Commissioners in 1907 lacked an actual harbor, they successfully formed bond campaign committees to raise the needed funds, and thereby emerged as a formidable bureaucratic apparatus. By 1932, the Port of Los Angeles was the most important on the Pacific coast and third in the nation in terms of total tonnage handled.[67]

While the Harbor Commission pursued a collaborationist strategy with the local business community (and enjoyed its continuous support), the Department of Water and Power (DWP) faced major business opposition.[68] Announced in 1905, the Los Angeles Aqueduct was opened in 1913, bringing sufficient water for two million potential consumers (at the behest of city water engineer William Mulholland) from the Owens River Valley on the eastern slopes of the Sierra Nevadas to the San Fernando Valley.[69] Mulholland vigorously lobbied to make annexation a precondition for receiving aqueduct water, thereby expanding the city's bonding capacity. In over 70 separate annexation elections between 1906 and 1930, the city's administrative area grew dramatically from 43 to 442 square miles.[70]

Los Angeles' new aqueduct also generated low-cost steam and electricity. The DWP used these resources between 1909 and 1932 to raise public capital to expand the Owens River system, to purchase LA's private utilities, and to secure water and power from the federal Boulder Canyon Dam project.[71] Because power dominated the political agenda, the DWP moved to center-stage in local politics during this period. DWP bureaucrats Mulholland, Matthews and Scattergood were instrumental in securing Congressional passage of the Boulder Canyon Project Act, a federal water project which ultimately permitted the city to grow beyond two million inhabitants. LA's electrical power rates became the lowest of any major city in the nation, and acted as a magnet for eastern industries.

Domesticating land-use planning, 1900–1941

The problem offered by Los Angeles is a little out of the ordinary.[72]

City and regional land-use planning emerged out of Los Angeles' post-1900 progressivism. The progressives' complaints about the negative consequences of uncontrolled development focused on "private enterprises's single-minded devotion to profits and public authority's exclusive dedication to material progress."[73] Their advocacy led in 1915 to the creation of a Los Angeles City Planning Association, and ultimately (in 1920) to a legally-constituted City Planning Commission. The President of the latter announced candidly that the Commission was not a conservative branch of city government, but would "Dream dreams and see Visions." [74] In reality, the burgeoning land-use planning apparatus was promptly pre-empted by real estate interests. A business ethos was clearly evident in the contemporaneous priorities set by one planning practitioner: "A city plan should be prepared from the economic standpoint first, the social or human standpoint second, and the aesthetic viewpoint last."[75] From his perspective on a century of transportation planning in Los Angeles, Brodsly concluded that:

> planners on all levels have consistently tried to play down their active role in public policy... [and] often had to guard against being considered utopian visionaries.[76]

Zoning was first introduced into the United States by a 1904 experiment in Los Angeles that separated residential and industrial land uses.[77] Interest in land-use planning was intensified when Charles Mulford Robinson (a renowned advocate of the City Beautiful movement) visited LA and prepared a series of grand designs for the city's future. In an inspirational conclusion to his report, Robinson wrote:

> I have tried to show what I thought should be the municipal ideal toward which Los Angeles should develop... Not to be simply big; but to be beautiful as well. Not to be content with narrow, crowded streets, with meanness of aspect and a modeling after cities where lives must be spent indoors; but to be spacious, handsome, as a capital city, the streets alluring one out of doors, and offering so many drives and giving one so much to do that tourists will not pass through Los Angeles. They will stay here, in a real "Paris of America" – a summer city, when the East is swept by wind and snow; and they will find a gay outdoor life where other cities are stamped with the grime and rush of earnestness that knows not how to play. It is a beautiful, enviable role.[78]

Despite these lofty thoughts, the practicalities of day-to-day zoning occupied the minds of many Angelenos. The Los Angeles Realty Board (LARB) campaigned on behalf of the first citywide zoning law in 1908, and pushed to establish the County Regional Planning Commission in 1923 – the first in the country – to "facilitate suburban growth and circumvent the need for involvement by the City of Los Angeles in land-use regulation, infrastructure and service provision, and property taxation."[79] However, the intervention of the LARB should not be understood as a naive or homogeneous instrumentality on the part of its members. The Board was frequently divided over issues, some members wanting to use zoning to promote speculation, others favoring protecting districts from sprawl and thereby stabilizing land values.[80] On other occasions, smaller landowners often found themselves at odds with large holders of land, the former generally resisting any and all controls on land and property development.[81] The subsequent growth and development of LA's land-use planning apparatus was inextricably linked with the interests of the LARB. For example, the collapse of the local real estate market in 1907, and the weak market associated with the 1914–15 nationwide depression led the LARB to press (successfully) for new zoning regulations.[82]

In other cities, the conflicting objectives of planners and private developers frequently developed into a classical stand-off, a constantly shifting dialectic between progressive visions and economic imperatives. But in LA, successive rushes of spectacular urban development erased most utopian overtones from a dialogue on the urban future. In 1918, 6,000 building permits were issued in Los Angeles; by 1923, the peak year of the boom, this had climbed to 62,548 permits with a total value of $200 million. By the end of 1925, LA had no less than 600,000 subdivided lots standing vacant; the city had already parceled out enough land to accommodate seven million people, fifty years before the reality of demographic growth would catch up with the realtors' speculative appetite.[83] These consistently high rates of expansion are often cited as a principal reason for planning's subservient role with respect to business. In addition, the city's planning department was usually chronically understaffed and almost exclusively concerned with zoning.[84] During the 1920s, for instance, zoning matters occupied 80 percent of the department's and the commission's time,[85] while in the first nine months of its operation, the Regional Planning Commission was obliged to review over 800 proposals for tract development in unincorporated territories.[86]

Fogelson claims that "nothing in Los Angeles demonstrated the tenacity of private development as convincingly as the course of public planning." [87] Indeed, there is little doubt that city planning was generally consonant with the ambitions of developers and residents alike. Los Angeles developers "fully understood the need for planned infrastructure to support their realty projects, and they were quite willing to utilize government for such purposes."[88] The potential of planning was thus effectively reduced to the exigencies of zoning practice,[89] which "merely sanctioned the preferences of private enterprise."[90] Brodsly underscores the confluence of convenience and conscience implicit in these alliances:

> Los Angeles' history has been one continuous real estate enterprise, with land speculation a driving force for its never-ending growth... [The] metropolis began to take shape, not according to any plan but rather at the subdivider's discretion.[91] ... Los Angeles' urban form has been, perhaps to an unprecedented degree, a reflection of choice.[92]

Whose choice? According to Fogelson: "In all essentials, the planners shared the populace's suburban ideals, and the populace agreed with the metropolitan aspirations."[93]

After a half century of truly unprecedented urban growth, in 1942 Los Angeles prepared for the long post-war boom. The prospects facing the city's planning apparatus at this time were succinctly summed up by planning commission member William H. Schuchardt: "The present situation of the City of Los Angeles, from the standpoint of the city planner, may be couched in one word: Chaos."[94]

Transportation palimpsest, 1941–54

[The] freeway system in its totality is now a single comprehensible place, a coherent state of mind, a complete way of life...[95]

The chaos of post-war planning was a consequence of staggering rates of demographic growth in Los Angeles during the preceding decades. Total population in Los Angeles and Orange Counties rose from under one million to over 2.3 million during the decade of the 1920s. A further 1.4 million was added during the 1940s, and 2.3 million in the 1950s. The population was already ethnically and racially diverse, and highly segregated into separate neighborhoods.[96] To complicate matters, the early Angelenos began early their love affair with the car. In 1915, LA County's 750,000 residents had over 55,000 cars – the highest ownership rates in the nation. By 1918, vehicle registrations rose to 110,000, and to over 400,000 by 1924.[97]

Transportation has always played an important role in Southern California's sprawling suburbanism. Architect Rayner Banham characterized the region as a "transportation palimpsest," by which he meant that it was a huge tablet of movement, constantly being revised by successive generations.[98] The first railroads defined the major intrastructural axes for the burgeoning multicentered settlement pattern, even though they themselves had followed routes that were used by Indian and colonial settlers, which in turn were a reflection of the region's topography.[99] However, the birth of the fragmented metropolis was made possible, in a most dramatic way, by Henry Huntington's Pacific Electric Railway Company[100] which (by 1925) gave LA the largest electric inter-urban railway system in the world.[101] The millions of newcomers streaming into Southern California (particularly from the Midwest) rode the streetcars in search of their suburban ideal.[102] Thus, despite LA's popular image as the "automotive city", Southern California's signature urban sprawl originated as a dispersed polycentric system of electric rail lines.[103]

The chief effect of the automobile was to provide an unstoppable impetus to the decentralization imperative.[104] Streetcars had facilitated suburbanization primarily along clearly-defined linear corridors; the car, however, permitted urban development in any area where a road could be cleared. Congestion levels rose. The first major step in establishing public control of automotive transport was undertaken via the 1924 report, "A Major Traffic Street Plan for Los Angeles," by Olmsted, Bartholomew and Cheney.[105] Fundamental to this plan was the notion that the "promiscuous mixing of different types of traffic" was harmful, and that all streets

should be divided into three use classes: major thoroughfares, parkways or boulevards, and minor streets.[106] Although little of immediate practical consequence
flowed from the Olmsted report, important seeds for future freeway planning were
thus planted. During the 1920s, there was a significant change in patterns of public
transportation patronage. Suburban routes were cut, and in the 1930s they began to
be replaced by bus lines. The Great Depression had a catastrophic effect on transit
operator revenues. What happened to rail in LA was no different from what was
happening to urban streetcar systems elsewhere in the country. Despite the popularity of a "conspiracy theory" that blamed General Motors for the demise of public
transit, Angelenos had simply come to dislike congested streetcars and prefer the
convenience of the private car.[107]

It did not take long for highway planning to develop quickly and effectively in
Southern California. The Regional Planning Commission's 1941 report, "Master
Plan of Highways," codified plans that it had been accumulating since 1923; the
Automobile Club of Southern California published its freeway plan in 1937; the
Arroyo Seco Parkway (later the Pasadena Freeway) had been opened in 1938; and
the highly influential "Transit Program for the Los Angeles Metropolitan Region"
was issued in 1939. This last was essentially adopted wholesale into the City Plan-
ning Department's "Parkway Plan for the City of Los Angeles and the Metropolitan
Area" in 1941.[108] However, planning highways was to prove easier than building
them, largely as a consequence of the absence of funds. But, once state and federal
monies were allocated, the freeway system was rapidly implemented. In 1947,
California's Collier–Burns Highway Act accelerated freeway construction in Los
Angeles, and was given further impetus when the National System of Interstate
and Defense Highways was launched in 1956. Most of the region's major freeways
were begun during this period. Brodsly commented on the "perceived lack of real
alternatives" in contemporary road transportation planning documents.[109] He notes
that highway planning could proceed confidently, assuming (usually correctly) that
the public supported the plans, and that the "science" of traffic engineering had
substituted for the political process.

For many years, the local land-use planning apparatus basked in the successes of
the highway planners. A 1941 city charter amendment authorized expansion of the
Department of City Planning.[110] Staffing levels doubled during the wartime expansion,[111] and several significant project initiatives were undertaken. For instance, a
new Comprehensive Zoning Ordinance became effective on June 1, 1946; in 1948,
Mayor Fletcher Bowron established the Community Redevelopment Agency of Los
Angeles (CRA), creating an institution that was to have a major impact in later
decades; and in 1954, Mayor Poulson approved the first redevelopment plan in the
State of California (the Ann Street Redevelopment Project).[112] It seemed that the
1930 prophesy of LA's City Planning Commission had at last come true: "City
planning is rapidly developing into an exact science."[113] Planning had arrived,
polished and glistening, confident in its modernist regalia.

High modernism, 1956–1991

It is then . . . the peculiar overlap of future and past, . . . the resistance of archaic feudal
structures to irresistible modernizing tendencies . . . that is the condition of possibility

for high modernism...[The] postmodern must by characterized as a situation in which...the archaic has finally been swept away without a trace.[114]

It did not take long for the sheen to become tarnished. A 1956 report by the consultant firm of Adams, Howard and Greely was highly critical of the LA City Planning Department. While acknowledging the enormity of the tasks facing the staff, the report pointed out that Los Angeles was still without a comprehensive master plan despite the mandate given by the 1941 city charter revision. It also highlighted problems of inadequate staffing, the absence of background research, excessive bureaucracy, and the lack of coordination between different branches of city government.[115]

The City responded to these complaints by searching for new technical and organizational rationalities that could improve the Department's performance. In January 1959, Stanford Optner and Associates submitted a report to the City Planning Department on the "Feasibility of Electronic Data Processing in City Planning." Insisting upon the increasingly technical and complex nature of planning, the report incorporated then-fashionable systems concepts into what was termed a "theory of planning through electronic data processing."[116] Two years later, in 1961, the ever-expanding planning department received yet another report, this time from UCLA's Department of Engineering. Entitled "Analysis of Land-Use Planning in Large Metropolitan Regions," the report had two objectives: "to examine the technique of master planning for a large metropolitan region...and to examine possible applications of high speed computers to the planning task."[117]

The continuing search for "science" and the "master plan" was to dominate the decades that followed the hegemony of the highway planners. For instance, in the early 1960s, three reports in the "Los Angeles Centropolis, 1980" series were issued. With a focus on downtown LA, the series analyzed the local economy, planning principles to guide future development, and transportation options. The reports were intended to provide the basis for a comprehensive plan for the central city area.[118] Then, in 1969, the City Planning Department, under the leadership of Calvin Hamilton, issued the Centers Concept, a master plan emphasizing the polycentric nature of the metropolitan region. The Concept's view of relative equality among the many competing centers was rejected the following year by the downtown LA Central City Association, which commissioned its own plan to deal with the post-Watts riot realities of Los Angeles. In 1971, the so-called "Silver Book" plan for downtown Los Angeles was published, ushering in two decades when the city's Community Redevelopment Agency became the dominant force in urban redevelopment schemes throughout the city, especially in the downtown and most spectacularly in Bunker Hill. For a brief moment, Mayor Bradley shifted the emphasis away from downtown LA when, in 1988, his corporate-dominated blue-ribbon committee produced a strategic plan for all of Los Angeles, entitled *LA 2000*.

The Postmodern Emerges?

[T]he essence of Los Angeles was revealed more clearly in its deviations from [rather] than its similarities to the great American metropolis of the late nineteenth and early twentieth centuries.[119]

The roots and precepts of modern urban planning lie deep in the history of modernity, especially the rationalities characteristic of the Enlightenment and the hegemonies of science and the state. Thus it is not difficult to reach back in time for evidence of appeals to unity, control and expert skills in the history of urbanization in Southern California. In the origins of Los Angeles, we have witnessed the imposition of an essentially colonial rationality inspired by the material and spiritual imperatives of the Spanish conquerors, bolstered by a thoroughly systematic code of city planning principles (handed down to the Spanish by the arch-rationalists, the conquering Roman Empire). An equally imposing example of early intentionality was the introduction of a market rationality following the Mexican then the US takeover of Alta California in the mid-nineteenth century. The Ord and Hancock surveys created an urban land and property market where there was as yet scarcely a city, thus enabling trading in the normal American way.

The maturation of a distinctly modernist urban planning in Los Angeles can be seen in the successive emergence of entrepreneurial and state-centered growth regimes at the turn of the century. During this time, an aggressive local boosterism promoted massive public infrastructure investment that pushed LA to the forefront of national urban consciousness. It was also a period when a fundamental split occurred between the material and the spiritual in modernist thought – when the modernist/modernization dialectic was sundered and an idealized utopian planning theory was divorced from the localized processes of capitalist urbanization. The most consequential practical manifestation of this fracture was the subordination of the land-use planning apparatus to the exigencies of local capital. In the ensuing instrumentality, planning practice created its own micro-level totalization in the form of detailed information-gathering and regulatory mechanisms. Although city and regional planning had been born from progressive ideas (which persisted, albeit as a muffled chorus), most utopian discourse was henceforward drowned in the sheer scale of the development tsunami in Southern California.[120]

The apex of twentieth-century modernist urban planning in Los Angeles is perhaps best represented by the freeway-building era. Transit-rationality was replaced by a freeway-rationality as freeways and roads provided an unstoppable impetus to a decentralization that existing rail lines had only prefigured. The freeways ultimately created the signature landscape of modernist Los Angeles – a flat totalization, uniting a fragmented mosaic of polarized neighborhoods segregated by race, ethnicity and class.

The transition to postmodernism begins in the period of high modernism, when social, political and economic structures begin to remake themselves against the backdrop of obsolescent institutional frameworks. The clash is evident in many ways: when the freeway rationality is confounded by Jane Jacobs' shout from the street; or when the Bronx imperative (still present as an escape to edge cities) is challenged in Los Angeles by an uprising – in 1965 and again in 1992 – by those left behind and unable or unwilling to uproot themselves to the new frontier. The postmodern hyperspace appears to be upon us though we remain uncertain about what it look like.

There is now, to my mind, a clear nonconformity between Los Angeles' persistently modernist urban planning and the emergent postmodern urbanism of Southern California. Land-use planning has become privatized, in a reversal of a century-long trend in which the profession has been progressively absorbed within the apparatus of the state. Yet the residual modernisms of conventional land-use planning are still evident in the postmodern built environment, e.g. the residential townscapes of Orange County, or downtown LA's Bunker Hill redevelopment scheme. But such schemes are essentially mausoleums of the modernist imagination. For instance, in 1991, the Los Angeles Community Redevelopment Agency commissioned a new downtown strategic plan (which I worked on) to replace the 1971 Silver Book; at the same time, about 40 other plans pertinent to downtown and its adjacent districts already existed; and although money for new freeways has dried up, a multi-billion dollar investment in rapid transit promises to reintroduce a transit-based rationality in the 1990s. But late twentieth-century land-use planning is detached from the spirit of the postmodern age. Free floating, it is a relict apparatus with only the most tangential relationship with the emergent postmodern city.

In 1961, John E. Roberts, who joined the LA City Planning Department in 1939 and became its director in 1955, issued this appeal:

> It is our objective to plan for the kind of City that the people of Los Angeles must prefer, for it is the people who make the City; it is the people who are the City. With the continued support of all civic-minded citizens, Los Angeles will steadily enhance its position as a truly Great City.[121]

The central irony in this appeal to "the people" who make Los Angeles a "truly Great City" is that it is no longer possible to identify *the* people of Los Angeles. This polycentric, polarized, polyglot metropolis long ago tore up its social contract, and is without even a draft of a replacement. There is no longer a single civic will nor a clear collective intentionality behind LA's urbanism; and the obsolete land-use planning machinery is powerless to influence the city's burgeoning social heterodoxy. This is the insistent message of postmodern Los Angeles: that all urban place-making bets are off; we are engaged, knowingly or otherwise, in the search for new ways of creating cities.

Notes

1. See, for example, Ward, D. and Zunz, O. (eds.), 1992: *The Landscape of Modernity*, New York: Russell Sage Foundation.
2. Dear, M. and Scott, A. (eds.), 1981: *Urbanization and Urban Planning in Capitalist Society*. London: Methuen.
3. Recent studies of Southern California urbanism include: Soja, E., 1991: *Postmodern Geographies*, New York: Verso; Davis, M., 1990: *City of Quartz: Excavating the Future of Los Angeles*, New York: Verso.; Kling, R., Olin, S. and Poster, M. (eds.), 1991: *Postsuburban California: The Transformation of Orange County Since World War Two*, Los Angeles: University of California Press; Sorkin, M. (ed.), 1992: *Variations on a Theme Park: The New American City and End of Public Space*, New York: Noonday Press; Zukin, S., 1991: *Landscapes of Power: From Detroit to Disney World*, Berkeley: University of California Press.
4. Wright, G., 1991: *The Politics of Design in French Colonial Urbanism*, Chicago: University of Chicago Press, Introduction.
5. Sorkin, M., (ed.) *Variations on a Theme Park: The New American City and End of Public Space*, Introduction, p.xii. Also see Soja, E. W., *Postmodern Geographies*.

6.	Ibid., p. xiii.
7.	Boyer, C. 1986: *Dreaming the Rational City*, Cambridge, MA: MIT Press, p. 3.
8.	Ibid.
9.	Ibid., p. 9.
10.	Ibid., pp. 13–26.
11.	Ibid., p. 27.
12.	Ibid., pp. 28–33.
13.	Quoted in Boyer, ibid., p. 54.
14.	Ibid., Chapter 4.
15.	Holston, J., 1989: *The Modernist City: An Anthropological Critique of Brasília*, Chicago: University of Chicago Press.
16.	Ibid., p. 40.
17.	Ibid., p. 91.
18.	Ibid., p. 95.
19.	The same process has essentially been observed in Le Corbusier's design for Chandigarh.
20.	Holston, J., *The Modernist City*, p. 98
21.	Berman, M., 1982: *All That is Solid Melts into Air: The Experience of Modernity*, New York: Penguin Books.
22.	Ibid., p. 16.
23.	Ibid., p. 15.
24.	Ibid., pp. 18–28.
25.	Ibid., pp. 133–332.
26.	Ibid., p. 159.
27.	Ibid. A similar logic underlies the essays in Dear, M. and Scott, A. (eds.), *Urbanization and Urban Planning in Capitalist Society*.
28.	Ibid., p. 166.
29.	Ibid., p. 328.
30.	Ibid., p. 332.
31.	Ibid., p. 346.
32.	The consequences of postmodernism are discussed in *inter alia* Best, S. and Kellner, D., 1991: *Postmodern Theory: Critical Interrogations*, New York: Guilford Press; Dear, M., 1988: "The Postmodern Challenge: Reconstructing Human Geography," *Transactions of the Institute of British Geographers*, NS 13(3), pp. 262–74; Smart, B., 1993: *Postmodernity*, London: Routledge.; Soja, E. W., *Postmodern Geographies*.
33.	The entire issue of *Society & Space*, 1986 volume 4(3) is devoted to an understanding of Los Angeles.
34.	Jameson, F., 1991: *Postmodernism, or the Cultural Logic of Late Capitalism*, Durham: Duke University Press, Chapter 1.
35.	Gregory, D., 1994. *Geographical Imaginations*, Oxford: Blackwell, pp. 171–182.
36.	Haraway, D. 1991 "Situated knowledge: the science question in feminism and the privilege of partial perspective," in her *Simians, Cyborgs and Women: the reinvention of nature*, London: Routledge, pp. 183–201; see also Rose, G. 1997. 'Situating knowledges: positionalities, reflexivities and other tactics,' *Progress in Human Geography* 21, pp. 305–320.
37.	City planning Ordinance number 5, Laws of the Indies of King Philip II of Spain, issued in 1573. See Crouch, D. P., Carr, D. J. and Mundigo, A. I., 1982: *Spanish City Planning in North America*, Cambridge: MIT Press, p. 7. Full information on the early planned settlements of the American West is contained in Reps, J. W., 1981: *The Forgotten Frontier: Urban Planning in the American West before 1890*, Columbia: University of Missouri Press. The standard history of Southern California is McWilliams, C., 1973: *Southern California: An Island on the Lane*, Salt Lake City: Peregrine Smith Books.

38. Robinson, W. W., 1959: *Los Angeles from the Days of the Pueblo*, San Francisco: California Historical Society, p. 12. The Southern California coast had been "discovered" by Juan Rodriguez Cabrillo in 1542, and more thoroughly explored by a merchant contractor, Sebastian Vizcaino during 1602–3.

39. Ibid.

40. Ibid.

41. Crouch, D. P., Garr, D. J. and Mundigo, A. I., *Spanish City Planning in North America*, p. 156.

42. Ibid.

43. Ibid., p. xviii.

44. Ibid., p. 2.

45. Ibid., p. 157. See also Robinson, W.W.: *Los Angeles from the Days of the Pueblo*, p. 17; Los Angeles Department of City Planning, 1964: "City Planning in Los Angeles: A History;" Hill, L. L., 1929: *La Reina: Los Angeles in Three Centuries*, Los Angeles: Security Trust and Savings Bank, p. 13; and Reps, J. W., 1981: *The Forgotten Frontier: Urban Planning in the American West before 1890*, Columbia: University of Missouri Press, pp.63–4.

46. Crouch, D. P., Carr, D. J. and Mundigo, A. I., *Spanish City Planning in North America*, p. 157.

47. Robinson, W. W.: *Los Angeles from the Days of the Pueblo*, p. 5.

48. Fogelson, R. M., 1967: *The Fragmented Metropolis: Los Angeles 1850–1930*, Cambridge: Harvard University Press, p. 5.

49. Crouch, D. P., Carr, D. J. and Mundigo, A. I., *Spanish City Planning in North America*, p. 167.

50. Ibid., pp. 167–8.

51. Fogelson, R. M., *The Fragmented Metropolis*, p. 6.

52. Nelson, H. J., 1983: *The Los Angeles Metropolis*, Dubuque: Kendall/Hunt Publishing Co., p. 143.

53. Crouch, D. P., Carr, D. J. and Mundigo, A. I., *Spanish City Planning in North America*, p. 162.

54. Ibid.

55. Ibid., pp. 171–2; Robinson, W. W., *Los Angeles from the Days of the Pueblo*, p. 49–50; Fogelson, R. M., *The Fragmented Metropolis*, pp. 15–16.

56. Ibid., p. 164.

57. Hill, L. L., *La Reina: Los Angeles in Three Centuries*, p. 12.

58. This history is cogently presented in Erie, S. P., 1992: "How the Urban West was Won," *Urban Affairs Quarterly* 27(4), pp. 519–554; and in Davis, M., City of Quartz, Ch.2.

59. Erie, S. P., "How the Urban West Was Won." An integral component of this early speculative era were the boulevards of LA; see Suisman, D. R., 1989: *Los Angeles Boulevard*, Los Angeles Forum for Architecture and Urban Design. An intriguing pictorial history of one important subdivision, Hollywood, is contained in Williams, G., 1992: *The Story of Hollywoodland*, Papavasilopoulos Press.

60. Erie, S. P., "How the Urban West Was Won," p. 525. For a full discussion of the local state, see Clark, G. L and Dear, M., 1984: *State Apparatus: Structures and Language of Legitimacy*, Boston: Allen & Unwin.

61. Erie, S. P., "How the Urban West Was Won: The Local State and Economic Growth in Los Angeles," 1880–1932, pp. 526–8. The emergence of the Progressive era in California is described in Mowry, G. E., 1951: *The California Progressives*, Los Angeles: University of California Press. See also Starr, K., 1985: *Inventing the Dream: California through the Progressive Era*, New York: Oxford University Press.

62. Fogelson, R. M., *The Fragmented Metropolis*, Chapter 6.
63. Erie, S. P., "How the Urban West Was Won," pp. 530–1; Davis, M. *City of Quartz*, pp. 110–114.
64. Erie, S. P., "How the Urban West Was Won," p. 532.
65. Ibid., p. 534. See also Fogelson, R. M., *The Fragmented Metropolis*, Chapter 10 on the politics of the Progressive era in Los Angeles.
66. Erie, S. P., "How the Urban West Was Won," p. 534.
67. Ibid., p. 538.
68. Ibid., pp. 538–40.
69. The story of water and Los Angeles has been told many times; see, for example Kahrl, W. A., 1982: *Water and Power*, Berkeley, University of California Press. The remarkable career of William Mulholland is recounted in Davis, M. L., 1993: *Rivers in the Desert: William Mulholland the Inventing of Los Angeles*, New York: Harper Collins.
70. Ibid., p. 540. Also useful is Bigger, R. and Kitchen, J. D., 1952: *How the Cities Grew: A Century of Municipal Independence and Expansion in Metropolitan Los Angeles*, Los Angeles: Haynes Foundation.
71. Erie, S. P. , "How the Urban West Was Won: The Local State and Economic Growth in Los Angeles, 1880–1932," pp. 541–47. For a discussion of Harry Chandler's leading role in this latter period, see Davis, M., *City of Quartz: Excavating the Future in Los Angeles*, pp. 114–120.
72. Robinson, C. M., The City Beautiful, *Report to the Mayor, City Council and Members of the Municipal Art Commission*, p. 4.
73. Fogelson, R. M., *The Fragmented Metropolis*, p. 247.
74. Ibid., p. 248; Whitnall, G., 1964: "1929–30, Tracing the Development of Planning in Los Angeles," *Los Angeles Board of Planning Commissioners Annual Report*, p. 38; Los Angeles Department of City Planning, 8–9.
75. Fogelson, R. M., *The Fragmented Metropolis*, p. 249.
76. Brodsly, D., 1981: *LA Freeway: An Appreciative Essay*, Berkeley: University of California Press, p. 134.
77. Los Angeles Department of City Planning (1964), 2–3; Smutz, H.E., "Zoning in Los Angeles," in Los Angeles Board of Planning Commissioners, Annual Report 1929–1930, p. 58
78. Robinson, C. M., The City Beautiful, p. 31. For Robinson's role in the city beautiful movement, see Wilson, W. H., 1989: *The City Beautiful Movement*, Baltimore: The Johns Hopkins University Press.
79. Weiss, M., 1987: *The Rise of Community Builders*, New York: Columbia University Press, pp. 80–1. Similar chapters in New York City's urban planning history are recounted in Ward, D. and Zunz, O. (eds.), *The Landscape of Modernity*, See also, Los Angeles Department of City Planning (1964), 10: Whitnall, G. "Tracing the Development of Planning in Los Angeles", p. 43.
80. Weiss, M., *The Rise of the Community Builders*, pp. 79–80, 100–1.
81. Ibid., p. 80.
82. Ibid., Chapter 4, "The Los Angeles Realty Board and Zoning." In 1939 the LARB also attacked the administration of zoning in LA, focusing on corruption and the "zoning variance racket."
83. Starr, K., 1990: *Material Dreams: Southern California through the 1920s*, New York: Oxford University Press, pp. 69–70.
84. Fogelson, R. M., *The Fragmented Metropolis*, p. 257.
85. Los Angeles Department of City Planning, 1964: *City Planning in Los Angeles: A History*, p. 13.

86. Brodsly, D. *L. A. Freeway*, p. 132.

87. Fogelson, R. M., *The Fragmented Metropolis*, p. 271.

88. Weiss, M., *The Rise of the Community Builders*, p. 79.

89. According to W. L. Pollard (in 1930), the LARB's planning and zoning attorney: "planning as it is generally known in Los Angeles consists of zoning." Ibid., p. 105.

90. Fogelson, R. M., *The Fragmented Metropolis*, p. 257.

91. Brodsly, D., *L. A. Freeway*, p. 132.

92. Ibid., p. 136. The spectacular urban design of the decade of the 1930s was one consequence of this confluence of interests; See Gebhard, D. and von Breton, H. 1989. *Los Angeles in the Thirties: 1931–1941*, Los Angeles: California Classic Books.

93. Fogelson, R. M., *The Fragmented Metropolis*, p. 250. While agreeing with the importance of the automobile, Fishman emphasizes that the "suburban idea" predated the automobile era; see Fishman, R., 1987: *Bourgeois Utopias: The Rise and Fall of Suburbia*, New York: Basic Books, (Chapter 6: "Los Angeles: Suburban Metro-polis").

94. Los Angeles Department of City Planning, p. 25.

95. Banham, R., 1971: *Los Angeles: The Architecture of Four Ecologies*, New York: Penguin, p. 213.

96. Brodsly, D., 1981: *L.A. Freeway*, Berkeley: University of California Press, p. 89, 109; Fogelson, R.M., *The Fragmented Metropolis*, pp. 79–84.

97. Brodsly, D., *L.A. Freeway*, p. 2.

98. Banham, R., *Los Angeles: The Architecture of Four Ecologies*, Chapter 4, especially p. 75.

99. Brodsly, D., *L.A. Freeway*, pp. 2–3, 64.

100. Ibid., p. 69.

101. Ibid., p. 69.

102. Ibid., p. 80. Something of the effect of the region's burgeoning decentralization is conveyed in the relative decline of downtown Los Angeles as a center of urban activities. By 1930, the central area was already the slowest-growing part of the metropolis.

103. Hall, P., 1988: *Cities of Tomorrow: An Intellectual History of Urban Planning and Design in the Twentieth Century*, New York: Blackwell, Chapter 9.

104. Brodsly, D., *L.A. Freeway*, p. 85. See also Fogelson, R. M., *The Fragmented Metropolis*, p. 250; and Bottles, S. L., 1987: *Los Angeles and the Automobile: The Making of the Modern City*, Berkeley: University of California Press, especially Chapter 4.

105. Brodsly, D., *L.A. Freeway*, p. 85.

106. Ibid., pp. 93–4; Bottles, S. L., *Los Angeles and the Automobile*, Chapter 1; and Fogelson, R. M., *The Fragmented Metropolis*, Chapter 8.

107. Brodsly, D., *L.A. Freeway*, pp. 96–106.

108. Ibid., 115–16; Bottles, S. L., *Los Angeles and the Automobile*, pp. 232–3.

109. Brodsly, D., *L.A. Freeway*, p. 136.

110. Los Angeles Department of City Planning, p. 23.

111. Ibid., p. 26.

112. Ibid., pp. 28–33.

113. Ibid., p. 46.

114. Jameson, F., *Postmodernism, or the Cultural Logic of Late Capitalism*, p. 309.

115. Adams, Howard and Greely, 1956: "Los Angeles City Planning Department," *Report to the Board of City Planning Commissioners*; see Los Angeles Department of City Planning, pp. 36–42.

116. "Los Angeles Department of City Planning," pp. 48–48.

117. Case, H. W., Campbell, B., Brenner, R., Mosher Jr., W. W. and Sheridan, R. B., 1961: "Analysis of Land-Use Planning in Large Metropolitan Regions," Department of Engineering, University of California at Los Angeles, p.1; pp. 51–2.
118. "Los Angeles Department of City Planning," pp. 57–9.
119. Fogelson, R. M., *The Fragmented Metropolis*, p. 134.
120. See Davis, M. *City of Quartz: Excavating the Future in Los Angeles*, prologue.
121. "Los Angeles Department of City Planning," p. 65.

6

Deconstructing Urban Planning

Urban & regional planning is a systematic creative approach to addressing and resolving social, physical and economic problems of cities, suburbs, metropolitan areas, and larger regions. It involves identifying problems and opportunities, devising alternative policies or plans, analyzing and implementing these options and evaluating implemented plans.[1]

After earning an undergraduate degree in geography, my first job was as a "town planner" in London, England. I have been an urban planner ever since, mixing both academic and practical interests. I find it hard to put these decades of experience into historical perspective, largely because my professional practice has been split among several different countries with very different planning traditions (in England, Canada, and the United States, plus a year in Australia). But I am now approaching that point when the longest stretch of my professional life will have been spent in the United States, and two unrelated events from the recent past strike me as symptomatic of what has happened to the planning profession during the last three decades.

The first of these was when I was shouted down at a public meeting in San Diego. I had been called in as the outside expert on the NIMBY (Not In My Back Yard) syndrome as it pertained to the siting of shelters for homeless people in that region. Now, I am accustomed to angry expressions of opposition in these contexts, but the people at that meeting were, in the majority, unwilling even to listen to arguments that went counter to their opposition. There was no room for dialogue, evidence, experience, conscience, knowledge, caring, or compromise. They were simply out for blood, preferably mine. In the end, I all but lost my temper and shouted back at them; so much for getting together to reason!

The second experience happened when a group of nationally-renowned architects and planners assembled to prepare a plan for downtown Los Angeles. (This experience warrants an entire book to itself!) At one point in the work, the principles of "new urbanism" were being applied to the downtown industrial eastside – an unimaginable mix of skid row, clothing, electrical, wholesale food markets, and toy importers. After a morning of plonking down schools, open spaces, and other undoubtedly desirable icons of civic amenity in totally infeasible locations, I suggested that we actually leave the office in order to go and look at the sites in question. This crudely utilitarian advice was immediately rejected because the intrusion of urban actualities would, so my colleagues believed, hinder the visionary process.

I felt badly about both experiences. I still do. I came away from San Diego overwhelmed by the incivility of public discourse, the absence of community, the disdain for those in need of help, and the irrelevance of planning. In Los Angeles,

Figure 6.1 (a) Piranesi City Plan, (b) Piranesi Carceri (University of Southern California Library Special Collections).

Giovanni Battista Piranesi (1720–78) was an 18th-century Italian engraver. He made his name and fortune by selling images of Rome's splendor to travelers on the Grand Tour. His topographic views were tinged with the fantastical, and often culminated in visionary plans for urban development. His work also included imaginary architectural interiors (of tombs, prisons, and torture chambers). Taken together, the works reflect less on the civilizing influences of the Roman empire, speaking more of its social control and oppression, of an authority that holds whole peoples in its thrall.

I simply could not fathom the depths of barren abstractness with which some professionals approached the urban design effort; it was solely a technical application of established principles without any necessary grounding in reality.

One should not perhaps make too much of small blips on the radar of life. So let me look at the broader field of planning experience, concentrating for the moment on the decades of the 1970s and 1980s because in my judgement these contain the pivotal moments in the birth of what may be called a "postmodern planning." For it was during this period that a radical shift began in an almost century-long tradition of increasing local state intervention in the urban process (as described in the preceding chapter). By taking a longer look at these decades of adjustment, I hope to situate the changes of emphases that led to a postmodern planning. Following the precepts developed in Chapter 2, I understand deconstruction to be principally an exercise in textual analysis, emphasizing the uses of language, the presences and absences in texts, and the sources of authority in discourse. In this chapter, I want to deconstruct the practices of urban planning, as revealed principally by the voices of planners themselves. My interest lies in the question of intentionality in the creation of urban landscapes from the planner's viewpoint. A corollary concern is the putative emergence of a postmodern planning, or pursuing the hypothesis of a radical break in urban planning theory and practice. I shall first outline a cognitive map of contemporary planning knowledge since 1945, then examine the pivotal importance of the trend toward privatization in planning, and finally reveal the impoverished rhetoric of the seventies and eighties that has led to a "proto-postmodern" urban planning.

A Cognitive Map of Planning Knowledge

Planning is about power. It is concerned with achieving urban outcomes that serve the purposes of powerful agents in society. Since there are many such agents, planning is also about the process of conflict, as agents attempt to maneuver to achieve their ends. The multiplicity of ends that characterize most land-use disputes is simply a reflection of the diverse intentionalities that the various agents bring to a dispute. In this context, "intentionality" is meant to convey nothing more complex that purpose, goal, or motive. In our society, markets, legal systems, and governments are examples of institutional frameworks through which individuals and groups can express intentionality. Sometimes, when larger coalitions form to express collective intentionality, we may speak of a civic will. On occasion, of course, small powerful groups may also find ways by which to express their minority intentionality as a civic will.

Land-use planning (or city planning, or urban planning – I will use the three terms interchangeably in this book) is often portrayed as a profession that seeks to achieve the rational, orderly and efficient use of land. Such a goal may often be overlain with sentiments pertaining to the public interest, altruism, and moral/ethical principles (this last concerning philosophy or theory in general; or idealized, even utopian, thoughts about urban futures). Such motivations tend to be a reflection of the planner's own intentionality. Other agents in the land and property development process usually have radically different goals, including maximizing tax revenues (a politician's goal), or generating maximum private profits for a building's tenants (a property manager's goal).

As we saw in the previous chapter, for most of the twentieth century the urban planning apparatus has become increasingly ensconced as part of the bureaucratic apparatus of the state. There, as Bent Flyvbjerg has shown in an important series of studies, it is buffeted by Machiavellian levels of intrigue, and even reduced to a sinister instrument of social control and oppression.[2] Not surprisingly, under such circumstances, the best laid plans often go astray, be they large or small in their vision. In an intriguing study of why things go wrong, James C. Scott zeroes in on a mistaken belief in the ability to design society in accordance with scientific laws. Such principles of rational design, Scott contends, are characteristic of a "high modernism", and they have usually failed. Scott cites as evidence two of our century's largest social experiments: urban renewal, and the rural resettlement of peasant farmers. He contends that the failure of these enterprises was due to:

- an administrative ordering of society by the state;
- faith in high modernist ideals;
- an authoritarian regime ready and able to use coercive powers; and
- a weak civil society unable to resist these powers.

Lest it be thought that Scott is merely anti-government, he also suggests that today, when ideas of planning are in disarray, high modernism has found a home in the ideology of free markets.[3]

To explain how we got to the present state, I need to go back to the end of the World War II, and trace the evolution of planning thought and practice during the past half-century. Five basic eras can be identified in the general histories of Canada, Great Britain and the USA (Figure 6.2)

1945–60: Postwar reconstruction and the pre-eminence of physical land-use planning

The period following World War II was one of massive physical and social reconstruction in Western Europe. Extensive war damage meant that nations were necessarily preoccupied with rebuilding efforts. For instance, this period spawned the British new town legislation which was to provide an important model for controlled urban growth in Western Europe for decades to come. In Canada, big cities such as Toronto tentatively moved toward large-scale comprehensive metropolitan plans. In the United States, which had not suffered significant physical destruction through war, new federal initiatives were undertaken especially in the field of housing. In short, the early postwar years were a period in which an extensive (renewed) mandate was granted for state intervention in the land and property development process. It was a time when the incipient planning profession consolidated its physical land-use planning identity.

1960–70: The new scientism and the rise of popular planning

The decade of the 1960s was a time of remarkable ferment in planning. Two major philosophies were to impact the discipline: first, a new scientism which suggested

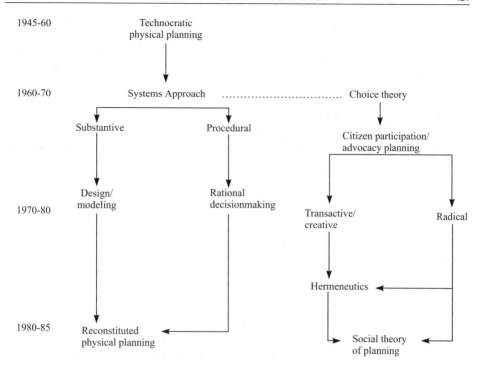

Figure 6.2 A Map of Planning Theory since 1945 (Pion, Society and Space, 1986, 4(3), 367–84)

that planning could and should take on the methodologies of the natural sciences; and, second, a rising tide of populism in planning, which arose largely out of a worldwide surge in participatory democratic politics and the consequent crisis in the profession's sense of legitimacy.

The new scientism shook most social sciences in the 1960s, and was represented in planning by a commitment to systems theory. It provoked a fundamental shift toward rationality which found expression in the impetus toward a "substantive-procedural" rift in planning. The substantive focus (on the objects being planned) served to propel the practice of land-use planning toward a scientific approach akin to the rationality of engineering. The approach received a strong reinforcement and consolidation through the advent of mathematical model-building. The use of quantitative methods in computer-based, large-scale land-use and transportation models was particularly prominent in the USA. It provided a considerable legitimacy for advocates of the scientific method of planning, which was further reinforced by the spillover from computer-assisted methods in architectural design. The movement toward scientific planning was accelerated by what was initially perceived as a competing theoretical domain. Procedural theories of planning also derived from rational systems models. As applied to planning, they emphasized the administrative and managerial context of planning decisions. Heavily influenced by operations research, they sought to establish rules of rational decision-making and to purge irrationality from the practices of planning. Although many have pointed to the damaging effects of the procedural–substantive dichotomy and the ultimate need for both in planning, the dichotomy had a strong appeal and its legacy persists to the present.

As well as being a period of scientific optimism, the 1960s was also a highly charged political decade. In planning, this took the form of growing citizens' involvement in planning decisions within the general context of an increasingly participatory democratic politics. Very importantly, at the same time, some professional planners were prompted to begin a deep search for the sources of their own legitimacy, beyond the authority granted by their status as expert or government bureaucrat. A loose coalition of essentially liberal-minded planners rallied under the banner of a choice theory of planning. This somewhat ill-defined theory emphasized the significance of citizen choice in, and even determination of, planning decisions. As it became obvious that citizen participation did not significantly alter the balance of power in development decisions, advocacy planning enjoyed a relatively brief vogue as a means of enfranchising citizen groups. The net effect of 1960s populism was to place planning overtly on the political agenda. Perhaps in no period before or after has the structure of urban political power been so rawly exposed as in these early community battles.

1970–80: The emergence of a critical left

The optimism and prosperity of the 1960s spilled over into the early years of the next decade. In this more committed, relatively tolerant climate, two overtly ideological concepts of planning emerged. The first was the movement toward transactive (or creative) planning; the second was a more radical critique – a firestorm of criticism ignited by a rejection of the studied apoliticism of the rationalists. The transactive–creative approach in planning emphasized "mutual learning," a creative synthesis of community intelligence and planners' skills to invent an urban future. The lineage of this approach can be directly traced to an underlying belief in rationality and a commitment to involving communities in planning their futures. Transactive–creative planning was essentially a participatory vision of planning practice, and as such, it was uncomfortable for those who did not share its essentially liberal-democratic ideology.

The radical critique that surfaced in the mid-1970s was largely provoked by the perceived inadequacy of the theoretical bases for city planning. Neo-Marxism was bursting out all over, and critics argued for a social theory of planning that would specifically incorporate a political–economic awareness. They emphasized the essentially subordinate role of planning in the context of capitalist urbanization. The radial critique provided a new way of thinking about planning, but the debate was often conducted at such a high level of abstraction that practitioners and theoreticians alike had difficulty in linking it to everyday practice. Many of its supporters themselves seemed incapable or unwilling to dig themselves out of the trap of "structuralist inactivity" into which this view of planning had led them. (The task of smashing capitalism being something of a tall order, one would simply repair to the pub instead.)

Then, in the late 1970s, a potential resolution of the liberal–radical split was plucked from the social theory of the Frankfurt School, and from Jürgen Habermas in particular. Phenomenology and hermeneutics became influential because hermeneutics offered a firmer theoretical basis for the essentially interpretive–ideo-logical approach of transactive–creative planning. It provided the option for a new alliance with the radical left without the need to espouse its Marxism. In short, hermeneutics provided a new theoretical and practical legitimacy where it was urgently needed.

1980–90: A frenzy of discourse and the retreat to origins

A recession-ridden 1980s canceled the optimism of the previous decades for all but the chosen few, and were accompanied by an increasingly frenzied discourse on planning. Doubts and uncertainties began to assail the left, and an increasingly bullish center-right began to reassert itself. The net effects have been a retreat from context, and a rediscovery of a technical instrumentalism in planning. Despite its promise and the eloquence of its advocates, the sparkle of hermeneutics did not translate readily into practice, nor was its theoretical promise realized. Secondly, radical critics became quiescent. For some, the increasingly strident political con-servatism of the Thatcher and Reagan eras was cause enough for retreat. Others were absorbed into the search for a wider social theory of planning to which the challenge of neo-Marxism and hermeneutics had given a noisome birth. Whatever political commitment remained became watered down as successive conservative governments attacked the ideologies of planning. Kiernan's politics of positive discrimination (for instance) built a new planning from the social context of Marx, plus Weberian notions of bureaucracy, in a system guided by Rawlsian notions of justice.[4]

In the vacuum of planning practice left by the apparent disarray of the social theorists, and in the conservative economic and political culture, attempts were launched to recapture the center ground in planning. Planning began again to be defined as physical land-use planning. This retreat to disciplinary traditions is at heart an attempt to reaffirm planning's core identity and a range of defensible professional expertise. The movement reveals itself in many ways, as (for instance) in direct attacks on social theories that are perceived as harming the professional credibility of planning, and in a renewed emphasis on public–private partnerships in the development process. The trend was celebrated in Breheny's revealingly-entitled article "A practical view of planning theory." Breheny identified with those "who are concerned to pin down the essential features of planning before proceeding with the task of theory building."[5] Not surprisingly, he is led to conclude that land-use planning is concerned with government intervention in the private land-development process, and that the planners' role is to assist governments in the administration of this activity. It's as simple as that!

The climactic moment in this return to origins was, for me at least, the birth of something called the "new urbanism," or "neo-traditional" planning. (Yes, it's the same creature that wrecked my day when I was planning downtown LA.) According to one of its chroniclers, Peter Katz, the new urbanism was born out of a distaste for "costly" and "destructive" urban sprawl, plus a yearning for compact, closely-knit communities where people can walk to needed services.[6] These sentiments should sound familiar to anyone with at least a passing knowledge of the history of urban thought, because they come right out of the nineteenth-century notebooks of

Ebenezer Howard, he of Garden City fame. Howard's plan for a neighborhood-based garden city has been repackaged and marketed (these words are carefully chosen) as the panacea for current urban ills. The undoubted popularity of the new urbanism has as much to do with the nostalgia for professional identity as the messianic zeal with which its message is being promulgated.

The 1990s: Ascendancy of pastiche

As our history enters the 1990s, let me immediately concede that there is a certain oxymoronic recklessness in even naming a "postmodern planning." How can we begin to engage as intentional activity as land-use planning in terms of an anti-rational philosophy like postmodernism? I want to skirt this difficulty for a moment, and ask you once again to postpone a decision. I shall only identify initially a concept of "proto-postmodern" planning, which takes the material form of a current pastiche of practices.

By the late 1980s, planning theory had become a conflictual Babel of separate languages, almost all of which were voluntarily ignored by practitioners. For its part, planning practice had devolved into a ritualized choreography of routines. One dimension of practice was already deeply embedded in the apparatus of the state. There it was relatively insulated and free from interference, serving to legitimize the actions of the state. The second dimension of practice had became ever more situated in the offices of private land and property development interests. There, it was equally insulated, a passive tool capable of only the most muted social criticism. In this case, planning was legitimizing the actions of capital. In its twin identities as legitimator of state and capital, planning had come to closely resemble architecture, but with one crucial and as yet inexplicable difference. Whereas architecture has traditionally sought to rationalize or even conceal its subordinate role by wider appeals to art, philosophy, and history, urban planning has so far strenuously resisted such engagement, including its specific links to social science, and has instead sought to bolster its credibility solely on the basis of appeals to utilitarianism.

This notion of a pastiche of practice is intended to convey the ensemble of free-floating, unsystematized planning theories, which together define a proto-postmodern planning (see Figure 6.2). By 1990, discourse around planning theory had splintered; and since each approach had its advocate, pastiche was in the ascendancy. Yet paradoxically, the dominant focus of discourse in all narratives became increasingly restricted. The long heritage of utopian concerns was excised from planners' vocabulary (I shall deal with the reasons for this later in the chapter). In addition, the ideological commitment of the 1960s and 1970s lost much of its persuasive powers, having retreated into its own version of pastiche (a little bit of Marx, a touch of Weber, stir with Rawls – there you go!). As planners were pressed to legitimize actions by state and civil society in the creation of the built environment, the planners' role diminished to that of facilitator; and the planning process itself was reduced to commodified "bits" susceptible to an instrumental logic. In both senses, we can already speak of a new depthlessness in planning. At the end of our history of the last three decades, we seem poised to create a truly postmodern planning style – a planning of filigree, of decoration alone.

Privatizing Planning

Privatization portends a fundamental, even irrevocable, change in the way in which planning is conducted. It is perhaps the single most important trend affecting the profession today. Privatization is a term that has acquired many meanings. It can refer, for instance, to the cessation or reduction of publicly-produced and provided goods and services; to the process of contracting-out for the provision of formerly-public services (such as garbage collection); to the sale of government assets (including the denationalization of state-run industries and the sale of public housing); and to the generic process of deregulation. As Paul Starr has succinctly stated, while there may be degrees of privatization, there can be little doubt about its overall ideology: "Privatization needs to be understood as a fundamental re-ordering of claims in society."[7] The functions and goals of the urban land-use planning apparatus are part of the privatization debate. A wealth of evidence exists to support the notion that planning is becoming increasingly privatized, e.g. the growth of planning personnel in private sector positions, the packaging and marketing of planning services for sale, and the prominent trend in planning education toward a development-oriented curriculum. Surprisingly, most of these tendencies seem to have been absorbed without comment into the realm of planning practice.

Urbanization may be understood as the outcome of the state–civil society dialectic.[8] As part of its mandate, the state developed a land-use planning apparatus which undertook a typical range of regulatory functions as applied to property and land development. On the other side of the urbanization equation were the myriad decisions of private firms and households. Urban form is the consequence of the tensions and contradictions that beset the interaction of state and civil society.[9] Thus in Chapter 5, the history of urbanization in Southern California was read as a series of mediations and temporary accords between these two relatively autonomous sectors. Urban outcomes vary according to whose star (state or civil society) is in the ascendant during successive periods. Until recently, the story of the planning profession has recounted the progressive professionalization of land-use planning within the apparatus of the state.

One characteristic of postmodern society's "disorganized capitalism" is a shift in the balance of power toward civil society.[10] This has been supported by a conservative ideology which has promulgated the need for a "retreat from the state," although Jennifer Wolch's account of the rise of a non-profit "shadow state" cautions against the too-ready adoption of such rhetoric into our thinking.[11] An increasing proportion of the state's planning functions have been shifted or surrendered to the private sector, so that two very different sets of rules now govern the practice of planning. Planners who continue as agents of the state can still shelter under the mantle of legitimacy afforded them by their elected officials, and even claim to act in the public interest. In contrast, planners who are agents of private capital are responsible only to the bottom line of the business' profitability. At issue is whether or not these two approaches are in any way compatible: they may efficiently streamline the process of negotiation and approvals; or they may take on an increasingly adversarial gloss, and thereby intensify decision-making gridlock.

In practical terms, the privatization of planning has developed within the state's planning apparatus, and through the creation of a private planning apparatus. In the first instance, planning has been affected (like many other sectors) by the general restructuring of the welfare state. This has taken many forms, including cutbacks and rechanneling of financial and programmatic commitments. In the United States, for instance, many federal programs that hitherto employed planners now no longer exist or have been drastically curtailed (including some Community Development Block Grant initiatives and the Department of Housing and Urban Development). There has been a parallel erosion of the mechanisms of public planning in Great Britain where some government functions have been abolished.[12] In other countries, there have been relaxations of planning regulations in order to promote economic development. The cumulative effect of these changes has resembled a death by a thousand cuts, rather than an outright abolition of the profession. For example, in 1987, members of the British Royal Town Planning Institute (RTPI) were informed that countryside planning was "outside the mainstream of Institute concern." It was something better dealt with by "ecologists, estate managers and leisure specialists rather than professional planners."[13] And in Canada, when it came time (in the early 1980s) to revise Ontario's Planning Act, members of the provincial planning institute voted decisively to exclude "social planning" from their mandate.

One of the key strategies in the push for privatization is commodification, referring to transformation of routine government functions into packageable units which can then be marketed and sold like private goods. Commodification is facilitated when a "user pays" philosophy can be adapted to public services and a simple fee for service devised (as is typically the case with many of planning's information services, including census data, traffic and market area facts, appraisals, and so on). Spurred on by the need to recover costs and demonstrate efficiency in public services, state-sponsored commodification strategies have proliferated. Purchases of government services are now a commonly accepted part of doing business; and governments increasingly contract out for their services. Representatives of capital have responded by intensifying their efforts to capture the state planning apparatus (through memberships on planning boards and commissions, lobbying, political contributions, and corruption). None of these strategies is new, of course; they have simply been accelerated by the privatization ethos, as well as by the increased competition between cities for a piece of the diminishing development pie.

Three other initiatives reinforce the trend toward a private-sector planning. First, as I have mentioned, private developers have already gone some way toward creating their own planning apparatus. This is often defended as a survival strategy because public planning-department staffing levels have declined while regulatory procedures have remained intact or even expanded. Hence, so the argument goes, private capital is obliged to take on board its own experts to help navigate a hopeless bureaucratic maze. Whatever the impetus, the net outcome is that the private sector is now buttressed by a new kind of advocacy planner, equipped to advance capital's case with expertise equivalent to that of the public-sector planner.

Second, active pro-development lobbies have been instigated, by such groups as the Urban Land Institute and the National Association of Homebuilders in the

United States. They have, almost unnoticed, created a climate in which the necessity and wisdom of public–private partnerships go unchallenged. This trend is, I believe, different from past practices in which the interrelatedness of state and capital was recognized as a reality and incorporated into everyday planning. We have witnessed a qualitatively different phenomenon in which planners, convinced by the rhetoric of a corporatist-style planning, concede in advance the rules of the development game in return for a seat at the negotiating table. A corporatist approach has also been embraced by governments anxious for development partnerships that create jobs and enable them to leverage private dollars in support of public projects.

Third, a corporatist ideology has extended into planning education. Private development interests have morally and financially supported the introduction of a more development-oriented curriculum. This has shifted the emphasis in planning education toward real estate development specializations, course work emphasizing marketing and entrepreneurial skills, and the hiring of new faculty to teach these courses. Courses not fitting the new mold (such as social planning) have been deleted from school calendars. Even within planning schools, an "anti-planning" ethos has been identified by Tridib Banerjee. The net effect of all these adjustments has been to dilute the traditions of the traditional planning school curriculum.[14]

Let it be said immediately that, in some ways, the profession's response to privatization is entirely predictable, even rational. Planners and educators are simply responding to a changing job market; and recently-qualified professionals are merely going where the jobs are. But from the evidence of their publications and conference calendars, most planners (academic and non-academic) are dangerously silent on the issue of privatization. My emphasis in the rest of this chapter is on how the discourses of professional planners are propelling the profession into a mutant form of practice that we have not yet begun to understand.

The Rhetorics of Planning, 1970–90

Conventional definitions of the term "rhetoric" draw attention to the structures of writing and speaking, as well as to classical notions of the art of persuasion.[15] In this analysis, three particular dimensions of the term are useful: (1) *Persuasion* emphasizing rhetoric as the art of speaking, or how people convince one another to adopt a particular line of thought or action;[16] (2) *Power* which is a view of rhetoric as a strategy to exercise control over others[17] and (3) *Community* in which the culture defined by the rhetor and the persuaded constitutes a community of interest, and rhetoric thus becomes a central art whereby culture and community are established, maintained and transformed.[18]

These elements of rhetoric are present in most discourses, to a greater or lesser extent. For instance, a planner's work typically involves speaking to a community audience. The presentation requires a creative process, because the planner often adjusts it to become more convincing or responsive (by, for example, playing down the unpopular aspects of a proposal). The speech act also involves – at least implicitly – a community of identity around the presentation; there is a shared understanding that the speech is about the kind of community we wish to create. Hence, in a typical planning encounter, planners are given a language to speak by their culture; they have the power to transform that language through argument; and they appeal through their dialogue to the often implicit commonalities of an interpretive community.[19] The analysis of rhetoric is therefore about "the study of the ways we constitute ourselves as individuals, as communities, and as cultures, whenever we speak."[20] In theoretical discourse, rhetoric may be used to win acceptance for a particular explanation or interpretation; in practical planning discourse, it argues for a specific proposal. Since it is impossible to defend the everlasting truth of one theory, or the unambiguous merit of one proposal over another, the power of the advocate's rhetoric becomes of central significance. In the absence of proof positive, all that advocates can aim do is to persuade their interlocutors of the merit of their position.

I shall use the phrases "speech acts" or "the speech of planners" to convey the totality of dialogues engaged in by the community of planners. These include statements of principle (what planners believe they should do); of intent (what they would like to achieve); of action (what they actually do); and of self-criticism (what they ultimately achieve). The relevant texts of planning practice will include not only transcripts of professional meetings but also legal documents, exhortations by professional leaders, guidelines on professional ethics, general plan statements, and so on. I want now to let planners speak for themselves through their texts (or more precisely, through my choice of their texts), in order to discover how planners represent their professional practice. Two caveats are necessary before I begin. First, my analysis is based primarily on a survey of papers addressing planning practice which have appeared during two pivotal decades, 1970–1990, in the principal journals in the United States, Britain and Canada. These sources were supplemented by consideration of the major texts and monographs that appeared during the same period. Such a sample is inevitably biased and incomplete. However, the dimensions of practice identified below will, I believe, represent an identifiable culture of planning practice which others should easily recognize.[21] Secondly, I have used many quotations from a wide variety of sources. With some effort, I could have selected several different sets of references to make exactly the same points. No personal criticism is intended of those individuals I have chosen to cite. Many have made enduring, important contributions to the field of planning, and I have no desire to impugn their motives or integrity. But, like me, they are caught in a web of words and traditions. In this book, I am attempting to look beyond these restraints, to search for a clearer understanding.

In the contemporary culture of planning practice, three styles of rhetoric predominate: what we say we are going to do; what we actually end up doing; and how we judge what we have done. In more formal terms, these concerns translate into three distinct rhetorics of practice:

(1) *the theory of practice*, being statements of principle about the nature of planning practice;
(2) *accounts of practice*, being analyses of the actual professional encounter; and
(3) *performance evaluation*, being post hoc judgements on the outcomes of planning practice.

I shall now examine a limited number of exemplars of each of these dimensions of practice.

The theory of practice

The theory of planning practice is relatively underdeveloped. There may be many reasons for this, not least because it poses difficult epistemological and ontological challenges.[22] There are also severe technical difficulties in developing a theory which takes account of the multitude of different planning environments in which practice occurs, or the proliferation of tasks undertaken in the name of planning. A focal theme in contemporary rhetoric on the theory of practice is the need to recover the traditional core of planning. As we have seen, this has successfully been translated into a reassertion of the central role of physical, or land-use planning as planning's key identity and society's judgement about what is useful in a planning profession (the planner's "tool-kit"). Planning discourse has become confined to a narrow range of technical support functions that practitioners feel they can defend as their unique area of expertise.

The retreat from a broader vision of planning was particularly evident in Britain when the Thatcher government launched a series of attacks on the profession. One government White Paper (i.e. a draft of legislative proposals) was revealingly entitled *Lifting the Burden*. It pulled no punches in arguing that planning was a convenient and manageable "burden" to be removed. The consequence, as noted by one British planner,[23] was that:

> The planning profession has a major task ahead of mobilising undoubted public support ... while also rehabilitating the concept of positive planning.

But what should this positive planning look like, if it was to convince the general public? Breheny's version of a positive planning[24] begins by arguing for a "practitioner-friendly" approach, blaming theorists for allowing theory and practice to drift apart. The reason for the separation (he claimed) was that Marxist-inspired work which held sway academically at the time he was writing (1983) was divorced from the specifics of practice.[25] Breheny suggested that a reassessment of planning could only come from a solid reappraisal of its roots:

> Land-use or town and country planning is concerned with government intervention in the private land-development process. The purpose of this intervention is to achieve particular social, economic, and physical outcomes by the control of land development.... The role of planners is to assist in the administration of this activity and in helping governments make and implement decisions.[26]

Breheny's solipsistic reconstruction of a practical theory of planning is thus neatly completed. He says, in effect, that these are the things that planners do, so (by extension) we should write theory to account for them, advocating a "rebuilding of planning from its core functions of control and policy in relation to land use."[27] It is hard to see how he could have concluded otherwise, given his starting point.

The appeal to planning's roots and for the development of a positive theory might, once again, be regarded as a rational response to a hostile political environment; or it could reflect nothing more than ideological bias on the advocate's part. But whatever its source(s), the appeal to restore the technical base of planning has strongly detracted from the social and utopian ideals that have hitherto characterized the history of planning discourse. Many positive planners now seem disinclined to raise their gaze above the technical details to consider the socio-economic and political groundedness of their work. As Mandelbaum[28] observed, there is a widespread ignorance about social theory, which is sometimes coupled with an apparent unwillingness to contemplate the implications of that theory. Take, for example, Britton Harris' 1978 rejection of the Marxist interpretation of planning practice suggested by Allen Scott and Shoukry Roweis:[29]

> The fundamental difficulty lies in the fact that the approach of Scott and Roweis[30] – at least in the hands of less experienced analysts, students, and critics of planning – provides an easy way out of the difficulties of learning, practicing, and accommodating to planning. The tasks, the difficulties, and the process of planning are imputed to the developmental tendencies of society as a whole, and these tendencies are in turn explained by standard Marxist concepts, frequently oversimplified. The effect on actual planning is either paralytic or revolutionary...

Harris then goes on to define his view of a "positive social theory" which attempts to "define and explain what happens in society."[31] In their response to Harris' attack, Scott and Roweis are understandably bemused:

> This allegation is predicated upon untenable reasoning; it is like calling for the abolition of pianos because the "less experienced" are likely to produce dissonant sound effects .... [One] of the prime tasks which confronts us as scholars and teachers is to participate ... in overcoming inexperience (including our own) rather than to ban the instruments by which it may be overcome.[32]

In contrast to those who ignore social theory in planning, Blowers comes to a conclusion that privileges social theory and ends up dismissing the profession:

> Town planners appear to be concerned with vague purposes such as the protection of the public interest, the rational allocation of land use or the promotion and preservation of an attractive environment. But these are matters of opinion and value requiring no special expertise. They amount to an ideology not a profession.... It is difficult to see how town planning constitutes a profession in the sense of specialized skills and knowledge and a commitment to specific goals.... The notion of professional town planning should be abolished.[33]

Blowers' pessimism takes an interesting turn when advocates the promotion of a "positive planning" but with a "focus on social effects." He asserts that this would require researchers, not professional planners as currently conceived. Planning should provide the "knowledge base for political decisions," but as part of a generic process of decision-making in a decentralized system of local government, where town planning would no longer be a separate, professional function of local government but an integral part of a process of local service delivery.[34] A clear message in Blowers is that an instrumental positive planning must be integrated with some notion of the public interest, or the study of social effects, in order to be planning. Without this "visionary dimension," planning becomes simply a management information function. But how to avoid becoming simply one more servant in the bureaucratic apparatus of the state, or unseen expert in the back rooms of private capital? Qadeer contends that this is, in fact, where an instrumental view of planning has taken us:

> By preoccupying itself with controls and grants, the profession has rendered itself peripheral to the public interest. It is now a minor activity of the government.... [P]lanning practice is little distinguishable from administrative routines. [35]

The professional encounter

During the 1980s, attention was directed to the study of actual planning practice. Its predominant concern was with what Bolan termed the "phenomenology of the professional episode,"[36] and focused on the importance of language and communication at the expense of technique and methodology. The approach derived great impetus and authority from John Forester's applications of Jürgen Habermas' critical theory. As Baum noted:

> critical theory gives us a new way of understanding action, or what a planner does, as attention-shaping (communicative action), rather than more narrowly as a means to an end (instrumental action). [37]

The study of actual practice has since attained a relatively high degree of prominence and sophistication, and found concrete expression in the planning curriculum. Forester himself continues to examine the rhetorical structure of planning encounters.[38] He developed a model of anticipatory practice, for example, in which planning's three elements were described as: "envisioning a problem situation, managing arguments concerning it, and negotiating strategically to intervene." In other work in this field, Baum[39] and Schon[40] have directly addressed the issue of the planner's personal politics in professional practice. Kaufman[41] offers a view of planner as ethicist, identifying three key dimensions of practice: *normative*, a belief that planners have an ethical responsibility to serve the public interest; *action-oriented*, attempting to intervene selectively for planned change; and *realistic* about the complex politics of decision-making.[42]

The analytical turn toward the phenomenology of the professional encounter was necessary and long overdue. It raised planners' consciousness about the political, socio-cultural and economic contexts in which their work is conducted, and had an honorable philosophical lineage. In practical terms, it filled an important theoretical vacuum left by the apparent demise of the rational comprehensive model, and the atheoreticism of transactive/creative planning. Upon this respectable theoretical foundation planners could drape their needs for dialogue, mutual learning, and legitimacy. The phenomenological turn facilitated debate around power in planning and rationalized planners' interventions without the need for recourse to idealism, ideology, or political commitment. Yet Peter Hall argued, in 1988, that these theoretical props were illusory:

> the practical prescription all comes out as good old-fashioned democratic common sense, no more and no less than Davidoff's advocacy planning of fifteen years before:

cultivate community networks, listen carefully to the people, involve the less-organized groups, educate the citizens in how to join in, supply information and make sure people know how to get it, develop skills in working with groups in conflict situations, emphasize the need to participate, compensate for external pressures.[43]

Whether or not Hall was correct in this judgement, his remarks have direct consequences for my analysis. He revealed that critical theory can provide a theoretical legitimacy for those who wish to maintain a social/democratic voice in planning. However, when stripped of its social vision, the rhetoric of the professional encounter becomes just one more form of instrumentalism in planning. In a bastardized version of phenomenology, planning practice has been distilled to an exercise in the mechanics of persuasion – what Bill Fulton refers to as "putting the deal together."[44] For believers, the only scholarly and practical game in town is getting to "yes." The planning curriculum is besieged by new course offerings in strategy and negotiation; and planners themselves now celebrate successful decision-making. As they strive for a satisfactory closure, planners aim to communicate effectively to anyone who is across the table. Sometimes it seems to matter little what kind of decision is being reached. In a defence of practice as negotiation, McDonic noted:

> Planning today is *not* the negative, rigidly bureaucratized, paternalistic or domineering function that it is often accused of being…Modern planning is sensitive, people-centered and "open" to a degree undreamed of in the past.[45]

But what exactly are we being open about? Is planning no more than correct conversation?

Performance

In contrast to the proliferation of studies on the professional encounter, there is a relatively small literature on performance assessment. By this, I mean retrospective analyses of planning's achievements and failures: the kind of study which asks "What would have happened if there had been no planning?"; or "How much better would things have been if they had been properly planned?" Such post-occupancy questions are important, and their answers should be sought urgently by those interested in the efficacy of planning practice.[46] The study of performance indicators poses no insurmountable technical difficulties. Why, then, is there such a dearth of such analyses? Could it be that we are too fearful of what the results of such research could show? Or of revealing our inability to truly influence the course of development?

The principal technical hurdle in performance analysis is the determination of the appropriate criteria for judging planning outcomes. For instance, Hall's classic study, *Great Planning Disasters*,[47] viewed success or failure in terms of public reaction to a planning scheme. (But public opinion is notoriously fickle; the Sydney Opera House, for instance, has shifted from status of pariah to a well-loved symbol of Australia.) Knudsen[48] evaluated Danish planning outcomes in terms of "degrees of control," i.e. how far plannners' original intentions were carried through to the final result. Other criteria are possible, but Reade[49] reminds us that performance analyses have not been limited by technical difficulties, rather by planners' unwillingness to recognize or concede the importance of such analyses.

In a most comprehensive survey of more than 250 urban programs spanning over 100 years, Alexander Garvin cautioned that we need more realistic expectations about what planning can achieve. According to Garvin, planning is about change: that is, "preventing undesirable change and encouraging desirable change."[50] And, by extension, successful city planning is "public action that generates a desirable, widespread, and sustained private market reaction."[51] He identified six ingredients for success:[52]

- an active market for land and property development
- good location
- available financing
- good design
- entrepreneurship (often in the form of public/private partnerships)
- good timing (to take advantage of wider trends).

Garvin concedes that government "can play a major role" in fostering positive interaction between various actors in the development process (through, for example, investment, regulation and incentive).[53]

Roeseler's *Successful American Urban Plans*[54] is another look at representative achievements of American urban planning over the past 30–40 years. It is a fascinating exercise to reread this book as a statement about a philosophy of planning practice. Planning should occur, according to Roeseler, in "an atmosphere of sincerity and result-orientation that represents the very best of enlightened conservatism and self-interest."[55] He views planning practice as a technical exercise that is part of the wider function of urban management: "Its sole purpose is to lay before the decision makers feasible alternative solutions to perceived issues of public concern."[56]

Roeseler's histories are primarily a retelling of the roles played by the many "great men" (sic) who molded the appearance of American cities, including businessmen, planners and politicians. The book is full of references to people who were "committed," had "brilliant leadership," possessed "fine guidance," were "sincere" and "tireless," had "timeless genius," showed "tolerant appreciation," and so on. Despite his protestations about the need for cooperation in successful planning, Roeseler builds a view of planning that is simultaneously antigovernment ("The role of government is . . . to intervene only when absolutely necessary");[57] antibureaucracy ("The work of these men could not be duplicated by a thousand bureaucracies");[58] antipolitics ("Politics never entered the picture");[59] and profoundly antitheoretical ("little was to be gained from the theoretical;"[60] "[He] wasted no time with theory").[61]

What exactly does Roeseler regard as a measure of success in planning? Somewhat akin to Knudsen, he begins by defining success as the achievement of "what you set out to do," including the achievement of *inter alia*: an extensive freeway building program; a Haussmann-like clearance of slums; cooperation between public and private sectors; the absence of political conflict; establishing an ongoing planning administration; and revision of a zoning code. Planning failure is epitomized in the "pathetic urbanization" of Houston[62] – a conspicuously unplanned city. Planning was unsuccessful there because of the "blatant failure of the economic power structure, the bankers and merchant princes, to do their part in the democratic process." Instead, public affairs were given over to "opportunists and fast-talking salesmen." The future of Houston, according to Roeseler, awaits the "return to enlightened self-interest for the good of all."

For Roeseler, planning practice is ultimately a matter of determining the public interest: "A proposition either is or is not in the public interest. If it is ... it may be implemented; if it is not, it must be rejected."[63] This is hardly a non-problematic assertion, and Roeseler concedes that things can go wrong: "It is all up to the people and their leaders. A public that tolerates corrupt and inept leadership deserves it. The image of the city is an unmistakable expression of its spirit – an expression of fair play, opportunity, and reasonableness."[64]

The Poverty of Practice

What, then becomes necessary [in planning] is *not* head-on confrontation – messy and often unsuccessful at the best of times – but, instead, the reinforcement of existing worthwhile initiatives and momentum. The trick is – judo-style – to give a jolly good shove to anything that is moving in the right direction.

F. Tibbalds, President of the Royal Town Planning Institute, 1988.[65]

If we heed planners, we discover three dominant discourses in current practice:

(1) *a rhetoric of instrumentalism*, seeking to reassert an obsolete professionalism;
(2) *a rhetoric of rhetorics*, which focuses on strategies of persuasion; and
(3) *a rhetoric of performance*, which judges planning mainly according to the extent to which it promotes its sponsors' interests.

Case 1 is what Mandelbaum would call the "contingency table" approach to planning.[66] Planning becomes a routinized technical response ("If this, do that...") to a set of well-defined professional tasks that deal with matters of land use. This retreat to this traditional orthodoxy is a reactionary attempt to retrieve the "cloak of competence" that was perceived to exist in association with that orthodoxy. To advocates, it seems to matter little that the world has irrevocably changed, that old legitimacies cannot be recovered intact, and that such a retreat may be viewed as an admission of obsolescence, panic, even defeat.

Case 2 is a powerful star in the skies. It has engaged many prominent scholars, promising to bridge theory and practice, and sometimes touted as the principal paradigm among the community of planning theorists. But to base planning knowledge in a theory of negotiation is a reductionist game, if we allow ourselves to forget why we are engaged in negotiation in the first place.

Case 3 may yet prove to be the Achilles heel of public planning. Under pressure, the profession has been transformed into an empty bureaucratic vessel, to be filled (and thus activated) by any public or private agency desiring it to operate (cf. my discussion of Brasília in Chapter 5). Planning becomes tolerable to the extent that it facilitates what its sponsors wish to achieve in the name of an elusive public interest. None of these developments may be intrinsically wrong, although Reade[67] *inter alia* is highly critical of current trends. But we have to ask: Is this all that we want planning to be? Are we even aware that this is what planning practice has become?

Former RTPI president Francis Tibbalds' advice to his professional colleagues was typical of his commonsensical approach to problem-solving. Yet his words have acquired an ominous dimension certainly not intended by the speaker. While in general it might be true that the trick is to give a good shove to anything that is moving in the right direction, on the evidence of this chapter significant portions of the discourse in planning are now immobilized or may actively be moving in the wrong direction. Present in our discourse are the rhetorics of land-use planning, negotiation, and performance. Powerful voices are heard persuading the community of planners to recover former skills; to facilitate; and to align themselves with a myriad public and private interests. Planners who adopt a more critical tone are less likely to be given a hearing, and dissent becomes equated with disloyalty. Manipulating discourse in this way is, of course, nothing new. It is the principal *modus operandi* of academic and professional life. But what happens when such social Darwinism extinguishes some truly important voices?

Deconstruction has taught us to look for absences as well as presences in discourse. The first glaring excision from our vocabulary has been identified: the rhetoric of reform. There have been very few explicit attempts to connect contemporary planning discourse with its progressive, utopian roots. By this, I do not mean a lugubrious, uncritical return to old obsessions and dreams, nor am I arguing for more intellectual biographies. Instead, I am pinpointing the need to restore the reform tradition to a prominent position and thereby to forge a politically-aware and socially-conscious planning agenda relevant for a postmodern era.[68] The planner's ability and responsibility to forge substantive visions of the urban future have been all but forgotten in the rush to become articulate, technically-proficient facilitators.

The demise of a rhetoric of reform is, I believe, the principal reason that planners have not balked at the privatization trend. But the broader impact of an impoverished discourse is to compromise the planning identity. The new tech-speak is fixated upon the instrumental logics of planning: "This is what we can do; isn't it useful?" If the answer is no, we still have our yes-speak capacities to help you get things done. Planning functions have been commodified and sold to anyone willing to pay the price. Under present fiscal realities, planners are selling themselves to the private sector because the state has begun to spurn them. As a corollary, those parts of planning that are not susceptible to commodification have been neglected or even discarded. The reform tradition has little identifiable market utility; so we have buried it.

It is highly unlikely that all planners deliberately conspired to limit their discourse, or to promote commodification and privatization. (Some planners, of course, did both.) The altered rhetoric was most probably stimulated by the desire to defend a profession that (like others) was manifestly under pressure. Nevertheless, the cumulative effects of a disorganized defence, plus a self-interested advocacy on behalf of particular rhetorics, have reduced planning to a series of instrumental functions. These can easily be annexed by private interests, most especially the development industries. The fact that the current political climate is actively supportive of privatization has translated what began as an opportunity into a steely mandate.

Another significant dimension of planning discourse that has been curtailed is the rhetoric of theory. By this, I mean a self-awareness of our own situatedness, plus a mode of comparative analysis for the various theories of planning (e.g. Peter Hall versus the critical theorists). Those who care only for their own theory will not care about this absence; nor will those lacking an interest in theory. But everyone who recognizes the need to examine the qualitative differences between theories (and the practice they frame) will understand that a curtailment of the discourse on theory is an unwelcome precedent in any era. It compromises our capacity to envision; it limits what we can speak about; it accounts for why planners have, for example, been slow to adopt feminist theory and postmodern thought (cf. Chapter 12); and it hides what is happening to the world. In short, the absence of theory reduces planners (not just planning) to empty vessels, passive automatons. It is difficult to invent a grounded planning theory that fits into a postmodern era celebrating intellectual relativism, but it is professional and scholarly suicide to ignore the obligation to do so. In James Boyd White's felicitous phrasing:

> When we discover that we have in this world no earth or rock to stand and walk upon, but only shifting sea and sky and wind, the mature response is not to lament the loss of fixity, but to learn to sail.[69]

There may be few valiant navigators in the present planning world, although Beth Moore Milroy has ably demonstrated the benefits that flow from direct engagement with this problematic.[70] I am uncomfortably reminded of Ed Bacon's words, albeit in a different context, who said that the "planning profession is committing suicide."[71] If the future proves him correct, it may be because the critical voices of the planning visionary and planning theorist have been excised from contemporary discourse. Without this vital groundedness, which paradoxically does not derive from real-world practice, planning has floated free of its roots. Ready or not, it has entered its postmodern era.

Notes

1. Patton, C. V. and Reed, K. (eds) 1986: *Guide to Graduate Education in Urban and Regional Planning*, Milwaukee: Association of Collegiate Schools of Planning, p. vii.
2. Flyvbjerg, Bent, 1998: *Rationality and Power: Democracy in Practice*, Chicago: University of Chicago Press.; also Yiftachel, O., 1998:"Planning and Social Control: Exploring the Dark Side," *Journal of Planning Literature*, 12 (4), pp. 395–406.
3. Scott, James C. 1998: *Seeing Like a State: How Certain Schemes to Improve the Human Condition Have Failed*, New Haven: Yale University Press.
4. Kiernan, M. J. 1983: "Ideology, Politics, and Planning," *Environment & Planning B, Planning & Design*, 10, pp. 71–87.
5. Breheny, M. J. 1983: "A Practical View of Planning Theory," *Environment & Planning B*,10, p. 106.
6. See Katz, P. 1994: *The New Urbanism: Towards an Architecture of Community*, New York: McGraw Hill, pp. ix–x.
7. Starr, P., "The Meaning of Privatization," in Kamerman, Sheila B and Kahn, Alfred J. (eds) 1989: *Privatization and the Welfare State*, Princeton: Princeton University Press,

p. 42. For a representative sample of the literature on privatization, see Ascher, K. 1987: *The Politics of Privatization*, London: Macmillan; LeGrand, J. and Robinson, R. 1984: *Privatisation and the Welfare State*, London: Allen and Unwin; Swann, D. 1988: *The Retreat of State*, Hemel Hempstead: Harvester Wheatsheaf; Veljanovski, C. 1987: *Selling the State: Privatisation in Britain*, London: Weidenfield and Nicolson.

8. Dear, M. and Scott, A. 1981: *Urbanization and Urban Planning in Capitalist Society*, London: Methuen; Clark, G. L. and Dear, M. 1984: *State Apparatus: Structures and Language of Legitimacy*, Boston: Allen & Unwin.

9. Wolch, J. and Dear, M. (eds) 1989: *The Power of Geography: How Territory Shapes Social Life*, Boston: Unwin Hyman.

10. Lash, S. and Urry, J. 1987: *The End of Organized Capitalism*, Cambridge: Polity Press; Offe, C. 1987: *Disorganized Capitalism*, Cambridge: MIT Press; Scott, A. 1989: *Metropolis: From Division of Labor to Urban Form*, Berkeley: University of California Press.

11. See, for example, Wolch, J. 1989: *The Shadow State: Government and the Voluntary Sector in Transition*, New York: The Foundation Center.

12. Reade, E. 1987: *British Town and Country Planning*, Milton Keynes: Open University Press.

13. Fyson, A. 1987: "New Country Planning," *The Planner* 73, 5, p. 3.

14. Bannerjee, T. 1993. "Antiplanning Undercurrents in U.S. Planning Education." *Environmental & Planning B*, Planning & Design, 20.

15. Cf. Clark, G. L. 1985: *Judges and Cities*, Chicago: University of Chicago Press; and Olsson, G. 1980: *Birds in Egg*, London: Pion.

16. McCloskey, D. N. 1985: *The Rhetoric of Economics*, Madison: University of Wisconsin Press, p. 29

17. Maranhao, T. 1986: *Therapeutic Discourse and Socratic Dialogue*, Madison: University of Wisconsin Press, p. 237.

18. White, J. B. 1985: *Heracles' Bow: Essays on the Rhetoric of the Law*, Madison: University of Wisconsin Press, p. 28.

19. Clark, G. L. and Dear, M. *State Apparatus: Structures and Language of Legitimacy*.

20. White, J. B. *Heracles' Bow: Essays on the Rhetoric of the Law*, p. 35.

21. Cf. Forester, J. 1989: *Planning in the Face of Power*, Berkeley: University of California Press; Friedmann, J. 1987: *Planning in the Public Domain*, Princeton: Princeton University Press; Hall, P. 1988: *Cities of Tomorrow*, Oxford: Blackwell; and Reade, E. *British Town and Country Planning*.

22. See, for example, Bourdieu, P. 1977: *Outline of a Theory of Practice*, Cambridge: Cambridge University Press.

23. Bailey, N. 1986. "What Burden," *The Planner*, p. 31.

24. Breheny, M. J. "A Practical View of Planning Theory."

25. Breheny, M. J., "A Practical View of Planning Theory," p. 103. See Hall, *Cities of Tomorrow*, Chapter 10 for an alternative interpretation of this separation.

26. Breheny, M. J. "A Practical View of Planning Theory," p. 106.

27. Ibid., p. 114.

28. Mandelbaum, S. 1987: "Open Moral Communities" (unpublished manuscript) p. 25. Available from the author at the Department of City and Regional Planning, University of Pennsylvania, Philadelphia, PA. 19104.

29. Harris, B. 1978: "A Note on Planning Theory," *Environment & Planning A*, 10(2), p. 221.

30. Scott, A. J. and Roweis, S. 1977: "Urban Planning in Theory and Practice," *Environment & Planning A*, 9, p. 221.

31. Harris, B., "A Note on Planning Theory," p. 221.

32. Scott, A. J. and Roweis, S. 1978: "A Note on Planning Theory: A Response to Britton Harris," *Environment & Planning A*, 10, p. 229.
33. Blowers, A. 1986. "Town Planning – Paradoxes & Prospects," *The Planner*, 72(4), p. 17.
34. Blowers, A. "Town Planning – Paradoxes & Prospects," p. 18.
35. Qadeer, M. 1987: "The Tensions between Planning Education and Practice," *Plan Canada*, (26(10), p. 276.
36. Bolan, R. S. 1980: "The Practitioner as Theorist," *Journal of the American Planning Association*, 46, p. 261.
37. Forester, J. 1980: "Critical Theory and Planning Practice," *Journal of the American Planning Association*, 46, p. 275.
38. Forester, J. 1987: "Teaching & Studying Planning Practice," *Journal of Planning Education and Research*, 6(2), p. 136.
39. Baum, H. S. 1983: *Planners & Public Expectations*, New York: Schenkman.
40. Schon, D. A. 1983: *The Reflective Practitioner*, New York: Basic Books.
41. Kaufman, J. L. 1987: "Teaching Planning Students About Strategizing Boundary Spanning and Ethics," *Journal of Planning Education and Research*, 6(2), p. 113.
42. Cf. Wachs, M. 1985: *Ethics in Planning*, New Brunswick NJ: Center for Urban Policy Research, on the matter of ethics in planning.
43. Hall, P. *Cities of Tomorrow*, pp. 339–340.
44. Fulton, W., 1997: *The Reluctant Metropolis: The Politics of Urban Growth in Los Angeles.*, Point Arena, CA: Solano Press Books, p. 86
45. McDonic, G. 1986: "Planning a Positive Service," *The Planner*, 72(3), p. 6.
46. Cf. Reade, E. *British Town and Country Planning*, Chapter 7; also, Dear, M. and Laws, G. 1986. "Anatomy of a Decision: Recent Land-use Zoning Appeals and Their Influence on Group Home Location in Ontario", *Canadian Journal of Community Mental Health*, 5(1), 5–17.
47. Hall, P. 1980: *Great Planning Disasters*, Berkeley: University of California Press.
48. Knudsen, T. 1988: "Success in Planning," *International Journal of Urban and Regional Research*, 12(4).
49. Reade, E. *British Town and Country Planning*, p. 88.
50. Garvin, A. 1996: *The American City: What Works and What Doesn't*, New York: McGraw Hill, p. 3.
51. Ibid., p. xi.
52. Ibid., Chapter 2.
53. Ibid., pp. 27–28.
54. Roeseler, W. G. 1982: *Successful American Urban Plans*, Lexington: D. C. Heath.
55. Ibid., p. 45.
56. Ibid., p. 21.
57. Ibid., p. 184.
58. Ibid., p. 19.
59. Ibid., p. 104.
60. Ibid., p. 134.
61. Ibid., p. 147.
62. Ibid., p. 73.
63. Ibid., p. 21.
64. Ibid., p. 69.
65. Tibbalds, F., 1988: "Presidental statement," Royal Town Planning Institute, 26 Portland Place, London W1N 4BE, p. 10.
66. Mandelbaum, S. "Open Moral Communities."
67. Reade, E. *British Town and Country Planning*, p. 216.

68. Honorable exceptions to the overarching silence on the rhetoric of reform include Brooks, M. 1988: "Four Critical Junctures in the History of the Urban Planning Profession," *Journal of the American Planning Association*, 54(2), 241–8; Friedmann, J. *Planning in the Public Domain*; and Hall, P. *Cities of Tomorrow*; Hall, P. "The Turbulent Eighth Decade," *Journal of the American Planning Institute*, 55(3), pp. 275–82. Also see my discussion of Leonie Sandercock's *Towards Cosmopolis*, in Chapter 15.

69. White, J. B. 1985: *Heracles' Bow: Essays on the Rhetoric of the Law*, p. 95.

70. Milroy, B. M. 1989: "Constructing and Deconstructing Plausibility." *Society and Space*, 7(3), 313–26.

71. Quoted in Fulton, *The Reluctant Metropolis: The Politics of Urban Growth in Los Angeles*, p.106.

7

Postmodern Urbanism

Sometimes, falling asleep in Santa Monica, he wondered vaguely if there might have been a larger system, a field of greater perspective. Perhaps the whole of DatAmerica possessed its own nodal points, infofaults that might be followed down to some other kind of truth, another mode of knowing, deep within the gray shoals of information. But only if there were someone there to pose the right question.[1]

One of the most innovative aspects of recent debates on the postmodern condition is the notion that there has been a radical break from past trends in political, economic, and socio-cultural life. There is no clear consensus about the nature of this ostensible break. Some analysts have declared the current condition to be nothing more than business as usual, only faster – a "hyper-modern" or "super-modern" phase of advanced capitalism. Others have noted that the pace of change in all aspects of our global society is sufficient for us to begin to speak of revolution. In this chapter, I follow an invocation of Jacques Derrida, who invited those interested in assessing the extent and volume of contemporary change to "rehearse the break," intimating that only by assuming a radical break had already occurred would our capacity to recognize it be released. Similar advice was offered by C. Wright Mills in *The Sociological Imagination*:[2]

> We are at the ending of what is called The Modern Age. Just as Antiquity was followed by several centuries of Oriental ascendancy, which Westerners provincially called The Dark Ages, so now The Modern Age is being succeeded by a post-modern period.

As I pointed out in Chapter 2, Mills believed that it was vital to conceptualize the categories of change in order to "grasp the outline of the new epoch we suppose ourselves to be entering."[3]

Based upon the evidence of the previous chapters, I shall now make a presumption in favor of something called a postmodern urbanism. I begin this search by examining a broad range of contemporary Southern California urbanisms. Then I will suggest a critical reinterpretation of this evidence that encompasses and defines the problematic of a distinctively postmodern urbanism. The inquiry is based on a simple premise: that just as the central tenets of modernist thought have been undermined, its core evacuated and replaced by a rush of competing epistemologies, so too have the traditional logics of earlier urbanisms evaporated, and in the absence of a single new imperative, multiple urban (ir)rationalities are competing to fill the void. The concretization and localization of these effects is creating the new geographies of postmodern society.

Well, what does a postmodern urbanism look like? One of the most prescient pieces anticipating a postmodern vision of the city is Jonathan Raban's *Soft City*, a reading of London's cityscapes.[4] Raban divides the city into hard and soft elements. The former refers to the material fabric of the built environment – the streets and buildings that frame the lives of city dwellers. The latter, by contrast, is an individualized interpretation of the city, a perceptual orientation created in the mind of every urbanite. The relationship between the two is complex, even indeterminate. The newcomer to a city first confronts the hard city, but soon:

> the city goes soft; it awaits the imprint of an identity. For better or worse, it invites you
> to remake it, to consolidate it into a shape you can live in. You, too. Decide who you are,
> and the city will again assume a fixed form around you. Decide what it is, and your own
> identity will be revealed.[5]

Raban makes no claims to a postmodern consciousness, yet his invocation of the relationship between the cognitive and the real leads to insights that are unmistakably postmodern in their sensitivities. First, he warns of the possibility and consequences of a breakdown in cognitive structures: "so much takes place in the head. So little is known and fixed. Signals, styles, systems of rapid, highly-conventionalized communication are the life blood of the big city...[But what happens]when these systems break down – when we lose our grasp on the grammar of life...?"[6] To show the consequences, Raban contrasts the organizing visions of nineteenth-century writers with those of present-day urbanists. Nineteenth-century planners, philanthropists and journalists used a metaphor of an encyclopedia to encapsulate the "special randomness of the city's diversity:"

> [T]he logic of the city is not of the kind which lends itself to straightforward narration or
> to continuous page-by-page reading. At the same time, it does imply that the city is a
> repository of knowledge, although no single reader or citizen can command the whole of
> that knowledge.[7]

Contrast this with the perceptual problems presented by the contemporary city, where conventional hierarchies fail:

> The social diversity of the city, which so delighted the eighteenth-century citizen, has,
> during the course of the twentieth century, multiplied to such an extent ... that no
> overview is possible. London now is not so much an encyclopaedia as a maniac's
> scrapbook.[8]

Raban abandons the search for a general theory, but retains his hold on place as a key to understanding the urban, because "place is important; it bears down on us, we mythicize it – often it is our greatest comfort, the one reassuringly solid element in an otherwise soft city."[9]

Ted Relph was one of the first to catalogue the built forms of that comprise the places of postmodernity. He describes postmodern urbanism as a self-conscious and selective revival of elements of older styles, though he cautions that postmodernism is not simply a style but also an attitude, a frame of mind.[10] He observes how the coincidence of many trends – gentrification, heritage conservation, architectural fashion, urban design, and participatory planning – has already caused the collapse of the modernist vision of a future city filled with skyscrapers, megastructures and other austere icons of scientific rationalism. The new urbanism is principally distinguishable from the old by its eclecticism. Relph warns that arbitrary repetition could result in "a chiaroscuro of increasingly flashy, unrelated and pointless patches, a postmodern, late-modern monotony-in-variety."[11]

Relph's periodization of twentieth-century urbanism involves a pre-modern transitional period (up to 1940); an era of modernist cityscapes (after 1945); and a period of postmodern townscapes (since 1970). The distinction between cityscape and townscape is the crucial to his diagnosis. Modernist cityscapes, he claims, are characterized by five elements:[12]

(1) *megastructural bigness*, few street entrances to buildings, little architectural detailing, etc.;
(2) *straight-space / prairie space*, city center canyons, endless suburban vistas;
(3) *rational order and flexibility*, the landscapes of total order, verging on boredom;
(4) *hardness and opacity*, including freeways, and the displacement of nature; and
(5) *discontinuous serial vision*, deriving from the dominance of the automobile.

Conversely, postmodern townscapes are more detailed, handcrafted and intricate. They celebrate difference, polyculturalism, variety and stylishness.[13] Their elements are:

(6) *quaintspace*, a deliberate cuteness;
(7) *textured facades*, aimed at pedestrians, rich in detail, often with an "aged" appearance;
(8) *stylishness*, appealing to the fashionable, chic, and affluent;
(9) *reconnection with the local*, involving deliberate historical–geographical reconstructions; and
(10) *pedestrian–automobile split*, to redress the modernist bias toward the car.

The experience of driving through the late-twentieth century city is, for Relph, one of repetition, where unity is achieved by contiguity and little else. He concludes that the modern urban landscape is a failure, littered with the dreams of Ebenezer Howard, Frank Lloyd Wright, le Corbusier, and other utopians. But the postmodern townscape may be nothing more than a disguise for an ever more subtle and powerful rationality on the part of government and corporations – a "pretty lie," as Relph calls it.[14] He concludes:

> For all the dramatic modifications that have been made to urban landscapes over the last 100 years I begin to suspect that the only fundamental social advances have been to do with sanitation. All the other changes – skyscrapers, renewal, suburban subdivisions, expressways, heritage districts – amount to little more than fantastic imagineering and spectacular window dressing.[15]

A Maniac's Scrapbook: Contemporary Southern California

This latest mutation in space – postmodern hyperspace – has finally succeeded in transcending the capacities of the human body to locate itself, to organize its immediate surroundings perceptually, and cognitvely to map its position in a mappable external world.[16]

Raban's emphasis on the cognitive and Relph's on the concrete underscore the importance of both dimensions in understanding socio-spatial urban process. The palette of urbanisms that arises from merging the two is thick and multidimensional. We turn now to the task of constructing that palette by examining empirical evidence of recent urban developments in Southern California (Table 7.1). In this review, we take our lead from what exists, rather than what we consider to be a comprehensive urban research agenda. From this, we move quickly to a synthesis that is prefigurative of a proto-postmodern urbanism (Figure 7.1) which we hope will serve as an invitation to a more broadly-based comparative analysis.

Table 7.1 A Taxonomy of Southern California Urbanisms
(Blackwell)

EDGE CITIES
PRIVATOPIA
CULTURES OF HETEROPOLIS
CITY AS THEME PARK
FORTIFIED CITY
INTERDICTORY SPACE
HISTORICAL GEOGRAPHIES OF RESTRUCTURING
FORDIST / POSTFORDIST REGIMES OF ACCUMULATION / REGULATION
GLOBALIZATION
POLITICS OF NATURE

Edge cities

Joel Garreau noted the central significance of Los Angeles in understanding contemporary metropolitan growth in the US. He asserts that: "Every single American city that is growing, is growing in the fashion of Los Angeles," and refers to LA as the "great-grandaddy" of edge cities. (He claims there are 26 of them within a 5-county area in Southern California).[17] For Garreau, edge cities represent the crucible of America's urban future. The classic location for contemporary edge cities is at the intersection of an urban beltway and a hub-and-spoke lateral road. The central conditions that have propelled such development are the dominance of the automobile and the associated need for parking; the communications revolution; and the entry of women in large numbers into the labor market. Although Garreau agrees with Robert Fishman that "all new city forms appear in their early stages to be chaotic,"[18] he is able to identify three basic types of edge city. These are: *uptowns*, peripheral pre-automobile settlements that have subsequently been absorbed by urban sprawl); *boomers*, the classic edge cities, located at freeway intersections);

and *greenfields*, the current state-of-the-art, "occurring at the intersection of several thousand acres of farmland and one developer's monumental ego."[19]

One essential feature of the edge city is that politics is not yet established there. Into the political vacuum moves a "shadow government" – a privatized proto-government that is essentially a plutocratic alternative to normal politics. Shadow governments can tax, legislate for, and police their communities, but they are rarely accountable, are responsive primarily to wealth (as opposed to numbers of voters), and subject to few constitutional constraints.[20] Jennifer Wolch has described the rise of the shadow state as part of a society-wide trend toward privatization.[21] In edge cities, "community" is scarce, occurring not through propinquity but via telephone, fax and private mail service. The walls that typically surround such neighborhoods are social boundaries, but they act as a community "recognizers," not community "organizers."[22] In the edge city era, Garreau notes, the term "master-planned" community is little more than a marketing device.[23] Other studies of suburbanization in LA, most notably by Hise[24] and Waldie,[25] provide a basis for comparing past practices of planned community marketing in Southern California.

Privatopia

Privatopia, perhaps the quintessential edge city residential form, is a private housing development based in common-interest developments (CIDs) and administered by homeowners' associations. There were fewer than 500 such associations in 1964; by 1992, there were 150,000 associations privately governing approximately 32 million Americans. In 1990, the 11.6 million CID units constituted over 11 percent of the nation's housing stock.[26] Sustained by an expanding catalogue of covenants, conditions, and restrictions (or CC&Rs, the proscriptive constitutions formalizing CID behavioral and aesthetic norms), privatopia has been fueled by a large dose of privatization, and promoted by an ideology of "hostile privatism."[27] It has provoked a culture of non-participation.

McKenzie warns that far from being a benign or inconsequential trend, CIDs already define a new norm for the mass production of housing in the US. Equally importantly, their organizations are now allied through something called the Community Associations Institute, "whose purposes include the standardizing and professionalizing of CID governance."[28] McKenzie notes how this "secession of the successful" (the phrase is Robert Reich's) has altered concepts of citizenship, in which "one's duties consist of satisfying one's obligations to private property."[29] In her futuristic novel of LA wars between walled-community dwellers and those beyond the walls, Octavia Butler has envisioned a dystopian privatopian future. It includes a balkanized nation of defended neighborhoods at odds with one another, where entire communities are wiped out for a handful of fresh lemons or a few cups of potable water; where torture and murder of one's enemies is common; and where company-town slavery is attractive to those who are fortunate enough to sell their services to the hyper-defended enclaves of the very rich.[30]

Cultures of heteropolis

One of the most prominent socio-cultural tendencies in contemporary Southern California is the rise of minority populations.[31] Provoked to comprehend the causes and implications of the 1992 civil disturbances in Los Angeles, Charles Jencks[32] zeroes in on the city's diversity as the key to LA's emergent urbanism: "Los Angeles is a combination of enclaves with high identity, and multienclaves with mixed identity, and, taken as a whole, it is perhaps the most heterogenenous city in the world."[33] Such ethnic pluralism has given rise to what Jencks calls a hetero-architecture, which has demonstrated that: "there is a great virtue, and pleasure, to be had in mixing categories, transgressing boundaries, inverting customs and adopting the marginal usage."[34] The vigor and imagination underlying these intense cultural dynamics is everywhere evident in the region, from the diversity of ethnic adaptations[35] through the concentration of cultural producers in the region,[36] to the hybrid complexities of emerging cultural forms.[37]

The consequent built environment is characterized by transience, energy, and unplanned vulgarity, in which Hollywood is never far away. Jencks views this improvisational quality as a hopeful sign: "The main point of hetero-architecture is to accept the different voices that create a city, suppress none of them, and make from their interaction some kind of greater dialogue."[38] This is especially important in a city where minoritization, "the typical postmodern phenomenon where most of the population forms the 'other'," is the order of the day, and where most city dwellers feel distanced from the power strucure.[39] Despite Jencks' optimism, other analysts have observed that the same Southern California heteropolis has to contend with more than its share of socio-economic polarization, racism, inequality, homelessness, and social unrest.[40] Yet these characteristics are part of a socio-cultural dynamic that is also provoking the search for innovative solutions in labor and community organizing,[41] as well as in inter-ethnic relations.[42]

City as theme park

California in general, and Los Angeles in particular, have often been promoted as places where the American (suburban) Dream is most easily realized. Its oft-noted qualities of optimism and tolerance coupled with a balmy climate have given rise to an architecture and society fostered by a spirit of experimentation, risk-taking, and hope. Architectural dreamscapes are readily convertible into marketable commodities, i.e. saleable prepackaged landscapes engineered to satisfy fantasies of suburban living.[43] Many writers have used the "theme park" metaphor to describe the emergence of such variegated cityscapes. For instance, Michael Sorkin describes theme parks as places of simulation without end, characterized by aspatiality plus technological and physical surveillance and control.[44] The precedents for this model can be traced back to the World's Fairs, but Sorkin insists that something "wholly new" is now emerging. This is because "the 800 telephone number and the piece of plastic have made time and space obsolete," and these instruments of "artificial adjacency" have eviscerated the traditional politics of propinquity.[45] Sorkin observes that the social order has always been legible in urban form; for example, traditional cities have adjudicated conflicts via the relations of public places such as the agora or piazza. However, in today's "recombinant city," he contends that conventional legibilities have been obscured and/or deliberately mutilated. The phone and modem have rendered the street irrelevant, and the new city threatens an "unimagined sameness" characterized by the loosening of ties to any specific space, rising levels of surveillance, manipulation and segregation, and the city as a theme park. Of this last, Disneyland is the archetype – described by Sorkin as a place of "Taylorized fun," the "Holy See of Creative Geography."[46] What is missing in this new cybernetic suburbia is not a particular building or place, but the spaces between, i.e. the connections that make sense of forms.[47] What is missing, then, is connectivity and community.

In extremis, California dreamscapes become simulacra. Ed Soja, identified Orange County as a massive simulation of what a city should be.[48] He describes Orange County as "a structural fake, and enormous advertisement, yet functionally the finest multipurpose facility of its kind in the country." Calling this assemblage "exopolis," or the city without, Soja asserts that "something new is being born here" based on the hyperrealities of more conventional theme parks such as Disneyland.[49] The exopolis is a simulacrum, an exact copy of an original that never existed, within which image and reality are spectacularly confused. In this "politically-numbed" society, conventional politics is dysfunctional. Orange County has become a "scamscape," notable principally as home of massive mail fraud operations, savings and loan failures, and county government bankruptcy.[50]

Fortified city

The downside of the Southern Californian dream has, of course, been the subject of countless dystopian visions in histories, movies and novels.[51] In one powerful account, Mike Davis noted how Southern Californians' obsession with security has transformed the region into a fortress. This shift is accurately manifested in the physical form of the city, which is divided into fortified cells of affluence and places of terror where police battle the criminalized poor. These urban phenomena, according to Davis, have placed Los Angeles "on the hard edge of postmodernity."[52] The dynamics of fortification involve the omnipresent application of high-tech policing methods to the "high-rent security of gated residential developments" and "panopticon malls." It extends to "space policing," including a proposed satellite observation capacity that would create an invisible Haussmannization of Los Angeles. In the consequent "carceral city," the working poor and destitute are spatially sequestered on the "mean streets," and excluded from the affluent "forbidden cities" through "security by design."

Interdictory space

Elaborating upon Davis' fortress urbanism, Steven Flusty observed how various types of fortification have extended a canopy of suppression and surveillance across the entire city. His taxonomy of interdictory spaces[53] identifies how spaces are designed to exclude by a combination of their function and cognitive sensibilities. Some spaces are passively aggressive: space concealed by intervening objects or grade changes is "stealthy;" and spaces that may be reached only by means of interrupted or obfuscated approaches is "slippery." Other spatial configurations are more assertively confrontational: deliberately obstructed "crusty" space surrounded by walls and checkpoints; inhospitable "prickly" spaces featuring unsittable benches in areas devoid of shade; or "jittery" space ostentatiously saturated with surveillance devices. Flusty notes how combinations of interdictory spaces are being introduced "into every facet of the urban environment, generating distinctly unfriendly mutant typologies."[54] Some are indicative of the pervasive infiltration of fear into the home, including the bunker-style "blockhome," affluent palisaded "luxury laager" communities, or low-income residential areas converted into "pocket ghettos" by military-style occupation. Other typological forms betray a fear of the public realm, as with the fortification of commercial facilities into "strongpoints of sale," or the self-contained "world citadel" clusters of defensible office towers.

One consequence of the socio-spatial differentiation described by Davis and Flusty is an acute fragmentation of the urban landscape. Commentators who remark upon the strict division of residential neighborhoods along race and class lines miss the fact that LA's micro-geography is incredibly volatile and varied. In many neighborhoods, simply turning a street corner will lead the pedestrian/driver into totally different social and physical configurations. One very important feature of local neighborhood dynamics in the fortified culture of Southern Californian cities is, of course, the presence of street gangs.[55]

Historical geographies of restructuring

Historical geographies of Southern California are relatively rare, especially when compared with the number of published accounts of Chicago and New York. For reasons that are unclear, Los Angeles remains, in my judgement, the least studied major city in the United States. Until Mike Davis' *City of Quartz*[56] brought the urban record up to the present, students of Southern California tended to rely principally on Carey McWilliams'[57] seminal general history and Fogelson's *The Fragmented Metropolis*,[58] an urban history of LA up to 1930. Other chronicles of the urban evolution of Southern California have focused on transportation,[59] the Mexican/Chicano experience,[60] real estate development and planning,[61] and oil.[62] The political geography of the region is only now being written,[63] but several more broadly-based treatments of Californian politics exist, including excellent studies on art, poetry and politics,[64] railways,[65] and the rise of suburbia.[66]

In his history of Los Angeles between 1965 and 1992, Soja attempts to link the emergent patterns of urban form with underlying social processes.[67] He identified six kinds of restructuring, which together define the region's contemporary urban process. In addition to *Exopolis* (noted above), Soja lists: *Flexcities*, associated with the transition to post-Fordism, especially deindustrialization and the rise of the information economy; and *Cosmopolis*, referring to the globalization of Los Angeles both in terms of its emergent world city status and its internal multicultural diversification. According to Soja, peripheralization, post-Fordism, and globalization together define the experience of urban restructuring in Los Angeles. Three specific geographies are consequent upon these dynamics: *Splintered Labyrinth*, which describes the extreme forms of social, economic, and political polarization characteristic of the postmodern city; *Carceral city*, referring to the new "incendiary urban geography" brought about by the amalgam of violence and police surveillance; and *Simcities*, the term Soja uses to describe the new ways of seeing the city that are emerging from the study Los Angeles – a kind of epistemological restructuring that foregrounds a postmodern perspective.

Fordist vs post-Fordist regimes of accumulation and regulation

Many observers agree that one of the most important underlying shifts in the contemporary political economy is from a Fordist to a post-Fordist industrial organization. In a series of important books, Allen Scott and Michael Storper have portrayed the burgeoning urbanism of Southern California as a consequence of this deep-seated structural change in the capitalist political economy.[68] For instance, Scott's basic argument is that there have been two major phases of urbanization in the United States. The first related to an era of Fordist mass production, during which the paradigmatic cities of industrial capitalism (Detroit, Chicago, Pittsburgh, etc.) coalesced around industries that were themselves based upon ideas of mass production. The second phase is associated with the decline of the Fordist era and the rise of a post-Fordist "flexible production." This is a form of industrial activity based on small-size, small-batch units of (typically sub-contracted) production that are nevertheless integrated into clusters of economic activity. Such clusters have been observed in two manifestations: labor-intensive craft forms (in Los Angeles, typically garments and jewelry); and high technology (especially the defense and aerospace industries). According to Scott, these so-called "technopoles" until recently constituted the principal geographical loci of contemporary (sub)urbanization in Southern California (a development prefigured in Fishman's description of the "technoburb."[69]

Post-Fordist regimes of accumulation are associated with analogous regimes of regulation, or social control. Perhaps the most prominent manifestation of changes in the regime of regulation has been the retreat from the welfare state. The rise of neoconservatism and the privatization ethos have coincided with a period of economic recession and retrenchment which has led many to the brink of poverty just at the time when the social welfare "safety net" is being withdrawn. In Los Angeles, as in many other cities, an acute socio-economic polarization has resulted. In 1984, the city was dubbed the "homeless capital" of the USA because of the concentration of homeless people there.[70]

Globalization

Needless to say, any consideration of the changing nature of industrial production sooner or later must encompass the globalization question.[71] In his reference to the global context of LA's localisms, Mike Davis claims that if LA is in any sense paradigmatic, it is because the city condenses the intended and unintended spatial consequences of post-Fordism.[72] He insists that there is no simple master-logic of restructuring, focusing instead on two key localized macro-processes: the overaccumulation in Southern California of bank and real-estate capital principally from the East Asian trade surplus; and the reflux of low-wage manufacturing and labor-intensive service industries following upon immigration from Mexico and Central America. For instance, Davis notes how the City of Los Angeles used tax dollars gleaned from international capital investments to subsidize its downtown (Bunker Hill) urban renewal, a process he refers to as "municipalized land speculation."[73] Through such connections, what happens today in Asia and Central America will tomorrow have an effect in Los Angeles. This global/local dialectic has already become an important (if somewhat imprecise) leitmotif of contemporary urban theory.

Politics of nature

The natural environment of Southern California has been under constant assault since the first colonial settlements. Human habitation on a metropolitan scale has only been possible through a widespread manipulation of nature, especially the control of water resources in the American West.[74] On one hand, Southern Californians tend to hold a grudging respect for nature living as they do adjacent to one of the earth's major geological hazards, and in a desert environment that is prone to flood, landslide and fire.[75] On the other, its inhabitants have been energetically, ceaselessly, and sometimes carelessly unrolling the carpet of urbanization over the natural landscape for more than a century. This uninhibited occupation has engendered its own range of environmental problems, most notoriously air pollution, but also issues related to habitat loss and dangerous encounters between humans and other animals.

The force of nature in Southern California has spawned a literature that attempts to incorporate environmental issues into the urban problematic. The politics of environmental regulation have long been studied in many places, including Los Angeles.[76] However, the particular combination of circumstances in Southern California has stimulated an especially political view of nature, focusing both on its emasculation through human intervention[77] and on its potential for political mobilization by grass-roots movements.[78] In addition, Jennifer Wolch's Southern California-based research has led her to outline an alternative vision of biogeography's problematic.[79]

Synthesis: Proto-postmodern urbanism

If these observers of the Southern California scene could talk with each other to resolve their differences and reconcile their terminologies, how might they synthesize their visions? At the risk of misrepresenting their work, I suggest a schematic that is powerful yet inevitably incomplete (Figure 7.1). It suggests a "proto-postmodern" urban process, driven by a global restructuring that is permeated and balkanized by a series of interdictory networks; whose populations are socially and culturally heterogeneous, but politically and economically polarized; whose residents are educated and persuaded to the consumption of dreamscapes even as the poorest are consigned to carceral cities; whose built environment, reflective of these processes, consists of edge cities, privatopias, and the like; and whose natural environment, also reflective of these processes, is being erased to the point of unlivability while at the same time providing a focus for political action.

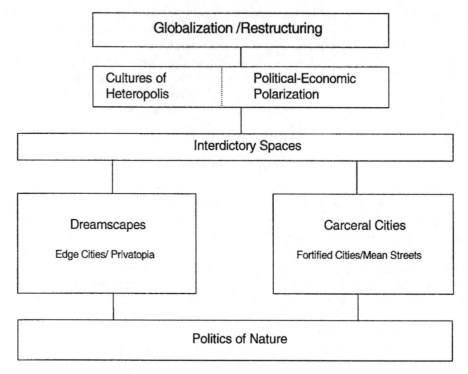

Figure 7.1 A concept of proto-postmodern urbanism (from Annals, Association of American Geographers 88(1), courtesy Association of American Geographers, 1998)

Postmodern Urbanism

The only theory worth having is that which you have to fight off, not that which you speak with profound fluency.

Stuart Hall[80]

Recognizing that I may have caused some offense by characterizing others' work in this way, let us move swiftly to reconstruct their evidence into a postmodern urban problematic (Table 7.2). We anchor this problematic in the straightforward need to account for the evolution of society over time and space. Such evolution occurs as a combination of deep-time (long-term) and present-time (short-term) processes; and it develops over several different scales of human activity (which we may represent summarily as micro-, meso-, and macro-scales).[81] The structuring of the time–space fabric is the result of the interaction among ecologically-situated human agents in relations of production, consumption, and coercion. We do not intend any primacy in this ordering of categories, but instead emphasize their interdependencies – all are essential in explaining postmodern human geographies.

Our promiscuous use of neologisms in what follows is quite deliberate.[82] This technique has been used historically to good effect in many instances and disciplines.[83] Neologisms have been used here in circumstances when there were no existing terms to describe adequately the conditions we sought to identify; when neologisms served as metaphors to suggest new insights; when a single term more conveniently substituted for a complex phrase or string of ideas; and when neo-logistic novelty aided our avowed efforts to rehearse the break. The juxtaposing of postmodern and more traditional categories of modernist urbanism is also an essen-tial piece of our analytical strategy. That there is an overlap between modernist and postmodern categories should surprise no-one; we are, inevitably, building on

Table 7.2   Elements of a Postmodern Urbanism
(Blackwell)

GLOBAL LATIFUNDIA
HOLSTEINIZATION
PRAEDATORIANISM
FLEXISM
NEW WORLD BI-POLAR DISORDER
Cybergeoisie
Protosurps
MEMETIC CONTAGION
KENO CAPITALISM
CITISTaT
Commudities
Cyburbia
Citidel
In-beyond
Cyberia
POLLYANNARCHY
DISINFORMATION SUPERHIGHWAY

existing urbanisms and epistemologies. The consequent neologistic pastiche may be properly regarded as a tactic of postmodern analysis; others could regard this strategy as analogous to hypothesis-generation, or the practice of dialectics.

Urban pattern and process

I begin with the assumption that urbanism is made possible by the exercise of instrumental control over both human and non-human ecologies (Figure 7.2). The very occupation and utilization of space, as well as the production and distribution of commodities, depends upon an anthropocentric reconfiguration of natural processes and their products. As the scope and scale of, and dependency upon, globally-inte-grated consumption increases, institutional action converts complex ecologies into monocultured factors of production by simplifying nature into a *global latifundia*. This process includes both homogenizing interventions, as in California agriculture's reliance upon vast expanses of single crops, and forceful interdiction to sustain that intervention against natural feedbacks as in the aerial spraying of pesticides to eradi-cate fruit-flies attracted to these vast expanses of single crops. Being part of nature, humanity is subjected to analogous dynamics. *Holsteinization* is the process of monoculturing people as consumers so as to facilitate the harvesting of desires, including the decomposition of communities into isolated family units and individuals in order to supplant social networks of mutual support with consumer-sheds of dependent customers. Resistance is discouraged by means of *praedatorianism*, i.e. the forceful interdiction by a praedatorian guard with varying degrees of legitimacy.

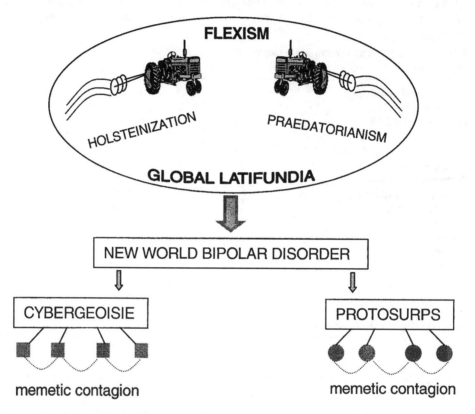

Figure 7.2 Postmodern Urbanism – 1 (from Annals, Association of American Geographers 88(1), courtesy Association of American Geographers, 1998)

The global latifundia, holsteinization, and praedatorianism are, in one form or another, as old as the global political economy; but the overarching dynamic signaling a break with previous manifestations is *flexism*, a pattern of econo-cultural production and consumption characterized by near-instantaneous delivery and rapid redirectability of resource flows. Flexism's fluidity results from cheaper and faster systems of transportation and telecommunications, globalization of capital markets, and concomitant flexibly-specialized, just-in-time production processes enabling short product- and production-cycles. These result in highly mobile capital and commodity flows able to outmaneuver geographically-fixed labor markets, communities, and bounded nation states. Globalization and rapidity permit capital to evade long-term commitment to place-based socio-economies, thus enabling a crucial social dynamic of flexism: whereas, under Fordism, exploitation is exercised through the alienation of labor in the place of production, flexism may require little or no labor at all from a given locale. Simultaneously, local down-waging and capital concentration operate synergistically to supplant locally-owned enterprises with national and supranational chains, thereby transferring consumer capital and inventory selection ever further away from direct local control.

From these exchange asymmetries emerges a *new world bipolar disorder*. This is a globally-bifurcated social order, many times more complicated than conventional class structures, in which those overseeing the global latifundia enjoy concentrated power. Those who are dependent upon their command-and-control decisions find themselves in progressively weaker positions, pitted against each other globally, and forced to accept shrinking compensation for their efforts (assuming that compensation is offered in the first place). Of the two groups, the *cybergeoisie* reside in the "big house" of the global latifundia, providing indispensable, presently unautomatable command-and-control functions. They are predominantly stockholders, the core employees of thinned-down corporations, and write-your-own-ticket freelancers (e.g. CEOs, subcontract entrepreneurs, and celebrities). They may also shelter members of marginal creative professions, who comprise a kind of para-cybergeoisie. The cybergeoisie enjoy perceived socio-economic security and comparatively long-term horizons in decision-making; consequently their anxieties tend toward unforeseen social disruptions such as market fluctuations and crime. Commanding, controlling, and prodigiously enjoying the fruits of a shared global exchange of goods and information, the cybergeoisie exercise global co-ordination functions that predispose them to a similar ideology and, thus, they are relatively heavily holsteinized.

Protosurps, on the other hand, are the sharecroppers of the global latifundia. They are increasingly marginalized "surplus" labor providing just-in-time services when called upon by flexist production processes, but otherwise alienated from global systems of production (though not of consumption). Protosurps include temporary or day laborers, fire-at-will service workers, a burgeoning class of intra-and international itinerant laborers specializing in pursuing the migrations of fluid investment. True surpdom is a state of superfluity beyond peonage – a vagrancy that is increasingly criminalized through anti-homeless ordinances, welfare-state erosion, and widespread community intolerance (of, for instance, all forms of panhandling). Protosurps are called upon to provide as yet unautomated service functions designed as to be performed by anyone. Subjected to high degrees of uncertainty by the omnipresent threat of instant unemployment, protosurps are prone to clustering into affinity groups for support in the face of adversity. These affinity groups, however, are not exclusive, overlapping in both membership and space, resulting in a class of marginalized indigenous populations and peripheral immigrants who are relatively less holsteinized.

The socio-cultural collisions and intermeshings of protosurp affinity groups, generated by flexist-induced immigration and severe social differentiation, serves to produce wild *memetic contagion*.[84] This is a process by which cultural elements of one individual or group exert crossover influences upon the culture of another previously unexposed individual/group. Memetic contagion is evidenced in Los Angeles by such hybridized agents and intercultural conflicts as Mexican and Central American practitioners of Afro-Caribbean religion, blue-bandanna'd Thai Crips, or the adjustments prompted by poor African Americans' offense at Korean merchants' disinclination to smile casually.[85] Memetic contagion should not be taken for a mere epiphenomenon of an underlying political economic order, generating colorfully chaotic ornamentation for a flexist regime. Rather, it entails the assemblage of novel ways of seeing and being, from whence new identities, cultures and political alignments emerge. These new social configurations, in turn, may act to force change in existing institutions and structures, and to spawn cognitive conceptions that are incommensurable with, though not necessarily any less valid than, existing models. The inevitable tensions between the anarchic diversification born of memetic contagion and the manipulations of the holsteinization process may yet prove to be the central cultural contradiction of flexism.

With the flexist imposition of global imperatives on local economies and cultures, the spatial logic of Fordism has given way to a new, more dissonant international geographical order. In the absence of conventional communication and transportation imperatives mandating propinquity, the once-standard Chicago School logic has given way to a seemingly haphazard juxtaposition of land uses scattered over the landscape. Worldwide, agricultural lands sprout monocultures of exportable strawberry or broccoli in lieu of diverse staple crops grown for local consumption. Sitting amidst these fields, identical assembly lines produce the same brand of automobile, supplied with parts and managed from distant continents. Expensive condominiums appear amongst squatter slums, indistinguishable in form and occupancy from (and often in direct communication with) luxury housing built atop homeless encampments elsewhere in the world. Yet what in close-up appears to be a fragmentary, collaged polyculture is, from a longer perspective, a geographically-disjoint but hyperspatially-integrated monoculture, i.e. shuffled sames set amidst adaptive and persistent local variations. The result is a landscape not unlike that formed by a keno gamecard. The card itself appears as a numbered grid, with some squares being marked during the course of the game and others not, according to some random draw. The process governing this marking ultimately determines which player will achieve a jackpot-winning pattern; it is, however, determined by a rationalized set of procedures beyond the territory of the card itself. Similarly, the apparently-random development and redevelopment of urban land may be regarded as the outcome of exogenous investment processes inherent to flexism, thus creating the landscapes of *keno capitalism*.

Keno capitalism's contingent mosaic of variegated monocultures renders discussion of "the city" increasingly reductionist. More holistically, the dispersed net of megalopoles may be viewed as a single integrated urban system, or *Citistät* (Figure 7.3). Citistät, the collective world city, has emerged from competing urban webs of colonial and post-colonial eras to become a geographically-diffuse hub of an omnipresent periphery, drawing labor and materials from readily-substitutable locations throughout that periphery. Citistät is both geographically corporeal, in the sense that urban places exist, and yet ageographically ethereal in the sense that communication systems create a virtual space permitting coordination across physical space. Both realms reinforce each another while (re)producing the new world bipolar disorder.

Materially, Citistät consists of commudities (commodified cybergeois residential and commercial ecologies), and the in-beyond (internal peripheries simultaneously undergoing but resisting instrumentalization in myriad ways). Virtually, Citistät consists of cyburbia, the collection of state-of-the-art data-transmission, premium pay-per-use, and interactive services generally reliant upon costly and technologically complex interfaces; and cyberia, an electronic outland of rudimentary communications including basic phone service and telegraphy, interwoven with and preceptorally conditioned by the disinformation superhighway (DSH).

Commudities are commodified communities created expressly to satisfy (and profit from) the habitat preferences of the well-recompensed cybergeoisie. They

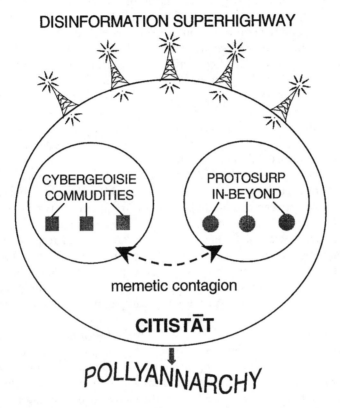

Figure 7.3 Postmodern Urbanism – 2 (from Annals, Association of American Geographers 88(1), courtesy Association of American Geographers, 1998)

commonly consist of carefully-manicured residential and commercial ecologies managed through privatopian self-administration, and maintained against internal and external outlaws by a repertoire of interdictory prohibitions. Increasingly, these pre-packaged environments jockey with one another for clientele on the basis of recreational, cultural, security, and educational amenities. Commonly located on difficult-to-access sites like hilltops or urban edges, far from restless populations undergoing conversion to protosurpdom, individual commudities are increasingly teleintegrated to form *cyburbia*,[86] the interactive tollways comprising the high-rent district of Citistāt's hyperspatial electronic shadow. (This process may soon find a geographical analog in the conversion of automotive freeways linking commudities via exclusive tollways.) Teleintegration is already complete (and de rigueur) for the *citidels*, which are commercial commudities consisting of high-rise corporate towers from which the control and coordination of production and distribution in the global latifundia is exercised.

Citistāt's internal periphery and repository of cheap on-call labor lies at the in-beyond, comprised of a shifting matrix of protosurp affinity clusters. The in-beyond may be envisioned as a patchwork quilt of variously-defined interest groups (with differing levels of economic, cultural, and street influence), none of which possesses the wherewithal to achieve hegemonic status or to secede. Secession may occur locally to some degree, as in the cases of the publicly-subsidized reconfiguration of LA's Little Tokyo, and the consolidation of Koreatown through the import, adjacent extraction, and community recirculation of capital. The piecemeal diversity of the in-beyond makes it a hotbed of wild memetic contagion. The global connectivity of the in-beyond is considerably less glamorous than that of the cybergeoisie's commud-ities, but it is no less extensive. Intermittent phone contact and wire-service remit-tances occur throughout *cyberia*.[87] The pot-holed public streets of Citistāt's virtual twin are augmented by extensive networks of snail mail, personal migration, and the hand-to-hand passage of mediated communications (e.g. cassette tapes). Such con-tacts occasionally diffuse into commudities.

Political relations in Citistāt tend toward polyanarchy, a politics of grudging tolerance of difference that emerges from interactions and accommodations within the in-beyond and between commudities, and less frequently, between in-beyond and commudity. Its more pervasive form is *pollyannarchy*, an exaggerated, manufactured optimism that promotes a self-congratulatory awareness and respect for difference and the asymmetries of power. Pollyannarchy is thus a pathological form of poly-anarchy, disempowering those who would challenge the controlling beneficiaries of the new world bipolar disorder. Pollyannarchy is evident in the continuing spectacle of electoral politics, or in the citywide unity campaign run by corporate sponsors following the 1992 uprising in Los Angeles.

Wired throughout the body of the Citistāt is the *disinformation superhighway* (or DSH), a mass info-tain-mercial media owned by roughly two dozen cybergeoisie institutions. The DSH disseminates holsteinizing ideologies and incentives, creates wants and dreams, and inflates the symbolic value of commodities. At the same time, it serves as the highly-filtered sensory organ through which commudities and the in-beyond perceive the world outside their unmediated daily experiences. The DSH is Citistāt's "consent factory",[88] engineering memetic contagion to encourage partici-pation in a global latifundia that is represented as both inevitable and desirable. However, since the DSH is a broad-band distributor of information designed prim-arily to attract and deliver consumers to advertisers, the ultimate reception of messages carried by the DSH is difficult to target and predetermine. Thus, the DSH also serves inadvertently as a vector for memetic contagion, e.g. the conversion of cybergeoisie youth to wannabe gangstas via the dissemination of hip-hop culture over commudity boundaries. The DSH serves as a network of preceptoral control, and is thus distinct from the coercive mechanisms of the praedatorian guard. Overlap between the two is increasingly common, however, as in the case of televised disin-fotainment programs like *America's Most Wanted*, in which crimes are dramatically re-enacted and viewers invited to call in and betray alleged perpetrators.

As the cybergeoisie increasingly withdraw from the Fordist redistributive triad of big government, big business and big labor to establish their own micro-nations, the social support functions of the state disintegrate, along with the survivability of less-affluent citizens. The global migrations of work to the lowest-wage locations of the in-beyond, and of consumer capital to the citidels, result in power asymmetries that become so pronounced that even the DSH is at times incapable of obscuring them, leaving protosurps increasingly disinclined to adhere to the remnants of a tattered social contract. This instability in turn creates the potential for violence, pitting Citistāt and cybergeoisie against the protosurp in-beyond, and leading inevitably to a demand for the suppression of protosurp intractibility. The praedatorian guard thus emerges as the principal remaining vestige of the police powers of the state. This increasingly privatized public/private partnership of mercenary sentries, police expeditionary forces, and their technological extensions (e.g. video cameras, helicopters, criminological data uplinks, etc.) watches over the commudities and minimizes disruptiveness by acting as a force of occupation within the in-beyond. The praedatorian guard achieves control through coercion, even at the international level where asymmetrical trade relations are reinforced by the military and its clientele. It may only be a matter of time before the local and national praetorians are administratively and functionally merged, as exemplified by proposals to deploy military units for policing inner city streets or the US–Mexico border.

An alternative model of urban structure

We have begun the process of interrogating prior models of urban structure with an alternative model based upon the recent experiences of Los Angeles. We do not pretend to have completed this project, nor claim that the Southern Californian experience is necessarily typical of other metropolitan regions in the United States or the world. Still less would we advocate replacing the old models with a new hegemony. But discourse has to start somewhere, and by now it is clear that the most influential of existing urban models is no longer tenable as a guide to contemporary urbanism. In this first sense, our investigation has uncovered an epistemological radical break with past practices, which in itself is sufficient justification for something called a Los Angeles School. The concentric ring structure of the Chicago School was essentially a concept of the city as an organic accretion around a central, organizing core. Instead, we have identified a postmodern urban process in which the urban periphery organizes the center within the context of a globalizing capitalism.

The postmodern urban process remains resolutely capitalist, but the nature of that enterprise is changing in very significant ways, especially through (for instance) the telecommunications revolution, the changing nature of work, and globalization. Thus, in this second sense also we understand that a radical break is occurring, this time in the conditions of our material world. Contemporary urbanism is a consequence of how local and inter-local flows of material and information (including symbols) intersect in a rapidly-converging globally-integrated economy driven by the imperatives of flexism. Landscapes and peoples are homogenized to facilitate large-scale production and consumption. Highly mobile capital and commodity flows outmaneuver geographically fixed labor markets, communities, and nation states, and cause a globally bifurcated polarization. The beneficiaries of this system are the cybergeoisie, even as the numbers of permanently marginalized protosurps grow. In the new global order, socio-economic polarization and massive, sudden population migrations spawn cultural hybrids through the process of memetic contagion. Cities no longer develop as concentrated loci of population and economic activity, but as fragmented parcels within Citistāt, the collective world city. Materially, the Citistāt consists of commudities (commodified communities) and the in-beyond (the permanently marginalized). Virtually, the Citistāt is composed of cyburbia (those hooked into the electronic world) and cyberia (those who are not). Social order is maintained by the ideological apparatus of the DSH, the

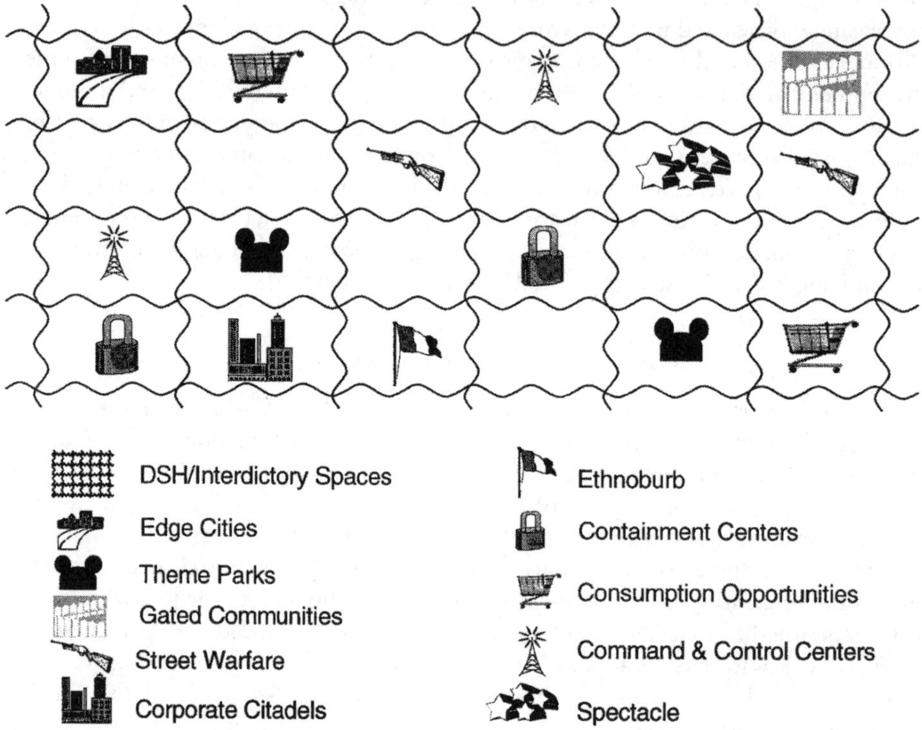
DSH/Interdictory Spaces
Edge Cities
Theme Parks
Gated Communities
Street Warfare
Corporate Citadels
Ethnoburb
Containment Centers
Consumption Opportunities
Command & Control Centers
Spectacle

Figure 7.4 Keno capitalism: a model of postmodern urban structure (from Annals, Association of American Geographers 88(1), courtesy Association of American Geographers, 1998)

Citistāt's consent factory, and by the praedatorian guard, the privatized vestiges of the nation-state's police powers.

Keno capitalism is the synoptic term that we have adopted to describe the spatial manifestations of the postmodern urban condition (Figure 7.4). Urbanization is occurring on a quasi-random field of opportunities. Capital touches down as if by chance on a parcel of land, ignoring the opportunities on intervening lots, thus sparking the development process. The relationship between development of one parcel and non-development of another is a disjointed, seemingly unrelated affair. While not truly a random process, it is evident that the traditional, center-driven agglomeration economies that have guided urban development in the past no longer apply. Conventional city form, Chicago-style, is sacrificed in favor of a

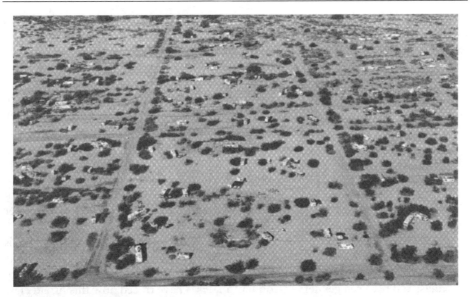

Figure 7.5   Slab City (Center for Land Use Interpretation)
Slab City is a community of mostly seasonal denizens, who live in RVs (Recreational Vehicles) and shacks on unregulated county property. Located at the site of a former military base, on the edge of the Chocolate Mountains (an active bombing range in the Imperial Valley), Slab City gets its name from the prevalence of concrete aprons – or slabs – at the site. A network of roadways and slabs accommodate a population of as many as a few thousand occupants in the cooler winter months.

non-contiguous collage of parcelized, consumption-oriented landscapes devoid of conventional centers yet wired into electronic propinquity and nominally unified by the mythologies of the disinformation superhighway. Los Angeles may be a mature form of this postmodern metropolis; Las Vegas comes to mind as a youthful example. The consequent urban aggregate is characterized by acute fragmentation and specialization – a partitioned gaming board subject to perverse laws and peculiarly discrete, disjointed urban outcomes. Given the pervasive presence of crime, corruption, and violence in the global city (not to mention geopolitical transitions, as nation-states give way to micro-nationalisms and transnational mafias), the city as gaming board seems an especially appropriate twenty-first century successor to the concentrically-ringed city of the early twentieth.

Invitation to A Postmodern Urbanism

Tell me, they'll say to me. So we will understand and be able to resolve things. They'll be mistaken. It's only things you don't understand that you can resolve. There will be no resolution.[89]

Our notion of keno capitalism is necessarily partial and positional, not a metanarrative but more a micro-narrative awaiting dialogical engagement with alternative conceptions of the urban, both from within Los Angeles and elsewhere. Although it is impossible for us to begin an exercise in comparative urban analysis at this point, we conclude with some general observations about a research agenda. Our knowledge of the literature suggests at least four broad themes that overlap with the substance of this essay.

(1) *World City*: In its contemporary manifestation, the emphasis on a system of world-cities can be traced back to Peter Hall.[90] The concept was updated by Friedmann and Wolff[91] to emphasize the emergence of a relatively few centers of command and control in a globalizing economy. Extensions and appraisals of the concept have been offered in, for example, Knox and Taylor[92] and special issues of *Urban Geography*[93] and the *Annals of the American Academy of Political and Social Science*.[94] A significant emphasis in the more recent work has been on the global-local connection, and on the implications of the sheer size of the emergent mega-cities.[95]

(2) *Dual City*: One of the most persistent themes in contemporary urban analysis is social polarization, i.e. the increasing gap between rich and poor; between the powerful and powerless; between different ethnic, racial, and religious groupings; and between genders.[96] Too few analyses have traced how this broad class of polarizations is translated into the spatial structure of cities.[97]

(3) *Hybrid City*: Another prevalent condition of contemporary urban existence is fragmentation, both in material and cognitive life. It has been noted by observers who place themselves both within and beyond the postmodern ethos.[98] Their concerns often focus on the collapse of conventional communities, and the rise of new cultural categories and spaces, including especially cultural hybrids.[99]

(4) *Cybercity*: No-one can ignore the challenges of the information age, which promises to unseat many of our cherished notions about socio-spatial structuring. Castells[100] has undertaken an ambitious three-volume account of this social revolution, but as yet relatively few people (beyond science-fiction authors such as William Gibson and Neal Stephenson) have explored what this revolution portends for cities. One pioneering exception is William J. Mitchell's *City of Bits*.[101]

Each of these themes (globalization, polarization, fragmentation and cultural hybrids, and cybercities) holds a place in our postmodern urbanism. But (as I hope is by now clear) none of them individually provide a sufficient explanation for the urban outcomes we are currently observing. A proper accounting of contemporary pattern and process will require a much more strenuous effort directed toward comparative urban analysis. Unfortunately, the empirical, methodological and theoretical bases for such analysis are weak. We lack, for instance, adequate information on a full sample of national and international cities, although valuable current syntheses are available in *Urban Geography*[102] and the *Annals, American Academy of Political and Social Sciences*.[103] There are a number of explicit comparative studies, but these tend to focus on already well-documented centers such as London, Tokyo, and New York City.[104] In contrast, the vibrancy and potential of important centers such as Miami still remain closeted.[105] Our methodological and theoretical apparatuses for cross-cultural urban analyses are also under-developed. Castells[106] offers an insightful engagement with global urban conditions, and the theoretical insights of Ellin,[107] King,[108] and Soja[109] on a putative postmodern urbanism are much needed excursions into a neglected field.[110] In addition, Chauncy Harris'[111] recent reworking of his multiple nuclei model into what he terms a peripheral model of urban areas reveals an acute sensitivity to the contemporary urban condition, but engages theoretical precepts quite different from ours. Finally, work on cities of the developing, post-colonial, and non-Western worlds remains sparse and unsustained, as well as being stubbornly immune from the broader lessons of Western-based theory – even though the empirical parallels between, for example, Seabrook's[112] "scenes from a developing world" and our construction of postmodern urbanism are striking.

Notes

1. Gibson, W, 1996: *Idoru*, New York: Putnam's, p. 39.
2. Mills, C. Wright, 1959: *The Sociological Imagination*, New York: Oxford University Press, p. 165–166.
3. Ibid., p. 166.
4. Raban, J., 1974: *Soft City*, New York: E. P. Dutton.
5. Ibid., p. 11.
6. Ibid., p. 15.
7. Ibid., p. 93.
8. Ibid., p. 129.
9. Ibid., p. 184.
10. Relph, E. C., 1987: *The Modern Urban Landscape*, Baltimore: Johns Hopkins University Press, p. 213.
11. Ibid., p. 237.
12. Ibid., pp. 242–250.
13. Ibid., pp. 252–258.
14. Ibid., p. 259.
15. Ibid., p. 265.
16. Jameson, F., 1991: *Postmodernism, or the Cultural Logic of Late Capitalism*, Durham: Duke University Press, p. 44.
17. Garreau, J., 1991: *Edge City: Life on the New Frontier*, New York: Doubleday, p. 3.
18. Ibid., p. 9.
19. Ibid., p. 116.
20. Ibid., p. 187.
21. Wolch, J., 1990: *The Shadow State: Government and Voluntary Sector in Transition*, New York: The Foundation Center.
22. Garreau, *Edge City*, pp. 275–281.
23. Ibid., p. 301.
24. Hise, G., 1997: *Magnetic Los Angeles: Planning the Twentieth-Century Metropolis*, Baltimore: Johns Hopkins University Press.
25. Waldie, D. J., 1996: *Holy Land: A Suburban Memoir*, New York: W. W. Norton and Company.
26. McKenzie, E., 1994: *Privatopia: Homeowner Associations and the Rise of Residential Private Government*. New Haven: Yale University Press, p. 11.
27. Ibid., p. 19.
28. Ibid., p. 184.

29. Ibid., p. 196.
30. Butler, O. E., 1993: *Parable of the Sower*, New York: Four Walls Eight Windows.
31. Cf. Ong, P., Bonacich, E., and Cheng, L. eds., 1994: *The New Asian Immigration in Los Angeles and Global Restructuring*, Philadelphia: Temple University Press; Roseman, C. Laux, H. D., and Thieme, G., eds., 1996: *EthniCity*, Lanham, MD: Rowman and Littlefield; Waldinger, R, and Bozorgmehr, M., 1996: *Ethnic Los Angeles*, New York: Russell Sage Foundation.
32. Jencks, C., 1993: *Heteropolis: Los Angeles, the Riots and the Strange Beauty of Hetero-Architecture*, London: Academy Editions; Berlin: Ernst and Sohn; New York: St. Martin's Press.
33. Ibid., p. 32.
34. Ibid., p. 123.
35. Park, E., 1996: "Our LA? Korean Americans in Los Angeles After the Civil Unrest", in Dear, M. Schockman, H. E., and Hise, G., eds., 1996: *Rethinking Los Angeles*, Thousand Oaks: Sage Publications.
36. Molotch, H., 1996: LA as Design Product: How Art Works in a Regional Economy in A. J. Scott and E. Soja (eds.) *The City: Los Angeles and Urban Theory at the End of the Twentieth Century*, Los Angeles: University of California Press.
37. Boyd, T., 1997: *Am I Black Enough for You?* Indianapolis: University of Indiana Press; Boyd, T., 1996: "A Small Introduction to the "G" Funk Era: Gangsta Rap and Black Masculinity in Contemporary Los Angeles," in M. Dear, H. E. Schockman, and G. Hise, eds., *Rethinking Los Angeles*.
38. Jencks, C., *Heteropolis*, p. 75.
39. Ibid., p. 84.
40. Cf. Anderson, S., 1996: "A City Called Heaven: Black Enchantment and Despair in Los Angeles," in A. J. Scott and E. Soja (eds.) *The City: Los Angeles and Urban Theory at the End of the Twentieth Century*, Los Angeles: University of California Press; Baldassare, M. (ed.) 1994: *The Los Angeles Riots*, Boulder, CO: Westview Press; Bullard, R. D., Grigsby, J. E., and Lee, C., 1994: *Residential Apartheid*, Los Angeles: UCLA Center for Afro-American Studies; Gooding-Williams, R., ed., 1993: *Reading Rodney King, Reading Urban Uprising*, New York: Routledge; Rocco, R., 1996: "Latino Los Angeles: Reframing Boundaries/Borders," in A. J. Scott and E. Soja (eds.) *The City: Los Angeles and Urban Theory at the End of the Twentieth Century*, Los Angeles: University of California Press; Wolch, J. and Dear, M., 1993: *Malign Neglect: Homelessness in an American City*, San Francisco: Jossey-Bass.
41. Pulido, L., 1996: "Multiracial Organizing Among Environmental Justice Activists in Los Angeles," in M. Dear, H. E. Schockman, and G. Hise, eds., *Rethinking Los Angeles*.
42. Cf. Abelmann, N. and Lie, J., 1995: *Blue Dreams: Korean Americans and the Los Angeles Riots*, Cambridge: Harvard University Press; Martínez, R., 1992: *The Other Side: Notes from the New LA, Mexico City, and Beyond*, New York: Vintage Books; Yoon, I., 1997: *On My Own: Korean Businesses and Race Relations in America*, Chicago: University of Chicago Press.
43. Such sentiments find echoes in Neil Smith's assessment of the new urban frontier, where expansion is powered by two industries: real estate developers (who package and define value), and the manufacturers of culture (who define taste and consumption preferences), Smith (1992), 75.
44. Sorkin, M. (ed.) 1992: *Variations on a Theme Park: The New American City and the End of Public Space*, New York: Hill and Wang.
45. Ibid., p. xi.
46. Ibid., p. 227.
47. Ibid., p. xii.

48. Soja, E., 1992: Inside Exopolis: Scenes from Orange County in M. Sorkin (ed.) *Variations on a Theme Park*, New York: Noonday Press.

49. Ibid., p. 101.

50. Ibid., p. 120.

51. The list of LA novels and movies is endless. Typical of the dystopian cinematic vision are *Blade Runner* (Ridley Scott, 1986) and *Chinatown* (Roman Polanski, 1974); and of silly optimism, *LA Story* (Mick Jackson, 1991).

52. Davis, M., 1992: "Fortress Los Angeles: The Militarization of Urban Space," in M. Sorkin (ed.) *Variations on a Theme Park*, New York: Noonday Press, p. 155.

53. Flusty, S., 1994: *Building Paranoia: The Proliferation of Interdictory Space and the Erosion of Spatial Justice*, West Hollywood, CA: Los Angeles Forum for Architecture and Urban Design, (1994), p. 16–17.

54. Ibid., pp. 21–33.

55. Cf. Klein, M., 1995: *The American Street Gang: Its Nature, Prevalence, and Control*, New York: Oxford University Press; Vigil, J., 1988: *Barrio Gangs: Streetlife and Identity in Southern California*, Austin: University of Texas Press.

56. Davis, M., 1990: *City of Quartz: Excavating the Future in Los Angeles*, New York: Verso.

57. McWilliams, C., 1946: *Southern California: An Island on the Land*, Salt Lake City: Peregrine Smith Books.

58. Folgelson, R. M., 1967: *The Fragmented Metropolis: Los Angeles 1850–1970*, Berkeley: University of California Press.

59. Cf. Bottles, S., 1987: *Los Angeles and the Automobile: The making of the Modern City*, Los Angeles: University of California Press; Wachs, M., 1996: "The Evolution of Transportation Policy in Los Angeles: Images of Past Policies and Future Prospects," in A. J. Scott and E. Soja (eds.) *The City: Los Angeles and Urban Theory at the End of the Twentieth Century*, Los Angeles: University of California Press.

60. Del Castillo, R., 1979: *The Los Angeles Barrio, 1850–1890: A social history*, Los Angeles: University of California Press.

61. Erie, S. P., Forthcoming: *Global Los Angeles: Growth and Crisis of a developmental City-State*, Stanford: Stanford University Press; Hise, G., 1997: *Magnetic Los Angeles: Planning the Twentieth-Century Metropolis*, Baltimore: Johns Hopkins University Press; Weiss, M., 1987: *The Rise of the Community Builders: The American Real Estate Industry and Urban Land Planning*, New York: Columbia University Press.

62. Tygiel, J., 1994: *The Great Los Angeles Swindle: Oil, Stocks, and Scandal During the Roaring Twenties*, New York: Oxford University Press.

63. Fulton, W., 1997: *The Reluctant Metropolis: The Politics of Urban Growth in Los Angeles*, Point Arena, CA: Solano Press Books; Sonenshein, R., 1993: *Politics in Black and White: Race and Power in Los Angeles*, Princeton: Princeton University Press.

64. Cándida Smith, R., 1995: *Utopia and Dissent: Art, Poetry, and Politics in California*, Los Angeles: University of California Press.

65. Deverell, W., 1994: *Railroad Crossing: Californians and the Railroad 1850–1910*, Los Angeles: University of California Press.

66. Fishman, R., 1987: *Bourgeois Utopias: The Rise and Fall of Suburbia*, New York: Basic Books, Inc.

67. Soja, E., 1996: Los Angeles 1965–1992: "The Six Geographies of Urban Restructuring," in A. J. Scott and E. Soja (eds.) *The City: Los Angeles and Urban Theory at the End of the Twentieth Century*, Los Angeles: University of California Press, pp. 426–62.

68. Scott, A. J., 1988: *New Industrial Spaces: Flexible Production Organization and Regional Development in North America and Western Europe*, London: Pion; Scott, A. J., 1988: *Metropolis: From the Division of Labor to Urban Form*, Berkeley: University of California Press; Scott, A. J. and Soja, E., eds., 1996: *The City: Los Angeles, and Urban Theory at*

the End of the Twentieth Century, Los Angeles: University of California Press; Storper, M. and Walker, R., 1989: *The Capitalist Imperative*, Cambridge, Mass: Blackwell.

69. Cf. Fishman, *Bourgeois Utopias*; Castells, M. and Hall, P., 1994: *Technopoles of the World: The making of the 21st Century Industrial Complexes*, New York: Routledge.

70. Cf. Wolch, *The Shadow State*; Wolch and Dear, *Malign Neglect*; Wolch, J. and Sommer, H., 1997: "Los Angeles in an Era of Welfare Reform: Implications for Poor People and Community Well-being," Los Angeles: Liberty Hill Foundation.

71. Cf. Knox, P. and Taylor, P. J., (eds), 1995: *World Cities in a World System*, Cambridge: Cambridge University Press.

72. Davis, *Chinatown Revisited*.

73. Ibid., p. 26.

74. Cf. Davis, M., 1993: *Rivers in the Desert: William Mulholland and the Inventing of Los Angeles*, New York: Harper Collins; Gottlieb, R. and FitzSimmons, M., 1991: *Thirst for Growth: Water Agencies and Hidden Government in California*, Tucson: University of Arizona Press; Reisner, M., 1993: *Cadillac Desert: The American West and its Disappearing Water*, New York: Penguin Books.

75. Cf. McPhee, J., 1989: *The Control of Nature*, New York: The Noonday Press; Darlington, D., 1996: *The Mojave: Portrait of the Definitive American Desert*, New York: Henry Holt and Company.

76. FitzSimmons and Gottlieb, *Thirst for Growth*.

77. Davis, M., 1996: "How Eden Lost Its Garden: A Political History of the Los Angeles Landscape," in A. J. Scott and E. Soja (eds.) *The City: Los Angeles and Urban Theory at the End of the Twentieth Century*, Los Angeles: University of California Press.

78. Pulido, "Multiracial Organizing."

79. Wolch, J., 1996: "From Global to Local: The Rise of Homelessness in Los Angeles during the 1980s," in A. J. Scott and E. Soja (eds.) *The City: Los Angeles and Urban Theory at the End of the Twentieth Century*, Los Angeles: University of California Press.

80. Hall, S. 1992. p. 280.

81. Dear, M., 1988; The Postmodern Challenge: Reconstructing Human Geography, *Transactions, Institute of British Geographers*, 13, 262–274.

82. One critic accused me (quite cleverly) of "neologorrhea."

83. Cf. Knox and Taylor, *World Cities*.

84. The term is derived from Rene Girard's "mimetic contagion" and animal ethologist Richard Dawkin's hypothesis that cultural informations are gene-type units, or "memes," transmitted virus-like from head to head. We here employ the term "hybridized" in recognition of the recency and novelty of the combination, not to assert some prior purity to the component elements forming the hybrid.

85. McGuire, B. and Scrymgeour, D., forthcoming: "Santeria and Curanderismo in Los Angeles," in Clarke, Peter, ed., *New Trends and Developments in African Religion*, Wesport: Greenwood Publishing Inc.

86. Dewey, F. and Rugoff, R., 1993: "The Floating World," *The Wild Palms Reader*, New York: St. Martin's Press.

87. Rushkoff, D., 1995: *Cyberia: Life in the Trenches of Hyperspace*, New York: Harper and Collins.

88. Chomsky, N. and Herman, E., 1988: *Manufacturing Consent*, New York: Pantheon Books.

89. Hoeg, P., 1993: *Smilla's Sense of Snow*, New York: Farrar Straus and Giroux, p. 453.

90. Hall, P., 1966: *World Cities*, New York: McGraw-Hill.

91. Friedmann, John and Wolf, Goetz, 1982: "World city formation. An agenda for research and action," *International Journal of Urban and Regional Research*, 6(3): 309–44.

92. Knox and Taylor, *World Cities*.

93. *Urban Geography*, Volume 17, No.1. Columbia: Bellwether Publishing, Ltd.

94. Annals of the American Academy of Political and Social Science, 1997: *Globalization and the Changing US City*, (May), Thousand Oaks: Sage Periodicals.

95. Cf. Dogan, M. and Kasarda, J., eds., 1988: *The Metropolis Era, Vol. I: A world of Giant Cities*, Beverly Hills: Sage Publications; Dogan, M. and Kasarda, J., eds., 1988: *The Metropolis Era, Vol. 2: Mega-Cities*, Beverly Hills: Sage Publications; Sudjic, D., 1992: *The 100 Mile City*, San Diego: Harvest Original.

96. Cf. O'Loughlin, John and Friedrich, Jürgen, 1996: *Social Polarization in Post-Industrial Metropolises*, Berlin: Walter de Gruyter; Mollenkopf, J. and Castells, M., eds., 1991: *Dual City: Restructuring New York*, New York: Russell Sage Foundation.

97. Ley, D., 1996: *The New Middle Class and the Remaking of the Central City*, New York: Oxford University Press; Sassen, S., 1994: *Cities in a World Economy*, Thousand Oaks: Pine Forge Press; Sassen, S., 1991: *The Global City*, Princeton: Princeton University Press.

98. Cf. Watson, S. and Gibson, K., eds., 1995: *Postmodern Cities and Spaces*, Cambridge, Mass: Blackwell.

99. Canclini, N. G., 1996: *Cultural Hybrids*, Minneapolis: University of Minnesota Press; Olalquiaga, C., 1992: *Megalopolis: Contemporary Cultural Sensibilities*, Minneapolis: University of Minnesota Press; Morley, D. and Robins, K., 1995: *Spaces of Identity: Global Media, Electronic Landscapes, and Cultural Boundaries*, New York: Routledge; Zukin, S., 1994: *The Culture of Cities*, Oxford: Blackwell.

100. Castells, M., 1996: *The Information Age: Economy, Society, and Culture, Vol. 1: The Rise of the Network Society*, Cambridge, Mass: Blackwell; Castells, M., 1997: *The Information Age: Economy, Society, and Culture, Vol. 2: The Power of Identity*, Cambridge, Mass: Blackwell.

101. Mitchell, W., 1996: *City of Bits: Space, Place, and the Infobahn*, Cambridge: MIT Press.

102. *Urban Geography*, 1996, Vol. 17 (1).

103. *Annals, American Academy of Political and Social Sciences*, 1997, "Globalization and the changing US City."

104. Cf. Fainstein, S., 1994: *The City Builders: Property, Politics, and Planning in London and New York*, Oxford: Blackwell; Sassen, *The Global City*.

105. Nijman, J., 1997: "Globalization to a Latin Beat: The Miami Growth Machine," *Annals of the American Academy of Political and Social Science*, May 1997, Thousand Oaks: Sage Publications; Nijman, J., 1996: "Breaking the Rules: Miami in the Urban Hierarchy," *Urban Geography*, Vol. 17, 5–22; Portes, A. and Stepick, A., 1993: *City on the Edge: The Transformation of Miami*, Berkeley: University of California Press.

106. Castells, *The Information Age*, vols 1 and 2.

107. Ellin, N., 1996: *Postmodern Urbanism*, Oxford: Blackwell.

108. King, R., 1996: *Emancipating Space: Geography, Architecture, and Urban Design*, New York: Guilford Press.

109. Soja, E., 1996: *Thirdspace: Journeys to Los Angeles and Other Real-And-Imagined Places*, Cambridge, Mass: Blackwell.

110. The collection of essays assembled in Benko and Strohmayer (Benko, C., and Strohmayer, U.(eds), 1997: *Space and Social Theory: Interpreting Modernity and Postmodernity*, Oxford: Blackwell) is an excellent overview of the relationship between space and postmodernism, including the urban question. Kevin Robins' valuable work on media, visual cultures, and representational issues also deserves a wide audience (e.g., Robins, K., 1996: *Into the Image: Culture and Politics in the Field of Vision*, New York: Routledge and Morley, D., and Robins, K., 1995: *Spaces of Identity: Global Media, Electronic Landscapes, and Cultural Boundaries*, New York: Routledge.

111. Harris, C. D., 1997: "The Nature of Cities," *Urban Geography*, Vol. 18, 15–35.

112. Seabrook, J. 1996: *In the Cities of the South: Scenes from a Developing World*, New York: Verso.

8

A Tale of Two Cities
1. Tijuana

"Tijuana is definitely postmodern."

Alfredo Alvarez Cardenas[1]

What can we say about postmodern ways of city-making? The remainder of this book follows two deceptively straightforward lines of inquiry: how does one read the city in an age when the urban grows increasingly to resemble televisual and cinematic fantasy?; and what does the politics of postmodern urbanism look like? The first of these issues is taken up in Chapters 8 through 11; and the second in Chapters 12 through 15.

Cities as Representations as Cities

In *The Truman Show* (Peter Weir, 1998), a young man named Truman Burbank (played by Jim Carrey) slowly uncovers a very painful secret: that his entire life is a television show. That he was raised by actors playing his parents; married to a woman cast as his wife; and sent out each day to live and work on an enormous, fabricated sound stage. His life, literally, was an on-going TV soap opera.

Already in 1961, Daniel Boorstin had warned of a society where fantasy is more real than reality. He described how the fabricated, the inauthentic, and the theatrical were driving out the genuine and the spontaneous until reality had been converted to stagecraft. And he cautioned:

> We risk being the first people in history to have been able to make their illusions so vivid, so persuasive, so "realistic" that they can live in them. [2]

Since Boorstin, many observers have commented on how the deliberate application of the techniques of "theater" to politics, religion, education, warfare, etc., have converted them all into branches of show business, i.e. the infotainment industry of Chapter 7. Neil Gabler describes entertainment as "arguably the most pervasive, powerful and ineluctable force of our time."[3] In what might qualify, he suggests, as the single most important cultural transformation of the twentieth century:

> ...life itself was gradually becoming a medium all its own, like television, radio, print and film, and that all of us were becoming at once performance artists in and audiences for a grand ongoing show...[4]

In short, Gabler asserts, life has become art, and the logic and rhythms of the entertainment industry are the controlling wellsprings of (American) life. He even suggests that entertainment unites Daniel Boorstin, Marshall McLuhan, deconstruction, and "so much of the general perspective we call postmodernism."[5]

This is a heady notion with deep roots in concepts of society as spectacle. What interests me here is one rather complicated corner of the "life as art" puzzle – how city life is represented, and how such representations themselves become guiding texts for emerging urbanisms. For example, what does it mean when Southern California is represented as dystopia or pollyannarchy? How quickly are we colonized by such caricatures/cartoons? And what happens when media giants such as Disney create the image, then the real-world prototype (Disneyland), which becomes the archetypal preference of millions of ordinary people (and manifest in the real town of Celebration, Florida, or Disney University)?

These are tough but slippery issues. I want to tackle them because: (a) they can teach us more (methodologically) about what it means to take a postmodern perspective on cities; and (b) they reveal further dimensions of the substantive nature of postmodern urbanism. I am here suggesting a further trope of postmodern urbanism: that televisual and cinematic representations of the urban increasingly define the physical form of the city. As cities become representations, so do representations become cities: cities as representations as cities...

To show this, I will extend my purview of little beyond the statistical boundaries of Southern California, to Tijuana and Las Vegas. Tijuana is south of the Mexican border across from San Diego, in Baja California, just over two hours' drive from LA (The State of California used to be called Alta California when it was part of Mexico.) Las Vegas, Nevada, is in the Mojave Desert east of LA, somewhat more distant, but still easily drivable in less than a day. Both cities sprang to life as offspring of the gargantuan urban appetites extending out from Los Angeles. Both are, today, among the fastest growing cities in their respective countries. Apart from these historical ties with Southern California, I am interested in both cities as exemplars of the "youthful" stages of postmodern urbanism. In this and the next two chapters, I shall build an argument about Tijuana and Las Vegas, uniting them as emblematic visions of the youthful postmodern city in which urban reality increasingly resembles urban fantasy. Linking these two essays (Chapters 8 and 10) will be a more discursive chapter (9) that forges a theoretical link between architectural spaces and film spaces.

Globalspace

The principal trope in artistic, cultural and intellectual representations of Tijuana is space. Spaces of the border, spaces of xenophobia, and spaces of liminality. In a 1930s documentary film of a US border patrol around Tijuana, two policemen are seen driving their vehicle into the desert. They stop at a pure white column, resembling an Egyptian obelisk but inscribed with the words "US–Mexico Border." They proceed to traverse the desert spaces on foot, occasionally dropping on one knee to inspect the sand for traces of *illegales, mojados*. They are like Indian scouts fleetingly the center of attention in a Western movie. Cut to a commercial silent movie, *Licking the Greasers* (also known as *Shorty's Trip to Mexico*). Here, *yanqui* cowboys rescue

Shorty's (Mexican) girl friend. As they high-tail it for home, they pass by the same white, border-defining obelisk and they are safe once again. The famous monolith in Stanley Kubrick's *2001* could not be a more potent symbol of spatial order and fealty.

During the past 150 years, political and economic relations between the US and Mexico have been characterized by an ever-increasing integration. The nineteenth-century pre-industrial period witnessed a border urbanization principally in centers that had been established under eighteenth-century Spanish rule, including Ciudad Juárez and San Diego. The growth impetus later spread to nineteenth-century towns established as civil centers and forts under Mexican rule, including Tijuana in 1840. And finally, after the 1848 Treaty of Guadalupe Hidalgo created the international boundary, it affected towns established as forts and supply stations (e.g. El Paso, Texas), and post-Civil War settlements such as Nogales (Arizona and Sonora), Tecate (Baja California) and San Ysidro (California).

Between the 1900s and 1960, the US economy moved rapidly toward industrialization, and inital linkages with Mexico were based on agriculture and tourism. Industrial growth and urbanization in the South West were rekindled after the Great Depression, and consolidated by World War II. Another boom (this time in agricultural employment) was stimulated by the 1942 US Emergency Farm Labor Program, also known as the *Bracero* Program. At first, the program employed about 50,000 Mexican workers in US agriculture; by the time it ended (in 1964) over 4.6 million contracts had been issued. Entire neighborhoods sprang up in cities like Tijuana and Ciudad Juárez, based largely on temporary residents. In the early 1950s, Tijuana was reputedly the fastest-growing city in Mexico. But in the recession following the Korean War, US unemployment rose and the government initiated "Operation Wetback" to return Mexican laborers to their homeland. Border cities

Figure 8.1 Tijuana Boundary Monument (postcard, Jesse Lerner)

grew at record levels as returning laborers resettled. In 1954 alone, over one million Mexican *braceros* were deported from the United States.

During the 1960s the global economy entered a period of economic restructuring, associated with international financial instability, the rise of competitive trading blocs, and the oil crises of 1973 and 1979. One of Mexico's responses to high unemployment was to initiate the Border Industrialization Project (BIP) which authorized the establishment of *maquiladoras* (assembly plants) in specially-designated zones. By 1992, there were over 2,000 such plants in Mexico, employing about half a million workers.[6] Several drastic devaluations of the peso also affected the industrialization process, and Mexican wage levels tumbled relative to the US The passage of the North American Free Trade Agreement (NAFTA) simply confirmed what was obvious to most border mavens: that the US and Mexican economies were increasingly being integrated and wired into the global economy. The spaces of the borderland became concrete manifestations of the emerging global-space.

Localspace

Globalization can be traced in Tijuana's evolving urban form. The city's five principal ecologies are: cattle town, border town, tourist town, industrial town, and emergent metropolis. Prior to the Treaty of Guadalupe Hidalgo, Tijuana was simply the largest of a collection of cattle-ranching villages stretching across the Tijuana River valley in Alta California. The dominant force in the region was the mission system. The treaty changed all this; the development and settlement of northern Baja California became far more influenced by the US than by Mexico. Tijuana's transition from a cattle town to a truly urban settlement was fueled principally by the economic boom in late-nineteenth century Southern California. Two wealthy Mexican families living in California (the Arguello and Olvera clans) realized that they could take advantage of the region's growth by developing lands they owned in Tijuana. The first plan for Tijuana was created in 1889, modeled after the plan for Indianapolis.[7] It consisted of a regular grid layout sliced at intervals by diagonal boulevards reminiscent of l'Enfant's plan for Washington DC and Haussmann's for Paris.

In the early decades of the twentieth century, real estate development was driven by the tourist economy, but only fitfully followed the formal plan structure. After 1916, when a racetrack was constructed less than one-quarter of a mile from the international border, Tijuana emerged as a playground for US visitors. Prohibition laws in the United States (1919–29) led to what has been called the "golden era" of tourism. Downtown Tijuana became awash with gambling houses, bars, cabarets, and prostitution. Then in 1935 President Lázaro Cárdenas ordered all gambling establishments to close, but it was too late to break Tijuana's ties with the United States. By 1950, the returning *braceros* had inflated the city's population to just under 60,000 people, more than tripling 1940 levels.

Between 1950 and 1980, Tijuana was one of the fastest-growing cities on the continent. By 1980, it had over 700,000 inhabitants, almost half of Baja California's population. About two-thirds of this growth was due to migration from the Mexican interior. Development was propelled by the expansion and diversification of the region's economic base, principally through the BIP-inspired *maquiladora* expansion. (Tijuana went on to employ almost two-third of Baja's *maquila* workers.) Other government programs provided further impetus, including the National Border Program (PRONAF) which was designed to beautify border cities in order to attract tourists. The Mesa de Otay industrial park just to the east of Tijuana was one such development; the redevelopment of the city's flood-prone River Zone was another. Set alongside these government-and private-sector economic development programs was the explosion of spontaneous *colonias populares* – irregular housing settlements established by newly-arriving residents who could not afford the high rents in serviced portions of the urbanized area.

By the mid-1980s, Tijuana and neighboring San Diego had effectively become a single functional urban region. San Diego was a sprawling, decentralized metropolis of 2 million inhabitants. Tijuana had a population of 1 million, its residents largely concentrated within approximately eight miles of the city center. Whereas San Diego's suburban expansion was relatively orderly, Tijuana's peripheral expansion was chaotic and dense. Nevertheless, a symbiotic pairing was established, as it was in twin cities elsewhere along the border (e.g. Brownsville-Matamoros, Laredo-Nuevo Laredo, and El Paso-Ciudad Juárez). As Larry Herzog observed,[8] these "transfrontier" metropolises embraced two contradictory dynamics: "the traditional cities, as defined by national culture, and the integrated metropolis, defined by evolving social, cultural, and economic processes that connect the United States and Mexico across the border on a daily basis." It is hard to predict which of these two cultures (national or migrant) will prevail, but Tijuana is already the most heavily trafficked border crossing in the world. About 50 million people make the crossing legally each year.

Filmspace/Borderspace

The spaces of the border, *la frontera*, loom large in the history of Mexican cinema. In her definitive study of the border in Mexican movie-making, Norma Iglesias identifies the characteristic obsessions of *frontera* films: migration, agricultural work, drugs, undocumented workers, poverty, and racism.

First period: 1938–69

In early Mexican films, the border was referred to simply as a place of transit, and migration to the United States became the central theme of movie-makers. The border was a place of danger, where hopes and lives could be realized or ruined. Images of loss and tragedy were countered by movies with more assertive approaches to Mexican cultural identity and nationalism. Typical of these was *Primero soy mexicano* (1950, Joaquin Pardave), a comedy about cross-border relations, in which *un pocho* sings of his true identity:

> *Si me gustan los hot cakes*
> *Digo hello sin dar la mano*
> *Y aunque pida ham and eggs:*
> *Primero soy mexicano!*

No hot cakes, sino tortillas,
Ham and eggs tampoco hermano;
Primero soy mexicano!
De esos que hay para semilla.

Ancho charro y no texano
Guayabera y no chamarra;
La moda a mi no me agrada
Primero soy mexicano!

If I like hot cakes
I say hello without shaking hands
And though I ask for ham and eggs
I am Mexican first and foremost!

No hotcakes, but rather tortillas,
No ham and eggs either, bro'
I am a Mexican first and foremost!
A prototype for future generations

Wide charro's sombrero and not a cowboy hat
A guayabera and not a dress shirt
Fashion means nothing to me
I am a Mexican first and foremost!

Toward the end of this first period, Mexican film-makers began to turn their attention to mimicking Hollywood westerns, which were to remain a popular staple of studio production until the late 1970s.

Second period: 1970–78

Mexican political reforms (*apertura politica*) in the 1960s and 1970s introduced a new dynamic into the local movie industry. Most notable was the appearance of films concerned with Chicano political movements. Westerns remained popular, and the earliest films on drug trafficking appeared. If the previous period of frontier cinema in Mexico outlined its basic themes, the second defined with much greater clarity the erosion of national and cultural identity associated with border cultures. To this extent, *el cine fronterizo* of the 1970s foreshadowed the development of "cultural hybrids" that were to become a dominant characteristic of present-day Tijuana.

Third period: 1979–89

In the last epoch identified by Iglesias, the border becomes predominantly a space where violent mythologies of the drug traffic are played out by *los hijos del controbando* (or, the Contraband Kids). The period also witnessed the rise of the sexy-comedia, which poked fun at US immigration authorities, *la migra*. One such movie was *Mojado...pero caliente* (1988) which promised provocatively that "to be a wet-back (*mojado*) is . . . Hot!"[9] A further thematic variation is the elevation of the tragic potential of the border spaces. The honorable struggles of poor people to improve their lives are presented against a backdrop of desperation, stoicism, God, and death.

El otro lado: Hollywood vistas

In Mexican cinema, the border hot-house produced a delirium of otherness with its own distinctive aesthetic. In contrast, Hollywood cinema tended to view Mexico and the border as an endless repository for cowboy and comedic adventures, at least until *Touch of Evil* (1958, Orson Welles). For the most part, it still does. But Welles' classic *film noir* altered this perspective irrevocably.

Adopting fairly conventional narratives of corruption, xenophobia, justice and betrayal, Welles conjures up a dark borderscape of claustrophobic intensity. Nicholas Christopher stressed that the "city as labyrinth" was the key to entering the psychological and aesthetic frameworks of *film noir*.[10] Welles represents the labyrinth both literally and metaphorically on the screen. The actual border is almost never visualized, as characters amble, stumble and run through anonymous streets. Janet Leigh, playing wife to Charlton Heston's Mexican cop, is literally led into an urban labyrinth for a fateful meeting with an underworld leader. Later, she is again led

Figure 8.2 The rhythm of cultural hybridity lies always in the potential for crossing, or not crossing, to the Other side. In *Touch of Evil*, corrupt cop Hank Quinlan (Orson Welles) looms in a doorway, blocking the threshold/border between the inner and outer worlds – a screening process reflected in both the mirror and our gaze (Universal Pictures; courtesy Kobal Collection)

(this time unwittingly by her husband) to a isolated desert motel where, in scenes shot with equivalent claustrophobic intensity, she is drugged and sexually compromised. And over everything looms the enormous figure of Welles himself, playing the corrupt detective Hank Quinlan. It is Quinlan who defines what passes as law in the city; it is Quinlan who casts the metaphorical shadow of a bloated northern neighbor across the border into Mexico.

Another paradigmatic moment in Hollywood's *frontera* history is *El Norte* (1985, Gregory Nava), which is actually about a Guatemalan brother and sister who depart for Los Angeles to escape political persecution. However, the movie's pivotal moments take place in Tijuana, where the couple patiently, desperately attempt to arrange an illegal border crossing. They finally cross over after a harrowing journey through rat-infested pipelines, an experience which ultimately has tragic consequences after the couple arrive in Los Angeles. More recently, Nava continued his bittersweet exploration of the immigrant experience in *Mi Familia* (1996).

Still, Hollywood has almost invariably viewed the border as a source of humor and bufoonery. In *Three Amigos!* (1986, John Landis), a group of Hollywood Western movie has-beens (played by Steve Martin, Chevy Chase and Martin Short) are offered good money to strut their stuff in a Mexican village. Only later do they discover that they will be expected to take on a vicious bandit who is terrorizing the village. Cheech Martin's *Born in East LA* (1987) satirizes border life in Tijuana and LA, discovering Mensa-levels of stupidity on each side as well as (naturally enough) redeeming doses of homespun humanity. More "serious" Hollywood westerns have blazed adventuresome trails into Mexico ever since Shorty went looking for his girl. Popular themes include saving a beautiful woman (e.g. *The Professionals*, 1966, Richard Brooks); escape from the law (*Butch Cassidy and the Sundance Kid*, 1969, George Roy Hill); and mercenary battles (Sam Peckinpah's definitive *The Wild Bunch*, 1969, and John Sturges' equally canonical *The Magnificent Seven*, 1960). In most of these movies, the border is little more than a narrative convenience, unless it affords the opportunity for some spectacular diversion (such as fording a rain-swollen Rio Grande, or mounting an ambush).

Thirdspace: *Culturas Hibridas*

Imperceptibly and almost without comment, Tijuana has emerged as the second-largest city on the western seaboard of North and Central America. It has done this though a fortuitous combination of proximity to a booming Southern California plus some home-grown political and economic strategies to encourage economic development. Now, as the world's attention shifts from the Atlantic to the Pacific Ocean, Tijuana's global connections will likely ensure that the city plays a significant role in the emerging Pacific century. At the same time, this openness to global trends has turned Baja California into a leading center of political ferment in Mexico.[11]

Commercial cinema on both sides of the border will take several years to catch up with the rapidly changing political, economic and social scene in Tijuana. In contrast, independent film-makers have already documented the sea-changes in Baja (so, too, have Mexican writers and intellectuals).[12] For instance, Frank Christopher's *The*

New Tijuana (1990) is an insightful overview of political ferment in the *colonias*: poverty alongside great wealth, the rise of the *maquiladoras*, the love–hate relationship with gringo tourists, and the urban redevelopment of the downtown and River Zone. Even more compelling is the evocative vision of border history in *Fronterilándia* (Jesse Lerner and Rubén Ortiz-Torres, 1995). In a lyrical juxtaposing of current fears about lost cultural identity and the Disneyfication of Tijuana, Lerner and Ortiz-Torres identify a second key trope in the burgeoning border vocabulary: the cultural hybrid.

Cultural production in present-day Baja California is a consequence of the tensions between the twin poles of Los Angeles and Mexico City, with Tijuana as their fulcrum. According the Néstor García Canclini, two tendencies embody the hybridization process: dislocation and deterritorialization, the former linked to migration, the latter to globalization. As a consequence, the paradigmatic emblem of contemporary border environments is the production of *culturas hibridas*. Tijuana, in Canclini's terms, is one of the major laboratories of postmodernity.[13] It is emblematic of Homi Bhaba's "third space," the liminal location between cultures, or perhaps Soja's "thirdspace." Guillermo Gomez-Peña speaks of the Tijuana-San Diego border as "the gap between two worlds"[14] – a metaphor for many things, including a literal crossing, a spiritual passage, and a place for struggle and transgression. Debra Castillo has captured the essence of the dynamic of hybrid cultures: the potential for crossing, or not crossing, to the other side is a constant presence in border-dwellers' lives.

An alternative mental cartography is thus being invented at the hybrid borderspaces. In it, national and regional identities, as well as other elements of cultural conditioning, are distilled and brought into question. Federico Campbell's writings are permeated by the enduring contradictions of Tijuana: between land and sea, United States and Mexico, fence and shoreline, English-speakers and Spanish-speakers.[15] Borderspaces are places where hybrid cultures are being constructed between

Figure 8.3 Tijuana – San Diego international border fence extending into the Pacific Ocean (Camilo José Vergara)

global and local spaces, and nourished in the liminal spaces of otherness. In the works of independent film-makers, we glimpse the unmasking of Tijuana as a future world city.

Notes

1. Cardenas is director of Tijuana's cultural center. *LA Times*, April 29, 1997, p. A-16.
2. Quoted in Gabler, N., 1998: *Life The Movie: How Entertainment Conquered Reality*, New York: Knopf , p. 4.
3. Gabler, N., *Life The Movie*, p. 9
4. Ibid., p. 4.
5. Ibid., p. 10.
6. Sklair, L., 1993: *Assembling for Development: The Maquila Industry in Mexico & the United States*. San Diego: Center for US Mexican Studies, University of California San Diego, p. 241.
7. Ramirez, D. P. (ed.) 1985: *Historia de Tijuana*. Tijuana: Universidad Autónoma de Baja California.
8. Herzog, L. 1990: *Where North Meets South: Cities, Space, & Politics on the US Border*, Austin: Center for Mexican American Studies, University of Texas at Austin, p. 140.
9. Iglesias, N. 1991: *Entre Yerba Polvo y Plomo: Lo Fronterizo visto por el cine Mexicano*, Volume 1. Tijuana: El Colegio de la Frontera Norte, p. 50.
10. Christopher, N. 1997: *Somewhere in the Night: Film Noir and the American City*, New York: The Free Press.
11. Rodriguez, V. E. and Ward, P. M, 1994: *Political Change in Baja California*. San Diego: Center for US–Mexican Studies, University of California, San Diego.
12. A definitive account of avant-garde film-making in Mexico is provided by González, R. and Lerner, J. 1998: *Cine Mexperimental/Mexperimental Cineria*. Santa Monica: Smart Art Press; for an interesting overview of the changing intellectual scene in Mexico, see Monsiváis, C. 1998: *Mexican Postcards*, New York: Verso.
13. Castillo, D. A. 1995. "Borderlining: An Introduction." in Campbell, F. 1995: *Tijuana*, Los Angeles: University of California Press, p. 19. See also Canclini, N. G. 1996: *Hybrid Cultures: Strategies for Entering and Leaving Modernity*, Minnesota: University of Minnesota Press; and Canclini, N. G. 1992. "Cultural Reconversion," in Yúdice, G., Franco, J., and Flores, J. (eds.) *On Edge: The Crisis of Contemporary Latin American Culture*, Minneapolis: University of Minnesota Press, p. 40.
14. Rouse, R. 1996. "Mexican Migration and the Space of Postmodernism," in Gutierrez, David G. 1996: *Between Two Worlds: Mexican Immigrants in the United States*, Wilmington: Jaguar Books, p. 248.
15. Campbell, F. 1995: *Tijuana*, Los Angeles: University of California Press, p. 13.

9

Film, Architecture and Filmspace

"Has cinema been the logical producer of Los Angeles, or is the city a mere projection in physical space of this singular industry?"[1]

J. A. Ramirez

If movies (and other kinds of representation) are capable of revealing new urban worlds to us, there are many questions about how such representations are achieved. In this chapter, I examine more formally the relationship between film and architecture (the built environment), and outline a concept of *filmspace* in which cinematic representation of urban spaces are manufactured. This will help show how postmodern cities are increasingly created out of representations of cities.

I begin with a vexed question: How do you recognize a postmodern movie? Everyone knows that Quentin Tarantino's much-acclaimed *Pulp Fiction* (1994) is postmodern, but why? Its habits of non-linear narrative, counter-climaxes, multiple plottings, elisions of time and space, and so on have been around since movies began. They are not so very different from equivalent techniques used in movies from Robert Weine's *The Cabinet of Dr.Caligari* (in 1926) to Robert Altman's *Short Cuts* (in 1994).

Giuliana Bruno's seminal essay on *Blade Runner* (Ridley Scott, 1982) is frequently cited as the first attempt to examine a film as metaphor for the postmodern condition.[2]

Figure 9.1 *Blade Runner* (movie still) Corporate control of the Citistāt, or global city, as imagined in *Blade Runner*. The pyramids of the Tyrell Corporation (recalling those of ancient civilizations) rise above polyglot streets of poisonous darkness and perpetual rain (Ladd Company/Warner Brothers; courtesy Kobal Collection)

Doel and Clarke especially isolate her references to spatiality (the city's architectural pastiche) and temporality (the film's fragmented experience of time) as emblematic of a postmodern sensibility. [3] Joel Schumacher's *Falling Down* (1992), about the violent demise of a laid-off defense-industry worker in Los Angeles, is also cited for its representation of the postmodern urban in terms of eclecticism, difference, and otherness – a city of stasis and rottenness. [4] But while these and other movies deal recognizably with what may be called the postmodern condition, do they possess a postmodern style?

In a critical study of social theory and the contemporary cinema, Norman Denzin is in little doubt about the influence of postmodern thought on such films as *Wall Street* (Oliver Stone, 1987), *Paris Texas* (Wim Wenders, 1984), and *Do the Right Thing* (Spike Lee, 1989). He identifies Los Angeles as the "quintessential postmodern city"; *Blue Velvet* (David Lynch, 1986) as the "quintessential postmodern film"; and Woody Allen as the "paramount postmodern film-maker".[5] Yet Denzin evades a clear prescription for postmodern cinematic style, relying principally on Jameson's specification of an "effacement of the boundaries between past and present (typically in the forms of pastiche and parody), and a treatment of time which locates the viewer in a perpetual present."[6] Denzin is more concerned to focus on cinematic representations of postmodernism which (he opines) fail to offer anything more than superficial solutions to the present conditions.[7]

Feminist film critics have grappled more successfully with the issue of postmodern style. Harmony Wu suggests a formulaic parody on Jameson's indicators of post-modernism:

postmodern film = pastiche + nostalgia + blurring of high and low culture + depthless-ness + schizophrenic experience.

A movie that matches these criteria is presumably postmodern, except that Wu insists that all these symptoms of the postmodern appeared in earlier eras (think of Hitch-cock's innovations in *Vertigo* and *Psycho*, for example, or the French New Wave of the 1960s). Wu regards the split between "classical" and "modern" film as more significant than any ostensible radical break with the postmodern. She appeals to Linda Hutcheon who locates the key difference between modernist and postmoder-nist film in the concept of subjectivity and its relation to a historically-determined ideology. From her analysis of the films of Gregg Araki, Wu concludes that:

postmodern film = city + style + queerness

since these three characteristics come together to display a distinctive postmodern sensibility. In the present context, we can understand queerness to refer to a broader idea of giving voice to the previously marginalized.[8]

A similar emphasis on recovered subjectivity is found in the work of Anne Fried-berg, who is at once accepting but also skeptical of the term "postmodernity." She recognizes that the proliferation of terms such as post-industrial society, multina-tional capitalism, society of the spectacle, and neocolonialism are attempts to describe the qualitative transformations of time, space, and subjectivity that char-acterize postmodernity. However, she prefers to conceive of a "gradual and indistinct tear along the fabric of modernity rather than proclaiming a single distinct moment of rupture." Consistent with the skepticism that I bring to the question of post-modern cinematic style, Friedberg concludes that the postmodern turn has had little effect on theoretical and historical accounts of the cinema, even though she concedes that there is a postmodern style or aesthetic.[9] Instead of a stylistic break between modern and postmodern movies, Frieberg appeals to another of Hutcheon's ideas, that of metareferentiality between the two styles. This emphasizes the constant re-telling that characterizes movie-making, but downplays the periodizing claims of postmodernity. Frieberg concludes:

> the subjectivity of the "postmodern condition" appears to be the product of the instru-mentalized acceleration of ... spatial and temporal fluidities. Postmodernity is marked by the increasing centralization of features implicit (from the start) in cinema spectator-ship: the production of a virtual elsewhere and elsewhen, and the commodification of a gaze that is mobilized in both time and space.[10]

This tendency is especially pronounced in an era when the cinema and television draw attention to the cultural centrality of the "mobilized virtual gaze."[11]

So: Is *Pulp Fiction* a movie in the postmodern style? Yes, of course it is. It deals with the condition of life in Los Angeles, the anointed postmodern city; and it has a style that is principally founded in a self-conscious irony and shifting subjectivities. As importantly, it is manufactured by film-makers who deliberately invoke postmo-dern stylistic references, and is viewed through a spectator subjectivity already alert to the possibilities of postmodernism. In short, it is context that makes it possible to define a postmodern filmic text.

Film Architecture

Over sixty years ago, Walter Benjamin argued for the constitution of the filmic as the modern critical aesthetic, and in so doing was instrumental in securing the link between film text and city text, particularly via his *Passagen-Werk*.[12]

> By close-ups of the things around us, by focusing on hidden details of familiar objects, by exploring commonplace milieus under the ingenious guidance of the camera, the film, on the one hand, extends our comprehension of the necessities which rule our lives; on the other hand, it manages to assure us of an immense and unexpected field of action. Our taverns and our metropolitan streets, our offices and furnished rooms, our railroad stations and our factories appeared to have us locked up hopelessly. Then came the film and burst this prison-world asunder by the dynamite of the tenth of a second, so that now, in the midst of its far-flung ruins and debris, *we calmly and adventurously go traveling*. With the close-up, space expands; with slow motion, movement is extended ....An unconsciously penetrated space is substituted for a space consciously explored by man.... The camera introduces us to unconscious optics as does psychoanalysis to unconscious impulses.[13]

Architecture and film, commonly referred to as the two "spatial arts," have tradi-tionally claimed center-stage in the film/city linkage. The relationship between them is often taken for granted, and yet it is highly ambiguous. Vidler claims that the "complex question of film's architectural role is again on the agenda." In truth, it never was off it, simply submerged under a welter of competing claims. One thinks, for example, of the cyclical recovery of Eisenstein's film theory, or of how film decor was a regular topic of 1920s and 1930s architectural mainstream. Vidler goes on to assert that of all the arts, "it is architecture that has had the most privileged and difficult relationship to film."[14]

At one level, there are obvious parallels between the manipulation of spaces in architecture and in film, as (for instance) in the literal creation and construction of film sets. Maggie Toy also referred to similarities in the perceptual experiences between the two media.[15] Yet while these linkages are frequently invoked, there seems to me to be an unmistakable asymmetry in the way each discipline approaches the other. Specifically, although architects frequently appeal to the filmic in both theory and practice, the converse is not always true of film makers and critics. This point has been made by Gibson:

> L'architecture, sous ses diverses formes, est l'une des matières du cinema, et ces deux arts, industrialisés, collectifs, automystifiants, ont beaucoup en commun. Mais les véritables échanges sont rares et chacun se nourrit des stereotypes de l'autre.

> [Architecture, in its diverse forms, is one of the elements of cinema, and these two arts, industrialized, collaborative, mystifying, have a lot in common. But true exchanges between them are rare; each nourishes stereotypes of the other.][16]

The resurgence of current interest in the connections between architecture and film is undoubtedly related to the rise of cultural studies. Already, slivers of a new synthesis are emerging, crystal-like, from the proliferation of critical studies.[17] Denzin identifies the pivotal significance of the "cinematization of contemporary life," in which "[r]epresentations of the real have become stand-ins for actual, lived experience."[18]

I want to examine the troubled relationship between architecture and film in more detail. Then, in the remainder of the chapter, I will introduce a critical third element into the discourse: *space-place*.

Architecture

In architectural theory and practice, there is a long pedigree of reference to film. For instance, Richard Ingersoll claimed that: "Architecture is the latent subject of almost every movie;"[19] and Ramirez leaves no doubt that the architecture of film is "absolutely central to an understanding of what...is happening in contemporary design."[20] Fischer has put architects on a par with directors and actors in German expressionist movies:

> Les architectes des films éxpressionistes ont la même importance que les metteurs en scène et les acteurs.

> [Architects are as important as directors and actors in expressionist films.][21]

Many practicing architects have sought deliberately to work in both mediums. Perhaps unsurprisingly, this interaction has been especially prominent in Los Angeles, in the work of inter alia Craig Hodgetts and Hsin-Ming Fung, Anton Furst, Frank Israel, and Syd Mead.[22]

In a concise historical overview, Vidler reveals the parallel evolution of modernism in architecture and film. A distinct theoretical apparatus emerged at the beginning of the twentieth century to posit architecture as the "fundamental site of film practice, the indispensable real and ideal matrix of the filmic imaginary, and, at the same time, posited film as the modernist art of space par excellence – a vision of the fusion of space and time"[23] Abel Gance, writing in 1912, hoped for a new synthesis of the movement of space and time. But it was Elie Faure who first coined the term that brought together the two aesthetics: "cineplastics." Ultimately such theorizing gave rise to the "totalizing plasticity" of German expressionist films, most notably in Robert Weine's *Das Cabinet des Dr. Caligari* (1919). Siegfried Kracauer comments on the "conspicuous role of architecture" in German films after *Caligari*, and how it expressed the structure of the soul in terms of space.[24] In *Der Golem* (Paul Wegener, 1920), a prominent architect, Hans Poelzig, was called in for the first time to design movie sets.[25]

From the mid-1920s, the more purely decorative and staged characteristics of expressionist film were denounced in favor of a greater realism. Kracauer, himself a former architect, argued against the decorative and artificial, favoring a critical vision of the real. He was especially enamoured of the street, with its potential for understanding the complexity of modernity.[26] The subsequent emphasis on physical reality led Erwin Panofsky to assert the unique possibilities of film "defined as *dynamization of space* and, accordingly, *spatialization of time*."[27]

Some of the earliest shots in this latest battle for the architectural mind have come from a diversity of sources.[28] Bernard Tschumi, Dean of Columbia's Architecture School, has made clear that: "The history of architecture is as much the history of its writings as its buildings".[29] And Andrea Kahn stresses the significance of the political in architectural space:

> all architecture...configures form and material in spatial constructs with ideological force. All architecture – whether it houses explicitly political programs or not – politicizes space.[30]

The emphasis on space is well-made. Feminist theorist Beatriz Colomina has demonstrated that space is not simply a metaphor for sexual relations, but that space is constituted through, mediated by, and constitutive of regimes of sexuality.[31] In addition, critic Herbert Muschamp has long argued that social and spatial forms are linked in more ways than architects traditionally recognize (through what some geographers refer to as the "socio-spatial dialectic"). For instance, in his analysis of Queer Spaces, Muschamp recognizes the transgressive nature of homosexual communities, and warns architects of the dangers of creating norms that at the same time define abnorms.[32] In an increasingly pluralist society, he cautions, too much emphasis is being placed on symbolic forms, and not enough on grappling with political and economic realities.[33]

In the history of architectural theory, postmodernism's obituary was written almost as soon as it appeared, and deconstructivism (that peculiar hybrid) never truly got a foothold. Now, as critics pick over the cemetery of conceptual corpses, hostilities and confusions proliferate. Jim Collins rues the disintegration of the project of postmodernism, which he claims has "boiled down to designer tea kettles or flattened out into coffee table books of simulated theory about America."[34] In other quarters, much effort is being invested in creating a "new urbanism," described by one of its organizers as "focused to the point of evangelism".[35] With its neo-traditional emphasis on garden-city suburbs,[36] the new urbanism seems little more than the last, lugubrious echo of the Ebenezer Howardists. The lack of a "grounded" (or contextualized) theory of architecture is the principal reason why I think the profession's current shift toward cultural studies and its rediscovery of movie and video culture are welcome trends.

Film

> There are people in the world who call themselves film architects. Poor people, who lead a strange life among diverse film artists – no one knows how and no one knows where. ... In no way are film sets architecture![37]

The history of film is replete with references to architecture. For instance, Eisenstein's classic work identified two paths of the "spatial eye:"

> the *cinematic*, where a spectator follows an imaginary line among a series of objects, through the sight as well as in the mind – "diverse impressions passing in front of an immobile spectator" – and the *architectural*, where "the spectator moved through a series of carefully disposed phenomena which he absorbed in order with his visual sense."[38]

In an essay on Piranesi, he went on to compare architectual composition to cinematic montage and develop a comprehensive theory of what he called "space construc-tions."[39] Yet, despite this early conflation of the two spatial arts, it is doubtful whether or not any real exchange has occurred between architecture and film. Take, for example, Andrea Kahn's critique of Jacques Tati's *Playtime* (1965). This is a film, she claims, where "architectural material...has a starring role."[40] Yet she is very clear about how Tati has constructed his cinematic Paris:

> Tati builds his city, unmistakably the city of Paris, not through recognizable monuments but through unmistakable movements. In a place constructed of illusive structure ... we find conclusive evidence arguing for the building body, and not, as we might think, the body of building ... The set (the buildings) is without character, but the space of action is teeming with site specificity. *Architecture, we learn, supports but cannot purport place.*[41] (emphasis added)

Ingersoll makes an analogous point, except that he identifies the essential unground-edness of cinematic space (and time):

> Architecture is the latent subject of almost every movie. The illusion of architectural space and the reliance on images of buildings are ineluctable devices for establishing mood, character, time, and the site of action in a film. In cinema there is fictive architecture in the tradition of theatrical *effimera*, and there is also the fictional use of real buildings. In both cases architecture is removed from the normal concerns for commodity and firmness to an accentuated cultivation of delight. *Film demands that*

architecture only serve the plot, and thus there are no constraints on structure or space.[42] (emphasis added)

It would be difficult to imagine a more surgical separation of architecture from film: all except the most abstract of architectures is inevitably place-bound, but cinematic conventions are aggressively tied to the compression, expansion, and even reversal, of space–time relations. And, as a consequence, there is a significant creative tension between "the place in film and the space of film."[43] Anton Furst, who won a 1990 Academy Award for his designs in *Batman* (Tim Burton, 1989), made an important distinction: "I translated images of architecture, not architecture itself, into set design."[44]

Contemporary film studies have stretched far beyond architecture for their cultural referents, drawing upon post-structuralism, semiotics, psychoanalysis, postmodernism and deconstruction, as well as from popular culture including video and rap music.[45] Jeff Hopkins captures some of the flavor of film's grounded theory:

> The pleasure of film lies partially in its ability to create its own cinematic geography, but so too does its power. The cinematic landscape is not, consequently, a neutral place of entertainment or an objective documentation or mirror of the "real", but an ideologically charged cultural creation whereby meanings of place and society are made, legitimized, contested and obscured. Intervening in the production and consumption of the cinematic landscape will enable us to question the power and ideology of representation, and the politics and problems of interpretation. More importantly, it will contribute to the more expansive task of mapping the social, spatial, and political geography of film.[46]

At the core of the search for a more grounded theory lies a crisis of representation in contemporary movie-making and criticism. Let me emphasize the obvious: that whatever appears on the screen is always a re-presentation of the "real." Nothing in the movie world is fixed or immutable. At its most fundamental, the space created by a film is simply the frame which, 24 times every second, passes before our eyes.[47] The composition and content of each frame are not random events, but as with any text the author cannot fully control the effect that each framing provokes. The quality of textual authenticity in representation is inherently unstable – which is, of course, precisely the characteristic that film-makers seek to exploit:

> The power of the film image to (mis)represent the material and social world lies...in its ability to blur the boundaries of space and time, reproduction and simulation, reality and fantasy, and to obscure the traces of its own ideologically based production.[48]

The power of the artist is, therefore, contingent upon the power of the spectator to experience a film critically, to engage in what Derrida described as an "incessant movement of recontextualization,"[49] (which, as I pointed out in the opening section of this chapter, is the key to unlocking filmic postmodernism). But we have to go beyond the simple equation of architecture with film; the two spatial arts need to bridge their dialogue with a third concept: that of place/space.

The Cinematic City

It is precise that "events take place."

Michael Snow[50]

City in film, film in place

Since his earliest work on the postmodern, Fredric Jameson has stressed the significance of architecture in unraveling the meaning of social change; he termed it the "privileged aesthetic language."[51] In a later work, he makes a sustained effort to connect film and politics, in part making use of architecture to affect the fusion.[52] Colin MacCabe isolates three concepts that are critical to Jameson's project: (a) the *political unconscious* which identifies the often opaque articulation between the economic base and the cultural forms; (b) *postmodernism*, being the cultural form of the current moment of late capitalism; and (c) *cognitive mapping*, referring to the intersection of the social and the political, and how individuals learn about, and function, in urban space.[53] As we saw in Chapters 2 and 3, Jameson believes that an individual's ability to cognitively map the current social experience is critically important in forging a postmodern politics. Yet he made little headway with the cognitive mapping project. I believe one reason for this might be his insistence on the value of architecture to the detriment of place/space.

MacCabe repeats the assertion that architecture is the traditional art "most fully integrated with the economy."[54] And Jameson himself makes much use of this perspective in his book's critical engagement with movies. For instance, speaking of *All the President's Men* (Alan J. Pakula, 1976), he refers to architecture as "of course supreme" in the film's narrative.[55] Yet he makes disparaging remarks about the more generic roles of space and place in cognitive understanding; referring to the methodological difficulties involved, Jameson claims:

> Space and demography offer the quickest short-cuts to this perceptual difficulty, *provided each is used as a ladder to be kicked away after it has done its work*.[56](emphasis added)

This seems to suggest that space is useful in outlining the rudimentary coordinates of human cognition, but may be discarded after its first rude sketches have served their introductory purpose. This is fatal to the task of cognitive mapping. The link between film and space is a critically important suture in understanding the creation of cultures and places.

In a most fundamental sense, the spatial problematic in human geography is concerned to understand the simultaneity of time and space in structuring social process. Unpacking this geographical puzzle is easier said than done. The surficial characteristics of everyday life are only crude caricatures of underlying structures. Yet the spatial organization of society provides many clues to related social processes; ways of seeing and representing landscape provide potent keys to unlocking the ground rules of the social order. In their study of the geography of film, Aitken and Zonn put it this way:

> The very heart of geography – the search for our sense of place and self in the world – is constituted by the practice of looking and is, in effect, a study of images.[57]

The potency of urban images in film is almost universally conceded. So effective has their presence been that Colin McArthur suggests:

> With regard solely to the representation of cities, there must hardly be a major city in the world which ... is not known primarily by way of Hollywood.[58]

The dialogic power of film to create the cognitive basis for our knowledge of the city is pinpointed by Jean Baudrillard:

> The American city seems to have stepped right out of the movies. To grasp its secret, you should not then begin with the city and move inwards toward a screen; you should begin with the screen and move outwards towards the city.[59]

Somewhat more prosaically, Anthony Easthope has generalized the three broad attitudes toward cinematic representations of cities: (1) the city is "simply there," as background; (2) a celebratory and/or utopian view of the city; and (3) the city as dystopia.[60]

Needless to say, the city in film carries with it a multitude of metaphorical meanings: e.g. as refuge, in *Enemies: a love story* (Paul Mazursky, 1989), *The Godfather* (Francis Ford Coppola, 1971), *Mi Familia* (Gregory Nava, 1995), and *Sophie's Choice* (Alan J. Pakula, 1982); and as progress, in *Berlin: Symphony of a Great City* (Walter Ruttman, 1927). It is extremely rare, if ever, that the city (or any other backdrop) is simply "there" in a movie. This would be tantamount to conceding the irrelevance or artlessness of setting. Usually, a city plays some more integral role in the execution and representation of narrative; it may even be the *sine qua non* for a narrative. For instance, in *Chinatown* (Roman Polanski, 1974), the physical expansion of urban Los Angeles is a vital plot mainspring. Woody Allen's beloved *Manhattan* (1979) and Mick Jackson's whacky vision of Los Angeles (in *LA Story*, 1991) are cinematic affirmations of city life. In contrast, Ridley Scott's *Blade Runner* (1982) is the concretization of everyone's dream of urban dystopia – again Los Angeles, this time in the year 2019. Other movies effectively juxtaposed utopian and dystopian visions of the city, perhaps most enduringly in Frank Capra's *It's a Wonderful Life* (1946).[61] And Paula Massood observes that cityscapes are recurrent tropes in African-American films which are concerned with "blurring the boundaries between utopia and dystopia."[62] She cites the optimistic and pessimistic views of life in the hood encompassed in the canonical visions of, respectively, *Boyz N the Hood* (John Singleton, 1991), and Allen and Albert Hughes' *Menace II Society* (1993).

Most critics concede that *film noir* occupies a special place in the pantheon of cinematic representations of the city.[63] Nicholas Christopher characterizes the American city as a "seedbed of noir," in which the "city as labyrinth becomes the key to entering the psychological and aesthetic framework."[64] Tina Olsin Lent identified six specific categories of urban setting used in noir films set in Los Angeles: residential imagery, topographical imagery, downtown imagery, landmark imagery (outside the downtown), industrial imagery, and Hollywood imagery.[65] Her view, like mine, is that the city is never a neutral background, but (usually at night) becomes a place of "danger and excitement, a wasteland and a carnival, and incipient dream and nightmare." Film classics such as *The Maltese Falcon* (John Huston, 1941), *Double Indemnity* (Billy Wilder, 1944), and *The Big Sleep* (Howard Hawks, 1946) hold a special place in the history of the city in film. Their legacy can be traced through to the current generation of movies, including Carl Franklin's wonderfully atmospheric evocation of Walter Moseley's novel *Devil in a Blue Dress* (1995), as well as in David Lynch's small-town noir epics, *Blue Velvet* (1986) and *Wild at Heart* (1990).

Christopher makes a strong case that *film noir* has periodically resurfaced in Hollywood productions during times of deep national stress. He suggests this is because noir is fundamentally "a way of seeing the world."[66] At the core of its vision is a certain cinematic style. Christopher quotes writer/director Paul Schrader to the effect that *noir* is:

> not defined, as are the western and gangster genres, by conventions of setting and conflict, but rather by the more subtle qualities of tone and mood ... Like its protagonists, *film noir* is more interested in style than theme.[67]

The series of essays on *film noir* edited by Joan Copjec seems to support this contention.[68]

Another way in which film is intimately tied to place is in the spheres of production and criticism.[69] The production of cultural objects cannot be separated from the place in which they are created. Thus in film studies, for instance:

> Certainly where cinema studies is practiced, where it gets produced, has everything to do with how it understands and writes history.[70]

Figure 9.2 Location shoot, Ocean Front Walk, Santa Monica (Michael Dear)
"The Industry" is a ubiquitous presence in LA, especially around the beaches. People live, in effect, on a movie set.

On the production side, Lent demonstrates how Hollywood cinema has mirrored both the golden and dark sides of the Los Angeles dream;[71] and Tony Williams argues that the return of Hong Kong to China "has seen the emergence of a particular apocalyptic and highly cinematic body of work responsive to a future historical situation."[72] However, as Paula Massood emphasizes, the transition from urban context to cinematic form is not always an unmediated affair:

> If one were to believe the plethora of images produced by mainstream Hollywood releases, Los Angeles is composed of Hollywood, Beverly Hills, and Bel Air, with a little Malibu and Venice Beach thrown in for a coastal touch.[73]

In addition, fashions change. Donald Albrecht has traced, for example, the rise and fall of the "celluloid city" of New York, especially as tracked by the rise of "Delerious Los Angeles."[74]

A complicated trialectic of film and power and place undoubtedly exists. Movies have always been used by the powerful to advance and consolidate their position; and minority voices have been systematically excluded. A brief but well-crafted account by Schulte-Sasse of the way Berlin was evoked in films of the Nazi era demonstrates this point very effectively. Before the Nazis came to power, their movies made explicit use of the antinomies between city and nature/pastoral life to advance a nationalist consciousness and political agenda within the country. Berlin stood as a point of reference, a "spatial metaphor for the threat of [international] capitalism" to German identity and security.[75] Common elements in the early films of Nazism were:

> the pejorative depiction of the nightclub ... the linkage of scantily clothed women and the capitalist "type," the predominance of foreign languages, foods, and drink, and of course the protagonist's revulsion.[76]

Such films allowed spectators a voyeuristic pleasure in the forbidden, but also a simultaneous feeling of indignation and moral superiority (partly directed against the city). They offered the message that Germany could only be saved by a "renaturalization" of the urban environment.[77] Schulte-Sasse also underscores that urban phenomena were viewed as feminine in fascist discourse, requiring a specifically male corrective action to overcome the city's decadence.[78] After the Nazis came to power, there is a shift in emphasis toward an external threat. Berlin, and especially the Olympic Stadium, acquire a fresh significance as collective symbols of German unity. The Stadium is especially potent as "a symbol both of containment – enhanced by its solidity and shape – and of ecstatic dissolution (*Entgrenzung*) within the contained boundaries, which allows the individual to merge safely with the whole."[79] (Not unlike a movie theater?)

Cinema city

Anyone even remotely interested in the relationship between place and the manufacture of film culture and criticism will inevitably encounter the work of Giuliana Bruno. Her *Streetwalking on a Ruined Map* is a brilliant reconstruction of the place–time of the films of Elvira Notari (1875–1946). In it, Bruno recounts Notari's film career in Naples, and incidentally portrays most of the elements of a spatial problematic of film. Bruno works on a ruined map because the documentary record is sparse (many of Notari's film have been lost), and adopts the streetwalking metaphor to emphasize her focus on female spectatorship. The fragments and silences surrounding Notari's history lead Bruno to an "archeological intertextual approach;"[80] she quotes Virilio: "The field of vision has always seemed to me to be comparable to the ground of an archeological excavation."[81]

Bruno takes her lead in space and place from Braudel, who wrote:

> For us geography will be above all a way of re-reading, re-estimating and re-interpreting ... Landscapes and panoramas are not simply realities of the present but also, in large measure, survivals from the past. Long-lost horizons are redrawn and recreated for us through what we see ... The value of geographical observation lies in the depth, the duration, and the abundance of densely-packed realities.[82]

Her analysis is consequently marked by "spatial practices and corporeal stories and forged by a topographical epistemology." She describes her purpose as:

> the reappropriation of geography in history, the redrawing of the cultural map as metonymy of fragmentations, the exploration of a territory of a subjugated popular knowledge, the mapping out of a scene of micro-histories in the terrain of cultural studies and through the lens of cultural theory.[83]

Notari's Dora Film company was a studio that made a cinema of the street. Movies were shot *dal vero* (from real life), using city views and street life as locations. "As film was implanted within the cityscape, the cityscape was implanted within film."[84] Bruno's own focus is on the "epistmological panorama" of female spectatorship[85] and the representation of female fantasy as spatial practices. Central to this construction was the role of Naples in Notari's cinematographic activity, especially the arcade known as the Galleria Umberto I (and its adjacent piazza) a place of open-air screenings:

> Cinema, housed in the arcade, was thus grounded in a locus of spectacle and circulation of people and goods, in a metropolitan setting of diverse social configuration – from those of a social elite and intelligentsia to that of the underworld.[86]

The genesis of Notari's Neopolitan cinema thus took place within what Bruno calls a new perceptual geography:

> Located in the arcade and around the railway, the art of motion pictures ... found in the cityscape its appropriate home. In Gaston Bachelard's phrase, the "unconscious is housed."[87]

At the core of this new cinematic urbanism lay the dynamic of mobility. Bruno refers to the notion of *transito*, for which no single English word suffices, but it is meant to convey movement, transition, transitory states, and circulation.[88] With echoes of Walter Benjamin (who also lived in Naples for part of his life), Notari's son Edoardo referred to the arcade as an *ombrello de pirucchi*, or umbrella for idlers.[89]

The arcade and the movies were particularly important in liberating women; the *flâneuse* shifted emphasis from the male gaze to female spectatorship and the spatial practices of transgression (leading ultimately to the *flâneuse du* mal(l) whom Friedburg describes.[90] As Bruno emphasizes, "the unconscious may be housed, but it is also moving." Cinema mapped a new "heterotopic topography" for Neopolitan women[91] where, to repeat Benjamin's phrase, "they calmly and adventurously go traveling." These observations recall de Certeau's spatial stories: "[N]arrative structures have the status of spatial syntaxes ... Every story is a travel story – a spatial practice ...geographies of action."[92] Together they evoke deep analogies from film to the urban and back again to everyday life.

The city of Naples provided the vital heart of Notari's films. According to Bruno: "The urban matrix produces Notari's narrative matrix in the sense that her films are always territorial."[93] Notari's travel stories were manufactured from the spaces of the city, including the royal palace and the street market, popular music and the newspaper's crime sheet. The social anatomy of the city became the corporeal geography of the film; each street was known for its practices.[94] Bruno is especially attentive to the ways in which Notari constructed female geographies and female fantasies out of the city and its maritime surroundings.[95] The city and its streets also became the locus of spectatorial topoanalysis, Bruno's term for the spaces of a spectator's engagement with the city through the experience of film. She defined this as: "the terrain of the cinematic apparatus, thereby expanding the range of its theorization and offering a reading of filmic pleasure."[96] Benjamin also commented about the special perceptual qualities of contemporary Naples when he and Asja Lacis coined the term "porosity" to refer to the fact that "the structuring boundaries of modern capitalism – between public and private, labor and leisure, personal and communal – have not yet been established."[97]

Filmspace, or A Spatial Theory of Film

Once spacing is introduced, as a sine qua non of linguistic expression and of sense-making processes in general, then the philosophies of language necessarily becomes a philosopher of spatial articulation(s). The task becomes, in effect, an architectural one, mapping out the limits and testing the boundaries of communicational space, or that of a plastic artist, exploring the relations among line, form, and shades of meaning.[98]

If film theory has any kind of unity, it derives (in Anthony Easthope's opinion) from rejection of the "naturalist fallacy" that dominated classical film theory in the past. The classical view was that film is successful to the extent that it reproduces the real world; this perspective was rejected when critics pointed out that film is not nature but culture, not reproduction but a sign. Since then critical theory has been directed at "not just the manifestly creative aspects of cinema but everything that happens when you enjoy a movie,"[99] The pivotal theoretical axes in contemporary film theory, in Easthope's view, are: "semiotics, theories of ideology, of subjectivity and of gender"[100] David Clarke reaches a broadly similar conclusion: "Today by far the dominant paradigm for the study of film covers a theoretical terrain triangulated by semiotics, psychoanalysis and historical materialism."[101] There is widespread agreement about these boundaries, although Lapsley and Westlake caution that diversity in discourse is needed, and care must be taken to avoid the totalizing nature of existing theoretical biases, especially psychoanalysis.[102]

Even though semiotics, psychoanalysis and historical materialism have radically different epistemologies and preoccupations, Easthope bravely concludes that contemporary film theory shares some common assumptions. These are:

- that the cinematic text should be grasped in its *full semiotic complexity,* including literal and symbolic meanings (present and absent on the screen), and that the film and human perceptions of the world are social constructs;
- that film is always *ideological,* dealing with power and offering a position or model/imaginary identity to the viewer for adoption (a process called interpellation);
- that film is a form of *fantasy,* offering scopophilic pleasures and meanings which require the use of psychoanalysis to understand how a viewer makes sense out of the barrage of images and sounds that comprise a movie; and
- that film is seen by a viewing subject as spectator, whose *subjectivity* is based in habits of film-going, the pleasures of the dark theatrical womb, and predispositions of the "gendered gaze" (meaning that women, men, children, gays, ethnic minorities, religious believers, etc., all see movies differently), even though a "sliding" between subject-positions may be "unstoppable."[103]

There is, you will note, no specific mention of space in this list of preoccupations, but this should not be taken as an absence of interest on the part of film theorists. Preliminary steps in this direction have been taken by Alexander Sesonske's series of articles on space and time in the cinema.[104] Sesonske develops parallel notions of normal (i.e. physical) space, screen-space, and action-space, which together define what he calls "cinema space;" and natural time, screen-time, and action-time, together comprising "cinema time." Mary Ann Doane has also pointed toward a more integrated theory beyond the mere instrumentalities of space in film. She identifies three types of space that are put into play in the cinematic situation: diegetic (the film's virtual space), visible (the screen), and acoustical (the sound in the theater). Together these define the "place where a unified cinematic discourse unfolds."[105]

The challenge of a fully articulated theory of film is expressed thus by Easthope; "The aesthetic text, including film, signifies all over, and film theory achieves maturity when it can respond adequately to that challenge."[106] For this challenge to be adequately met, I believe that a focus on place/space is vital. Geographers have begun to take film seriously and have extended consideration of filmspace. To date, two principal edited collections have begun to define the field, a pioneering effort by Aitken and Zonn, and another by David Clarke, which contains a number of essays by non-geographers.[107] Although I have alluded to a number of these essays already, in what follows, I shall draw most particularly on Bruno's study of Notari for a theory of filmspace.

There are four primitives in my spatial theory of film:

- *The place of production,* i.e. where the film is made. Just as the place-time of early twentieth-century Naples had its own conventions, panoramas, and observers

(Walter Benjamin and Benedetto Croce among them), so does present-day Hollywood.

- *The production of place*, i.e. the narrative conventions of the film. These embrace
  the spatial practices involved in creating of the corporeal geographies of the
  cinematic narrative (e.g. the use of the street, *dal vero*, and cityspaces); as well
  as the spatial tools of film-making (e.g. sets, camera angles, composition) used to
  create the epistemological panorama of a film's narrative.
- *The film text*, i.e. the movie itself.
- *The spectator*, the whole panoply of perceptual apparatus the viewer brings to a
  text, (i.e. the viewer's subjectivity in relation to the film, including especially the
  place of viewing, and the delights and dangers of fantasy, flânerie, *transito*.

Broadly speaking, the film text is the nexus between the production and consumption sides of the theory (Figure 9.3).

A *viewer* is someone who watches a movie simply for pleasure; a *critic* views for
professional reasons of one kind or another (e.g. journalism, scholarship). Spectators
(a category taken to include viewers and critics) occupy two basic geographic locales:
the screening site, and their subjective positionality. For most people, the act of going
out to a movie theater and sitting for a couple of hours in the dark staring at a screen
with moving images among a host of other terrified, tearful, or laughing people is a
pleasurable experience.[108] Segregated from the screen, yet contained within the
theatrical womb, the *consumer in place* simultaneously experiences detachment
and belonging. On the other hand, sitting at home alone with your VCR is an
entirely different *cartography*, with its own distractions and pleasures, like being
able to rewind and play again the scenes that you just enjoyed.

One of the strongest themes in contemporary film scholarship is the subjectivity of
the viewer, who arrives at the screening site with a complex, internalized cartography

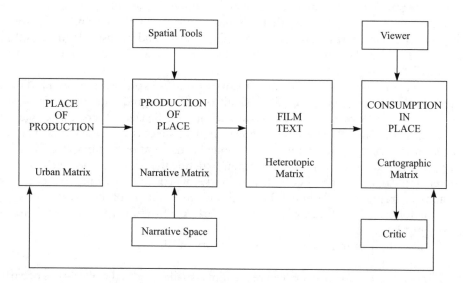

Figure 9.3   A Theory of Filmspace (Michael Dear)

of presuppositions and prejudices. These biases are captured in the phrase the "gendered gaze," which although it was originally intended to distinguish between female and male ways of seeing, may also be taken to stand for the multitude of different ways of seeing. The biases of gaze interact with what is being screened to produce pleasure and meaning. However, Laura Mulvey has emphasized how the quickly the voyeuristic gaze can shift to becoming a fetishistic scopophila, especially in portrayals of the female body.[109] (It was not for nothing that the night club in Kathryn Bigelow's *Strange Days*, 1995, was named "The Retinal Fetish.") The production of meaning is, needless to say, complicated by the cinematic conventions used in producing a movie. Viewer pleasure might derive from knowing these conventions, but also from unexpected breaches of convention.

The critical gaze is subject to analogous perceptual and situational biases that of as the casual viewer, but also to the critics' own theoretical apparatuses and situatedness. A contemplative scholar is likely to approach the critical exercise diffently from a journalist with an urgent deadline; and critical conventions in Los Angeles are different from those in Paris or Melbourne. We should also beware of those who occupy what Rosalyn Deutsche refers to as "commanding positions" on the battleground of representation, because the coherence in such positions has usually been won at the expense of silencing other voices.[110]

The narrative conventions of a movie text largely derive from the *production of place*. They can give rise to the comfortably familiar – the Paris of Jacques Tati, the Hong Kong of Jackie Chan, or the Rome of Charlton Heston – as well as the deliberately deranged. There are dual aspects to this production process: the techniques of spatiality used by film-makers (their *spatial tools*), and the actual filmic spaces on the screen that are produced by those tools. The spatial tools are a box of tricks used by the film-maker to produce a required representational space. Such techniques include the use of camera angles (high, level, low); depth of focus; framing (e.g. close-up); camera mobility; altered motion (slow, accelerated, reverse, etc.), special lenses and other special effects; and lighting.[111] The list of such basic building blocks is long, and all the tools can be regarded as having at least a potential effect on the production of the narrative spaces on the screen. Edward Dimendberg identifed "the three great variables – territory, communication, and speed" that must be controlled; they define a "centrifugal space" that create spatial forms which "exceed received understandings of the architectural."[112]

The construction of *narrative space* lies at the core of a spatial problematic of film. It is surprising, therefore, that so little has been written about it. Discussions invariably fall back on Stephen Heath's excellent 1976 article entitled "Narrative Space."[113] The construction of the narrative matrix begins with the framing of the actors and action, sets and lighting, etc. to produce the *mise-en-scène*, or the art of the image. The techniques of spatiality are crucially important in this exercise. Derrida draws attention to the role of "spacing" (*éspacement*) in language. In *Of Grammatology*,[114] he showed how in its material form of writing, language always entails a spacing that works at a remove from its author. In film, distance between observer and observed is principally created by the camera. Kracauer has suggested that "distance is necessary to lessen the shock that would result from the spectator's direct confrontation with certain phenomena."[115] In the case of pornography, for instance, the camera plays off spectator fear of crudity, coarseness, and sexuality. The camera becomes a device for creating distance and the medium of a harmless voyeurism.[116] Yet in the Canadian anti-pornographic movie, *Not a Love Story* (Bonnie Sher Klein, 1981), camera distance is deliberately foreshortened to confront the viewer with pornographic representations. Mary Ann Doane[117] makes the case that female specificity is theorized in terms of "spatial proximity" and the dynamics of fetished looking (think, for example, of the extreme close-up of Isabella Rosellini's rouged lips in *Blue Velvet*, as she pleads "Hit me," to her abusive lovers.)

Other examples of narrative spatiality are discussed in an insightful essay by Wolgang Natter in his analysis of Walter Ruttman's *Berlin, Symphony of a Great City* (1927). Natter observes how a shot (an uninterrupted sequence of film time) differs from a cut (an instantaneous change from one shot to another), and thus "thoroughly defines film as spatial."[118] The close-up and its connections to medium- and long-shots also renders scale an important element of filmic spatiality. Natter concludes: "The passage from place to cinematic space is marked not by repetition, but by alterity, whose visual element is the fragment."[119] Similar effects are often attempted in manufacturing the movie image, as for instance in the placing of actors within the frame, who are thus accorded more or less weight in our perspective on the action. Lighting, sets and scenography also have powerful effects on structuring the cinematic experience. Such literal distancing has broader connections to theory. For instance, Iain Chambers (discussing the possibilities of criticizing the present) recommends immersing oneself in the local while also observing from a distance.[120] "Distance" in this context is provided by the use of theory. Both local immersion and a more distant theoretical stance are needed for understanding a text.

The third component of filmspace is the *place of production* (Figure 9.3). This refers generically to the broad context for film production. Film-making conventions differ from place to place, as do audience expectations, conditions of film financing and distribution, and so on. These material and interpretive variations will have a significant effect on local practices. As we have seen, stressful times in a national economy will tend to be accompanied by increased output of *films noir*; and movies made in Hollywood's postmodern place-time will differ from those of India or Weimar Germany. Another important geographical question is the simple availability of movie screens. In Los Angeles, for instance, the enormous glut of movie houses cannot hide the paucity of foreign film released in the city. Outside the major metropolitan areas, most movies (irrespective of source) remain unscreened. The questions of marketing and distribution of film are significant part of my spatial problematic, but the topic is too large to go into at this point. A very good introduction to "Hollywood" in all its glory is given by Richard Maltby,[121] and some of the best accounts of independent film-making in Los Angeles are those by David James.[122]

The three elements I have so far described are linked by the dynamic of viewing of the *film text*, during which spectators enter into an *heterotopic cartography* of their own making. They calmly and adventuresomely go traveling in the movie's virtual geographies. Everything comes together at this moment – the production process and artistry, the film distribution system, and the movie-goers preferences and pleasures. But things do not end there, just as they come together. Quite the contrary. The heterotopic experience will alter the spectators' perceptions, perhaps briefly, even permanently. Thus, in Figure 9.3, the hatched lines returning from the film to the broader context of urban life underscores the dialogical relationship between seeing and living. It recalls the Bakhtinian "chronotope," i.e. that which oscillates between (literary) representation and the space–time of everyday life. It exactly invokes Bruno's *spectatorial topoanalysis*, referring to the change in viewers' engagement with the city and streets of Naples as a consequence of movie-going. In this way, the film fantasy contextualizes the subsequent experience of reality. Needless to say, most movies are instantly forgotten. But whether their makers intend them this way or not, certain movies lodge in our conscious and subconscious, later to frame the way we perceive, think, and act. In other words, our desires and actions become conditioned by the movies and similar forms of entertainment. We may even go on to imagine and create a life, a city, that mimics the movies...[123]

Figure 9.4/a–b   Police evict squatters from house near Munt-Plein, Amsterdam, 1998 (Michael Dear)
(left) Police secure the street and hoist a container up to the top floor of the building to invade, after it and its occupants had been thoroughly doused by water canon.
(right) The eviction was to permit demolition of the property, and the construction of a multiple-screen movie theatre complex. The sign hung from the building read: "PATHE CINEMA presents THE EVICTION – How 15 people became homeless because a cinema is more important. Based on a true story."

Notes

1. Ramirez, J. A., 1992: "Ten Lessons (or Commandments) about Architecture and the Cinema," *Design Book Review*, Spring, p. 12

2. Bruno, G., 1987: "Ramble City: Postmodernism and *Blade Runner*", *October* 41: pp. 61–74.

3. Doel, M. A. and Clark, D. B., 1997: "From Ramble City to the Screening of the Eye: *Blade Runner*, Death and Symbolic Exchange", in Clarke, D. B. (ed.): *The Cinematic City*, New York: Routledge.

4. Mahoney, E., 1997: "The People in Parenthesis: Space Under Pressure in the Postmodern City," in Clarke, D. B. (ed.): *The Cinematic City*, pp. 173–4.

5. Denzin, N. K., 1991: *Images of Postmodern Society: Social Theory and Contemporary Cinema*. London; Newbury Park: Sage Publications, see respectively pp. 33, 65, and xi

6. Ibid., p. 68.

7. Ibid., p. 150.

8. Wu (personal communication); Wu, H., 1997: "Queering L.A.: Gregg Araki's Hero-Pomo Cinema-City," *Spectator* 18(1), p. 58–69; see also Hutcheon, Linda, 1990: *The Politics of Postmodernism*, London; New York: Routledge.

9. Friedberg, A., 1993: *Window Shopping: Cinema and the Postmodern*. Berkeley: University of California Press, p. 7.

10. Ibid., p. 179.

11. Ibid., p. 2.

12. Buck-Morss, S., 1989: *The Dialectics of Seeing: Walter Benjamin and the Arcades Project*, Cambridge: MIT Press.

13. Walter Benjamin, quoted in Vidler, A., 1993: "The Explosion of Space: Architecture and The Filmic Imaginary," *Assemblage* 21, p. 43, my emphasis.

14. Vidler, A., 1993: "The Explosion of Space: Architecture and The Filmic Imaginary," *Assemblage* 21, p. 43.

15. Toy, M. (ed.), 1994: *Architecture and Film*. London: Academy Editions; New York: St. Martin's Press, p. 7.

16. Gibson, B., 1984: "Architecture et Cinema," *Images et Imaginaires d'Architecture*. Paris: Centre National d'Art et de Culture George Pompidou, p. 113.

17. See especially Colomina, B., 1992: *Sexuality and Space*, New York: Princeton Architectural Press; Jameson, F., 1992: *The Geopolitical Aesthetic: Cinema and Space in the World System*. Bloomington: Indiana University Press; London: British Film Institute.

18. Denzin, N. K., *Images of Postmodern Society*, p. x.

19. Ingersoll, R., 1992: "Cinemarchitecture," *Design Book Review*, Spring, p. 5.

20. Ramirez, J. A., 1992: "Ten Lessons (or Commandments) about Architecture and the Cinema," *Design Book Review*, Spring, p. 9.

21. Fischer, V., 1984: "Le Décor, Element de Psychogramme sur Architecture dans le Film Expressioniste," *Images et Imaginaires d'Architecture*. Paris: Centre National d'Art et de Culture George Pompidou., p. 110.

22. Giovanni, J., 1994: "LA Architects: They Did It Their Way," *Los Angeles Times Magazine*, May 15.

23. Vidler, A., "The Explosion of Space," p. 40.

24. Kracauer, Siegfried., 1947: *From Caligari to Hitler: A Psychological History of the German Film*, Princeton: Princeton University Press, p. 75; Rotha, P., 1930: *The Film Till Now: A Survey of the Cinema*, London: Jonathan Cape.

25. Neumann, Dietrich (ed.), 1996: *Film Architecture: Set Designs from Metropolis to Blade Runner*, Munich; New York: Prestel.

26. Neumann, Dietrich (ed.), *Film Architecture*, p. 19; also see Kaes, Anton, 1996: *The Weimar Republic Sourcebook*, Berkeley: University of California Press, on the use of the street in Weimar film.
27. Quoted in Vidler, A., "The Explosion of Space," p. 50, my emphasis.
28. See, for example, Agrest, D. I., 1991: *Architecture From Without: Theoretical Framings for a Critical Practice*, Cambridge: MIT Press; Ockman, J., 1993: *Architecture Culture, 1943–1968: A Documentary Anthology*, with the collaboration of Edward Eigen, New York: Columbia University Graduate School of Architecture, Planning, and Preservation: Rizzoli.
29. Tschumi, B., 1993: "Foreword," in Ockman J. (ed.), *Architecture Culture 1943–1968*, New York: Rizzoli, p. 11.
30. Kahn, Andrea, 1991: *Drawing/Building/Text: Essays in Architectural Theory*, New York: Princeton Architectural Press, p. 109.
31. Colomina, B., *Sexuality and Space*.
32. Muschamp, H., 1994: "Designing a Framework for Diversity," *New York Times*, June 19, p. 34.
33. Ibid., p. 36.
34. Collins, J., 1991: "A Clear Vista of the Edge of Civilization: Urbanism, Mass Culture and True Stories," *Cinema and Architecture*, Paris: Iris., p. 127.
35. Solomon, D., 1994: "Rallying Around the New Urbanism," *Places* 9(1), p. 74.
36. Katz, P., 1994: *The New Urbanism: Toward an Architecture of Community*, New York: McGraw-Hill.
37. Walter Reimann (1926); quoted in Neumann, Dietrich (ed.), *Film Architecture*, p. 193.
38. Vidler, A., "The Explosion of Space," p. 56.
39. Ibid., p. 55.
40. Kahn, 1992, p. 22.
41. Ibid., p. 27.
42. Ingersoll, R., "Cinemarchitecture," p. 5.
43. Aitken, S. C. and Zonn, L. E. (eds), 1994: *Place, Power, Situation, and Spectacle: A Geography of Film*, Lanham: Rowman & Littlefield, p. 17.
44. Quoted in Neumann, Dietrich (ed.), 1996: *Film Architecture: Set Designs from Metropolis to Blade Runner*, Munich; New York: Prestel, p. 162.
45. Cf. Boyd, T., 1997: *Am I Black Enough For You?: Popular Culture from the 'Hood and Beyond'*, Bloomington: Indiana University Press; Colomina, B., 1992: *Sexuality and Space*; Easthope, A. (ed.), 1993: *Contemporary Film Theory*, London; New York: Longman; and Denzin, N. K., *Images of Postmodern Society*.
46. Hopkins, J., 1994: "A Mapping of Cinematic Places," in Aitken, S. C. and Zonn, L. E. (eds), *Place, Power, Situation, and Spectacle*, p. 47.
47. Aitken, S. C. and Zonn, L. E. (eds), *Place, Power, Situation, and Spectacle*, p. 15.
48. Hopkins, J., "A Mapping of Cinematic Places," p. 48.
49. Quoted in Natter, W., 1994: "The City as Cinematic space: Modernism and Place in Berlin, Symphony of a Great City," in Aitken, S. C. and Zonn, L. E. (eds), *Place, Power, Situation, and Spectacle*, p. 205.
50. Quoted in Heath, 1981, p. 24.
51. Jameson, F., 1991: *Postmodernism, or the Cultural Logic of Late Capitalism*, Durham: Duke University Press, p. 37.
52. Jameson, F., *The Geopolitical Aesthetic*.
53. MacCabe, Colin, 1992: "Preface," in Jameson, F. *The Geopolitical Aesthetic*, p. x–xv.
54. Ibid., p. xiii.
55. Jameson, F., *The Geopolitical Aesthetic*, p. 75.
56. Ibid., p. 2.

57. Aitken, S. C. and Zonn, L. E. (eds), *Place, Power, Situation, and Spectacle*, p. 7.
58. McArthur, C., 1997: "Chinese Boxes and Russian Dolls: Tracking the Elusive cinematic City," in Clarke, D. B. (ed.), *The Cinematic City*, p. 34.
59. Baudrillard, J., 1988: *America*, London; New York: Verso, p. 56.
60. Easthope, A., 1997: "Cinecites in the Sixties," in Clarke, D. B. (ed.), *The Cinematic City*, p. 131.
61. Edward Dimendberg has written an excellent series of essays on film, architecture, and the city. He has also made the connection with the work of Henri Lefebvre. See especially: Dimendberg, E. 1997. "From Berlin to Bunker Hill: Urban Space, Late Modernity and Film Noir in Fritz Lang's and Joseph Losey's M" *Wide Angle*. 19 (4), pp. 62–93; and his "Film Architecture" Winter/Spring 1999, *Harvard Design* Magazine, pp. 81–83. On Lefebvre, see Dimendberg, E. 1998. "Henri Lefebvre on Abstract Space," in Light, A. and Smith, J. M (eds) 1998: *Philosophy and Geography II: The Production of Public Space*, Lanham: Rowman & Littlefield, pp. 17–47.
62. Masood, P. J. 1996. "Mapping the Hood: The Genealogy of City Space in *Boyz N the Hood* and *Menace II Society*," *Cinema Journal* 35.2: p. 94.
63. McArthur, C., "Chinese Boxes and Russian Dolls," p. 28.
64. Christopher, N., 1997: *Somewhere in the Night: Film Noir and the American City*, New York: The Free Press, p. 37.
65. Lent, Tina Olsin. "The Dark Side of the Dream: The Image of Los Angeles in Film Noir," *Southern California Quarterly*, (Winter 1987), p. 337.
66. Christopher, N., *Somewhere in the Night*, p. 64.
67. Ibid, p. 48.
68. Copjec, J. (ed.), 1993: *Shades of Noir: A Reader*, London; New York : Verso.
69. Hay, J., 1997: "What Remains of The Cinematic City," in Clarke, D. B.(ed.), *The Cinematic City*.
70. Ibid., p. 210.
71. Lent, T. "The Dark Side of the Dream: The Image of Los Angeles in Film Noir."
72. Williams, T. "Space, Place, and Spectacle: The Crisis Cinema of John Woo," *Cinema Journal* 36.2 (Winter 1997), p. 67.
73. Masood, P. J. "Mapping the Hood: The Genealogy of City Space in *Boyz N the Hood* and *Menace II Society*," p. 89.
74. Albrecht, in Neumann, Dietrich (ed.), *Film Architecture*, p. 42.
75. Schulte-Sasse, L., 1990: p. 170; A similar observation is made by Neumann, Dietrich (ed.), *Film. Architecture*.
76. Ibid.
77. Ibid., p. 174.
78. Cf. Haxthausen, C. W. and Suhr, H. (eds), 1990: *Berlin: Culture and Metropolis*. Minneapolis: University of Minnesota Press, for a wide-reaching discussion of contemporary culture in Berlin; also Theweleit, K., 1989: *Male Fantasies*, translated by Stephen Conway in collaboration with Erica Carter and Chris Turner. Minneapolis: University of Minnesota Press, on male fantasies of the period.
79. Schulte-Sasse, 178–9.
80. Bruno, G., 1993: *Streetwalking on a Ruined Map*. Princeton: Princeton University Press, p. 3.
81. Ibid., 148.
82. Ibid., p. 12.
83. Ibid., p. 4.
84. Ibid., p. 37.
85. Ibid., p. 37
86. Ibid., p. 43.

87. Ibid., p. 45.
88. Ibid., p. 46.
89. Ibid., p. 47.
90. Ibid., p. 51.
91. Ibid., p. 57.
92. de Certeau, M., 1988: *The Writing of History*, translated by Tom Conley, New York: Columbia University Press, p. 115–16.
93. Bruno, G., *Streetwalking*, p. 177.
94. Ibid., pp. 163–77.
95. Ibid., p. 226.
96. Ibid., p. 37.
97. Buck-Morss, S., *The Dialectics of Seeing*, p. 26.
98. Derrida, quoted in Brunette, P. and Wills, D. (eds), 1994: *Deconstruction and the Visual Arts: Art, Media, Architecture*. Cambridge: Cambridge University Press.
99. Easthope, A. (ed.), *Contemporary Film Theory*, p. 19.
100. Ibid.
101. Clarke, D. B (ed.), *The Cinematic City*, p. 7
102. Lapsley, R. and Westlake, M., 1993. "From *Casablanca* to *Pretty Woman*: The Politics of Romance" in Easthope, A. 1993: *Contemporary Film Theory*, London: Longman.
103. The terms are due to Cowie, E., 1993: From *Fantasia*, in P. Adams, and E. Cowie (eds), *The Woman in Question*. London: Verso, pp. 149–96.
104. See Sesonke, A., 1990: "Time and Tense in Cinema," *The Journal of Aesthetics and Art Criticism* 33.4, pp. 419–26; Khatchadourian, Haig: 1987: "Space and Time in Film," *British Journal of Aesthetics* 27.2, pp. 169–77, provides a short critique.
105. Doane, M. A., 1980: "The Voice in the Cinema: The Articulation of Body and Space," *Yale French Studies*, 60, p. 340.
106. Easthope, A. (ed.), *Contemporary Film Theory*, p. 19.
107. Aitken, S. C. and Zonn, L. E. (eds), *Place, Power, Situation, and Spectacle*.
108. Kracauer, S., 1995: *The Mass Ornament: Weimar Essays*, translated by Thomas Y. Levin, Cambridge, Mass.: Harvard University Press, p. 323, reverentially called Berlin's theaters "picture palaces."
109. See also Mulvey, L., 1981: "A Phantasmagoria of the Female Body: The Work of Cindy Sherman," *New Left Review*, 188, pp. 136–50
110. Deutsche, R., 1991: "Boys Town." *Environment and Planning D: Society and Space*; Deutsche, R., 1990: "Men in Space." *Artforum*.
111. Easthope, A., *Contemporary Film Theory*, p. 3.
112. Dimendberg, E. 1995. "The Will to Motorization: Cinema, Highways, and Modernity." *October 73*, p. 91.
113. Heath, Stephen, 1976: "Narrative Space," *Screen*, 17(3); see also Lapsley, R. and Westlake, M. From *Casablanca* to *Pretty Woman*: The Politics of Romance, in Easthope, A., *Contemporary Film Theory*, for a critique of Heath.
114. Derrida, J., 1976: *Of Grammatology*, translated by Gayatri Chakravorty Spivak. Baltimore: Johns Hopkins University Press.
115. Quoted in Gibson, P. C. and Gibson, R. (eds), 1993: *Dirty Looks: Women, Pornography, Power*, London: BFI Publishing, p. 37.
116. Koch, G., 1993: "The Body's Shadow Realm," in Gibson, P. C. and Gibson, R. (eds), *Dirty Looks*, p. 37.
117. Doane, M. 1992. "Film and the Masquerade: Theorizing the Female Spectator." The Sexual Subject: A Screen Reader in Sexuality. New York: Routledge, pp. 232–3.
118. Natter, W., "The City as Cinematic Space," p. 211.
119. Ibid.

120. Chambers, I., 1997: "Maps, Movies, Musics, and Memory," in Clarke, D. B. (ed.), *The Cinematic City.*

121. Maltby, R., 1995: *Hollywood Cinema*, Oxford: Blackwell.

122. See, for example, James, David E., 1989: *Allegories of Cinema: American Film in the Sixties*, Princeton: Princeton University Press; James, David E., 1996: *Power Misses: Essays Across (Un)popular Culture*, London: Verso; James, D. E. and Berg, R., 1996: "The Hidden Foundation: Cinema and the Question of Class," Minneapolis: University of Minnesota Press.

123. The topics of film and visual culture more generally have enjoyed an enormous upsurge in popularity, and it is simply impossible to undertake a comprehensive coverage of the vast popular and scholarly visual literatures, let alone of the artifacts themselves. The case of television is especially important. Lynn Spigel (1992, *Make Room for TV: Television and the Family Ideal in Postwar America*, Chicago: University of Chicago Press), among others, has written extensively on the rise of television in post-1945 America including (most interestingly in the present context) the theory and history of spectators at home, and the emergence of a discursive space within suburban televisual culture. Margaret Morse (1990, "An Ontology of Everyday Distraction: The Freeway, the Mall, and Television," in *Logics of Television: Essays in Cultural Criticism*. Patricia Mellencamp (ed.), Bloomington & Indiana University Press, pp. 194–221), draws strong parallels among the worlds of television, the shopping mall, and freeway culture (life seen through the windshield) in the production of space/place and nonspace. Anne Friedberg (1993, *Window Shopping: Cinema and the Postmodern*, Berkeley: University of California Press) extends the analogies by comparing the pleasures of cinema with shopping mall, in what Benjamin referred to as the "phatasmagoria of the interior," or a mixture of levels of consciousness and objects of attention. According to Friedberg (1993, p. 4), the "gradual shift into postmodernity is marked ... by the increased centrality of the mobilized and virtual gaze as a fundamental feature of everyday life." I have not dealt either with avant-garde film nor video, still less documentary film (see respectively, D. E. James, 1996: *Power Misses: Essays Across (Un)Popular Culture*, Verso, London, UK, and Renov, M. (ed), 1993: *Theorizing Documentary*, New York: Routledge). For the general context of cultural production in place, see T. Boyd (1997, *Am I Black Enough for You?*, Indianapolis: University of Indiana Press), and R. Deutsche (1997, *Evictions: Art and Spatial Politics*, Chicago: Graham Foundation for Advanced Studies in the Fine Arts; Cambridge, MIT Press). On photography, see V. Burgin (1996, *In/different Spaces: Place and Memory in Visual Culture*, Berkeley: University of California Press), B. Kruger (1993, *Remote Control: Power, Cultures, and the World of Appearances*, Cambridge: MIT Press), and L. Mulvey's wonderful essay on Cindy Sherman (1991, "A Phantasmagoria of the Female Body: The Work of Cindy Sherman," *New Left Review*, 188, pp. 136–150). On public art, see E. Doss (1995, *Spirit Poles and Flying Pigs: Public Art and Cultural Democracy in American Communities*, Washington: Smithsonian Institute Press), and S. Lacy (1995 Lacy, S. (ed.), 1995: *Mapping the Terrain: New Genre Public Art*, Seattle: Bay Press).

10

A Tale of Two Cities
2. Las Vegas

Las Vegas takes some established trends in the Los Angeles townscape and pushes them to extremes where they begin to become art, or poetry, or psychiatry.

Reyner Banham [1]

On Friday 13th of September 1996, Tupac Shakur, rap artist and actor, was shot and killed in Las Vegas as he was riding in the passenger seat of a BMW 750 sedan, driven by Marion (Suge) Knight, head of Death Row Records. The murder could not be contained by the 11 o'clock news bulletins, and has since spread into the larger public consciousness. With the Las Vegas Strip as backdrop, TV images of the car quarantined behind yellow "Police: Do Not Cross" tapes are replayed on the slightest pretext ... [2]

Like Tijuana, Las Vegas shares pride of place in the honor roll of the visual and cinematic absurd. Life is a tale told by idiots, full of sound and fury but signifying very little, in movies as diverse as Martin Scorsese's *Casino* (1995) and Steven Kessler's *National Lampoon's Vegas Vacation* (1997). And like Los Angeles, Las Vegas continues to be regarded as an exception to the conventions of American urbanism. But many before me have pleaded for its broader relevance, including Alan Hess: "Today it is more and more difficult to view Las Vegas as an anomaly. ... These changes have catapulted Las Vegas to the leading edge of American urbanism." [3] Others, including Reyner Banham, Ada Louise Huxtable, and Venturi, Scott Brown and Izenour have described Las Vegas as a work of art. [4] But Robert Goodman is appalled by the prospect of Las Vegas as a blueprint for urban society, and warns of the "Las Vegasing of America." [5] Let me briefly examine the history of this remarkable city before going on to consider the meanings of its evolving casino architecture, where cinematic fantasies progressively invade the urban.

Cowboys and Cadillacs

Las Vegas, like so many other Western towns, grew along with the railroad. Montana Senator William Clark bought what was to become the town site from a widowed wife of a rancher in 1902, and put lots on sale in 1905 just after the railroad was completed. Some settlers were already living on an adjacent site owned by J. T. McWilliams, who had surveyed and platted a townsite, and been advertising his lots in Los Angeles newspapers throughout 1904. Clark's site was an instant success, and Las Vegas soon received another boost when a railroad spur was extended to the booming silver towns of Bullfrog and Rhyolite. Las Vegas became a trans-shipment point and railroad repair center. Crucial to the town's early success was a strongly supportive press and a "progressive" business leadership.[6] Despite promises from the Union Pacific Railroad to take care of the problem, townsfolk took it into their own hands to secure a water supply by creating the Vegas Artesian Water Syndicate in 1907. And when Union Pacific decided to close the repair facility in Las Vegas, the town began to diversify its base by becoming a resort city (building on its boisterous reputation). Local entrepreneurs were already wise to the money that could be made out of the Western image.[7]

In the 1930s, a series of events conspired to set the scene for the expansion of Las Vegas. First, and perhaps most important was what Moehring called "the federal trigger" – a sudden outpouring of federal reclamation, relief, and (later) defense spending that benefited towns across the sunbelt. As part of Franklin D. Roosevelt's New Deal, $19 million was set aside to build the Boulder Dam or, as it came to be called, the Hoover Dam. More funds were allocated to improve the city's physical infrastructure, including water and electricity supplies. In this respect, Las Vegas was no different from many other sunbelt cities of the era:

> Las Vegas ... is a western phenomenon, tied to the car, the suburban strip, and a postindustrial society emerging after World War II. Los Angeles, providing many of Las Vegas' architects and most of its customers in this period, was its model.[8]

The legalization of gambling in 1931 was the second major mark on the region's evolution. Of course, gambling had been legal in Nevada since 1869, even though a 1911 law had closed all casinos. Repeal of the prohibition was given a sharp push by events in Los Angeles, where the 1938 election of Mayor Fletcher Bowron was followed by crusades to clean up prostitution and gambling in LA. Those who fled easily found their way to Las Vegas. A third trigger was the expansion in the highways program of the federal government's Bureau of Public Roads, which included improving the all-important connection between LA and Las Vegas.

Population grew, and so did gambling, since construction workers had to have something to spend their wages on. Other quirks of Las Vegas life made their early appearance; for instance, the divorce business thrived. And domestic technological advances, such as "swamp coolers," made the desert heat more tolerable. Tourism helped Las Vegas ride out the depression, especially since federal dollars had dried up. Then World War II came. Las Vegas joined the war effort in a big way after 1940. The conflict shifted the region's economy away from "mining and agriculture to an expanded role in manufacturing and science."[9] The region would soon acquire a magnesium factory, an air base, and (ultimately) a nuclear testing ground. The war also helped stimulate gambling and urban growth. For instance, the massive Basic Magnesium Inc. was scheduled in 1940 to deliver ten times Germany's total production to factories in Los Angeles, and gave rise to the new industrial suburb of Henderson. Soldiers and workers flooded into Las Vegas and other emerging sunbelt centers which were free of wartime building restrictions that characterized many frostbelt cities. By 1945, "[f]ifteen years of frantic federal spending [had] changed Las Vegas forever."[10]

After Hours Architecture

For the grand debut of Monte Carlo as a resort in 1879 the architect Charles Garnier designed an opera house for the Place du Casino; and Sarah Bernhardt read a symbolic poem. For the debut of Las Vegas as a resort in 1946 Bugsy Siegel hired Abbot and Costello, and there, in a way, you have it all.[11]

In his superlative architectural history of the Las Vegas casinos, Hess suggests that visitors to present-day Las Vegas are likely to make the mistake of seeing the city as "a unified tapestry," when in fact it is "a collage of many different eras and styles."[12] I want to examine this historical trajectory, taking it beyond 1993 when the Hess study stops.

The geographical center of gambling of wartime Las Vegas was Fremont Street in the city's downtown core. Few people took much notice of the handful of casinos sprinkled along Highway 91, the Los Angeles Highway, just beyond the city limit in Clark County. This all changed in 1941 when Thomas Hull, a Los Angeles hotel magnate, opened El Rancho Las Vegas, the first lavish motor hotel on Highway 91. The roadside motel might seem an odd cornerstone for urban development, but the motel was to become the basic building block of the Vegas Strip. As importantly, El Rancho Vegas was the first themed hotel in Las Vegas. Hess defines theme architecture in this context as: "the thorough depiction of a particular historical era or geographical area in the architecture, ornament, costumes, and service of the hotel."[13] As the Strip grew, the "motel archetype, organized along the linear highway and given meaning by themes ... [was]the seed planted by El Rancho Las Vegas. In the next decades it would grow into a new type of city."[14] It was, as Hess urges, Thomas Hull who was responsible for the characteristic pattern of luxury resorts strung out along a highway; he was Las Vegas' Pierre l'Enfant, and not mobster Bugsy Spiegel who opened his Flamingo Hotel five years after Hull's innovation.

After El Rancho Las Vegas, new resort hotels followed each other up and down the Strip with a breathtaking persistence. The Last Frontier opened in 1942. Next came the Flamingo, and brought along with it Bugsy Siegel and organized crime.[15] Each hotel vied to outdo its predecessors in terms of opulence. During the 1950s, hotel-building took off at a feverish pace, and headed in the direction of the mass market. In the process, it introduced a remarkable popular architecture which incorporated neon into the hotel facade to such an extent that the signage became the architecture. Signage had always been important on the Strip as a means of visually connecting the hotel with the roadside, and the new hotels such as the Flamingo had given spectacular new meaning to neon. But the Stardust was something else. This is how Hess described it:

In the summer of 1958, the year of a record seventy-seven above-ground atomic tests, the Young Electric Sign Company (YESCO) built a vision of heaven along the desert roadside. Stretching 216 feet long and 27 feet high, it displayed planets and comets from an undiscovered galaxy that pulsed neutrons and radiated cosmic rays. Mixing neon, incandescent bulbs, plexiglass, and painted sheet metal, the shimmering universe was brought to earth and the Strip.[16]

Figure 10.1   Downtown Las Vegas during a nuclear test, 1950s (Las Vegas News Bureau)

As the logic and grammar of Strip architecture evolved, the giant signs were to give greater coherence and form to adjacent buildings.

Needless to say, not everything went according to plan for the new casino kings. Even gangsters had financial setbacks. But the example of the Dunes Hotel shows what happened in Las Vegas when cash-flow problems were combined with over-heated imaginations. In quick succession, the Dunes introduced a floor show with Las Vegas' first-ever topless showgirls, opened a gourmet restaurant, attached an 18–hole Dunes golf course, and doubled (later quadrupled) room capacity, recogniz-ing that room occupancy rates were related to casino profits.[17]

The unbridled growth of the Strip divided Las Vegas casinos into two basic categories: 'carpet joints' and 'sawdust joints.'[18] By the mid-1960s, owners had worked out an architectural package for profitable casino operation, and the casinos themselves had reached sufficient numbers and mass to constitute a distinct-ive urban framework along the Strip. The architectural equation was described thus by Hess:

> A certain number of rooms meant a certain number of customers losing money at the casino. These rooms had to be within easy walking distance of the casino, so highrises became part of every hotel game plan. ... Elevators were placed so that customers had to walk through the casino to get to them. Restaurants, lobby, and entertainment were all accessible from the casino, which became the central plaza of the hotel. Casino cages were located away from entries to make robberies more difficult. Each hotel tried to keep the customers in their own casinos, and the distances from hotel to hotel helped. So

did air conditioning. Proximity to newly opened Interstate 15, which paralleled the Strip half mile to the west, also figured in the game plan.[19]

But Vegas was not finished with re-inventing itself. In the next phase, hotels would make themselves into self-contained islands.

Caesars Palace [sic] opened in 1966 after an eight-year hiatus in new hotel construction. It broke with the roadside motel tradition. Casual site arrangement and frontal parking lots were rejected in favor of a monumental style that pushed cars off to the side. The building's bulk and symmetrical wings were said to be reminiscent of St Peter's Square in Rome. Instead of signage placed tangentially to face oncoming traffic, Caesars faced directly onto the Strip. But the purpose was the same: to attract gamblers, at which Caesars was very successful at doing. So, naturally enough, it attracted competitors, each with its own theme to differentiate it from the herd. In retrospect, perhaps the pivotal moment in the Strip's contemporary history was the 1968 opening of Circus Circus. Attempts had been made previously to attract families to Las Vegas, but Circus Circus literally suspended the acrobats above the gamblers' heads in the gaming pits below, and put their children on a separate, second-level midway with a clear view of the circus attractions. Then in 1968, Nevada law was changed to allow corporations to own casinos, where previously only individuals could.[20] Hotels rapidly got bigger, and the Las Vegas experience was packaged and commodified for general sale. This is the era (1981–92) that Hess dubs 'Corporate Splendor'.[21]

Blockbuster corporate architecture now took over on the Strip, elbowing out the glorious neon signs. These unornamented obelisks were initally large anonymous slabs plonked unceremoniously onto a site. Their most innovative idea was the *porte cochere*, a vast canopy that could shelter a fleet of limousines. (And, incidentally, create a wind tunnel effect that made you rush inside for shelter! But perhaps that too was intentional, since then you were in the gaming area?) In general, however, the corporate legacy has been megahotels and more megahotels with increasingly outlandish theming. The South-Sea-island-themed Mirage Hotel (1989) is set back from the Strip and fronted by a volcanic island that erupts every fifteen minutes after dark. The Excalibur opened in 1990, resembling a false-front movie-set inspired by a Disney-style Magic Kingdom. And Treasure Island (1993) features a mock pirate battle in front of the hotel.

Not surprisingly, large customer volume and sidewalk spectacles have given rise to a lively pedestrian scene along the Strip. But pedestrians ambling on a sidewalk present a challenge to the casino owners, who would prefer that those people were inside spending money. So owners keep on inventing ingenious ways to get them inside, especially since distracting sidewalk shows tend to keep them outside. In Caesars Palace, for instance, a moving pavement and covered pavilion have been extended 135 feet from the sidewalk to the casino entrance. And when Bally's took over the first MGM Grand, they retired the old *porte cochere* and invited lighting engineer John Levy to construct a spectacular moving pavement with light and acoustical canopy to transport customers from sidewalk onto casino. The effect Levy has created is that you are in the casino as soon as you step on the escalator.

Screening Las Vegas

The particular urban patterns that characterize Las Vegas were an inspiration for my thoughts on keno capitalism in Chapter 7. The population of the City of Las Vegas grew 14 percent between 1990 and 1992, totalling 300,000 people; meanwhile surrounding Clark County grew by 37 percent between 1990 and 1995. The metropolitan area is now well over a million people. The city's land area grew from 80 square miles in 1988 to 92 square miles by 1995. Some 15,000 land use permits and requests for zoning changes come into the county offices every month.[22] As early as 1978, consultant Charles Paige drew attention to the peculiar "checkerboard effect" of urbanization to the south and west of Las Vegas, which was dominated by "large residential subdivisions connected by commercial strips along major streets and separated by equally large squares of undeveloped land".[23] In his history of gambling in the US, John Findlay shrewdly observed that Las Vegans did not attempt to build a 'home town' in any conventional sense; instead they were preoccupied with creating a city that would appeal to tourists.[24]

Las Vegas is since 1990 the fastest-growing metropolitan area in the United States. Somewhat like Tijuana, this former 'suburb' of Los Angeles seems to have shaken off its subordinate role and gone solo. Gaming flourishes. The convention business has joined golf, divorce, and defense as mainstays of the local economy;[25] Moehring says that Las Vegas has been a "martial economy" since 1941;[26] I presume he was referring only to the last of these three functions. Although a more traditional manufacturing base has eluded Las Vegas, the region has begun to attract high-tech, white-collar industry, and is increasingly a retirement destination. Nevertheless, one quarter of the work force is directly employed by the hotel and casino industry; and some estimates put two-thirds of the region's half-million workers in "gambling-related" jobs.[27]

In casino architecture, form continue to follow fantasy. The most recent generation of hotels – among them the Egyptian pyramid of the Luxor and the new MGM Grand (the largest hotel in the world) – were both completed in 1993. They redefine destination resorts. The Luxor in particular is detached from the Strip with a broad setback occupied by the figure of a god, a *porte cochere*, and an elaborate sunken garden with a fountain upon which plays a laser light show at periodic intervals (again designed by John Levy). The Luxor makes no pretense at attracting casual passers-by off the street; its physical arrangement actually discourages this. It is designed instead to bring people by car to this particular hotel where they will find everything they can possibly want in a visit to Las Vegas, including gambling, accommodation, good service, parking, a variety of restaurants and casual food vendors, and an indoor theme park suitable for all ages. In 1992, Caesars Palace opened the Forum shopping mall adjacent to its casino, and thereby not only anchored customers within the casino perimeter but also attracted people off the streets. Inside, it is an easy stroll from the casino proper into a shopping street and piazza reminiscent of an Italian town, except that all the stores are somewhat upscale (Gucci, Versace, Dior, etc.). Statues of Bacchus and other gods grace a smaller piazza; every hour the statues move and speak in a synchronized light and sound show (Bacchus invites the crowds: "Come one, come all; and welcome to the mall". The lighting in the Forum (courtesy of John Levy) cycles through several rounds of day and night within a single 24–hour period. It is most convincing. Nearly everyone stops by the Fountain of the Gods for a souvenir photograph.

The Strip mega-projects have in turn caused a major renovation in the old Fremont Street gambling core of downtown Las Vegas. The length of the street was canopied (1400 feet long, 90 feet high, in a design by Jon Jerde) and landscaped in an effort to maintain customer interest. And yet competition from the Strip escalates. The Hard Rock Cafe Hotel and Casino opened in 1995 with an 82–foot Gibson guitar out front, and has exceeded its projected share of the younger gaming set. The Strato-sphere Tower/Hotel/Casino/Thrill Ride opened atop a 1,149–feet tower in 1996. And in 1997, a facsimile of the Manhattan skyline was concertina'd into one gigantic 2,000–bedroom theme hotel and casino called New York–New York. More, larger hotels are planned. Note how gambling has been renamed gaming. Resorts like Treasure Island now receive less than half their revenues from casino operations (the rest comes from restaurants, retail and entertainment).[28] Much effort is also going into connecting the major hotels by monorail, so that once again the necessity to leave the hotel and go hiking off on one's own is obviated; instead, you go where the monorail goes, which is into another casino! This suggests another dimension to Friedberg's *flânerie du* mal(l); perhaps monorailing the mall, or streetwalking the slots?

Alan Hess is convinced that people ought to take Las Vegas seriously as a model of American urbanism, even though he concedes it might not be an ideal model. He is energized by the architectural experimentation and the rise of the hotels as mini-cities that rearrange the neighborhoods of the traditional city. At the same time, he despairs of the centrifugal nature of urban development, environmental pollution,

Figure 10.2   Luxor Hotel, Las Vegas (Las Vegas Visitors' Bureau from website, in public domain)

traffic congestion, water shortages, etc.[29] Late in his survey of casino architecture, Hess muses:

> The Strip's theme architecture makes it a video screen of the national consciousness.[30]

By this, he is referring to the consecutive effacement of various stereotypical images that might have been considered part of American national identity (for example, the sophisticated Old West is today nowhere to be seen in Las Vegas today). But I take this to imply something broader. And this is that the architecture and urbanism of today's Strip takes its lead quite literally from the movies. The hotels are film sets and sound stages on which ordinary people come to live, play, and act out. Architects are mimicking the screen; and film-makers have stepped out from behind the camera into the realm of public events production (e.g. the 1996 Atlanta Olympics). Architecture critic Ada Louise Huxtable has turned to Las Vegas somewhat ruefully for insight:

> The theme park has no such problem of degenerative authenticity. Nothing in it is admired for its reality, only for the calculated manipulation and simulation of its sources. It is not surprising that much of the most popular and profitable development of the genre is spearheaded and bankrolled by the masters of illusion; the movie and entertainment businesses have become the major innovators and investors in theme parks and related enterprises.[31]

And New Yorkers, who reflexively sneer at anything to do with Southern California now face their own apocalypse: the Disneyfication of Times Square.

It is no longer possible to recognize the boundary between the screen and the street, between cinematic fantasy and the creation of the urban. Representations of cities are becoming cities. Life is becoming a virtual reality?

Notes

1. Banham, R. 1970: "Las Vegas", *Los Angeles Times West Magazine*, November 8, p. 38.
2. Bruck, C. 1997: "The Takedown of Tupac," *The New Yorker*, July 7, pp. 46–64.
3. Hess, A. 1995: *Viva Las Vegas: After-Hours Architecture*, San Francisco: Chronicle Books, p. 114.
4. Banham, R. "Las Vegas;" Huxtable, A. L. 1997: "Living with the Fake and Liking It," *New York Times*, March 30, pp. 2–1; Venturi, R., Scott Brown, D., and Izenour, S. 1997: *Learning from Las Vegas*, Cambridge: MIT Press.
5. Goodman, R. 1995: *The Luck Business: The Devastating Consequences and Broken Promises of America's Gambling Explosion*, New York: Martin Kessler Books: Free Press; also Alvarez, A. 1996: "Learning from Las Vegas," *The New York Review of Books*, January 11, pp. 15–20.
6. Moehring, E. P. 1995: *Resort City in the Sunbelt: Las Vegas, 1930–1970*, Reno: University of Nevada Press, p. 5.
7. Hess (1993), 1993: *Viva Las Vegas*, pp. 14–17.
8. Ibid., p. 40.
9. Moehring, E. P. *Resort City in the Sunbelt: Las Vegas, 1930–1970*, p. 3.
10. Ibid., p. 40.

11. Wolfe, T. 1995: "Las Vegas (What?) Las Vegas (Can't Hear You! Too Noisy) Las Vegas!!!!" in Tronnes, M. (ed.) *Literary Las Vegas*, New York: Henry Holt, p. 13.

12. Hess, A. *Viva Las Vegas*, p. 11.

13. Ibid., p. 33.

14. Ibid.

15. There are numerous accounts of the Vegas gaming/gambling industry and its connection with organized crime. Nicholas Pileggi proves to be a knowledgeable and entertaining guide; see, for example, his *Casino* (1996), and the movie *Casino* (1995), scripted by Pileggi and Martin Scorsese, and directed by Scorsese. The drollest perspective on mob life in Vegas is that by Susan Berman, whose father was Davie Berman, confidante of Meyer Lansky, Frank Costello, and Bugsy Siegel. At Davie's Jewish funeral service, just before the Kaddish, one mourner grabbed daughter Berman, exclaiming: "Susie, your dad was the greatest gangster that ever lived. You can hold your head up high." (Berman, S. 1995: "Memoirs of a Gangster's Daughter," in Tronnes, M (ed.) *Literary Las Vegas*, New York: Henry Holt, p. 104).

16. Hess, *Viva Las Vegas*, p. 66.

17. Moehring, E. P., *Resort City in the Sunbelt: Las Vegas, 1930–1970*, pp. 79–80.

18. Ibid., pp. 82.

19. Hess, A., *Viva Las Vegas*, pp. 74–5.

20. Hess, A., *Viva Las Vegas*, p. 100; Moehring, E. P., *Resort City in the Sunbelt: Las Vegas, 1930–1970*, p. 55.

21. Hess, *Viva Las Vegas*, p. 100.

22. Clayton, D. 1995: "Las Vegas Goes for Broke," *Planning*, 61(9), pp. 4–9.

23. Quoted in Moehring, E. P. *Resort City in the Sunbelt: Las Vegas, 1930–1970*, p. 238.

24. Findlay, J. 1986: *People of Chance: Gambling in American Society from Jamestown to Las Vegas*, New York : Oxford University Press, p. 177.

25. On Las Vegas weddings, see Joan Didion's 1968 essay "Marrying Absurd," in her collection *Slouching Toward Bethlehem*, New York: Noonday Press (Farrar, Straus, and Giroux).

26. Moehring, E. P. *Resort City in the Sunbelt: Las Vegas, 1930–1970*, p. 97.

27. Clayton, D. "Las Vegas Goes for Broke," p. 4.

28. Gorman, T. 1997: "From Craps to Cranberry Juice," *Los Angeles Times Magazine*, March 16, p. 19.

29. Hess, *Viva Las Vegas*, p. 117–118.

30. Ibid., p. 119.

31. Huxtable, A. L. "Living with the Fake and Liking It," p. 40.

11

From Sidewalk to Cyberspace (and back to Earth again)

"You know that we have lost the sense of space. We say 'space is annihilated,' but we have annihilated not space, but the sense thereof. We have lost a part of ourselves."
Kuno, to his mother Vashti, in E. M. Forster's *The Machine Stops*[1]

The Puzzle of Postmodernity: from Boulevard to Metaverse

Watch.

Even if you've been reading this book very carefully, you might have missed something very important. To show what this is, I will break one of my own cardinal rules of writing: never let quotations do the talking for you. But, just this once, let me pull some key quotes from the text so far, and add a few others to make the point.

The transition to modernity was captured as Baudelaire moved fearfully into the traffic-laden boulevards of Haussmann's Paris:

> I was crossing the boulevard, in a great hurry, in the midst of a moving chaos, with death galloping at me from every side.[2]

But Le Corbusier, instead of fighting it, merged into the traffic:

> On that first of October 1924, I was assisting in a titanic rebirth of a new phenomenon: traffic. Cars, cars, fast, fast! One is seized, filled with enthusiasm, with joy ... the joy of power. The simple and naive pleasure of being in the midst of power, of strength. One participates in it, one takes part in the society that is just dawning. One has confidence in this new society: it will find a magnificent expression of its power. One believes in it.[3]

The liberating power of the personal gaze was uncovered by Walter Benjamin within the microcosmic world of an urban arcade:

> The *flâneur* goes botanizing on the asphalt. But... strolling could hardly have assumed the importance it did without the arcades... "An arcade is a city, even a world in miniature." The street becomes a dwelling for the *flâneur*; he is as much at home among the facades of houses as a citizen in his four walls.[4]

Yet Benjamin also recognized the significance of the filmic gaze:

> Our taverns and our metropolitan street, our offices and furnished rooms, our railroad stations and our factories appeared to have us locked up hopelessly. Then came the film

and burst this prison-world asunder by the dynamite of the tenth of a second, so that now, in the midst of its far-flung ruins and debris, *we calmly and adventurously go traveling.*[5]

Now let Roland Barthes describe how the subjective experience of driving a car takes on a cinematic quality – a constant alternation of spatial situatedness that defines a continuous elsewhere:

If I am in a car and I look at the scenery through the window, I can at will focus on the scenery or on the window-pane. At one moment I grasp the presence of the glass and the distance of the landscape; at another, on the contrary, the transparency of the glass and the depth of the landscape; but the result of this alternation is constant: the glass is at once present and empty to me, and the landscape unreal and full.[6]

A fundamental shift that incorporates the spectatorial gaze and mobility is made even more explicit in Paul Virilio:[7]

What goes on in the windshield is cinema in the strict sense.

Or television, according to Jean Baudrillard:

The vehicle now becomes a capsule, its dashboard the brain, the surrounding landscape unfolding like a televised screen.[8]

Virilio takes this one further step, the screen interface supplanting real geography, and creating a kind of virtual space:[9]

On the terminal's screen, a span of time becomes both the surface and the support of inscription; time literally...surfaces....[T]he dimensions of space become inseparable from their speed of transmission. Unity of place without unity of time makes the city disappear into the heterogeneity of advanced technology's temporal regime.

For Anne Friedberg, the advent of postmodernity is heralded by:

the increasing centralization of features implicit (from the start) in cinema spectatorship: the production of a virtual elsewhere and elsewhen, and a commodification of a gaze that is mobilized in both time and space.[10]

Postmodernity is "the increased centrality of the mobilized and virtual gaze as a fundamental feature of everyday life.[11] We are now light years from Baudelaire. Friedberg captures part of this revolutionary dynamic:

For Benjamin, the *flâneur*'s ambulatory and distracted gaze found its most commanding outlet in the...arcade's curious temporality...Like the arcade, the cinema embodies this conflated temporality...film provides an explosive charge to burst asunder the "prison world" of nineteenth-century temporality. As arcades have become shopping malls, and as dioramas and panoramas have evolved into multiplex cinemas and videotheques, this new temporality has become a key component of postmodern subjectivity.[12]

This plethora of voices suggests that our geographies have radically shifted: from sidewalk into traffic; from car to screen; from arcade to inside your head; from stasis to speed. Your postmodern, mobile/virtual gaze dwells in a phantasmagoria of the interior, a hyper-real society of spectacle. And yet you are still in place, no matter where your senses are. Kuno was right.

The conflation between material and virtual worlds, between spaces of the screen and spaces of the street, is part of the postmodern condition that we are only now confronting. In *Snow Crash*, science-fiction writer Neal Stephenson domiciled his literary hero, Hiro Protagonist, in a storage locker in Inglewood, Los Angeles County. Hiro lived cheap so that he could afford to live high in his virtual world:

> So Hiro's not actually here at all. He's in a computer-generated universe that his computer is drawing onto his goggles and pumping into his earphones. In the lingo, this imaginary place is known as the Metaverse....
>
> Hiro is approaching the street. It is the Broadway, the Champs Elysées of the Metaverse.... It does not really exist. But right now, millions of people are walking up and down it....
>
> The sky and the ground are black, like a computer screen that hasn't had anything drawn into it yet; it is always nighttime in the Metaverse, and the Street is always garish and brilliant, like Las Vegas freed from constraints of physics and finance.[13]

Figure 11.1   Storage Facilities, Venice, California (Michael Dear)
In Neal Stephenson's *Snow Crash*, Hiro Protagonist lived in a Inglewood storage facility like this one, spending all his money instead on a Metaverse virtual property. In real life, homeless people rent out personal storage space here to live in and protect possessions.

This material/virtual world is what postmodern hyperspace is. And, Jameson was right, we cannot yet ascertain its coordinates. It may never be possible to do so. The puzzle of postmodernity (another trope?) is that it is about a space that has no bounds, yet it remains resolutely in place. Postmodern hyperspace is a virtual/material world that is as fundamental a break with the past as one can possibly imagine. And it is real. Now.

Watch.

Citistät as City of Bits

Fictional accounts of the brave new digital world are frequently dystopian in character. For instance, E. M. Forster imagines a future world of billions of people, each of whom lives in articulated multimedia chambers that automatically take care of the necessities of life, and link everyone to a stimulating web of ideas.[14] The only problem is that most people have forgotten they lived in The Machine. In William Gibson's *Idoru*, a post-earthquake Tokyo is not even where it used to be. The new islands are randomly constructed of "quake-junk," and colonized by "nanotech," stuff that grows buildings by itself.[15] The stuff grew so quickly that some people became implanted, forming part of the new infrastructure. The human world was composed of "aggregates of subjective desire ... [in which] the modular array would ideally constitute an architecture of articulated longing."[16]

Struggling to catch up with these imagined worlds, scholars are casting around for preliminary concepts to describe the virtual worlds of information and communications technologies.[17] Graham and Marvin[18] reveal the depths of confusion implicit in the proliferation of metaphorical characterizations of this new society – informational city, wired city, telecity, virtual city, cyberville, and so on. The visions are both optimistic and pessimistic: the virtual world will either revitalize democracy, or create a totalitarian global order; it will annihilate space, or produce an entirely original urban geography; it will numb the people, or it will liberate them.

More than most, William J. Mitchell has imagined what a digitally-mediated environment would look like. Calling himself an "electronic flâneur,"[19] Mitchell embraces the digital revolution:

> Just as Baron Haussmann had imposed a bold spider's web of broad, straight boulevards on the ancient tangle of Paris... these post-whatever construction crews were putting in place an infobahn... some local, fiber-optic fragments of what was fast becoming a worldwide, broadband, digital telecommunications network.[20]

Mitchell seems convinced that the way cities are organized will undergo profound changes as the economic, socio-cultural, and political action shifts into cyberspace. As a consequence, all the familiar urban design issues are up for radical reformulation.[21] In Mitchell's "city of bits," what we might refer to as the soft cities of cyberspace, the principal economic engine is the production, transformation, distribution, and consumption of digital information.[22] For urbanists, the task of the twenty-first century will be to build what he calls the "bitsphere" – a worldwide, electronically-mediated environment in which networks are everywhere:[23]

Networks at these different levels will all have to link up somehow; the body net will be
connected to the building net, the building net to the community net, and the community
net to the global net. From gesture sensors worn on our bodies to the worldwide
infrastructure of communications satellites and long-distance fiber, the elements of the
bitsphere will finally come together to form one densely interwoven system within
which the knee bone is connected to the I-bahn.[24]

The value of a network connection in the global Citistāt is determined by bandwidth.
In the city of bits, the "bandwidth-disadvantaged" are the new have-nots.[25] The
absence of network communication, known as "zero bandwidth," defines what it is
to be a "digital hermit," the marginalized outcasts of cyberia.[26]

Urbanists in the digital era will need to recognize that the body is differentially
related to space.[27] Because we are all cyborgs now, the boundary between interior
and exterior is undermined; distinctions between self and other become provisional,
positional, and open to reconstruction:[28]

> Think of yourself on some evening in the not-so-distant future, when wearable, fitted,
> and implanted electronic organs connected to your bodynets are as commonplace as
> cotton; your intimate infrastructure connects you seamlessly to a planetful of bits, and
> you have software in your underwear.[29]

As humans morph into cyborgs (prefigured in Kathryn Bigelow's *Strange Days*),
telecommunication systems will replace traditional circulation systems and conventional building types.[30] And as familiar forms vanish, so does our ability to cognitively map our surroundings (echoes of Jameson again); we are forced to rely
increasingly on our electronic extensions to make sense of the unfolding hyperspace.[31] It becomes more difficult to locate ourselves with respect to power, wealth,
workplace, community, and subsistence; just as long as basic needs are met, the rest
is mobile virtual gazing. We can become agitated, in an Orwellian manner,
by telebroadcasts concerning some (fake?) intercontinental war occurring
somewhere on the globe; or sedated by the sensual seductions of Forster's mechanical
cocoons.

In this cyberworld, lines on the ground will matter little:[32]

> a new logic has emerged. The great power struggle of cyberspace will be over network
> typology, connectivity, and access – not the geographic borders and chunks of territory
> that have been fought over in the past.[33]

Traditional dimensions of civic legibility will be erased. In a conventional city,
Mitchell insists, geography is destiny; where you are frequently tells who you
are.[34] But the Net despatializes everything:

> In the familiar, spatial, synchronous style of city, there is a time and a place for every-
> thing. ... But now extrapolate to an entirely asynchronous city. Temporal rhythm turns
> to white noise ... anything can happen.[35]

But what happens next can hardly be devoid of geography? Taking a lead from
Manuel Castells, Mitchell concedes that the emerging cybercity will be:

a complex interaction between established geographically located urban and regional economies and the increasingly powerful effects of long-distance, almost instantaneous flows within worldwide virtual communities.[36]

In the consequent tension between centralizing and decentralizing forces, "the initial development of an advanced telecommunications infrastructure is likely to favor existing urban centers (with their high and profitable concentrations of information work)."[37] Kevin Robins[38] strongly disputes the "post-geography" of Mitchell's city of bits. He takes a lead from Paul Virilio, who is concerned that the apparent collapse of geographical space is a fundamental threat to human liberty. In Virilio's terms, the compression of distance associated with the rise of the global village represents a "intellectual and spiritual enclosure".[39] So, even in the global Citistāt, geography matters, and inequalities will continue to plague the human condition.

Digital Democracy or Information Aristocracy?

Kevin Robins has shrewdly navigated his way right up against one of Gibson's infofaults – those nodal points (worm-holes?) in cyberspace, which may be followed down to another kind of truth, "deep within the gray shoals of information." Gazing into the abyss, Robins asserts:

> what is really at issue is the more fundamental question of creating a more plural and democratic culture, and we must not let this be reduced to being simply a technological issue.[40]

This is easier said than done. According to Mitchell, we have already entered "the era of dataveillance,"[41] in which power is vested in those systems operators who control the operating codes.[42] Howard Rheingold pinpoints even more precisely one of the principal political dangers implicit in virtual communities: the false utopian promise of the 'technological fix;' and the potential erosion of democracy. Rheingold quotes Langdon Winner to highlight the danger of belief in a technologically-driven utopia:

> ...there is none more poignant [political ideal] than the faith that the computer is destined to become a potent equalizer in modern society. ...

> In a contest of force against force, the larger, more sophisticated, more ruthless, better equipped competitor often has the upper hand.[43]

Rheingold issues an important warning: that there is nothing intrinsically democratic about electronic technologies. We seem prepared to forget this, just as we ignored lessons from earlier times. Rheingold connects our faith in Enlightenment progress with pollyannarchic hopes for a technological utopia. He points out that humans have an entire world-view embedded within the word "progress," which associates scientific innovation with improvement in the human condition:[44]

> The myth of technological progress emerged out of the same Age of Reason that gave us the myth of representative democracy, a new organizing vision that still works pretty

well, despite the decline in vigor of the old democratic institutions. It's hard to give up on
one Enlightenment ideal while clinging to another.[45]

And yet, Rheingold asserts:

> We've had enough time to live with steam, electricity and television to recognize that
> they did indeed change the world, and to recognize that the utopia of technological
> millenarians has not yet materialized.[46]

If virtual utopia is not just around the corner, what is the shape of democratic politics
in cyberspace? For now, it seems that the situation could go either way. Virtual
communities may help revitalize democracy, or they may simply become attractively-
packaged substitutes for democratic discourse. Rheingold underscores the prospects
of abuse, emphasizing the effects of commercializing cyberspace and the penetration
of the means of social control, thus foreshadowing the static on the Disinformation
Super Highway (DSH). For instance, he warns that a channel for authentic communication could just as easily become a channel for manufacturing commercial
desire.[47] If people ignore the hard work involved in online democracy, asserts
Rheingold, they run the danger of becoming "unwitting agents of commodification."[48] We might then anticipate the replacement of democracy with a global
mercantile state that exerts control through the media-assisted manipulation of
desire.[49] Thus, the most insidious attack on democracy might come not from political dictatorship, but from the marketplace:[50]

> The assault on privacy ... takes place in the broad daylight of everyday life. The
> weapons are cash registers and credit cards. When Big Brother arrives, don't be surprised
> if he looks like a grocery clerk.[51]

According to Rheingold, the simulation (and therefore destruction) of authentic
discourse is what Guy Debord would call the first leap into the "society of the
spectacle," or what Jean Baudrillard would identify as a milestone in the world's
slide into hyper-reality.[52] That is, the use of communications technology as a total
replacement of the natural world and social order with a technologically-mediated
hyper-real spectacle:

> Hyper-reality is what you get when a Panopticon evolves to a point where it can
> convince everyone that it doesn't exist; people continue to believe they are free, although
> their power has disappeared.[53]

And yet, despite prognostications of a sedated and controlled populace, optimistic
visions of cyberdemocracy persist. Many observers have discovered good government in virtual communities, especially in the democracy of the WELL (Whole Earth
Lectronic Link).[54] In other examples, Dallas Dishman showed how coming out was
easier for gay men on the Internet, and how it allowed isolated individuals to find
community.[55] On a geopolitical scale, David S. Bennahum makes a forceful argument about how important the new technologies have been in the liberation of the
former Soviet block.[56] He observed that the protests in Serbia are the "first mature

example" of the Internet playing a role in a popular uprising against an authoritarian regime.[57] Critically important is the way the Internet allows outsiders to receive news about internal events, and to provide moral support for dissenters. One revolutionary put it this way:

> Without media attention [we] were powerless in the face of physical force. ... We get more overseas reporting because of the Net... This is why we call it the Internet Revolution. It has led to real support from people outside.[58]

Bennahum argues that the experience of using the Internet bolsters people's confidence so that they can take care of their own affairs and govern themselves: "There is something inherent about the Net that supports democracy... it appears clear that access to the Internet is incompatible with authoritarianism."[59] One example may be the way in which a global anti-landmines coalition was expeditiously formed via the Net, leading to a United Nations resolution, and a Nobel Peace prize for the coalition's leader.

Sometimes, however, democracy does not endure. After a rape in cyberspace, the LambdaMOO community faced the difficult problem of inventing self-governance from scratch.[60] They could come to no consensus, so a community 'wizard' finally imposed more formal structures of governance. The community was never the same after that.

The tendency toward totalitarianism was uppermost in the mind of science-fiction writer William Gibson when he visited Singapore, which he described as "Disneyland with the death penalty."[61] He predicted that eventually "whole highways of data will flow into and through" Singapore as it becomes a wired city. Yet local inhabitants "seem to expect that this won't affect them."[62] Gibson is skeptical, warning that if a wired Singapore comes to pass, it will prove that is "possible to flourish though the active repression of free expression."[63]

In another of his perceptive essays on contemporary media culture, Kevin Robins plunges deeper into the infofault to show how the screen works to make moral responses more difficult.[64] He draws upon John Berger, who argued that screen voyeurism has permitted an unprecedented ruthlessness and indifference to life. Robins' concern is with the effects of the televising of the Gulf War by the national entertainment state. He makes a revealing connection between the use of high technology and the claims of moral purpose during war – the clear message of the televised confrontation was that 'smart' weapons were good, since they actually saved the lives of soldiers and civilians in the Gulf. Thus, to reduce error by deadly accuracy and efficiency reflected the moral triumph of Western technology. Robins sums up the new techno-morality this way:

> The Gulf War demonstrated that the power and the dominance of the *technological order* had become so well secured that it *is now the criterion of what is moral.*[65] (emphases added)

The conflation of the DSH, the infotainment industries, and politics is pervasive. Postmodern cyberspace is characterized by a promiscuous blurring of authority and order, politics and corporate wealth, consumption and entertainment. Thus in

October 1995, the Alliance Gaming Corporation announced that it was acquiring Bally Gaming International Inc. for $215 million. Craig Fields is vice chairman of Alliance, and former director of Defense Advanced Research Projects Agency at the Pentagon, an agency that helped create the Internet. Mr Fields hopes to use the computer network to bring casino gambling to home computers. Every state in the United States except Hawaii and Utah permit some form of gambling, and in 1994 the take in casinos alone was $18 billion, more than consumers spent on movie, theater, and concert tickets combined. A newly-unified trade group, the American Gaming Association, chose as its head Frank J. Fahrenkopf Jr, former chair of the Republican Party.[66]

The creatures and cultures of postmodern cyberspace are characterized by a 'society of spectacle' (Debord), a 'phantasmagoria of the interior' (Benjamin), a 'hyper-reality' (Baudrillard). Within its spaces, consumption-wracked, privatized human beings are satiated into submission. Postmodern styles are integral to this seduction. So are techno-rationalities, the latest in a centuries-old game of Enlightenment-inspired technological/utopian false consciousness. It is precisely this consciousness that is radically threatened by postmodern thought. But, for now, it is far from clear whether postmodernists can convince others of the explosive nature of the volatile mixture that places the telecommunications revolution alongside the disenchantment with representative democracy.

Postmodern Cyberspace: Simulation and Screen

In a surprising and counter-intuitive twist, in the past decade, the mechanical engines of computers have been grounding the radically nonmechanical philosophy of postmodernism.[67]

The culture of a "postmodern cyberspace" has been powerfully articulated by Sherry Turkle, one of the most perceptive observers of the relationships that people have with computers, and how these relationships change the way we think and feel – about mind, body, self, and machine. Since 1984, Turkle has called the computer a "second self," showing how windows have became a powerful metaphor for thinking about the self as a "multiple, distributed system."[68] In a radical shift of the way we create and experience human identity, life on the Internet stretches the windows metaphor so that real life (RL) can become "just one more window."[69] Some dedicated inhabitants of virtual space go so far as to challenge the idea of giving priority to RL, since the non-corporeal self is able to have so many adjacent experiences.

In a deft perceptual shift that I have been obliquely negotiating from a different direction in the last four chapters, Turkle conflates cyberspace with postmodernism. Her dazzling achievement, in a few brief pages of *Life on the Screen*, is to show how technology is bringing the ideas of postmodernism (especially the instability of meanings, and the lack of universal truths) into everyday life. In her words:

Computers embody postmodern theory and bring it down to earth.[70]

According to Turkle, until very recently, it was almost impossible to think of the computer as anything but a calculating machine. It employed centralized structures, systematic technical knowledge, and knowable rules. Turkle identifies this "modernist computational aesthetic" as one of the great metanarratives.[71] Yet computing today is less about calculation and programmed rules, and more about simulation, navigation, and interaction. We have moved toward a postmodern aesthetic of complexity and decentering, i.e. from "a modernist culture of calculation toward a postmodernist culture of simulation."[72] If these simulations remain opaque to us (in the sense of being too complex to be completely analyzed), Turkle advises against panic, since "our brains are opaque to us, this has never prevented then from functioning perfectly well as minds."[73]

As the traditional separation between human and machine is eroded, we ourselves approach the status of cyborg, a mixture of technology, biology and code (Haraway). Earlier distinctions between what is specifically human and specifically technological become fuzzy. Turkle asks: "Are we living life on the screen or life in the screen?"[74] In another bold connection, she finds an answer to this question in the diaries of Ralph Waldo Emerson. Writing in 1832, Emerson observed that:

> Dreams and beasts are two keys by which we are to find out the secrets of our nature...they are our test objects.[75]

Freud and his followers would go on to measure humans against their dreams, just as Darwin and his heirs were to measure human nature against Nature itself. So, Turkle claims:

> Dreams and beasts were the test objects for Freud and Darwin, the test objects for modernism. In the past decade, the computer has become the test object for postmodernism. (emphasis added)[76]

In this new world, we have become accustomed to an opaque technology and Learned to take things at "interface value" (where representations of reality substitute for the real). Our relationships with technology have caused us to reflect on what it is to be human, in a culture that is still deeply attached to the quest for modernist understanding. And we are discovering the computer as an intimate, rather than inanimate, machine.[77]

In short, Turkle concludes: "Today, life on the computer screen carries theory."[78] The power of simulation, virtual communities, and cyberspace derives from their ability "to help us think through postmodernism."[79]

Nature and Postmodernity

The spectacular, wondrous views of Planet Earth taken from the Apollo spacecraft furnish acute reminders that the earth and its resources are finite, precarious. And, no matter how virtual our world becomes, our feet are necessarily firmly planted on the ground. We remain, as I have pointed out many times, resolutely in place. And (to paraphrase Wittgenstein) it is quite literally from this position that you write your truths.

Figure 11.2   LA River (Michael Dear)
Symbolizing the control of nature and social division (between the *pinche* Westside and the *barrios* of East LA)

Environmental politics

It seems incontrovertible that the world is facing a debilitating accumulation of environmental problems. These include resource depletion and degradation, habitat loss and diminished biodiversity, pollution and global warming. When people are dying across a sub-continent because of the smoke from forest fires, it is time to take notice; when holes in the ozone layer threaten life on this planet, it is time to stop what we are doing! Yet the ability to act on these problems is compromised by uncertainties in our knowledge base; and wherever there is ambiguity, the door is open to political irresolution. The fact is that there is precious little agreement about the earth and its problems.

A useful summary of four perspectives on environmental politics is provided by David Harvey:[80]

(1) *environmental management*, involving corrective intervention, usually after the event, characteristically taking the form of government-mandated regulatory frameworks;

(2) *ecological modernization*, emphasizing the human propensity to produce environmental harms, and hence the need to adopt a proactive, prevention-oriented stance to protect the rights of future generations;

(3) *"wise use,"* a plea for private property arrangements as the best protection against environmental abuse; and

(4) *environmental justice*, a movement that attempts to alleviate the unequal geographical distribution of environmental harms, especially among communities of poor and peoples of color.

The variety of these approaches barely hints at the enormous complexities that engulf environmental issues. Consider, for a moment, some of the more prominent of these issues. For instance: is global warming truly happening? Those who agree with this proposition are steadily accumulating climatic data to prove their case. At the same time, dissenters undermine the reliability of the statistical base, asserting the impossibility of providing definitive answers to this question. I vividly recall when photographs of a climate station over a hundred years were compared; the instrumentation facility had originally been sited on an exposed, barren heathland, but in later shots had been almost entirely engulfed by forest! Or to take another example: should we stop burning fossil fuels? Yes, say the advanced industrial nations, because we are depleting our finite resources and poisoning the air. No, counter the emerging industrial nations, who mock the hypocrisy of those nations that have already had their fossil-fuel-based industrial revolution, and who interpret the proposed ban as a geo-economic ploy to maintain emerging nations in their subordinate roles.

Whether or not our science is accurate, there can be little doubt that the survival of our planet depends on how we deal with these questions. We are poisoning our world, even as we invent heroic new ways of maintaining the environment. But to act responsibly, how much do we really need to know about the extent of a problem? How can you be certain that the members of some species are diminishing to a level that threatens its survival? And, even if survival is compromised, ecological disturbance theorists will point out that natural history is (in effect) one long narrative of the rise and fall of different species. Which species loss is truly important? Which losses matter? And before you even broach those decisions, recall that you will need proof of population decline, habitat loss, etc.

Postmodern environmentalism

On the face of it, postmodernism and environmentalism have a lot in common. Commenting on their complementarity, Matthew Gandy queries "the extent to which postmodernism embodies the emergence of a new social and political paradigm more conducive to environmental sustainability and whether postmodern philosophies of science hold out the hope for more ecologically sensitive scientific epistemologies."[81] K. J. Donnelly is unequivocal about his position: "The green movement and environmental awareness are specifically postmodern phenomena, fundamentally new attitudes to the natural environment."[82] Whether or not this conflation is correct need not worry us, but the links between postmodern perceptions and environmental attitudes are undoubtedly strong.

A collection of essays edited by Max Oelschlaeger is focused on the linguistic turn in postmodernism and its application to environmental ethics, but also provides a useful summary of some of the broader preoccupations of postmodern environmentalism. Asserting the revolutionary significance of language, Oelschlaeger claims that:

> Deconstructive analysis, literally, the close reading of a text that exposes its underlying ideology and assumptions (subtexts) has been brought to bear on the reality of history, truth, God, democracy, the soul, objectivity, science, and technology.[83]

Much follows from this, as you might expect. Various contributors to the Oelschlaeger collection call for a language based in "ontological humility" that attempts to connect human projects to the earth community, and move beyond a preoccupation with humankind. However, critics warn of the debilitating mysticism in the language of deep ecology (i.e. a focus on the union of self and world), and plead for more action-oriented thinking. Part of the problem in freeing language from its constraints has been the biases of science, which have tended to marginalize other voices and non-anthropocentric ethics. This is sometimes referred to as the 're-enchantment' of nature.

A postmodern-sensitive environmentalism has moved away from Enlightenment-style master narratives, toward a social construction of science. Some of this work has its philosophical roots in Lewis Mumford, Rachel Carson, and Murray Bookchin, as well as Hobbes and Heidegger.[84] One strong consensus among contemporary environmental philosophers and ethicists blames the discourse of the Enlightenment for many of our difficulties.[85] This is because it is a discourse about power, about privileging humans above non-humans, and silencing the voice of nature; in short, it is a discourse of domination. We may need an entirely different story about nature and otherness.

Perhaps the strongest counter-narrative has been constructed by ecofeminists:

> Ecological feminism, or "ecofeminism"...is the position that there are important connections between how one treats women, people of color, and the underclass [sic]on one hand and how one treats the non-human natural environment on the other.[86]

Jody Emel and Jennifer Wolch observe that the concatenation of multiple critiques – feminism, postmodernism, and multiculturalism – has created a space for reconsidering the 'animal question.'[87] Challenging the male patriarchal voice is, however, only the first stage in ecofeminist discourse. Elder *et al.* call for an end to the "cultural imperialism" with which we treat animals, a valorization of difference (whether amongst humans or between animal and humans), and an abandonment of our obsession with domination in favor of an approach that considers the needs of other life-forms.[88] Elder *et al.* also note how racial differences between humans are constructed by casting Others as different, on the basis of their interactions with animals (e.g. practices regarding eating, wearing, or killing animals). They suggest that such oppressive practices could be translated into a new popular politics which (following Spivak) they term a *practique sauvage*.[89]

Postmodern, postcolonial, and feminist voices have especially begun to unpack the meanings of the culture of Nature. For instance, Jennifer Price has argued that shopping at the Nature Company stores is a safe way to express environmental concern within the frame of a comfortable consumerism, at the same time as the environmentally-exploitative aspects of mass consumption are effectively masked.[90] Susan G. Davis examined the representation of nature in commercial culture, deconstructing the textual complexities of Sea World, in San Diego. She notes how cultural constructions of nature closely relate to concepts of gender, and (most intriguingly) shows how the performances of Shamu the killer whale have been revised to refocus their gender and ethnic alignments.[91] And she leaves no doubt about the reasons that nature is packaged for us in a particular way:

"Sea World [marine park] is like a mall with fish," and underwater life is the story that helps keep us shopping.[92]

Beyond culture, postmodernity has drawn attention (necessarily, and sometimes brutally) to the material conditions of life on this planet. 'Ecological footprint' studies measure the 'load' imposed by people on natural resources; the 'footprint' represents "the land area necessary to sustain current levels of resource consumption and waste discharge by that population."[93] For instance, Folke *et al.* estimated that the 29 largest cities of Baltic Europe appropriate for their resource consumption and waste assimilation an area of forest, agricultural, marine, and wetland ecosystems that is "at least 565–1130 times larger than the area of the cities themselves."[94] Very often, resource consumption occurs in distant regions elsewhere in the world, thus also potentially disturbing the harmonies of the global bioregions (through clearance and monoculture, for example). Under these circumstances, it is hardly surprising that sustainability has become a key word in environmental debates. Like all important terms, it has several meanings that tend to confuse as much as enlighten. But, roughly, it refers to the ability to meet "the needs of the present without compromising the ability of future generations to meet their own needs."[95]

The postmodern age (postmodernity) has also by now outstripped nature. For example, it is possible to buy, from Monsanto, a pest-resistant strain of potato that comes with its own Operating System, which is copyrighted and licensed only to the purchaser (a kind of *Potato 3.1*). In another case, the race toward scientific progress has already made possible the cloning of sheep; and despite the concerns of ethicists, politicians, and everyday people, you can be sure that someone, somewhere is currently working on cloning human beings.

Zoöpolis: an urban (postmodern) environmental ethic

A principal culmination of five thousand years of human history is a world of giant cities, or 'mega-cities.' In 1950, there were 78 cities with over 1 million inhabitants; by 1985, there were 258 such cities. The United Nations estimates that there will be more than 500 cities with over 1 million people by 2010, and 640 by 2025. By that time, over 1.25 billion people will live in cities with over 4 million inhabitants. Already, more than half the world's population is living in cities. The Los Angeles five-county region (Los Angeles, Orange, Riverside, San Bernardino and Ventura counties) is part of this global pattern of accelerated urbanization. Between 1960 and 1990, the region doubled in size to 14.5 million people. (It took New York City 150 years to grow by an equivalent number of people.) If current trends continue, Los Angeles will surpass New York as the nation's largest urban center sometime around the turn of the century. Southern California will then be one of only a score of mega-cities with populations over 10 million.

Because of the impact of ecosystem appropriation (our ecological footprint), and because of the synergies between postmodern thought and a revitalized environment-alism, the postmodern urban condition is axiomatically an environmental issue. This position is echoed in another of Donnelly's claims:

Figure 11.3   Navy Target 103A (Center for Land Use Interpretation)
One of five practice targets used by the Navy and Air Force in the Imperial Valley. Each target is approximately 300-feet, across, and consists of three concentric circles, made of dirt and old tires, that surround a central bulls-eye mound. Some of the center mounds are topped with target objects, such as the hulks of tanks and other military vehicles, or large metal objects, like water tanks. The targets are struck with inert practice bombs and strafed with 20mm and 50 caliber machine gun fire.

> The city, and especially suburbia, has become a locus for... [a] changed situation, with animals and plants [playing roles] that would have been unheard of thirty years ago.[96]

He also draws attention to the rise of the natural world as a "mainstay of televisual culture" – the principal screen locus for postmodern visual culture.[97]

In his political history of the Los Angeles landscape, Mike Davis underscores the voraciousness of the urban appetite. The emblematic irony is that the nation's "most picturesque and emblematic landscapes," which had attracted hundreds of thousands of immigrants to Southern California, had been "systematically eradicated."[98] Davis documents how, for most of the twentieth century, warnings about the degradation of the natural landscape had been sounded, but then studiously ignored. For instance, a 1930 report by the Olmsted Brothers and Bartholomew & Associates cautioned that "the things that make [Los Angeles] most attractive are the very ones that are first to suffer from changes and deteriorate through neglect."[99] Later, in the mid-1960s, the environmental planning firm of Eckbo, Dean, Austin and Williams urged the California Legislature to "treat the area as a total system of air, land and water relationships, not simply as real estate to be developed."[100] The enormous influx of population throughout the twentieth century, and the extent of speculation in land and property development contributed to the massive eradication of Southern California's canonical landscapes. But Davis also draws attention to the extent of corruption in municipal government,[101] and the unfailing capacity of public and

Figure 11.4 Seals and homeless people shelter together under Santa Monica Pier (Whale Rescue Team)

private interests to ignore environmental hazards.[102] Local wags quip how Southern California has only four kinds of weather: earthquakes, floods, fires, and riots.

In one of the boldest of recent moves to redress the ecological and epistemological balance in favor of nature, Jennifer Wolch has described the "zoöpolis" – a city in which human and non-human animals co-exist to their mutual benefit.[103] From her Southern California base, she advocates a "transspecies urban theory" founded in an "eco-socialist, feminist, anti-racist urban praxis."[104] Such a viewpoint treats animals as subjects, not objects, and challenges us to "think like a bat,"[105] i.e. to consider the animal standpoint. Wolch concludes:

> I call this renaturalized, re-enchanted city *zoöpolis*. The reintegration of people with animals and nature in zoöpolis can provide urban dwellers with the local, situated everyday knowledge of animal life required to grasp animal standpoints or ways of being in the world, interact with them accordingly in particular contexts, and motivate political action necessary to protect their autonomy as subjects and their life spaces. Such knowledge would stimulate a thorough rethinking of a wide range of urban daily life practices: not only animal regulation and control practices, but landscaping, development rates and design, roadway and transportation decisions, use of energy, industrial toxics and bioengineering–in short, all practices that impact animals and nature in its diverse forms. ...And, at the most personal level, we might rethink eating habits, since factory farms are so environmentally destructive *in situ*, and the western meat habit radically increases the rate at which wild habitat is converted to agricultural land worldwide (to say nothing of how one feels about eating cows, pigs, chickens or fishes once they are embraced as kin).[106]

Like many others, Wolch is concerned to dissolve the dualisms separating culture and nature, city and country. Although she makes no explicit reference to postmodernism in her zoöpolis, she embraces some of its main precepts in later writings, incorporating notions of difference, body, multiculturalism, and postcolonialism, linking these with strands in feminist and postmodern thought.[107] However, Wolch's activist stance also anchors her critique firmly in the traditions of a materialist political economy. Although she is cognizant that contemporary urban planning has embraced notions of sustainability and environmental management, she recognizes the essential instrumentality (and rationalist biases) of such interventions (cf. Chapter 6 above). For instance, she notes the irony that Malibu's policy of "total fire suppression" – in an area where periodic burns are a part of normal ecological process – is not only very costly to taxpayers, but also intensifies the severity of any fire that does occur. She also observes government's complicity in the loss of nature in Southern California, even as the region makes significant improvements in managing other environmental hazards (most especially human-induced difficulties such as air pollution).

Another important claim made by Wolch for her transspecies urban theory is that zoöpolis would deter the marginalization of animal and human Others, and thereby induce a different, more progressive local politics (the *practique sauvage* referred to above). Evidence for this trend has been documented by other analysts of Southern California environmentalism. Roger Keil, in particular, notes that Angelenos have developed unique, emancipatory, and successful ways of dealing with nature in their emerging world city.[108] In addition, Laura Pulido has documented the rise in

Southern California of grassroots social movements based in environmental concerns.[109]

(De)limiting Postmodernism: Nanotechnic Biocentrism

Credible environmental policy requires a reliable environmental science, which is something we do not possess. The postmodern ethos has demonstrated the contingent nature of scientific knowledge. So, while science is necessary, its limitations palpably undermine its credibility. Herein lies a beautiful contradiction. Postmodernists can point to a victory ("Science is contingent! Get it?"). Yet, after reflection, they may also concede the necessity of some modicum of precision. ("Well, I know you don't know, but I'd still like your best guess before we act.") The conundrum invites us to consider the limits of postmodernism, in a precipitous, life-threatening context. This is not some salubrious session in a fashionable salon. It is a question of species and planetary survival.

The contingencies of postmodernism are well-suited to the shadowy infofaults of cyberspace. And yet, cyborgs in the metaverse are unavoidably in place even as they surf the net. Embedded in a place-specificity, we cyborgs are engulfed by the nanotech – the organically-expanding city around us. In *Idoru*, William Gibson's post-earthquake Tokyo was speedily rebuilt using nanotech, stuff that "just grows":

> "you could see those towers growing, at night. Rooms up top like a honeycomb, and walls just sealing themselves over, one after another. Said it was like watching a candle melt, but in reverse. ... Doesn't make a sound. Machines too small to see. They can get into your body, you know? ...
>
> [Eddie] says the infa, infa, the *structure* was wide open then. He says ... you could come in and root around, quick, before it healed over and hardened up again. And it healed over around Eddie, like he's an implant or something, so now he's part of the infa, the infa-"
> "Infrastructure"[110]

Cut to Jennifer Wolch's zoöpolis, one of the most compelling postmodern concepts in this book. Even while she insists on the role of biology, political economy, and ecofeminism in her transspecies urban theory, she also adopts an animal standpoint to explicate a political strategy for attaining zoöpolis. Thus, on one hand, conventional science and social theory are vital to her imagining; on the other, the essential contingencies of science and politics are also engaged. In merging these sensibilities with her personal politics, Wolch adopts a kind of biocentrism that is indistinguishable from her world view, her own ontological positioning.[111]

If we join nanotech together with biocentrism, we get *nanotechnic biocentrism*, a clumsy-sounding but effective metaphor for the postmodern urban condition; it can be used to define the edges of postmodernism (the task of delimiting), as well as opening up its horizons (the task of de-limiting, or if you prefer, un-limiting).

A nanotechnic biocentrism describes how we ourselves and our perceptions are nurtured within and around the confines of the technological and natural environments. It accords center-stage to our complicity in building the emergent hyperspace, both materially and cognitively; *we are engulfed in the infrastructure even as we ourselves give form to it.* Just as I cannot think like a bat, I cannot fully comprehend my position in the infrastructure. But knowledge about the cognitive and material constitutions of the urban is what I am seeking. Nanotechnic biocentrism may be an awkward term to describe this dual search, but its very unfamiliarity is likely to deter a too-ready rationalizing and stereotyping of what I intend. Nanotechnic biocentrism is a focus on the way I am positioned in, and create knowledge about, nature and the material urban world. The juxtaposition of nature's limits and the real/virtual urban is a deliberate ontological strategy of displacement and contradiction. It is simultaneously a position of knowing and unknowing. More precisely, nanotechnic biocentrism is an interrogatory attitude for confronting the postmodern urban condition.

Figure 11.5   Nanotechnic Biocentrism (Michael Dear)
(Corporate Head, Terry Allen, 1990)

Notes

1. Forster, E. M. "The Machine Stops," in Forster, E. M., 1928: *The Eternal Moment*, New York: Harcourt, Brace & Company, p. 17.
2. See page 97 of this book.
3. See page 97 of this book.
4. Quoted in Bruno, G. 1993: *Streetwalking on a Ruined Map*, Princeton: Princeton University Press, p. 47.
5. See page 178 of this book.
6. Quoted in Morse, M., "An Ontology of Everyday Distraction," in Mellencamp, P. (ed.) 1990: *Logics of Television*, Bloomington: Indiana University Press, p. 203.
7. Paul Virilio, quoted in Friedberg, A. 1993: *Window Shopping: Cinema and the Postmodern*, Berkeley: University of California Press, p. 203.
8. Baudrillard, J., "The Ecstasy of Communication," in Foster, H. (ed.) 1985: *Postmodern Culture*, London: Pluto Press, p. 127.
9. Colomina, B. 1994: *Privacy and Publicity: Modern Architecture as Mass Media*, Cambridge: MIT Press, p. 251.
10. Friedberg, A., *Window Shopping* , p. 179.
11. Ibid., p. 4.
12. Ibid., p. 184.
13. Stephenson, N. 1993: *Snow Crash*, New York: Bantam Books, p. 24–6.
14. Forster, E. M. "The Machine Stops," in Forster, E. M. 1928: *The Eternal Moment*, New York: Harcourt, Brace & Company.
15. Gibson, W. 1996: *Idoru*, New York: G. P. Putnam's Sons, p. 46.
16. Ibid., p. 178.
17. Cf. Castells, M. 1996: *The Rise of Network Society*, Cambridge, Mass: Blackwell; Loader, B. D. (ed.) 1997: *The Governance of Cyberspace: Politics, Technology and Global Restructuring*, New York: Routledge.
18. Graham, S. and Marvin, S. 1996: *Telecommunications and the City: Electronic Spaces, Urban Places*, London: Routledge, p. 9.
19. Mitchell, W. J. 1995: *City of Bits: Space, Place, and the Infobahn*, Cambridge: MIT Press, p. 7.
20. Ibid., p. 3.
21. Ibid., pp. 160–1, p. 106.
22. Ibid., p. 134.
23. Ibid., p. 167.
24. Ibid., p. 173.
25. Ibid., p. 17.
26. Ibid., p. 18.
27. Ibid., p. 28.
28. Ibid., p. 31.
29. Ibid.
30. Ibid., p. 48.
31. Ibid., p. 43.
32. Ibid., p. 147.
33. Ibid., p. 151.
34. Ibid., p. 10.
35. Ibid., p. 16.
36. Ibid., p. 138.
37. Ibid.

38. Robins, K. 1997: "The New Communications Geography and the Politics of Optimism," *Soundlings* 5, Spring, p. 198.
39. Ibid., p. 200.
40. Ibid., p. 202.
41. Mitchell, W. J., *City of Bits* , p. 157.
42. Ibid., p. 112, p. 149.
43. Rheingold, H. 1993: *The Virtual Community: Homesteading on the Electronic Frontier*, Reading: Addison-Wesley Publishing Company, p. 288.
44. Ibid., p. 287.
45. Ibid., p. 288.
46. Ibid., p. 287.
47. Ibid., pp. 285–286.
48. Ibid., p. 286.
49. Ibid., p. 27.
50. Ibid., p. 292.
51. Ibid., p. 291.
52. Ibid., p. 285.
53. Ibid., p. 297.
54. Cf. Rheingold, H. *The Virtual Community: Homesteading on the Electronic Frontier*; Hafner, K. 1997: "The Epic Saga of the Well," *Wired*, 5.05; Utne Reader: The Best of the Alternative Media. March/April 1995.
55. Dishman, D. 1996: "Digital Dissidents: The Formation of Gay Communities on the Internet," MA Thesis, Department of Geography, University of Southern California.
56. Bennahum, D. S. 1997: "The Internet Revolution," *Wired*, April, 122–173.
57. Ibid., pp. 123–124.
58. Ibid., p. 168.
59. Ibid., p. 172.
60. Dibbel, J., "A Rape in Cyberspace" in Derry, M. (ed.) 1993: *Flame Wars: The Discourse of Cyberculture*, Durham: Duke University Press.
61. Gibson, W. 1993: "Disney Land with the Death Penalty," *Wired Magazine*, Issue 1.4 September/October, p. 51.
62. Ibid., p. 115.
63. Ibid.
64. Aksoy, A. and Robins, K., "Exterminating Angels: Morality, Violence, and Technology in the Gulf War," in Mowlana, H., Gerbner, G. and Schiller, H. I. (eds.) 1992: *Triumph of the Image, The Media's War in the Persian Gulf – A Global Perspective*, San Francisco: Westview Press, p. 325.
65. Ibid., 331.
66. Sterngold, J. 1995: "Imagine the Internet As Electronic Casino," *New York Times*, October 22.
67. Turkle, S. 1997: *Life on the Screen: Identity in the Age of the Internet*, New York: Touchstone Books, p. 17.
68. Ibid., p. 14.
69. Ibid.
70. Ibid., p. 18.
71. Ibid., pp. 18–-19.
72. Ibid., p. 20.
73. Ibid.
74. Ibid., p. 21.
75. Quoted in ibid., p. 22.
76. Ibid.

77. Ibid., pp. 23–6.
78. Ibid., p. 49.
79. Ibid., p. 47.
80. Harvey, D. 1996: *Justice, Nature and the Geography of Difference*, Cambridge, Mass: Blackwell, pp. 373–91.
81. Gandy, M. 1996: "Crumbling Land: The Postmodernity Debate and the Analysis of Environmental Problems," *Progress in Human Geography* 20 (1), p. 23–4.
82. Donnelly, K. J. 1994: "A Ramble Through the Margins of the Cityscape: The Postmodern as the Return of Nature" in Dowson, J. and Earnshaw, S. (eds) *Postmodern Subjects/Postmodern Texts*, Postmodern Studies 13. Amsterdam; Atlanta: Rodopi, p. 50.
83. Oelschlaeger, M. (ed.) 1995: *Postmodern Environmental Ethics*, New York: State University of New York Press, p. 8.
84. See Macauley, D. 1996: *Minding Nature: The Philosophers of Ecology (Democracy and Ecology)*, New York: Guilford Press.
85. For example Birch, T. H. 1995: "The Incarceration of Wildness: Wilderness Areas as Prisons" in Oelschlaeger, M. (ed.) *Postmodern Environmental Ethics*; Frodeman, R. "Radical Environmentalism and the Political Roots of Postmodernism: Differences That Make a Difference" in Oeschlaeger, M. (ed.) 1995: *Postmodern Environmental Ethics*; and Manes, C. "Nature and Silence" in Oelschlaeger, M. (ed.) 1995: *Postmodern Environmental Ethics*.
86. Warren, K. and Erkal, N. (eds.) 1997: *Ecofeminism: Women, Culture, Nature*, Bloomington: Indiana University Press, p. xi.
87. Wolch, J. and Emel, J. (eds.) 1998: *Animal Geographies: Place, Politics and Identity in the Nature–Culture Borderlands*, New York: Verso Books, Chapter 1.
88. Elder, G., Wolch, J, and Emel, J. 1998: "*Le Pratique Sauvage*: Race, Place and the Human–Animal Divide," in Wolch, J. and Emel, J. (eds.) *Animal Geographies: Place, Politics and Identity in the Nature-Culture Borderlands*, p. 88.
89. Ibid., p. 72.
90. Price, J., "Looking for Nature at the Mall: A Field Guide to the Nature Company," in Cronon, W. (ed.) 1995: *Uncommon Ground: Toward Reinventing Nature*, New York: W. W. Norton, pp. 186–202.
91. Davis, S. G. 1996: *Spectacular Nature: Corporate Culture and the Sea World Experience*, Berkeley: University of California Press, pp. 11–12.
92. Ibid., p. 2.
93. Wackernagel, M. and Rees, W. 1996: *Our Ecological Footprint: Reducing Human Impact on the Earth*, Gariola Island, BC: New Society Publishers, pp. 5, 9.
94. Folke, C., Jansson, A., Larsson, J. and Costanza, R. 1997: Ecosystem Appropriation by Cities, *Ambio* Vol. 216 No. 3, p. 167.
95. Wackernagle, M. and Rees, W. *Our Ecological Footprint: Reducing Human Impact on the Earth*, p. 33.
96. Donnelly, K. J. "A Ramble Through the Margins of the Cityscape: The Postmodern as the Return of Nature", p. 44.
97. Ibid., p. 52.
98. Davis, M. 1996. "How Eden Lost Its Garden: A Political History of the Los Angeles Landscape" in Scott, A. and Soja, E. 1996: *The City: Los Angeles and Urban Theory at the End of the Twentieth Century*, Berkeley: University of California Press, p. 171.
99. Ibid., p. 161.
100. Ibid., p. 174.
101. Ibid., p. 176.

102. Davis, M. 1996. "How Eden Lost Its Garden: A Political History of the Los Angeles Landscape" in Scott, A. and Soja, E. 1996: *The City: Los Angeles and Urban Theory at the End of the Twentieth Century*, Berkeley: University of California Press, p. 174.

103. Wolch, J. 1996: "Zoöpolis" *Capitalism, Nature, Socialism* 7 (2), pp. 21–48.

104. Ibid., p. 23.

105. Ibid., p. 27.

106. Ibid., pp. 29–30.

107. Cf. Wolch, J. and Emel, J. (eds.) *Animal Geographies: Place, Politics and Identity in the Nature-Culture Borderlands*, especially Chapters 3 and 4.

108. Keil, personal communication. See also Keil, R. 1998: *Los Angeles*, New York: Wiley.

109. Pulido, L. 1996: "Multiracial Organizing Among Environmental Justice Activists in Los Angeles" in Dear, M., Schockman, H. E., and Hise, G. (eds) *Rethinking Los Angeles*, Thousand Oaks: Sage Publications, pp. 171–89.

110. Gibson, W. *Idoru*, p. 46.

111. Readers should in fairness be advised that Wolch and I are spouses. She made the insistences to which I refer over breakfast one morning. Her reaction to my accusation that she is an archetypal postmodernist is best left unrecorded.

12

The Personal Politics of Postmodernity

Gradually, it has become clear to me what every great philosophy has so far been: namely, the personal confession of its author and a kind of involuntary and unconscious memoir...

Friedrich Nietzsche[1]

You cannot write anything about yourself that is more truthful than you yourself are. That is the difference between writing about yourself and writing about external objects. You write about yourself from your own height. You don't stand on stilts or on a ladder but on your bare feet.

Ludwig Wittgenstein[2]

One of the most intriguing of puzzles is the nerveless rage of negative reactions to postmodernism. It is not as though truth were an uncontested topic – something we

Figure 12.1   Yo! (Michael Dear)
Spanish-speaking Toyota owners adjust the car-maker's logo to read: YO (I, or me).

could straightforwardly read off the surfaces of the text, word, or landscape. If this were the case, then there would be no desire to search for knowledge, no privilege in its possession. The intense longing for truth is evidence that it is not simply there for the taking. Then why has postmodernism's relativism caused such intensely negative reactions? I think the answer lies in two related conditions: the politics of the personal, or the way postmodernism challenges deep theoretical commitments of whatever stripe; and the place–time specifics of the contemporary culture of criticism. To show this connection, I examine my own and the politics of others in context. I am working toward the rather unsettling conclusion that critics are not seeking nor do they wish to reconcile their prejudices with the challenges of postmodernism.

Archeologies of the Personal

When I was a very young child, one of the high points of my day came when Chris Kinsey finished delivering bread to various homes in the mining village of Treorchy, in Wales. He used to carry the pungent slabs in a voluminous basket attached to the front of a bicycle, and when the basket was empty, he would grab me and dump me inside it. Then he would ride off at breakneck speed through the narrow streets back to the bakery, making my eyes water. I preferred those white-knuckle excursions to what was another routine event in my daily childhood round, when my father would pull me aside to talk politics. His sermons used to take place at the oddest hours, because he usually worked shifts at the coal-mine and his "free time" was (to me) painfully unpredictable. His perennial favorite was the tale of how Winston Churchill sent in the troops to break up the miners' strike during the depression. Everybody in the Rhondda hated Churchill, even after World War II, and my father was determined that I should understand my political birthright. It mattered not a jot that his history was a trifle shaky. I also passed a lot of time with a cousin, Marian, who was quite a bit older than me. She spent most of her short life in a psychiatric hospital. Relatives euphemistically whispered that Marian was "in the sanatorium," or, even more cryptically, "in Bridgend" (after the hospital's location). But I knew she was mad. It never bothered me; she was simply the most entertaining relative one could ever wish for.

When I was an undergraduate, my moral tutor (yes, they were called that!) invited me into his office during my freshman year specifically to say: "You are exactly the kind of student we don't want at this university." He never bothered to explain why. It was true that I was a teenager (thus automatically worthy of intergenerational scorn), but I suspect his censure had more to do with matters of class and nationality. I had been born into a family of Welsh coal miners and was destined to follow the tradition; he was a middle-class Englishman in an English university.

As a graduate student in England during the late 1960s, I spent a lot of time marching around London's Grosvenor Square, calling out the names of soldiers killed in Vietnam into a megaphone directed toward the Embassy of the United States of America. Later, completing my doctorate in Philadelphia, I discovered that my working-class and anti-war credentials (though belonging to different places and times) brought an unexpected legitimacy to many of my arguments in progressive circles. These were the same credentials that almost got me expelled as an undergraduate.

Many decades have gone by. Since my childhood in Wales, I have lived for long periods in Australia, Canada, England, and the United States of America. Throughout this time, my scholarly work has resolutely remained focused on the mentally disabled and the homeless, always seen through left-tinted lenses. I cannot shake off the commitments from a particular time and place; nor do I want to. They are who I am.

The postmodern emphasis on difference has placed an intense spotlight on the subject, body, and personal identity. As authors struggle to engage the political in themselves and their works,[3] the questions of identity and authenticity have arisen in two related but nevertheless distinct ways. In the first place, disguise is a consequence of what happens once a work is received by others. It is not uncommon for multiple layers of disguise to become the 'person' or the 'thought' irrespective of the intentions of the author or the text.[4] Secondly, disguise is an integral component in the work of many artists and scholars, whether it is deliberate or unconscious. Many intellectuals (and others) have chosen to exploit the ambiguities inherent in disguise by deliberately occupying the margins of discourse.[5] The significance of such personal positioning cannot be doubted, for, as Olsson has observed: "who questions his body, thereby questions his culture."[6] Adorno also placed the question of human subjectivity at the center of his critical inquiry into authenticity and domination.[7] The problems and pitfalls inherent in a postmodern politics of identity have been acutely pinpointed by Jacques Derrida. His *Otobiographies* invites us to consider what is at stake when an author signs a work, because it is impossible to control its fate by any power of the author once it is released upon the world.[8] In the case of Nietzsche's writings, Derrida is less interested in the fact that Nietzsche's works were appropriated by proto-Nazi ideologues than with exactly why his texts lent themselves to such interpretations in the first place.[9] He concludes that there are many competing versions of Nietzsche, none with an absolute claim to the truth, but all made possible by something in the structure of his writings.

In this chapter, using a series of examples of the Nazi legacy, I explore the relationships among place, time, identity, authenticity, and memory. The two forms of disguise I have just mentioned form the framework for this inquiry. First, using the examples of Martin Heidegger and Paul de Man, I examine the ways in which people are inevitably the products of particular places and times, but also how interpretive contexts (or 'cultures of criticism') overwhelm and reconstitute the ideas and the person, no matter how specific or forthcoming the texts/authors are. Next, I explore the way in which individuals deliberately manipulate their identities, by interrogating the lives and writings of Albert Speer and Philip Johnson. Finally, I show how the commemoration of memory, at later times and in different places, distorts the identity and authenticity of individuals, peoples, and ideas. In this way, it becomes possible for fictions to supersede truths. Such cultural distortions of place and time have special relevance for the practice of politics in a postmodern era, which has placed new emphasis on the subject, difference, and polyvocality in discourse.[10]

Authenticity and the Culture of Criticism

If philosophy is simply understood as a search for truth and politics as the pursuit of power, the two appear to have very little in common. In reality, however, both are concerned with the production, use, and control of truth, with generating, channeling, and manipulating streams of power – though in admittedly very different ways – and from this comes their closeness and their conflict. Philosophy and politics are, in fact, inextricably tied together, but their relationship is also precarious and unstable.

Hans Sluga[11]

Martin Heidegger remains one of the most influential philosophers of the twentieth century. He was also a Nazi. Paul de Man was one of the founders of deconstructionism. He also wrote antisemitic newspaper articles during World War II. Using these two examples, I now examine in more detail the relationship between individuals, their work, and the time–space specificities of the contemporaneous cultures of criticism.

The case of Martin Heidegger catapulted to a new public prominence in 1987 following the appearance of *Heidegger et le Nazisme* by Victor Farias.[12] Elements of the debate have been concisely and meticulously reconstructed by Thomas Sheehan, who described Heidegger as "a provincial, ultraconservative German nationalist" who was from 1932 a Nazi sympathizer.[13] Three months after Hitler came to power, Heidegger became rector of Freiburg University. He also joined the Nazi Party. Heidegger's record, as rector and teacher, is deeply distasteful. Soon after his 1933 appointment at Freiburg, he wrote that his goal was to bring about "the fundamental change of scientific education in *accordance with the strengths and the doctrines of the National Socialist State*."[14] He introduced the Nazi cleansing laws into Freiburg, so that Jews, Marxists, and non-Aryan students were denied financial aid. He secretly denounced colleagues and students. He declined to supervise Jewish doctoral students, and betrayed his mentor, Edmund Husserl.[15] Hugo Ott's political biography portrays a man who was disloyal, self-obsessed, mendacious, and spiteful.[16] In 1945 an internal de-Nazification committee at Freiburg charged Heidegger with the following: "having an important position in the Nazi regime; engaging in Nazi propaganda; and inciting students against allegedly 'reactionary' professors."[17] After a protracted debate, during which his health suffered badly, Heidegger was in 1949 declared a Nazi fellow traveler and was prohibited from teaching. By 1951, however, the political climate had altered sufficiently to allow emeritus status to be granted, thus enabling him to teach once again at the university. Heidegger's postwar defence of his political actions leaves little doubt that he remained convinced of their rectitude.[18]

The case of Paul de Man is more ambiguous. Between 1940 and 1942 the young de Man wrote 169 articles for *Le Soir*, a Belgian newspaper that had been taken over by collaborationists following the 1940 Nazi occupation. During the same period he wrote 10 other articles for a Flemish journal, *Het Vlaasmsche Land*, which was also under German control. These pieces were mainly book reviews, concert notes, and general literary and cultural criticism. In 1942, de Man resigned as critic of *Le Soir* for reasons that remain obscure. When Belgium was liberated from the Nazis in 1944, de Man appeared before a military tribunal but no collaborationist charges were brought against him.[19] The attack on de Man principally hinges on a single article, "Jews in Contemporary Literature," published as part of a special section on antisemitism in *Le Soir* of March 4, 1941. In it, de Man argues that European literature would not be weakened if Jews were to be placed in a separate colony. The crucial passage in this article reads:

> En plus, on voit donc qu'une solution du problème juif viserait à la création d'une colonie juive isolée de l'Europe, n'entraierait pas, por la vie littéraire de l'Occident, de conséquences déplorable.[20]

Since so much hangs on these words, I shall provide only the most literal of translations:

> "In addition, one sees therefore that a solution of the Jewish problem that aims for the creation of a Jewish colony isolated from Europe, would not entail, for the literary life of the West, deplorable consequences."

With its isolationist sentiments, it is easy to see why this sentence is the principal target of de Man's detractors. However, it is also likely that this is the single instance in de Man's complete *oeuvre* where such sentiments are so plainly stated.[21]

How do we read, see, and listen through the horrific images associated with Nazism? Should we now discard Heidegger and de Man, just as we routinely discount the rhetoric of our political enemies? To begin to answer these questions, let me first identify some important distinctions between the time- and place-specificities of the two cases.

Heidegger's involvement with Nazism is beyond doubt (although, as Sluga points out, many philosophers on both sides were all too willing to align themselves with their respective national interests).[22] Wolin concludes that philosophers will never again be able to read Heidegger without taking account of his odious politics.[23] Sheehan draws a similar conclusion: "Heidegger's engagement with Nazism was a public enactment of some of his deepest and most questionable philosophical convictions."[24] Although there is little to be gained from revisiting Heidegger's political past in order to pass judgement yet again, Sheehan argues that his philosophy must now be reappraised:

> One would do well to read nothing of Heidegger's any more without raising some political questions.... [One] must re-read the works for what might still be of value, and what not. To do that, one must read his works...with strict attention to the political movement with which Heidegger himself chose to link his ideas. To do less than that is, I believe, finally not to understand him at all.[25]

Some of the works, such as the commentaries on Plato and Aristotle, may be unaffected by Heidegger's Nazism. Other positions will require a complete review. Sheehan identifies the problem areas with a forensic precision: "Above all, I believe we can ill afford to swallow...his grandiose and finally dangerous narrative about the 'history of Being' with its privileged epochs and peoples, its somber insistence on the fecklessness of rational thought, its apocalyptic dirge about the present age, its conclusions that 'only a god can save us.'"[26] The point, according to Sheehan, is not to stop reading Heidegger but to begin demythologizing him.

Paul de Man's lesser offense has unleashed a violent attack on (and subsequent defense of) the man, his work, and his politics. One of his principal detractors, Stanley Corngold, is absolute in his denunciation: "I believe that de Man's critical work adheres to and reproduces, in literary masquerade, his experiences as a collaborator."[27] In other words, de Man's role in the invention of deconstruction is nothing more than an elaborate subterfuge to whitewash a duplicitous past. Other critics have ransacked de Man's private life for evidence. For instance, Georges Goriely asserted that de Man "was 'completely, almost pathologically dishonest', a crook who bankrupted his family. 'Swindling, forging, lying were, at least at the time, second nature to him.'"[28] A more temperate and ultimately more persuasive critique was offered by Jacques Derrida, an Algerian Jew and friend of de Man. Derrida confesses that when he was shown de Man's wartime journalism: "My feelings were first of all that of a wound, a stupor, and a sadness that I want neither to dissimulate nor exhibit."[29] He then proceeds with an analysis of the texts, making a strong argument for the undecidability of de Man's position. Even when de Man discussed the solution of a Jewish literary colony isolated from the rest of Europe, Derrida asserts that this "could not be associated with what we now know to have been the project of the 'final solution.'"[30] He also points out that de Man had publicly explained his behavior in a 1955 letter, written shortly after his arrival in the United States; that fame came late in life to de Man; and that further announcements about a distant past would have been "a pretentious, ridiculous and infinitely complicated gesture."[31] Derrida insists that we view the totality of de Man's work before condemning him on the basis of his wartime journalism.

Cultures of criticism can be transitory and volatile, but they are always highly time-and place-specific (one obvious example is fin-de-siècle Vienna).[32] The divergent receptions that have greeted the revelations about Heidegger and de Man provide insight into contemporary influences on our collective critical psyche. These influences include:

(1)   the timing of the revelations (Heidegger's Nazi affiliation was well-known for many years; de Man's antisemitism is newly revealed);
(2)   the magnitude of the crime (Heidegger's unrepentant Nazism is extensively documented and quite unequivocal; de Man's offense may be reducible to a single long-lost essay);
(3)   the nature of the offense (Nazism is a twentieth-century phenomenon and almost universally reviled; antisemitism has its roots in previous millennia and still has many adherents);
(4)   the perpetrator's stature (Heidegger is too important and central a figure to dismiss; de Man is a somewhat lesser figure); and
(5)   the critic's agenda (what is to be gained from this attack? why is it being launched now?).

The fluidity of the cultural climate following World War II explains the rapid fluctuation in Heidegger's fortune, and the proliferation of disguises surrounding his works. In 1949, he was punished for his Nazism; yet by 1951 the climate had changed sufficiently to allow for a limited rehabilitation. Since then (and especially since his death in 1976) there has been an almost continuous reappraisal of his

contribution, albeit in an atmosphere of heightened skepticism and critical intentionality. Paul de Man's journalism was written in a war-torn Europe in which German
hegemony seemed inevitable.[33] Some have blamed this context for his youthful
antisemitic lapse. According to Miller, de Man "stupidly wrote the deplorable
essay in order to please his employers and keep his job."[34] Following his arrival in
the United States, de Man's academic reputation developed slowly, to be secured only
by the rise of deconstructionism during the past decade. When his wartime journalism received widespread publicity in 1988, a chaotic flood of condemnation was
released. The intent of many critics was to establish de Man as a duplicitous person
who, by extension, had devised a duplicitous theory. *In extremis*, critics attacked de
Man's deconstructionism as an elaborate invention to blur the meaning of his
political writings (although less taxing subterfuges are surely available to an intelligent man intent on concealing his past).

How do these events reflect on our present culture of criticism? It is clear that
different standards are being applied to the legacies of the two men. Heidegger,
the unrepentant Nazi and major twentieth-century philosopher, is being handled
for the most part with care and respect. De Man, part of our urgent present even
though he died only seven years after Heidegger, is being vilified for a lesser offense.
Why this double standard? Why this unseemly rush to condemn de Man? I have
already mentioned that status, timing, and the nature of the offense influence critical
reactions at different times and in different places. But the full answer lies deep in our
critical culture. Some have argued that the crescendo of distortions surrounding de
Man are not solely or even principally directed against him. According to Miller:

> It is fear of this power in "deconstruction" and in contemporary critical theory as a
> whole, in all its diversity, that accounts better than any other explanation for the
> unreasoning hostility, the abandoning of the canons of journalistic and academic
> responsibility, in the recent attacks on de Man, on "deconstruction" and on theory in
> general.[35]

In a similar vein, Derrida angrily criticized those who use the revelations about de
Man to condemn deconstructionism, accusing them of using the same "exterminating gesture" they claim that de Man made during the war.[36]

If these interpretations are correct, there is something poisonous in the present
culture of criticism. Postmodernism in general, and deconstruction in particular, have
introduced unsettling levels of ambiguity and uncertainty into our discourses. Their
advocates have emphasized that we cannot move forward with the same imperious
certainty that we previously espoused. Instead, we must live with interpretive uncertainty, with a world we will never fully understand. Critics of de Man, postmodernism and deconstruction appear to find such ambiguity intolerable. Their
counterattack has spilled over into the personal life and politics behind the philosophy, discrediting the person in order to bury the thought.

The Nazi regime was evil. Heidegger's Nazism was wrong; so was de Man's
(putative) antisemitism. But such moral lapses do not nullify the philosophy and
criticism of either. As Pierre Bourdieu argued, Heidegger's thought cannot be reduced
to an ideological product of his socio-political circumstances; but neither can it be
treated as having no relation to its historical context.[37] The same caveat should apply

to Paul de Man. The proper way to read these (and other) texts is neither in isolation from the author's politics nor as reducible to them. The ramifications of this conclusion are enormous. Hans Sluga closes his meditation on the Heidegger controversy by recommending that we "rethink the whole question of philosophy's relation to politics."[38] The specific place–time circumstances within which a work is written and subsequently interpreted can no longer be regarded as innocent.

Identity

I believe that ... a writer is not simply doing his works in his books, but that his major work is, in the end, himself in the process of writing his books. The private life of an individual, his sexual preference, and his work are interrelated, not because his work translates his sexual life, but because the work includes the whole life as well.

Michel Foucault[39]

Everyone leads a life replete with contradiction, including the Gucci Marxist and the materialist evangelist. Such contradictions will come as no surprise to anyone with even the slightest experience of human nature. The significant question is what are we to do with our knowledge of difference and inconsistency? We can usually recognize when the limits of our personal tolerance have been reached; but what about the myriad ambiguous cases? How do we strike a balance between admiration and antipathy, between skepticism and persecution? These questions are especially pertinent when individuals themselves reconstruct their legacies, as in the examples of the disguises of Albert Speer and Philip Johnson.

Albert Speer was an architect who fell in with Hitler's inner circle during the 1930s.[40] Rapidly establishing himself as one of Hitler's favorites, Speer garnered increasingly prominent commissions including the plan for rebuilding Berlin as the world capital at the end of World War II. After the death of the German armaments minister in 1942, Hitler appointed Speer to that position, giving him authority over an industrial army of 14 million workers, many of them slave laborers and concentration camp inmates. The war crimes tribunal at Nuremberg found Speer guilty of exploiting slave labor, but innocent of complicity in genocide; he was sentenced to twenty years in Spandau prison. Speer himself denied all knowledge of the particularities of the Nazi genocide, claiming that pressure of work and Hitler's personal charisma prevented him from inquiring after potentially discomfiting details.

In the conclusion of his study on *The Last Days of Hitler*, Hugh Trevor-Roper identified Speer as "the real criminal of Nazi Germany" – not because he was a murderer, anti-Semite, or fanatic, but because he was a sophisticated, intelligent man who personified the educated Germans' disdain for politics.[41] This same aura, however, carried Speer through Nuremberg with his life intact; Bradley F. Smith noted that his Western judges looked with sympathy on such a "clean-cut and apparently repentant professional man with strong anti-Soviet tendencies."[42] For much of the remainder of his life, Speer devoted himself to self-examination through friendships with *inter alia* a Protestant chaplain, a Catholic monk, and a Jewish rabbi.

In a penetrating account of Speer's life, Gitta Sereny focuses not on what Speer did but on what he knew and why he acted the way he did.[43] She accepts Speer's own account of his early infatuation with Hitler and Nazism. Referring to his first lunch with Hitler, Speer says to Sereny:

> Can you conceive of what I felt?...Here I was, twenty-eight years old, totally insignif-icant in my own eyes, sitting next to him at lunch . . .as virtually his sole conversation partner. I was dizzy with excitement.[44]

Speer was not without selfish professional and political ambitions, however self-effacing he appears in this portrayal. Reflecting on his life after release from Span-dau, he frankly confesses:

> During the twenty years I spent in Spandau prison I often asked myself what I would have done if I had recognized Hitler's real face and the true nature of the regime he had established. The answer was banal and dispiriting: My position as Hitler's architect had soon become indispensable to me. Not yet thirty, I saw before me the most exciting prospects an architect can dream of.[45]

Sereny also stresses the power of the personal bond between Hitler and Speer, which kept him in thrall long after he recognized Hitler's criminality.

The almost palpable ambiguities in Speer's life are anticipated in the epigraph to Sereny's book, where she quotes W. A. Visser't Hooft (leader of the World Council of Churches, 1948–66):

> People could find no place in their consciousness for such...unimaginable horror... they did not have the imagination, together with the courage, to face it. It is possible to live in a twilight between knowing and not knowing.[46]

Historian Claudia Koonz suggests that truth for Speer was an "elaborate intellectual game," and that Sereny's dissection reveals a "slick opportunist who brilliantly served Hitler, outwitted the justices at Nuremberg and found power in postwar West Germany."[47] These are Koonz's words. Sereny herself concedes that Speer lied on occasion but that "truth" is evasive, each turn of the kaleidoscope producing different variations on the pattern of truth.

In 1977, after decades of dissembling and subterfuge, Speer ultimately conceded:

> to this day I still consider my main guilt to be my tacit acceptance (*Billigung*) of the persecution and murder of millions of Jews.[48]

Speer died from a stroke on December 14, 1981.

The 1994 publication of Franz Schulze's biography of architect Philip Johnson reveals a great deal about the human penchant for disguise.[49] Schulze himself underplays Johnson's 1930 flirtations with Nazism and his attempts to form a right-wing political party (lacking a definite political program, "their only firm decision was that members of their party would wear grey shirts").[50] Paul Goldberger is more critical of what he calls the architect's "ghastly political escapades" which reveal a man of stunning intelligence but equally stunning amorality, "not evil but lacking any clear center."[51] Johnson himself determinedly separated aesthetics from morality. When he attended a 1933 Nazi rally he responded less to the political content and more to Hitler's charisma and "all those boys in black leather."[52]

Hitler's armies entered Poland on September 1, 1939. Soon after, the German Propaganda Ministry invited Johnson to follow the Wehrmacht to the Front. Later he reported:

> The German green uniforms made the place look gay and happy. There were not many Jews to be seen. We saw Warsaw burn and Modlin being bombed. It was a stirring spectacle.[53]

About this same time, five articles by Johnson appeared in the magazine *Social Justice*. According to Schulze:

> The first, published July 24, attacked Britain and "aliens" for turning France into "an English colony": "Lack of leadership and direction in the [French] state has let one group get control who always gain power in a nation's time of weakness – the Jews."[54]

Schulze tries to account for the lack of critical attentiveness to the young Johnson's dubious politics. He notes Johnson's unassailable position in the architectural firmament; that (unlike Heidegger and de Man) he is still very much alive; and that his later activities in causes identified with Judaism may be interpreted as effort toward atonement.[55] Johnson also enlisted the help of powerful defenders. Abby Aldrich Rockefeller, one of the New York Museum of Modern Art's founders, is reported to have defended Johnson thus: "every young man should be allowed to make one large mistake".[56] And biographer Schulze himself somewhat disingenuously concluded:

> In any case, to the extent that his actions can be made out, they were decidedly unheroic, meriting little more substantial attention than they have gained.[57]

Apart from his politics (disreputable), his status as an architect (derivative, opportunistic), and his role as iconoclast (unmatched in twentieth-century architecture), reviewers of Schulze's biography have dwelled much on Johnson's sexuality. Critic Allan Temko argues that Johnson's "unabashed homosexuality" complicates everything we know about him.[58] He was deeply excited by the rallies that Speer staged for Hitler, and Temko describes Schulze's "major discovery" that Johnson felt a "sexual thrill" watching the destruction of Polish villages.[59] Martin Filler has written critically of the amount of prurient attention devoted to Johnson's sexuality which (he claims) has distracted attention from the virulence of his political activities, writings and correspondence. He expresses disbelief in the face of Johnson's ability to avoid accountability, even though his past has caught up with him.[60] Johnson captured some facets of his kaleidoscopic personality in a 1953 Smith College talk:

> I studied philosophy as an undergraduate, instead of architecture. Perhaps that is why I have none now. I do not believe there is a consistent rationale or reason why one does things...I am too far gone in my relativistic approach to the world really to care very much about labels. I have no faith whatever in anything.[61]

Schulze politely sanitizes Johnson's credo thus:

> Whatever the irreducible core of Philip's personality, it lay beneath multiple layers of motivations manifest in an almost unnatural facility at the intermingling of activities and interests, not all of them discernably consonant with one another.[62]

As he grew older, Johnson's studied ambivalence allowed him to champion successive emergent architectural fashions, including postmodernism and deconstructivism. He attracted increasing controversy, not least because he recognized it as one way of attracting attention.[63] His fundamental amorality is perhaps best revealed after his 1980 commission (with John Burgee) to build the Crystal Cathedral in Garden Grove, Los Angeles County. The Cathedral is the center of widely-televised evangelical Christian ceremonies. In 1990, invited to share Robert Schuller's pulpit at the dedication of the church's new bell tower, Johnson was asked:

> "Tell us, Philip, what went through your mind when you designed this beautiful building?". . . Philip responded by drawing close to the preacher and speaking in a subdued, almost inaudible voice. "I thought I knew history. I thought I knew what the Gothic spires of old stood for. The Romantic period and the thirteenth-century periods were the highest periods, in spiritual Christianity. I thought I knew how to combine these things to create a great tower. I was wrong. I could not have done this – I have to say it humbly, and I don't ever feel humbly, but I do this morning – I got help, my friends. I think you all [voice breaks] know where that help came from." Schuller beamed in transcendent acknowledgement. "Philip Johnson we love you!" he cried.

> Later, when asked by an interviewer who knew him well enough, "Philip, how could you?", Philip briefly buried his head in his hands in mock shame, then grinned and replied, "Wasn't that *awful*!"[64]

Andrew Ballantyne concludes that Johnson was prepared to go further than most to obtain a commission; that he was more cynically and effectively manipulative than other architects. He quotes Johnson: "I wanted to do the job. I got very religious." According to Ballantyne, it was as simple as that.[65]

Memory

> I used to think I would be rewarded for good behavior. Therefore if I wasn't understood, I must not be understandable; if I wasn't successful, I must try harder; if something was wrong, it was my fault. More and more now I see that context is all. When someone judges me, anyone or anything, *I ask: Compared to what?*
>
> Gloria Steinem[66]

Memories are recollected for a myriad reasons: we recall only good times we spent with lost loved ones, turning our thoughts away from painful images of their death or departure; or we reconstruct meaning in our lives by constantly reordering past experiences into a narrative of coherence; and we seek to atone for past wrongs, struggling for redemption and reconciliation. The problems of remembrance and forgetting – of disguise – are rarely more acute than in the case of institutionalized commemoration.

In 1995, a dispute emerged over the portrayal of Jewish victims of the Holocaust, at Yad Vashem, the Jerusalem-based museum and memorial.[67] Alongside stark photographs of carnage and mayhem is one image of unidentified Jewish women about to die; the women are stripped of their clothes and have arms folded across their breasts presumably to hide part of their nakedness and/or to keep warm. A group of Orthodox Jews in Jerusalem objected to the display of dead or near-dead people without their clothing, on the basis that the victims are being degraded yet again by their nakedness. Defenders of the photographs objected to the sanitization of Nazi cruelty that would be implied by the removal of the images. If their demands were not met, the Orthodox complainants threatened to establish their own museum to memorialize the victims "properly and objectively," in the words of one leader, Rabbi Moshe Zeev Feldman. Efraim Zuroff, Israel director of the Simon Wiesenthal Center responded: "You would think that on this one thing there would be a willingness to stand silently together. . . . Do you think the Nazis distinguished between Jews when they killed them?"[68] More than half a century later, in the new state of Israel, Jews are in conflict over whose version of the Holocaust should be preserved.

Distaste and resentment also simmer under the surface of negotiations to commemorate the Holocaust in Berlin.[69] In 1987, talk-show host Lea Rosh announced that she would ensure that Berlin would have a memorial to the six million Jews who died. She was granted permission to erect the memorial on a prominent site by Chancellor Helmut Kohl. As Jane Kramer emphasized, Rosh is not a Jew.[70] She changed her name from "Edith", and then took up the cause of commemoration. Berlin historian Reinhard Rürup called the proposed site "inappropriate" as a memorial to a single victimized group, the Jews, when in fact many groups suffered under the Nazis, including gypsies, homosexuals, and mentally retarded people.[71] Rosh responded that she would see to the erection of memorials for other victims, once the Jewish memorial was completed. This proposal did not appeal to Rürup. He predicted that when other persecuted groups stepped forward to press their cases, all memory would be lost to the "banality of conflicting claims."[72] The question of the Berlin memorial has since stalled. Some Jewish critics have entered the debate, objecting to any Holocaust memorial in the place–time of contemporary Germany, on the grounds that it would imply a German mediation of Jewish suffering and identity.[73]

The question of memory extends even to national identity. The complicity of ordinary Germans in Nazi atrocities is a highly-contested topic. Most commentators have denied the existence of a collective complicity with the Holocaust. In contrast, Daniel Goldhagen dismisses the ideas that ordinary Germans disapproved of the Holocaust and its methods, or that they participated in genocide only under duress. Instead, Goldhagen insists, the vast majority of Germans shared Hitler's antisemitism and willingly collaborated in its brutal implementation.[74]

Hitler, it is generally conceded, never disguised his intention of ridding Germany of the Jews. Yet his murderous vendetta had to await the beginning of the Russian campaign when circumstances and geography (specifically the annexation of Poland) contrived to facilitate his program.[75] Central to this effort was "the camp," a generic term that included the concentration camps, extermination camps, detention facilities, work camps, transit camps, and ghettos – together described by Goldhagen as Nazi Germany's largest institutional creation. He shows that the killings, usually assumed to take place out of sight in gas ovens run by the SS, actually involved ordinary German people often in full view of other ordinary German people. Goldhagen focuses on three specific instruments of death: police battalions, work camps, and death marches. The police battalions (*Ordnungspolizei*) were recruited haphazardly, minimally trained, and then sent out to round up Jews for transport to camps, or to shoot them. Members of such units were not compelled to take part in these activities. In work camps, Jews were forced into unproductive tasks with inadequate food and rest, and constantly abused by brutal guards until they died. (At Majdanek work camp, the mortality rates were not significantly lower than at extermination camps such as Auschwitz.) Forced marches involved food deprivation, beatings, and shootings. They continued even during the last phases of the war, demonstrating (for Goldhagen) the intensity of Germany's commitment to genocide.[76]

The history of the extermination camps betrays an equally broadly-based enthusiasm and commitment to their grisly goal.[77] Initial gassings of prisoners were affected at the front with crudely re-rigged vehicles; later, stationary gas vans were delivered custom-built to occupied territories. And finally, gas chambers capable of mass extermination were built, and refined into ever more capable killing factories.[78] One ambitious young physician, Dr Freidrich Mennecke, wrote enthusiastically to his wife about the latest technology at Dachau: "There are only two thousand [prisoners], who will be quickly done, as they can be examined only in assembly-line fashion."[79]

The Place–Time of Postmodern Politics

The arrival at a theory of identity is also an arrival at a certain theory of space, apparatus, body and structure.

Catherine Ingraham[80]

Where do identity and authenticity lie in the mutable folds of place–time? If they exist they are nowhere at rest. They float like fragments of a continent on a molten sea – always in motion, sometimes disappearing under one another like tectonic plates, only to return to the surface in a reconstituted form. The geological metaphor is apt. It reminds us that very little is new; we are merely sifting through the metamorphosed foundations of previous eras, albeit under different circumstances.

For me, the value of the postmodern (both in theory and practice) derives from its emphasis on the contingent nature of knowledge; its openness to the consequences of difference; its deliberate engagement with conflicting ideologies; its steadfast occupation of the margin; and its refusal to be co-opted.[81] This is not an abdication of political obligation, nor a case of anything goes. Instead, it is a more adequate dramatization of the dilemmas of personal politics in the contemporary world. Our lives as scholars and practitioners are everywhere compromised by forced and unforced complicities.[82]

So: what is it about relativistic scholarship that drives conventional academics so quickly from debate to defensive vituperation? Postmodernists, deconstructionists, post-structuralists and many others are already convinced of the contingent nature of explanation, recognizing a world of difference all around us. Yet the defenders of traditional "objective" scholarship – whether from the right or the left – are unwilling

Figure 12.2 Marlene (produced in Germany)
The name of a street in the unified Berlin was to be changed to honor Marlene Dietrich. The effort failed because of the action of protesters who objected to the film star's sympathy with the Allies during World War II. In 1997, a street in the reconstructed Potzdamer Platz was named after her, and a commemorative stamp was issued.

to allow that truth can be determined only on a more limited, temporary, or even singular basis. Instead, they claim transcendence for their private visions, under the guise of some kind of universalism, thereby insinuating that they alone hold the keys to knowing.[83] While traditionalists continue the search for solid ground, they seem constitutionally incapable of conceding that postmodernists are just as dedicated in the pursuit of truth and reality – although theirs is a different kind of dedication, one which recognizes that these are elusive concepts, subject to multiple, often divergent interpretations. Postmodernists reject traditional hegemonies, refusing to seek permission from others about what can and should be known, or how to go about knowing it. The keepers of the keys cannot stomach this; to defend themselves, they have invented the arcane obligations of the canon and the caricatures of political correctness.

In my professional work on homelessness I have encountered analogous misunderstandings between people who are unable/unwilling to speak the same language. I once worked on a large-scale, collaborative, strategic planning project with experts in architecture, urban design, economic development, transportation engineering, and historical preservation. It was amazing how quickly the consultant teams divided into two broad groups: those who draw, and those who write. The distinction, somewhat oversimplified, was between the line and the word: the draw-ers' method consisted primarily of sketching, and they valued above all the quality of being a visionary untrammeled by past and present realities; the writers used words and figures to imagine futures that were firmly rooted in an analysis of past trends and constrained by predictions about emerging socioeconomic and political futures. The two camps ended up working separately for the duration of the project. The draw-ers, for their part, seemed oblivious to the multiple groundings that inevitably frame architectural practice, ignorant of Andrea Kahn's warning that "architecture is...understood to encompass texts and drawings as well as buildings, and the discipline of architecture is instituted by and erected between these three modes of production.[84] For my part (as a writer, not a draw-er), I learned that placing a line on paper was a far too final way for me to begin a discourse on urban futures. Such lacunae are inevitably linked to biases in professional education; but they also pertain to a crude credentialism, and the fear of losing professional authority and autonomy.[85] I have observed similar dogmatism in other practical situations, as when experts argue fruitlessly over the 'true causes' of homelessness.

The yawning gaps separating postmodernists from traditionalists, draw-ers from writers, etc. are far from trivial. They stem from misunderstandings that are usually blamed on long-standing convictions about fundamental incommensurabilities between different methodologies. But these legendary incommensurabilities are founded on a falsehood. Given the seductive unknowability of the real world, and the different ways of seeing and representing that we have invented, it is inevitable that observers will produce different texts and divergent political agendas based on their personal experiences. But nothing in a text nor its assumptions automatically presages incommensurability (which is not to say that intertextual comparison is an easy, uncomplicated task; quite the contrary). A much more likely explanation for incommensurability – one that is rarely broached in polite discourse – is that proponents of conflicting explanations simply do not want reconciliation and prefer not to search for it. This is primarily because no-one is prepared to relinquish or compromise the languages, theories, texts, and methods that represent the bases for their identity and authority; no-one is willing to abandon ideology in favor of communicative competence.

Postmodernism is a contested terrain, but there can be little doubt about the significance of the challenge it poses. Once again to adapt Stephen Toulmin's felicit-ous phrases, what modernism regarded as timeless and universal, postmodernism has revealed to be particular and local;[86] and modernism's rational/utopian political agenda is betrayed as specific and malleable in both time and place. As the cacoph-ony of postmodern voices vies for attention in the interstices between existing hegemonies, the Babel of different theorists may be the closest thing we have to a common language, since most of the engaged interlocutors are prepared to forgo (even if temporarily) the authority of their preferred discourse.[87] At the same time, however, such critical openness tends also to provide convenient ammunition for those committed to attack on the basis of revealed personal beliefs. This is the source of an unhappy double standard, as when critics are scornful of those who concede subjectivity, yet defend their own universals without being forthcoming about their own proclivities.[88]

It is an elemental folly to erect artificial barriers between knowledge and personal politics. Feminists have emphasized that writers who include autobiographical details in their 'scientific' writings may assist in overcoming this false opposition and, in Norris' words, "inaugurate a reading attentive to the various points of exchange, of inter-textual crossing and confusion, between life and work."[89] Person, text, and politics cannot be separated; a contextual reading of Heidegger, de Man,

Speer, and Johnson (or anyone else for that matter) is unavoidable. Unfortunately, we seem neither well-equipped nor well-disposed to undertake the subtle, informed readings that contextual analysis requires. But as a beginning, I believe that there is an imperative favoring the polyvocality of postmodernity. Static place–time norms are the consequence of domination and subordination, those invisible glues that a critical social science seeks to dissolve. Without communication across ideologies, places, and times, all is silence.

Notes

1. Kaufmann, W. (ed.) 1968: *Basic Writings of Nietzsche*, New York: The Modern Library, p. 203.
2. Wittgenstein, L. 1980: *Culture and Value*, translated by Peter Winch. Chicago: University of Chicago Press, p. 33e.
3. See, for example, Blomley, N. 1994: "Activism and the Academy," in *Society and Space, Environment and Planning D*, 12(4) pp. 383–85.
4. Derrida, J. 1984: *Otobiographies: L'enseignement de Nietzsche et la politique du nom propre*, Paris: Galilee.
5. There is an important and ambivalent tension between those who choose to occupy the margins and those who feel excluded from the mainstream. On marginalism, see the collection of essays by Ferguson, R., Gever, M., Minh-ha, T., and West, C. (eds.). 1990: *Out There: Marginalization and Contemporary Culture*, Cambridge, MIT Press. The essay by Gayarti Chakravorty Spivak, "Explanation and Culture: Marginalia," (pp. 377–93), is especially relevant to my text.
6. Olsson, G., 1991: *Lines of Power/ Limits of Language*, Minneapolis: University of Minnesota Press, p. 150.
7. Adorno, T. W. 1973: *The Jargon of Authenticity*, Evanston, Northwestern University Press. Trent Schroyer has written a perceptive foreword to this translation by Knut Tarnowski and Frederic Will.
8. Derrida, J. *Otobiographies*. Also see Norris, C. 1986: *Derrida*, London: Fontana, for a critical summary of Derrida's argument (especially Chapter 8).
9. Friedrich Wilhelm Nietzsche was born in 1844. His father died when he was five, and the young Nietszche was forced into the company of grandmother, mother, sister and aunts, a situation he apparently did not much care for. He turned to philosophy after studying theology and classical philology, but was never content at the University of Basel, where he had taken up a professorship. He left the university after a few years and devoted himself to a life of writing, isolation and sexual asceticism. Friedrich's sister Elizabeth, a dominant personality, traveled in 1886 with her husband, Bernhard Förster, to Paraguay in order to establish an Aryan colony called Nueva Germania. Upon her return to Germany, the dreadful Elizabeth took control of her brother's work and reputation: it was she who largely rewrote Nietzsche's posthumous masterwork *The Will to Power*, investing it with her own proto-Nazi views; it was she who invented and promulgated the cult of his philosophy, inserting it into the new order emerging out of war-ravaged Europe. She died just before the outbreak of World War II and was given a full Nazi funeral, which was attended by Adolf Hitler. No other woman, with the possible exception of Cosima Wagner, was so celebrated in the cultural world of pre-war Nazism. And no-one did more to secure (her vision of) her brother's reputation.
10. I would like this essay to be viewed as an analysis of the political culture of changing place–time, especially as it relates to postmodernity. My inquiry is situated at the intersection between what would conventionally be described as "political geography"

and "cultural geography." But this essay is part of an ongoing re-writing of "political geography" in the light of the agenda established by contributors to Keith, M. and Pile, S. (eds) 1993: *Place and the Politics of Identity*, London; New York: Routledge. And in its emphasis on culture, this inquiry shows how the production of knowledge is never innocent of the place–time circumstances in which it is created and (later) received. As such, it is about the relationship between altered human subjectivities and cultural transformations, appealing to an agenda already prefigured in the collection of essays edited by Pile, S. and Thrift, N. (eds), 1995: *Mapping the Subject: Geographies of Cultural Transformation*, London; New York: Routledge, especially Chapters 1, 2, and 18.

11. Sluga, H. 1993: *Heidegger's Crisis: Philosophy and Politics in Nazi Germany*, Cambridge: Harvard University Press, p. vii.
12. Published in English as Farias, V. 1989: *Heidegger and Nazism*, translated by Paul Burrell and Gabriel Ricci. Philadelphia: Temple University Press.
13. Sheehan, T. 1988: "Heidegger and the Nazis", New York Review of Books. p. 39.
14. Quoted in ibid., p. 39; the emphasis was Heidegger's own.
15. As well as in the Farias volume cited earlier, the basic case against Heidegger has been assembled by Ott, H. 1993: *Martin Heidegger: A Political Life*, translated by Alan Blunden. New York: HarperCollins. Many of the original texts by Heidegger in support of Nazism are reprinted in Wolin, R. (ed.) 1993: *The Heidegger Controversy: A Critical Reader*, Cambridge: MIT Press.
16. Ott, H., *Martin Heidegger*.
17. Sheehan, T. "Heidegger and the Nazis", p. 47.
18. See Heidegger's final interview, published posthumously in *Der Speigel* in May 31, 1976; translated as "Only a God can save us" by Maria Alter and John Caputo, in *Philosophy Today*, xx(4/4): 267–85. The translation is reprinted in Wolin, R. (ed.), *The Heidegger Controversy*.
19. The basic facts in the case of Paul de Man are contained in Lehman, D. 1991: *Signs of the Times: Deconstruction and the Fall of Paul de Man*, New York: Poseidon Press. (although the reader is warned that this account is basically hostile toward de Man and deconstructionism).
20. Hamacher, W., Hertz, N. and Keenan, T. (eds) *Paul de Man, Wartime Journalism 1940–1942*, Lincoln: University of Nebraska Press. De Man's words were published seventeen months before the first deportations of Belgian Jews to the death camps; see Miller, J. H. 1988: *"NB," Times Literary Supplement* June 17–23. p. 685. While it is unclear whether de Man intended this opinion to imply a literal or a figurative ghettoization of the Jews, it is hardly possible to read his statement as an invitation to genocide.
21. Derrida draws this conclusion after reviewing de Man's writings; see Derrida, J. 1988: "Like the Sound of the Sea Deep within a Shell: Paul de Man's War," *Critical Inquiry*, 14, pp. 590–652. He concludes: "in the sum of the total articles from that period that I have been able to read, I have found no remarks analogous or identical to this one." (p. 631).
22. Sluga, H., *Heidegger's Crisis*..
23. Richard Wolin, "French Heidegger Wars," in Wolin, R. (ed.), *The Heidegger Controversy*, p. 273.
24. Sheehan, T. "Heidegger and the Nazis," p. 38.
25. Ibid., p. 47.
26. Ibid.
27. Corngold, S. 1988: Letter to the Editor, *Times Literary Supplement*, 26 August-September 1. p. 931.
28. Quoted in Atlas, J. 1988: "The Case of Paul de Man," *The New York Times Magazine*, August 28. p. 37.

29. Derrida, J. "Like the Sound of the Sea Deep within a Shell," p. 600.
30. Ibid., p. 632.
31. Ibid., p. 638.
32. See, for instance, Schorske, C. E. 1980: *Fin-de-Siècle Vienna: Politics and Culture*, New York: Knopf; and Janik, A. and Toulmin, S. 1973: *Wittgenstein's Vienna*, New York: Touchstone.
33. Kaplan, A. 1993: *French Lessons: a memoir*, Chicago: University of Chicago Press.
34. Miller, J. H. "*NB*," p. 685.
35. Ibid.
36. Derrida, J. "Like the Sound of the Sea Deep within a Shell." p. 651.
37. Quoted in Zimmerman, M. 1988: "L'Affaire Heidegger," *Times Literary Supplement*, October 7–13. p. 1116.
38. Sluga, H. *Heidegger's Crisis*, p. ix and Chapter 10.
39. Quoted in Miller, J. 1993: *The Passion of Michel Foucault*, New York: Simon and Schuster, p. 19.
40. Speer's life is recounted in a remarkable autobiographical account, Speer, A. 1970: *Inside the Third Reich: Memoirs*, New York: MacMillan.
41. Trevor-Roper, H. R. 1962: *The Last Days of Hitler,*. New York: Collier, p. 302. This is how Trevor-Roper accuses Speer:
    Nevertheless, in a political sense, Speer is the real criminal of Nazi Germany; for he, more than any other, represented that fatal philosophy which has made havoc of Germany and nearly shipwrecked the world. For ten years he sat at the very centre of political power; his keen intelligence diagnosed the nature and observed the mutations of Nazi government and policy; he saw and despised the personalities around him; he heard their outrageous orders and understood their fantastic ambitions; but he did nothing. Supposing politics to be irrelevant, he turned aside, and built roads and bridges and factories, while the logical consequences of government by madmen emerged.
42. Smith, B. F. 1981: *The Road to Nuremberg*, New York: Basic Books, p. 248; quoted in Craig, G. A. 1995: "In Love with Hitler," *New York Review of Books* November 2. p. 9.
43. Sereny, G. 1995: *Albert Speer: His Battle with Truth*, New York: Knopf.
44. Ibid., p. 103.
45. Speer, A. *Inside the Third Reich* p. 32.
46. Sereny, G. *Albert Speer*, p. vii.
47. Koonz, C. 1995: "Blind By Choice," *New York Times Book Review*, October 8. p. 12.
48. Sereny, G. *Albert Speer*, p. 707. Professor Richard J. Evans concludes that "Albert Speer lived his lie to the last." See Evans, R. J. 1995: "The Deceptions of Albert Speer", *The Times Literary Supplement*, September 29, p. 6.
49. Schulze, F. 1994:*Philip Johnson: Life and Work*, New York: Knopf.
50. Ballantyne, A. 1996: "Doing the Devil's Work," *Times Literary Supplement*, April 7, p. 7.
51. Goldberger,P. 1994: "The Man in the Glass House," *New York Times Book Review*, November 27, p. 14.
52. Ballantyne, A. "Doing the Devil's Work."
53. Schulze, F. *Philip Johnson*, p. 139.
54. Ibid., p. 138.
55. Ibid.
56. Ibid., p. 143.
57. Ibid., p. 144.
58. Homosexuality was also a factor in the intellectual agenda, career, and manner of Michel Foucault's dying. Critic James Miller sees Foucault as an essentially private moralist who begins and ends his career by attempting to orient himself in relation to society and his own desires. His early life was dominated by coming to terms with his homosexuality,

but the mature Foucault focused on social boundaries and their transgression. Powered by the Nietzschean injunction to become what one is, Foucault sought potentially transformative "limit-experiences," and under the influence of Georges Bataille, the limits of erotic transgression, especially sado-masochistic practices. According to Miller, Foucault's conscious efforts at scripting the self allow us to directly observe the relationship between the man and his work: "*all* of Foucault's books, from the first to the last, comprise a kind of involuntary memoir, an implicit confession." Indeed, Foucault himself invited such investigations. Not surprisingly, the somewhat prurient and sensational overtones in Miller's study have been denounced by Foucault's supporters as homophobic gossip. Others, less sympathetic to the man and his work, have used the revelations to mount what has been called a campaign of "intellectual liquidation" – claiming, in essence, that because Foucault's acclaim was founded on a lie, his work could now legitimately be discredited. Aspects of this reaction are discussed by Ryan, A. 1993: "Foucault's Life and Hard Times," *New York Review of Books*, April 8, p. 14. The phrase "intellectual liquidation" is used by Gordon, C. in "A Maverick Insider," *The Times Literary Supplement*, August 27, 1996, p. 27.

59. Temko, A. 1994: "Bad Boy Builder," *Los Angeles Times Book Review*, December 25, p. 1.
60. Filler, M. 1994: "Prince of the City," *New York Review of Books*, December 22, p. 46.
61. Schulze, F. *Philip Johnson* p. 271.
62. Ibid., p. 105.
63. Ibid., p. 273.
64. Ibid., p. 341–2.
65. Ballantyne, A. "Doing the Devil's Work," p. 7.
66. Steinem, G. 1994: *Moving Beyond Words*, New York: Simon and Schuster, pp. 282–3 (emphasis in original).
67. Haverman, C. 1995: "In a Museum of Hell, Qualms About Decorum," *New York Times*, March 7, p. A-6.
68. Ibid.
69. Kramer, J. 1995: "The Politics of Memory," *The New Yorker*, August 14, pp. 48–65.
70. Ibid., p. 50.
71. Ibid., p. 51.
72. Ibid., p. 52.
73. In Atlanta, Georgia, there is an analogous dispute between the family of Dr Martin Luther King Jr and the US National Park Service over how to commemorate the civil rights' leader's memory. See Smothers, R. 1995. "Issue Behind King Memorial: Who Owns History?" *New York Times* January 16, p. 1, p. 7.
74. Goldhagen, D. J. 1996: *Hitler's Willing Executioners: Ordinary Genius and the Holocaust*, New York: Knopf.
75. Craig, G. A. 1996: "How Hell Worked," *New York Review of Books*, April 18, p. 6.
76. Clive James has written that Goldhagen overstates his case; James emphasizes the coercive powers of the Nazi state, Hitler's obsession with Jews, and the multiple acts of local resistance by Germans as evidence of the absence of a monolithic antisemitism in Germany during World War II. See: James, C. 1996: "Blaming the Germans" *The New Yorker*, April 22, pp. 44–50.
77. Feig, K. G. 1981: *Hitler's Death Camps: The Sanity of Madness*, New York: Holmes and Meier; Fleming, G. 1984: *Hitler and the Final Solution*, Berkeley: University of California Press.
78. Kogon, E., Langbein, H. and Rucherl, A. (eds) 1993: *Nazi Mass Murder: a Documentary History of the Use of Poison Gas*, translated by Mary Scott and Caroline Lloyd Morris, New Haven: Yale University Press.
79. Ibid., p. 41.

80. Ingraham, C. "Lines and Linearity: Problems in Architectural Theory," in Kahn, A. (ed.) 1991: *Drawing/Building/Text*, New York: Princeton Architectural Press, pp. 83–4.
81. On marginalism, see the collection of essays by Ferguson, R., Gever, M., Minh-ha, T. and West, C. (eds), *Out There: Marginalization and Contemporary Culture*.
82. For a brilliant series of essays on complicity in the public lives of individuals, see three books by Malcolm, J. 1984: *In the Freud Archives*, New York: Knopf; Malcolm, J. 1990: *The Journalist and the Murderer*, New York: Knopf; and Malcolm, J. 1994: *The Silent Woman: Sylvia Plath and Ted Hughes*, New York: Knopf.
83. One thinks, for instance, of Gertrude Himmelfarb's caustic attack on recent trends in historical scholarship, Himmelfarb, G. 1994: *On Looking into the Abyss: Untimely Thoughts on Culture and Society*, New York: Knopf. For a well-judged critique of Himmelfarb's position, see Ryan, A. 1994: "The Two Himmelfarbs," *The Times Literary Supplement*, August 5, p. 7. See also Chapter. 15 below.
84. Kahn, A. (ed.) 1991: *Drawing, Building, Text*, New York: Princeton Architectural Press, p. 6.
85. The significance of the line in architectural thought is discussed in an interesting essay by Catherine Ingraham, entitled "Lines and Linearity: Problems in Architectural Theory," in Kahn, *Drawing, Building, Text*, pp. 63–84. See also Olsson, G. 1991: *Lines of Power/Limits of Language*, Minneapolis: University of Minnesota Press.
86. Toulmin, S. 1990: *Cosmopolis: The Hidden Agenda of Modernity*, New York: The Free Press, especially pp. 330–35.
87. This point has also been made by Nesbitt *inter alia*; see Lois Nesbitt, "Postscript," in Kahn, A. (ed.) *Drawing, Building, Text*, p. 169.
88. For instance, I am unable to read Gertrude Himmelfarb's defense of the canon of Western thought without awareness of her family connections to Irving Kristol (editor of the neoconservative *New Criterion*) and William Kristol (a leading Republican voice in the refashioning of American conservatism).
89. Norris, C. *Derrida*, p. 213.

13

The Power of Place

There is an immediate relationship between the body and its space, between the body's deployment in space and its occupation of space. Before *producing* effects in the material realm . . . , before *producing itself* by drawing nourishment from that realm, and before *reproducing itself* by generating other bodies, each living body is space and has space: it produces itself in space and it also produces that space.

Henri Lefebvre[1]

Personal politics and personal identity are defined by place, at the same time as they are constitutive of place. This is the principal lesson from Chapter 12. Heidegger, de Man, Speer and Johnston were all creatures of specific space–times, just as they produced works that reconstituted those space–times. In this chapter, I shall focus on the production of (postmodern) urban spaces, with a special emphasis on monuments and public memory. Once again, Henri Lefebvre provides a key to unlocking our understanding.

Lefebvre contrasts the banality of buildings (notwithstanding their importance) with the poetry of monuments. He claims that monuments make space legible, providing the signs by which such spaces may be read, while also masking the powers that produced them. Through what they represent, Lefebvre suggests, monuments close off multiple readings and portray communal values, thus rendering spaces incontestable. Steve Pile sums up Lefebvre's position in this way:

> Monuments are not just spaces of the body, subjectivity and language, but are also grids of meaning and power, which are complicit in the control and manipulation of simultaneously real and metaphorical space, where for example chairs become thrones, buildings become monuments, and so on.[2]

For these very same reasons, I might add, monuments occupy contested spaces. Precisely because they are so potent, they are conflicted sites of identity and power, culture and memory. They incorporate global and national sentiments, just as they find expression in the personal and everyday places.

Postmodern Memory, Postmodern Places

What does it mean for a culture to have memory? According to Marita Sturken, cultural memory is distinct from personal memory and history:

I use the term "cultural memory" to define memory that is shared outside the avenues of formal discourse yet is entangled with cultural products and involved with cultural meaning....

The self-consciousness with which notions of culture are attached to these objects of memory leads one to use the term "cultural" rather than "collective."[3]

In *Tangled Memories*, Sturken explores the politics of the Vietnam Veterans' War Memorial (by Maya Lin) in Washington, DC and the AIDS Memorial Quilt, among other objects and sites. She points out the importance of the image and representation in memory, and shows how memory is so often located in specific places and objects, quoting Pierre Nora: "Memory attaches itself to sites, whereas history attaches itself to events."[4] Sturken's analysis underscores just how important sites, places, and representations become in the commemoration process:

The debates over what counts as cultural memory are also debates about who gets to participate in creating national meaning.[5]

The huge arguments that dogged the Vietnam Memorial and the AIDS Quilt were emblematic of deep differences over who controlled the memory and what form that memory should take. Sturken places both the Vietnam War and the AIDS epidemic in the context of postmodern culture, "not only because they have disrupted previously held truths but also because they force a rethinking of the process of memory itself."[6] The war and the epidemic, she asserts, have disrupted American master-narratives of "imperialism, technology, science and masculinity."[7]

The condition of postmodern memory is also emphatically about forgetting. This is sometimes a strategic act of burying those events that are too painful to contemplate, but as importantly, forgetting emphasizes the difficulty of relating memory to original experience. As Linda Hutcheon has characterized the postmodern condition:

It does not deny the existence of the past; it does question whether we can ever know the past other than through its textualized remains.[8]

I would expand that last phrase to emphasize the "(con)textualized" nature of our knowledge.

Both the Vietnam Veterans' War Memorial and the AIDS Quilt are powerful, extraordinarily moving experiences. Set within the context of the nation's primary focus of commemoration (The Washington Mall), the War Memorial is a subdued, unheroic gesture, a plain open wound scored in the grassy surface of the Mall. The sight of people weeping as they touch the names of the dead soldiers, or leaving small tokens of memory and love, are all but unbearable. It made me remember calling out some of those same names in a Grosvenor Square demonstration over two decades earlier. The Quilt has on occasion also been spread over a vast acreage of the Mall, each piece commemorating a lost loved one. But the Quilt's power lies in its very ephemerality, its mobility. It reminds us of how brief all human life is. It travels. Sections of the Quilt have visited many parts of the United States. In this sense, the site of commemoration is brought home to you. It is a profoundly unheroic gesture in any public sense, even though each individual section is a history of life of personal

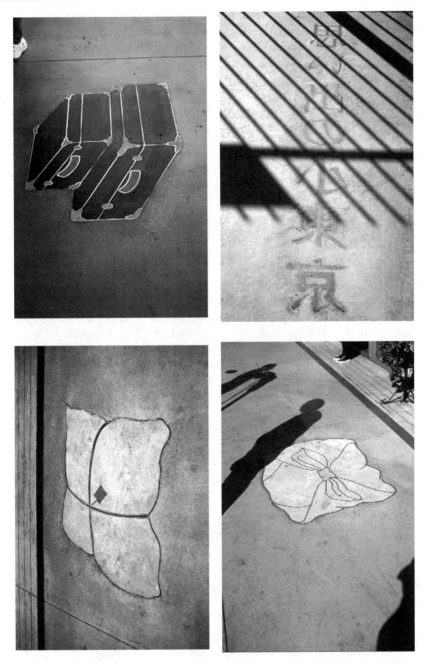

Figure 13.1/a–d "Remembering Old Little Tokyo," Power of Place Project (Shiela Levrant de Bretteville, designer) (ADOBE, LA, photos by (a) Alessandra Moctezuma (top); and (b) Ulises Diaz (bottom))

De Bretteville's design consists predominantly of words and images set in the sidewalk. These representations of packages and cases are poignant reminders of the few possessions that Japanese-American internees were allowed to carry when they were incarcerated during World War II.

heroism. There is now also a traveling version of the Vietnam Veterans War Memorial. Official commemoration and mourning in a nationally-sanctioned place is now less important than localized and personal memory.

In postmodern places, memory becomes a process, a constant renegotiations of mood and meaning.[9] Monuments have slipped (or been wrested) from the hands of the powerful, and masks of authority have been discarded. Street corners, walls, and vacant lots have been invaded, commandeered, and press-ganged into local service. In LA, the archetypal moment in popular memorials is Watts Towers, built between 1921 and 1954 by Simon Rodia, an Italian immigrant. The collection of towers rises to about 100 feet above the street; it is made from concrete, seashells, bottle fragments, old piping, etc. Once threatened with collapse and demolition, the Towers are now a protected cultural site, and an internationally recognized work of art.

Another highly prominent presence in Southern California cities is the mural movement. Imported from Mexico, the spread of formal and informal mural-making has been little short of phenomenal. For example, the Great Wall of LA tells California's popular history in an extended sequence along the walls of the Tujunga Wash. Under the direction of Judy Baca, large numbers of community artists were enrolled in the mural-making process. Murals in LA are now painted by artists from many racial and ethnic groups, and distinctive styles are blooming into amazing hybrids. Mural also makes gestures across racial/ethnic lines. In South-Central LA, for instance, many African-American store-owners paint Virgénde of Guadalupe murals on their storefronts to attract Mexican and Chicano customers.

Even formal commemorations in LA now have a way of remembering ordinary lives in a non-monumental fashion. For instance, Dolores Hayden's *Power of Place* project has recovered lost or erased memories and re-placed them in the cityscape.[10] One example is in the ingenious Biddy Mason project in downtown LA. From her origins in slavery, Ms Mason traveled to LA to become a pillar of the African-American community, a landowner and well-loved midwife. She is commemorated now in a wall display of a parking structure. Artifacts, such as her image, local maps, narrative moments, and a midwife's bag are set into the wall; as they pass by on their own journeys, pedestrians can trace the steps of Biddy Mason's life.[11]

Modern vs. Postmodern Production of Place

Ruins are products of modernity. In ancient times the debris of the past was freely used as the foundation for subsequent building or, if too sacred to be discarded, was often buried. At least since the Renaissance, however, ruins have occupied a central position in our collective imagination, provoking reactions ranging from nostalgia to foreboding, from dreams of grandeur to fears of mortality.[12]

In 1994, Luis Donaldo Colosio seemed destined to become the next president of Mexico. Then he was shot dead in one of the *colonias* of Tijuana. He was popular among many ordinary people, some of whom erected an informal altar at the site of the assassination. The Mexican government soon replaced the people's memorial with a formal plaza. The so-called Plaza de la Unidad y la Esperanza ('Unity and Hope') featured a statue of Colosio, one enormous left hand raised in salute, or perhaps a friendly wave.[13]

I use this example to suggest that modernist rationality still has a way of imposing itself on the landscape. The battle for architectural supremacy between the modernist establishment and an upstart postmodern movement has been the defining move-ment in the rebirth of Berlin as the German capital.[14] Called the "Architects' Debate" by Gavriel Rosenfeld, the struggle was about who could control the content and representation of memory.[15] Brian Ladd, who has published a number of wonderful books on the relationship between German national identity and city form, portrays this war in the starkest terms:

> German architecture and urban design cannot escape the crisis of German national identity. All cities' buildings display their cultural traditions, but the sandy soil of the German capital conceals the traces of a history so fiercely contested that no site, however vacant, is safe from controversy.[16]

Figure 13.2./a Altar a Colosio, Tijuana (Michael Dear)
Luis Donaldo Colosio was assassinated in Tijuana in 1994. An informal altar was quickly erected by mourners at the site of the shooting; it was later replaced by a sterile govern-ment-sponsored plaza in Colosio's honor.

Figure 13.2/b   Plaza de Colosio (Michael Dear)

Michael Wise's analysis of Germany's search for a new architecture of democracy demonstrated that, in Berlin's renaissance, we encounter a literal concretization of Germany's efforts at reconceptualization. This is occurring now principally because national leadership is passing to a younger generation, which has no personal memory of World War II. Wise asks: "Will time and new occupants ever erase the stigma associated with Berlin's buildings?"[17] He answers that while Berliners were anxious to distance themselves from Nazi-era buildings, they were "even more at pain to distance themselves from the built legacy of the German Democratic Republic."[18] But while the goal of disassociation from diverse pasts was widely shared, exactly how to achieve such distancing was deeply disputed.

In Rosenfeld's account, architect Leon Krier argued during the mid-1980s that the "true villains" of the Third Reich were "modern industry and technology." Krier wrote:

> Industrial civilization is unable...to create meaningful and beautiful places. It erects suburbs, zones transportation systems...and concentration camps. It is always concerned with mass housing...mass transport...and mass extermination. Auschwitz–Birkenau and Los Angeles have the same parents [sic].[19]

Having linked modernism to Nazism (and Southern California), Krier appealed for the rehabilitation of a neo-classical architecture, especially the work of Albert Speer (yes, the same A. Speer of the previous chapter), insisting that "architecture is not political; it is merely the tool of politics."[20]

Needless to say, the modernists screamed their objections, but Krier's appeal to traditions gained support, and such sentiments reappeared in the early 1990s as an

Figure 13.3/a Billboard Advertising the New Checkpoint Charlie, Berlin (Michael Dear)
Figure 13.3/b What remained of Checkpoint Charlie, Berlin 1997 (Michael Dear)
Figure 13.3/c Homage to the Architect of the New Checkpoint Charlie Office Complex, Philip Johnson (Michael Dear)

appeal to "Berlin Architecture." Critic Fritz Neumeyer argued that Berlin's urban identity had been eroded by modernism and postmodernism – the former involving a too-sharp break with traditions, the latter being an alien "hypermultiplicity." A cry that "Berlin must look like Berlin" led to the ascendancy of an architecture of convention rooted in Rationalist aesthetics of "simplicity, clarity, quiet ... [and] order."[21] Although the echoes of fascism were clear to many, supporters of the revamped rationalism practiced a "strategy of forgetting" with regard to the Nazi overtones of their precepts.[22]

To cut Rosenfeld's story short: the architectural rationalists triumphed in Berlin. Avant-garde architects of many persuasions found themselves increasingly excluded from the enormous projects of Potsdamer Platz, Pariser Platz, and elsewhere. Rem Koolhaas was on the hit list, for instance, and Daniel Libeskind (architect of Berlin's new Jewish Museum) protested the new rules of the game by moving his practice from Berlin to Los Angeles.[23] So now, when you stand overlooking Potsdamer Platz (one of the largest construction sites in Europe), the panorama your eyes struggle to encompass is actually a triumph of corporate rationality. Each multinational corporation (Sony, Daimler–Benz, etc.) has employed its own 'starchitect' to design a monument commemorating its global presence.

At the on-site Info-Box, one of the most popular tourist attractions in Berlin, for a few Marks you are bombarded by information about the reconstruction as well as futuristic visions of Potsdamer Platz.[24] But the holiest room of the Info-Box is reserved for busts of the most prominent architects, displayed in plinth-like clear plastic cases. All the architects so honored are male. They only female in the room stands, full-figure, looking out of a window at the construction site, her back to the architect masters in the room's center. She is meant to reflect the spirit of artistic creativity; and yes, she is naked.

But the most delicious irony of the renewed Berlin lies close by at Checkpoint Charlie. I first visited this historically important but fairly nondescript street corner many years ago in the rain when streets and building were still intact. Even though the infamous checkpoint control buildings had been removed, the place reeked of history. I felt John le Carré at my shoulder; he, too, was soaked to the skin. But in 1997, walking with my friend Ute Lehrer, I could not find Check-point Charlie. Ute, who knows more about the Potsdamer Platz redevelopment than anyone else, led me to it. The old streetscape had been almost totally obliterated to make way for the new Checkpoint Charlie Office Complex. The famous sign proclaiming "You are now leaving the American Sector" (in English, Russian and French) balances precariously on a scaffolding; the trace of a painted sign on behalf of a former East German newspaper (*Neue Zeit*, or "New Times") is fading from a building's wall behind it. And, in perhaps the best irony of all, the complex is being designed by Philip Johnson, (yes, the same P. Johnson of the previous chapter).

From Individual to Nation–Space

In concluding his account of the Architects' Debate, Rosenfeld observes that no matter what we think about architecture, it does not occur "in a vacuum but in a cultural context shaped by history."[25] And we understand now that this context is constantly shifting, reshuffled like tectonic plates, and re-evaluated by altered personal and collective ethos.

I have spent so much time in Berlin because so many of the paradigmatic post-modern issues (of identity, memory, politics, and place) are thrown into such high relief there. The German situation also problematizes acutely the link between individual and nation in postmodern society. Brian Ladd neatly expresses this concern:

> Germany has been called the first postmodern nation and the first postnational society. Those labels refer to the tendency of German intellectual to reject any unselfconscious German identity and to insist on questioning its nature and genesis.[26]

The urban and the personal are inextricable tied to the national. We cannot account for the personal and everyday spaces without knowing about the national and global contexts. Thus, it is appropriate for me to edge toward a conclusion by considering the nation state and a postmodern geopolitics.

Notes

1. Lefebvre, H., 1996: *The Production of Space*, Oxford: Blackwell, p. 170.
2. Pile, S., 1996: *The Body and the City*, London: Routledge, p. 214
3. Sturken, M., 1997: *Tangled Memories: The Vietnam War, The AIDS Epidemic, and the Politics of Remembering*, Berkeley: University of California Press, p. 3.
4. Ibid., p. 11.
5. Ibid., p. 12.
6. Ibid., p. 16.
7. Ibid.
8. Quoted in Sturken, M., *Tangled Memories*, p. 17.
9. See Kramer, J., 1996: *The Politics of Memory: Looking for Germany in the New Germany*, New York: Random House; and Linenthal, E. T. and Engelhardt, T. (eds), 1996: *History Wars: The Enola Gay and Other Battles for the American Past*, New York: Metropolitan Books.
10. Hayden, D., 1995: *The Power of Place*, Cambridge: MIT Press.
11. Hayden, D., 1998: *"Biddy Mason's Place: A Midwife's Homestead,"* poster designed by Shiela Levant de Bretteville, Los Angeles: The Power of Place.
12. From inside front cover, Roth, M. with Lyons, C. and Merewether, C., 1997: *Irresistible Decay: Ruins Reclaimed*, Los Angeles: The Getty Research Institute.
13. A fascinating account of Mexican attitudes to monuments is to be found in Rawls, W. (ed.), 1989: *Mexican Monuments: Strange Encounters*, New York: Abbeville Press.
14. A good general account of Berlin's history is to be found in Read, A. and Fisher, D. 1994: *Berlin Rising: Biography of a City*, New York: Norton. A beautifully-illustrated architectural history of twentieth-century Berlin is given in Balfour, A. 1990: *Berlin: The Politics of Order, 1737–1989*, New York: Rizzoli, which emphasizes the origins and consequences of the division of the city following World War II.
15. Rosenfeld, G. D., 1997: "The Architects' Debate: Architectural Discourse and the Memory of Nazism in the Federal Republic of Germany, 1977–1997," *History and Memory*, 9 (1/2), pp. 189–225.
16. Ladd, B., 1997: *The Ghosts of Berlin: Confronting German History in the Urban Landscape*, Chicago: University of Chicago Press, p. 234.

17. Wise, M., 1998: *Capital Dilemma: Germany's Search for a New Architecture of Democracy,* New York: Princeton Architectural Press, p. 93.
18. Ibid., p. 109.
19. Krier L., quoted in Rosenfeld, G. D., "The Architects' Debate," p. 205.
20. Ibid.
21. Ibid., pp. 210—11.
22. Ibid., p. 212.
23. Ladd, B., *The Ghosts of Berlin,* p. 233.
24. A thick promotional catalogue is available on-site in several languages (see INFOBOX: The Catalogue, Berlin: INFOBOX.)
25. Rosenfeld, G. D., "The Architects' Debate," p. 215.
26. Ladd, B., *The Ghosts of Berlin,* p. 234.

14

The Geopolitics of Postmodernity

The city has indeed emerged as a site for new claims: by global capital which uses the city as an "organizational commodity," but also by disadvantaged sectors of the urban population, which in large cities are frequent as internationalized a presence as is capital. The denationalizing of urban space and the formation of new claims by transnational actors... raise the question – whose city is it?

Saskia Sassen[1]

At first glance, it might seem odd that a book about urbanism should end up looking at global geopolitics. But truth be told, a large part of the world's history is a history of its cities. (Think about Amsterdam during the Dutch Golden Age.) In a world where the global is increasingly linked to the local, it is likely that the world's future will evermore be determined by the urban. This was exactly my intent, of course, in discussing the emergence of a global Cititstāt in Chapter 7, albeit using a somewhat different terminology.

As Peter Hall recounts in his sweeping review of 2,500 years of urban history, cities have always been the locus of distinctive 'civic innovations.'[2] He identifies four types of innovation: *artistic* (e.g. Renaissance Florence); *technological* (assembly-line Detroit, high-tech Palo Alto); *culture plus technology* (Hollywood and movies); and *problem solving* (London's nineteenth-century sewage treatment). To simplify, I can say that cities do the work (sometimes very difficult work) of culture, politics, livelihood, community, and so on. But what of the postmodern city? In *Globalization and its Discontents*, Saskia Sassen suggests that an incipient transnational urban system is presently evolving. A newly-emerging geography of centrality is binding together major international and financial business sectors; but this is simultaneously a geography of marginality, as traditional manufacturing centers decline and socio-economic polarization intensifies the gap between rich and poor. In political and social terms, one of the most significant consequences has been what Sassen refers to as the "transnationalization of labor" (a new lens on what has been conventionally analyzed through the language of immigration), and the "transnationalization of identities." These together offer sites for new types of politics especially the role of women in the global economy, and the role of postcolonial spaces.[3]

Sassen does not support a too-glib adoption of the view that globalization and the various transnationalizations signal the demise of the nation state. As she wryly points out, the new geographies of centrality "had to be produced by the state as well as capital."[4] However, she readily concedes that the contemporary "unmooring"

Figure 14.1   Hong Kong, 1989 (Michael Dear)
I. M. Pei's Bank of China building sits adjacent to the former British Legislative Council build-ing. The juxtaposition incensed *feng shui* – sensitive locals, who termed the Bank of China building a dagger in the heart of Hong Kong.

of identities has loosened traditional loyalties, including those toward nation and community. And, consequently, the new "city users" have made immense claims on the city, reconstituting city spaces for their own purposes. At the other extreme, Sassen observes that when legitimate claims are denied, urban violence may be sparked.[5] I do not think it is exaggerated or fanciful to link the 1992 urban civil unrest in Los Angeles to aspects of globalization, most especially the deindustrializa-tion process that impoverized so many workers and communities in LA. In an earlier study, Jennifer Wolch and I attempted to trace the connection between changes in the aggregate global economy and the individual homeless person adrift on the sidewalks of Skid Row.[6] It is not easy to make such connections, but they can sometimes be traced in (for example) the personal histories of unfortunate or unlucky individuals.

For present purposes, in this chapter I will extend my earlier concerns with personal politics to a geopolitics of postmodernity. This turns out to be vitally important because just as individuals have become "unmoored" by their own post-modernities, so are the foundations of nation states and global politics shifting. It should not be a surprise if I assert that these two trends are related.

Contemporary Geopolitics

A civilian is shot in a [Sarajevo] street; a television camera man, waiting at a dangerous crossroads to see somebody killed or mutilated, films the shooting; a soldier sent by the United Nations as a "peacekeeper" to a city officially called a "safe area" watches, unsure of what to do and paralyzed by fear. ...The elements of this troubling collage are also elements of what some military analysts are now calling "postmodern" or "future" war.[7]

If politics begins from fragmented personal identities, how then can we speak of a collective politics in a postmodern age? The traditional class-centered, corporatist politics of Fordism and the Welfare State have been evacuated in postmodernity. The politics of capital and labor have been transformed into a multi-hued identity politics, based in gender, age, religion, race, ethnicity, sexual preference, (dis)-ability, class, etc. Yet the translation from personal to identity politics is far from simple, because individuals have multiple allegiances. Multipositionality (or political hybridity) becomes the norm, and the practice of politics is made possible only through the submergence of at least some of the multiplicities. Thus, the anti-abortionist swallows religious misgivings in order to forge alliances with mainstream church organizations in pursuit of the cause; or a voter accepts distasteful elements of a party's platform in order to ensure solidarity. Identity politics (like other forms of coalition) require some emasculation of personality.

Postmodernity is also marked by the collapse of the Cold War, the pivotal geopolitical logic of the past fifty years, and the emergence of a postcolonial world of multiple (ir)rationalities. Former allegiances to nation states have splintered and new/old nationalisms have stirred, often with virulent and destructive consequences. Samuel Huntington has suggested that culture will form the basis for geopolitical turmoil in the twenty-first century, especially differences based on religion. Could this be the form of a twenty-first-century geopolitical identity politics?[8]

In his study of *The Rise and Fall of Great Nations*, Paul Kennedy surveys several centuries of global political-economic history.[9] He argues that world history has been cyclical, in the sense that geopolitics can be understood as the rhythmic rise (and subsequent demise) of single nations to global dominance. The hegemony of a particular nation is based in economic and political (especially military) power, and may last for a century or more; its ultimate collapse is due to over-extension of the political-economic resources of the hegemon, plus the tendency for competing nations to strive constantly to overtake the leader. After the hegemons collapse, Kennedy observes, there is a protracted period of instability, a multipolar world when nations compete until another hegemon emerges as the new world leader, usually as a result of war. Today, the end of the Cold War and the demise of the Soviet Union have once again given rise to a multipolar world, but to whom does the twenty-first century belong? To Japan, Germany, China, or a united Europe? Or will the United States continue its supremacy, but this time in solitary splendor?

I do not rule out the possibility that the answer is: None of the above. According to political scientist Ken Jowitt, the very absence of a hegemonic nation capable of shaping a new geopolitical order is the critical factor in current global instability:

> Nothing is more central to this [present] reality than the disorientation, disorganization and disintegration of state power. The collapse of the Soviet Union, Czechoslovakia ... the violent chaos of Somalia, Liberia, Sierra Leone, Afghanistan; the potential disorganization/disintegration of China, India, Canada and Mexico; coupled with profound regime-disorganization in Italy and Japan, and political disorientation in the United States; all these suggest the genuine possibility of fundamental change and the corresponding need to formulate new paradigms.[10]

Jowitt seems convinced that something original is happening – what we might refer to as a radical break.[11] He draws attention to the emergence of dispersed and random forms of violence, to the threatening consequences of social polarization, quoting Hans Magnus Enzensberger thus:

> [I]n New York as well as Zaire, in the industrial cities as well as the poorest countries, more and more people are being excluded from the economic system because it no longer pays to exploit them.[12]

The relative impotence of the nation state in this emerging world order is a theme taken up by Martin Walker who identified money, in the form of the new global currency markets, as the greatest threat to the authority of nation states. In 1995, currency markets alone were trading $1,200 billion in a single day. Walker comments:

> The global markets are the modern [sic] equivalent of the medieval papacy. Like the medieval popes, they embody a power that transcends frontiers, commands an alternative allegiance from citizens of individual states and can humble governments and leaders.[13]

The priestly class of this new papacy, he claims, owes allegiance only to "the theology of the market"[14] As if in acknowledgment of the new mercantilism, in July 1995, President Clinton ordered the US Central Intelligence Agency "to make economic espionage of America's trade rivals a top priority."[15] The CIA is acting with some reluctance, it is reported, because of the difficulty in an era of multinational corporations "of determining which firms should be considered American and which should not."[16]

Many military analysts regard as obsolete the notion of wars between states and their standing armies, signaling another break with the past. According to Roger Cohen (who must have been thinking about the situation in the former Yugoslavia), war will be replaced by a new kind of conflict in which "armies and peoples become indistinguishable."[17]

> In such wars, states are replaced by militias or other informal – often tribal – groupings whose ability to use sophisticated weaponry is very limited. Moreover, the wars are intractable. Live images of suffering, distributed worldwide, sap whatever will or ability

there may be to prosecute a devastating military campaign. The absence of effective central authority makes the war very difficult to end through negotiation. The United Nations ends up trying to palliate a chaos that is likely to endure over many years.[18]

But if money is to become a principal weapon in future global wars, the arsenals of nation states are already severely compromised. One difficulty is hinted at in accounts of a near-perfect counterfeit $100 bill that is being manufactured somewhere in the Middle East. It is called the 'supernote' because it is so authentic. There is evidence that the supernote printing is being protected by the military power in Syria – a government essentially hostile to the United States – although actual production of the counterfeit may occur in Lebanon.[19] Syria, some claim, is as much a "racketeering enterprise as it is a nation, and for years it has allegedly been involved in the international drug trade."[20] According to Dannen and Silverman, US Federal Reserve and Treasury officials fear the supernote less than the 'confidence problem' that might result if they publicly acknowledged its existence.[21] In the next war, it may not be necessary to fire a shot if you can instead destabilize your enemy's currency...

In the odiferous debris of scores of local wars, revolutions, terrorism, and repression lie the scattered shards of the old geopolitical order, unheeded as the postmodern transformation of politics unfolds.[22] Not only is the nation state's legitimacy compromised, its ability to secure the conditions for its own survival is being questioned. Into the consequent vacuum rush competing forces that will require a rethinking of the nature of postmodern geopolitics.

Corruption and the Legitimacy Crisis of the US State

"We're going to prosecute – got to prosecute everybody," the President said. "Does that bother you as being repressive?"
Mr. Haldeman replied: "We've got to be repressive".
                                            Extract from transcripts of tapes made by Richard Nixon during the
                                            Watergate scandal, which ultimately led to his resignation.[23]

Since Watergate, and the consequent resignation of Richard Nixon, corruption has been a become a prominent, commonplace feature of US political discourse. The Iran–Contra affair subsequently confirmed the presence of lawlessness at the highest levels, leading ultimately to the imprisonment of John Poindexter, former national security advisor and close aide to then President Ronald Reagan. Analogous practices exist at other levels of government in the United States. They also can be found in civil society, including private business and local communities. In this section, I shall explore some evidence of corruption and its consequences in government, private business, and community.

Scandals at HUD

For several decades, the Department of Housing and Urban Development (HUD) was the principal federal agency stimulating the housing market in the United States. Its major focus was on the production of new housing through mortgage insurance schemes, although it was also a direct provider of assisted housing for low-income families. During the Reagan Administration, the Secretary at HUD was Mr Samuel Pierce. Investigations of the Pierce tenure at HUD have revealed over $4 billion losses in waste, fraud and abuse. By the end of 1989, over 600 separate criminal investigations had been instigated.[24]

Complaints abut HUD fell into four broad categories:

(1) *Mismanagement* The Reagan/Pierce doctrine of privatization, which extolled the virtues of private-sector takeover of selected government functions, bit deeply into HUD. The department's budget dropped by more than half, to $15 billion; staff numbers fell from 16,000 to 13,000.[25] HUD relinquished many control and oversight duties to private agencies. This 'hands-off' approach meant that in-house staff were unable to keep track of finances. The books on $290 billion of Federal Housing Administration-insured home mortgages were reportedly so chaotic that outside auditors were unable to sign audit statements for ten years.[26]

(2) *Influence peddling* This is not illegal, but is viewed as an important indicator of the 'sleaze factor' in government operations. The record of Samuel Pierce's eight-year tenure at HUD was impressive even by Washington standards. For instance, almost $6 million was handed out as consultancy fees for major projects between 1984 and 1988. Top of the list of beneficiaries was Joseph Strauss, Pierce's former special assistant, with $1.68 million.[27] In another case, former Interior Secretary James G. Watt made a few phone calls to prominent decision-makers and got $300,000 in return.[28] The former chair of the Republican Party in Florida, W.L. Taylor, received over half a million dollars in cash and property for consulting work on behalf of developers seeking HUD benefits (prompting one Republican committee member to comment: "I wish you were a Democrat").[29] Joseph Monticciolo, HUD's New York regional administrator from 1981–8, testified that while in office, he made decisions that benefited developers he went to work with immediately upon departing from HUD.[30]

(3) *Theft* Instances of theft and fraud are the only scandals where criminal prosecution was possible. In the primary case in this category, federal investigators estimated that private escrow agents (hired by HUD to assist in the sale of $3 billion-worth of government-owned property each year) may have pocketed $20 million from proceeds of the sales.[31] Some think this figure will rise to $100 million. The escrow work used to be done internally by HUD employees, until the Reagan administration decided to privatize this activity. HUD records were reputedly so bad that auditors either ignored or failed to detect cases where escrow agents had not forwarded sales proceeds to the government.[32]

(4) *Deceit and cover-up* In an effort to distance himself from the activities of his subordinates (presumably equating ignorance with blamelessness), Mr Pierce told a Congressional inquiry in the summer of 1989 that he had little direct involvement in project approvals at HUD. Since then, a spate of public documents linked him directly with the approvals process.[33] He even overrode HUD staff to give personal approval to projects that staff believed to be of dubious merit. Key staff members, including Deborah Gore Dean (Pierce's executive assistant), avoided testifying by taking the Fifth Amendment (a constitutional

guarantee protecting against self-incrimination). In August 1989, signs of a cover-up emerged: HUD officials were found to have systematically hidden from Congress the true extent of political favoritism in the HUD subsidy programs.[34]

Political analyst John Ellis likened HUD to an abandoned building waiting to be stripped of its saleable assets.[35] The only difference, he suggested, is that stripping buildings is illegal; gutting HUD of its assets required only a few well-placed phone calls. Such 'insider trading,' the lack of oversight capacity, plus the habit of former political appointees to return as lobbyists to HUD all explain how the well-connected were able to profit from HUD's demise.[36] Apologists for HUD have argued that favoritism in government contracting is as American as apple pie. But long-time housing analyst Anthony Downs bluntly sums up the differences between the Carter and the Reagan administration as follows: "The big difference is that people who were in HUD under the Carter Administration had some interest in the subject and were interested in serving the constituencies the department worked with – cities, poor people and the housing industry. The Reagan Administration put people in HUD who couldn't give a damn about housing or HUD policies."[37]

Naturally enough, it is what could have been done with the diverted HUD dollars that annoys most people. In one evocative comparison, Martha Brown Hicks, President of the Los Angeles Skid Row Development Corporation, estimated that a $250,000 grant from HUD would have put over 400 homeless into her 60–day program at LA's Transition House.[38] There, they would have been fed, sheltered, and helped to get off the streets. Extrapolating from this estimate, the projected $4 billion HUD losses could have helped 640,000 homeless people – equal to the Urban Land Institute's early 1900s estimate of the total number of US homeless.

The collapse of the savings and loan industry

The US Savings and Loan (S & L) industry has long played a key role in helping people realize their dream of homeownership. It began as a simple agency for home-mortgage lending, but was transformed in the early 1980s by sweeping new investment freedoms granted by the US Congress and State legislatures. Following deregulation, the S & L business became a magnet for new owners who saw federally-insured savings deposits as an irresistible source of funds for multifarious investments, including office buildings, residential property, shopping malls, fast-food chains, and even 'junk bonds.'[39]

By the late 1980s, many S & Ls were in financial difficulty. Some had over-extended themselves by offering inflated interest rates to depositors, only to find themselves facing a collapsing real estate market. Others had been overtly-optimistic, excessively aggressive, and (in the opinion of some regulators) potentially fraudulent in their pursuit of real-estate profits.[40] Because it had guaranteed the deposits, the federal government was obliged to repay the depositors of the failed S & Ls (up to certain limits). In situations of this kind, depositors are sometimes reimbursed directly out of the general revenue; or (as happened in this case) the government may sell the repossessed assets in order to recoup its debts. The cost of the S & L bail-out was estimated in 1990 at around five hundred billion dollars ($500,000,000,000) – equivalent to $100 for every person on earth, or $2000 for every individual in the United States.[41]

Regional variations in the impacts of the S & L failure and bail-out were considerable. Their net effect is likely to be a significant transfer of wealth from the North-East and Mid-West to Texas and other states in the South-West.[42] This redistribution is related to a number of factors:

(1)   the original flow of individuals' savings deposits out-of-state in search of higher interest rates;
(2)   the movement of bank investment capital toward more prosperous regions;
(3)   the stock of empty buildings, built over the last decade by failed S & Ls, and now on the market at relatively low prices for businesses that want to relocate;
(4)   the inequitable tax bill for the bail-out (for instance, the net outflow of tax dollars from the state of Connecticut is estimated as $1,237 per person; the net inflow to Texas is $4,775, assuming a net bail-out cost of $203 billion); and
(5)   a tighter credit situation in the North-East and Mid-West, as regulators strive to avoid past mistakes made in Texas and elsewhere.

Progress in prosecuting potentially fraudulent behavior in the S & L scandal has been painfully slow. Initial reticence was blamed on the fact that both Democratic and Republican members of Congress were implicated in the crisis.[43] Later, Democrats attacked the Republican administration of George Bush for its tardiness in and maladministration of the bail-out effort. They referred to the 'second S & L crisis,'[44] in which government auditors reported on misconduct in the bail-out.[45] For instance, the rules appeared to encourage a holder of property, whose value has plummeted in a depressed market, to default on the loan and then repurchase the property from the government at a substantially lower price.[46] And, in what Congressional investigators called the "worst abuse found in the Federal bailout program," one Arizona insurance executive with a history of legal and regulatory problems was allowed to buy 15 insolvent Texas S & Ls using only $1,000 of his own money, $70 million in loans, and promises of $1.85 billion in Federal subsidies.[47] Overall, it has been estimated that there was criminal misconduct by insiders in fully three-quarters of the failed institutions.[48]

Militias

Beyond the halls of government and the board rooms of the rich and powerful, there are ordinary people who are fed up with their lot. These include, for instance, the young Nazi Low Riders of Antelope Valley in northern Los Angeles County.[49] The rise to prominence of militia groups in the United States is one symptom of mistrust toward government. Gary Wills has called militia members the 'new revolutionaries,' arguing that their analysis of government repression[50] makes an "internally consistent case for the illegitimacy of federal acts."[51] He summarizes their manifesto thus:

(1) The whole system of *taxation* is unconstitutional;

(2) the *courts and jury system* are ineffective and have abrogated too much power that rightfully belongs to ordinary citizens;

(3) there are too many intrusive government *regulations*;

(4) *police power* is out of control and citizen posses should restore order;

(5) *public education* is a failure, only brainwashing children in order to control them;

(6) the nuclear *family* is the cornerstone of the social fabric;

(7) the government has removed *religion* from American life;

(8) *citizen militias* are essential to prevent governmental oppression;

(9) respect for and restoration of the original *Constitution* and its ten amendments are necessary elements of reconstruction;

(10) current government is *corrupt*, degenerate and imperfect; and

(11) citizens have the right to protect themselves with *guns*, without which all preceding conditions will be rendered nugatory.

Many ordinary people who are not militia members will agree with this analysis, or at least parts of it. Wills links this burgeoning public animosity to the dissolving mandate for government intervention that followed the end of the Cold War. He paraphrases the militia-members' assessment this way:

> If the government is only good for fighting Communists, and it no longer fights Communists, then what good is it?[52]

Lacking convincing answers to this question, Wills argues, some citizens take it upon themselves to do something about the post-Cold War inertia in favor of big government. But there is also something new in the current paranoia. Certainly, elements of old extremisms persist (e.g. antisemitism); but, he avers, there is also a "constitutional anti-governmentalism" that connects militias to the broader discontent of the general public:

> The militias and their supporters are not the most central social symptom of our time, but they are among the more dramatic symptoms of a general crisis of legitimacy. The authority of government can no longer be assumed. It has to be justified from the ground up.[53]

Thus, Wills' central point – and, I believe, a vitally important one – is that it is no longer so extreme to believe that government is the greatest enemy to freedom. The relatively widespread diffusion of mistrust is manifest in, for example, a hatred of government agents, many of whom fear for their lives in rural western states, and in the unprecedented, vengeful vilification of Hillary Rodham Clinton and Bill Clinton. Wills sums up the cumulative drift toward a crisis of legitimacy in this way:

> The heaping of filth on the personnel and symbols of government has a delegitimating effect in itself; and the assault is joined to the disillusion, anger, and disorientation that have marked recent electoral behavior. *Where the heated deny legitimacy and the cool are doubtful of it, a crisis is in the making.*[54]

He should have added that politicians of all ideological persuasions are themselves contributing mightily to this climate of mistrust, and bringing on themselves such electorate backlashes as term limits for elected officials.

Gangster Nations

It's all just business, business that's bringing the world together for the first time ever, together in one big gangster nation.

Mitchell Koss

During the past decade or more, there has been a growing recognition that crime and criminal organizations have gone global. According to James Richards, this expansionism has coincided with

> the collapse of the Soviet Union, the growth of capitalism in China, the enactment of the North American Free Trade Agreement, and the lowering of European customs, currency, passport controls...[55]

Not only are these international criminal organizations (ICOs, or transnational criminal organizations, TCOs) operating globally,

> they are also forming strategic alliances with each other, with rogue governments, and with terrorist organizations.[56]

Although strategic alliances among TCOs are still in their infancy,[57] the TCOs have already developed a highly diversified portfolio, including:

> smuggling of everything from everywhere to everywhere, including radioactive material, human organs, and illegal immigrants; prostitution; gambling; loan-sharking; kidnapping; racketeering and extortion; counterfeiting of goods, bank notes, financial documents, credit cards, and identity cards; killers for hire; traffic of sensitive information, technology, or art objects; international sales of stolen goods; or even dumping garbage illegally from one country into another.[58]

Richards recognizes three types of TCOs:

(1) The traditional Big Five, including the Italian and American mafias, the Russian Mafiya, the Japanese Yakusa, the Chinese Triads, and the Colombian cartels (to which he adds the Mexican federation of drug cartels);
(2) A second tier of organized crime that essentially works as franchisees to the Big Six, including groups based in Nigeria, Panama, and Jamaica; and
(3) Terrorist groups that deal in drugs, etc. simply to finance their political objectives (e.g., Peru's Shining Path).[59]

Many TCOs find an immediate expression in world cities when they employ pockets of expatriates as bases for their operations (e.g. "Chinatowns").[60]

The most common manifestation of changing geopolitical order is also expressed through the multiple logics of criminality. Many nation states are themselves guilty of criminal behavior, but corruption takes many forms on both global and local scales. This is also evident in the rise of TCOs in a robust trafficking in young women for the sex industry,[62] and a global network of money laundering services often using legitimate commercial banking services.[63] In general terms, corruption is the used by the powerful of fraud, deceit, bribery, discrimination, threat and abuse in pursuit of influence and material gain. The practices of corruption warrant attention because they are immoral, exploitative, harmful, and even lethal; and they are destructive of public trust and political accountability in many countries around the world. In a pioneering, if somewhat quirky study, Peter John Perry comments on the general silence in academic studies on the topic of corruption, especially in geography.[64] However, Gordon Clark counters that graft and corruption are "recurrent themes in urban studies."[65] In his own pathbreaking work on pension fund management, Clark asserts that "corruption is a social practice with an indentifiable social structure."[66] In pension fund trustee decision-making, he defines corruption as:

> (1) knowingly to place one's interests (or a third party's interests) ahead of those interests one is directly responsible for protecting; (2) to choose a course of action which one would not ordinarily countenance; and (3) to benefit directly from those actions.[67]

Emphasizing the moral dimension of corruption, Clark identifies a *weapons frame* (forces influencing the suspension of customary rules), a *strategies frame* (mechanics of concealment), and an *emotions frame* (the emotional cost of violating trustrelationship).[68] Reading Clark, it is hard to avoid the conclusion that systematic lying

Table 14.1 Most and Least Corrupt Nations, 1996–98 (Scores are from 0 through 10, 0 being the most corrupt)

1996[1]		*1997*[2]		*1998*[3]	
Most Corrupt		*Most Corrupt*		*Most Corrupt*	
Rank	*Score*	*Rank*	*Score*	*Rank*	*Score*
1. NIGERIA	0.69	1. NIGERIA	1.76	1. CAMEROON	1.4
2. PAKISTAN	1.00	2. BOLIVIA	2.05	2. PARAGUAY	1.5
3. KENYA	2.21	3. COLOMBIA	2.23	3. HONDURAS	1.7
4. BANGLADESH	2.29	4. RUSSIA	2.27	4. TANZANIA	1.9
5. CHINA	2.43	5. PAKISTAN	2.53	4. NIGERIA	1.9
Least Corrupt		*Least Corrupt*		*Least Corrupt*	
Rank	*Score*	*Rank*	*Score*	*Rank*	*Score*
1. NEW ZEALAND	9.43	1. DENMARK	9.94	1. DENMARK	10
2. DENMARK	9.33	2. FINLAND	9.48	2. FINLAND	9.6
3. SWEDEN	9.08	3. SWEDEN	9.35	3. SWEDEN	9.5
4. FINLAND	9.05	4. NEW ZEALAND	9.23	4. NEW ZEALAND	9.4
5. CANADA	8.96	5. CANADA	9.10	5. ICELAND	9.3

[1] Source: *New York Times*, Nov 28, 1996, p. CI
[2] Source: *New York Times*, p. C-1, Transparency International, March 6, 1998
[3] Source: *New York Times*, Oct 4, 1998, p. 5
http://www.transparency.de/documents/cpi/index.html

and misrepresentation are commonplace in all countries at all levels of public and private practice.[69]

The notion of corrupt states is, needless to say, nothing new. It is easy to look back and condemn earlier states for their moral laxity, e.g. in the practice of slavery; or to examine the myriad contemporary examples of totalitarian and repressive regimes (e.g. Nazism and Communism).[70] But a new term has now entered the political lexicon to describe contemporary corruption – the gangster nation. According to film documentarian Mitchell Koss, the term applies to countries that are "controlled or highly influenced by organized criminal groups."[71] He uses Bolivia, Colombia, and Mexico as examples, but quotes US government officials as identifying a list of 32 gangster nations in 1996, and the number is growing. One of the principal reasons for their expansion is linked to globalization, which permits transnational organizations (legitimate and otherwise) to cross international borders with impunity, thereby weakening the authority of the nation state. Koss quotes a US Embassy official in Bolivia: "Drugs, Development, Democracy. You can't separate them."[72]

Another factor in the rise of state gangsterism is that rich and poor nations alike frequently turn to crime cartels to finance local development, thus permitting the cartels to enter legitimate business and to launder their illicit profits. For instance, the role of organized crime (the yakuza) in the modernization of Japan has long been conceded. A belated self-examination of yakuza influence in Japan's banking system was provoked by a financial crisis in which banks made up to $800 billion in bad loans. Over-priced real estate, and a 'bubble economy' in the late 1980s was followed by a land price collapse, when the value of the loan collateral dropped to less than half the amount of the loans. Many of the bad loans were to companies with yakuza ties. Critics argue that if the banks were to cave in and write off their losses, clear title on 50–80 percent of the assets put up as loan collateral will pass to corporations controlled or owned by yakuza, who will thus become entrenched in the legitimate economy.[73] In some ways, such a concern seems too little too late, since the yakuza already pockets at least 2–3 percent of all construction spending in Japan. The biggest yakuza gang has its headquarters in Kobe, where reconstruction costs following the 1995 earthquake were expected to exceed $120 billion.[74]

The levels of legitimate and illegitimate corruption in the world's nations have gotten so bad that a group pleasingly-entitled 'Transparency International' now publishes rankings of national corruption, identifying the most and the least corrupt nations (Table 14.1). Since the late 1970s, the United States has been the only country in the world with a law prohibiting its corporations from bribing foreign officials to win contracts; in one year (1994) American companies were reported to have lost $45 billion in overseas contracts because of the bribery ban.[75] In the 1996 corruption Top 20, the United States ranked number 15 with a score of 7.66, higher than Japan, France and Belgium, but lower than Israel, Britain, Germany and Singapore.

Of course, corruption is a risky business for governments which often undertake well-publicized campaigns to eradicate it.[76] For instance, recent decades have been marked by the spectacular fall of US president Richard Nixon, and senior ministers and governments have been toppled by corruption scandals in (for instance) Ireland, Japan, and South Korea. Italy's business capital, Milan, has come to be called *Tangentopoli*, or 'kickback city.' Britain usually favors sex scandals over financial hanky-panky. But exactly how are gangster nations created? The simple answer is that some nations are born corrupt, and others have corruption thrust upon them.

Myanmar Mafia and Mexican narco-democracy

In a 1988 coup, the ruling dictatorship known as the State Law and Order Restoration Council (SLORC) seized power in Myanmar (formerly Burma). Since then, according to Dennis Bernstein and Leslie Kean, SLORC has "incorporated the booming heroin trade into the permanent economy of the country,"[77] and the country's illicit drug exports have more than doubled. The United Nations Drug Control Program (UNDCP) estimated in 1997 that the Asian heroin trade reaped $63 billion in profits annually, and Myanmar supplies more than half the world's supply.[78] Bernstein and Kean provide a vivid account of the penetration of the drug economy into Myanmar society. They explain, for instance, how the state-controlled national bank actually solicits drug money and then "openly provides money-laundering services for a 40 percent cut,"[79] how opium "is warehoused at military bases,"[80] and how rural communities are "succumbing to the supplies of cheap heroin distributed unchecked in their villages."[81] Bernstein and Kean conclude:

> Burma's ruling junta appears willing to addict an entire nation to drugs, both by setting up long-term financial dependency on the heroin trade and by fostering a massive upsurge in drug usage. And the enormous financial payout from the SLORC's pro-drug policies helps the narco-dictatorship secure its hold on power against the struggling democracy movement.[82]

In Mexico, Jorge Casteñada has speculated that Colombian drug traffickers were actually invited in to set up operations. Whether or not this is true, the links between the highest levels of the federal government and drug dealers became deeply entrenched during the administration of Carlos Salinas, who ultimately took refuge in the United States and later in Ireland to avoid inquiries into his personal involvement in drug-related corruption. As a consequence of the introduction of drugs into the national economy, many commentators have identified a new sense of national insecurity in Mexico. According to journalists Mark Feneman and Sebastian Rotella, this is associated with the way in which the increasing power of the drug cartels is threatening the nation's stability, even to the point of making the country "ungovernable."[83] Former Mexican prosecutor Eduardo Valle Espinosa (who now lives in the United States) coined the term 'narco-democracy' to describe political conditions in Mexico. The term reflects the contradiction between a nation governed by elected officials and a democratic constitution increasingly influenced by international drug cartels.[84]

Now, it would be naive to assume that corruption exists only on the southern side of the US–Mexico border.[85] In one of the most controversial cases, nearly eight tons of Columbian cocaine (with a street value in the United States of $200 million) disappeared in the central Mexican state of Zacatecas. The drugs did not in fact disappear; it was later ascertained that they crossed the border into Southern California soon after the shipment was hijacked by one Mexican federal police unit from another.[86] A continuing probe of US border inspections has also resulted in charges against (for instance) two Calexico inspectors for "waving across [the border] tons of smuggled cocaine in exchange for bribes."[87] As one border official in San Diego put it: "When you've got an inspector you've got the keys to the kingdom."[88]

The Mexican narco-democracy is also democratic when it comes to death, having produced some 'excellent cadavers' – to borrow the term used by Alexander Stille in his study of Sicilian Mafia wars.[89] The slaying of Juan Jesus Posadas Ocampo, the Archbishop of Guadalajara at an airport attack in 1993 was the first major sign of a crisis in Mexican narco-politics. The gunmen reputedly fled on a commercial flight to Tijuana that had been held for them on the runway; and they were met and driven away in Tijuana by allies in the federal police.[90] In 1994, Luis Donaldo Colosio, the presidential candidate of the ruling Partido Revolucionario Institucional (PRI), was assassinated in Tijuana. Carlos Salinas appointed Ernesto Zedillo as his successor. After Zedillo's election, there was yet another assassination, this time of PRI secretary-general Jose Francisco Ruiz Massieu, which may have been orchestrated by Salinas' brother Raul.

Sebastian Rotella provides a vivid picture of the confusion at the US-Mexico border as the drug wars boil over into the streets:

> [In Tijuana] state police, in league with the drug lords, were accused of killing a federal commander in a shoot-out. An assassin had killed the presidential candidate [Colosio], whose own campaign guards were suspects in the assassination. The federal police, in league with drug lords, were suspected of killing the city police chief. The federal police had arrested the deputy state attorney general and charged him with corruption. The scandalous parade of stolen vehicles [Chevrolet Suburbans and Jeep Cherokees are the favored models] taking Ortiz to jail crystallized the sense that the institutions of social order had broken down.[91]

A hellish conflation of social change, involving "drugs, immigrants, trade, political reform, foreign investment, transnational industry, [and] cultural collision" conspired to make the San Diego–Tijuana line "ground zero" in a global–local war.[92]

Alma Guillermoprieto, one of the most perceptive observers of the Latin American scene, is in no doubt that these murders are clear evidence that the country is falling apart and that there is no one who can put the old order back together again.[93] She located this turn of events very precisely with the exile of former President Carlos Salinas to the United States. As he departed, she says, "[all] the old certainties went with him."[94] Not since the aftermath of the 1910 Revolution has Mexico lived through comparable times – of economic crisis, politically influential drug outlaws, and the disintegration of the PRI's one-party system. Guillermoprieto sums up: "It's not that the old rules don't apply anymore but that there is no longer any way of knowing when they do."[95] And, she adds, there is no guarantee that even the best-intentioned reforms can be effective.[96] It may be that the federal government in Mexico has forfeited its ability to govern?

Russian bazaar states and Italian clientelism

Analagous outcomes might be occurring on the other side of the world in Russia, although the forces of change there are obviously different.[97] Is there anyone who was not surprised by the demise of the Soviet Union? How could such a powerful and still-functioning state so quickly disintegrate? Robert D. Kaplan commented that as the social cement holding the Soviet Republics together began to erode, the former empire was replaced by 'bazaar states' run by local ethnic mafias – although these too are threatened as adjacent nations (e.g. China, Turkey, and Iran) seek to extend their cultural and economic influence.[98]

According to the US Central Intelligence Agency, approximately 400 metric tons of highly enriched uranium are missing in Russia. This is the equivalent of 16,000 nuclear warheads. And no one seems to know what has happened to it. The picture painted by Stephen Handelman is of a Russian state hijacked by organized crime; of hit men operating brazenly in Russia and abroad; of politicians amassing huge fortunes in bribes; and of army generals peddling anything from rifles to nuclear weaponry.[99] The country, in Handelman's words, is "awash in corruption, opportunism and crime."

Organized crime in Russia is emphatically not part of a single gargantuan organization. There are thousands of organized groups with origins in the former Communist party apparatus, the state industries, the military, and the KGB (the former USSR secret police).[100] The problem of the burgeoning criminal sectors might have been alleviated by even modestly-effective law enforcement had it not been for the fact that 'conventional' criminals have been joined be a flood of newcomers from the Communist Party of the Soviet Union. Even before the fall, party officials were diverting resources into commercial enterprises and foreign banks. Jack Matlock tells of Red Army officers who sold off petroleum and arsenals that they controlled in order to provide a capital base for subsequent entrepreneurial activities.[101]

Such relatively straightforward opportunism has become intimately entwined with other criminal activities, including drug trafficking and use, gang warfare, illicit arms trade, white slavery, and an underground trade in fissionable materials.[102] According to Anders Aslund of the Carnegie Endowment, "official corruption has a bigger impact than organized crime"[103]- a situation presenting the most significant impediment to the growth of investment and a market economy.[104]

Concern about the epidemic of criminal activity extends beyond Russia's borders. Russian hit men have struck in London and been arrested in Brooklyn; raw materials smuggled out of Russia play havoc in Western markets; and Russia's underground millionaires are beginning to acquire Western real estate.[105] More than 600,000 emigrés from the former Soviet Union now live in Los Angeles. They have brought with them huge proceeds from the privatization of the Soviet economy, and are spending this wealth in LA – changing the architectural aspect, the entertainment industry, business practices, and a violent organized crime (much to the chagrin of earlier emigrés who fled the Soviet Union's repression).[106] According to Matlock, these trends create conditions that

> could bring a dictator to power or... begin a process of fragmentation that would destroy any effective central government in the country.[107]

The question of internal legitimacy of the Russian state might prove to be decisive. Matlock observes that the Communist Party was associated with organized crime since its inception.[108] But today's 'wild capitalism' will be tolerated only insofar as it can deliver widespread prosperity. Modern Russia has always been highly stratified, but rarely so overtly polarized as it is today. According to official statistics, in 1994, 0.7 percent of the population were earning in excess of $300,000 per year; 27 percent were classified as 'poor' (i.e. able to buy food but not much else); and 33 percent had incomes at or below that required for subsistence.[109] As might be expected, tensions between the haves and have-nots is rising. According to Stephen Holmes, Moscow "symbolizes the total disregard of the Russian rich for the Russian poor."[110] Could this be analogous to the kind of First World/Third World dichotomy that I mentioned in connection with Los Angeles in Chapter 1? And many comment-ators have observed that legitimate society has little chance of flourishing while the government does little to control or hide its criminal activities, and in some cases even flaunts them.[111]

In a perceptive commentary, Holmes identified the legitimacy problem of the Russian state. The 'destatization' of the former Soviet Union is not a solution, he contends, but a problem insofar as there are no longer rules to live by (thus echoing Guillermoprieto's comment on not knowing when the rules of the Mexican federation apply). There is no law until the Mafia needs lawyers. The consequent social contract is "an exchange of unaccountable power for untaxable wealth."[112] The roots of popular discontent in this postcolonial situation, according to Holmes, "lie less in deplorable habits of dependency than in accurate perceptions of betrayal." [113]

Let me conclude this survey with a brief glance at Italy, an important European nation that has long been held up as an example of endemic state corruption. Symptoms of dysfunctionality are evident everywhere in Italian political life: separ-atist yearnings, political corruption, the Mafia, and an uncontrollable public debt. Patrick McCarthy puts the blame for this state of affairs on clientelism, which he defines as "the attainment and retention of power through the private expropriation of public resources, and through the use of the state to expropriate private resources."[114] Historically, the chief practitioners of clientism were the Christian Democratic Party and the Vatican.[115] Now it has been left to flourish in an unin-hibited manner throughout the country.[116] According to Matt Frei, "The bribe was not only used as a lubricant for business, it was often its sole purpose."[117] Politicians who demanded bribes before they took action thereby reputedly delayed rescue operations to save Venice from flooding; they also siphoned off millions of dollars from African relief funds.

The connection between the Northern establishment and Southern organized crime is by now well-documented.[118] When this immense collective fraud began to crumble in the 1990s, the legitimacy of the Italian state was openly questioned. Michele Salvati places the roots of this crisis in the middle-class perception that their taxes, extracted in the name of social and regional solidarity, were being consumed by corruption and state parasitism.[119] The network of dysfunctionality was cast widely: social services were taken over by politicians who distributed benefits in return for electoral support,[120] and the Italian secret services often frustrated judicial investigations of terrorism while maintaining links with the Mafia and right-wing terrorists.[121]

Unsurprisingly, the example of the Italian establishment was followed by many ordinary Italians. With leaders who were apparently unable to make a connection between politics and moral or civic obligation, Italians have made wholesale tax evasion a national pastime. Smith noted that "half the value-added tax seems not to have been paid" in Italy, and that without tax evasion the astronomical national debt could have been contained.[122] As successive leaders (Craxi, Andreotti, and Berlusconi) found themselves indicted or on trial for bribery or corrupt practices, many commentators doubt the ability of the Italian political system to rescue itself.[123] As Smith states: "Italian-style politics still seem an almost insuperable obstacle to good government."[124]

The Viability Crisis of the Postmodern State

The realization dawned that crime might be the new form that politics was taking in this unpredictable era.[125]

Why do certain nations/peoples and not others cross the line into corruption and lawlessness? Let me first concede the obvious: that human beings are imperfect creatures, and that the boundary between moral and immoral is sometimes fuzzy, and always contested. Hence, lawless individuals and conflicting moralities are the norm, even though most public officials act honestly.[126] Nevertheless, contemporary circumstances seem to have promoted a tilt toward corruption, even vindictiveness. Little and Posada-Carlo argue convincingly that one-party systems (especially in Latin America) have facilitated political corruption.[127] Postcolonial transitions in Africa have been accompanied by widespread criminalization of the state,[128] and genocide base on old tribalisms.[129] The USA, like other capitalist nations, became significantly more unequal during the decades of the seventies and eighties.[130] The growth of socio-economic and political inequality was accompanied by greater individual competitiveness and a consequent sense of personal insecurity. Many sectors of US capital suffered in the face of global competition and have been forced into strategies of survival. This provoked an on-going examination of the national psyche, in an attempt to fathom what it would take to maintain US political and economic hegemony in the world. Recession also undermined labor's authority, as shown in the dramatic decline in the membership and influence of the trade-union movement; the rise of an informal sector and of a drug-based economy are but two examples of survival strategies by class fractions now existing beyond the wage-labor sphere.

The most potent policy espoused by the corporatist alliance of the Reagan years (1981–8) was deregulation. This took many forms, including the break-up of monopolies (in communications, for instance), privatization of social services, and the rollback of government oversight. The policy's impact is only now being assessed.[131] Whatever its practical outcome in terms of specific localities and sectors, the generalized effect of deregulation has been to obscure the lines of public and private authority, responsibility, and accountability. For much of the period following the 1960s, central government politics in the United States was transformed into a 'dual sovereignty,' represented by a Republican executive (the presidency) and a Democratic Congress.[132] Both political parties became estranged from the electorate, almost half of whom no longer bothered to vote. This arrangement suited the sovereigns. The practices of democracy and electoral politics were reduced to strategic coalition-building among interest groups committed to maintaining the dual sovereignty (through sophisticated lobbying mechanisms, etc.).

Thus, while capital and labor contended with recession, the deregulating state engineered the decline of public welfare. As a result, economically-secure individuals felt more insecure and fearful of the consequences of economic failure; those who were already 'failures' perceived that they owed nothing to a society that had shown them no compassion. The former became more resentful and selfish; the latter were emboldened in 1992 to the worst civil disturbances seen in urban America during this century. Social unrest appeared to be on the rise during the 1990s, as witness the resurgence of racism; the shrill antagonisms surrounding the abortion debate, and, more generally, the place of women in American society; the anger of minorities and the poor; the outcry against environmental degradation; the intolerance of the homeless and people with AIDS; the despair and disgust over drugs; and the murderous depredations of the gang culture. Shining like beacons across this malevolent landscape are the thousand points of malfeasance ignited by prominent public persona who, on the evidence, regard themselves as above the law.

The examples of the Japan, Myanmar, Mexico, Russia, Italy and the United States suggest some common, disturbing inferences for the future of the postmodern nation state. The demonstrable facts of political life in each of these countries are:

- state corruption, including the police apparatus;
- political influence of organized crime;
- new levels of socio-economic polarization separating the haves from the have-nots;
- a legitimacy crisis of the nation state; and
- a viability crisis of the nation-state, i.e. the sense that the state cannot rescue itself.

These conditions hold under very different circumstances: in Japan, where organized crime is infiltrating the legitimate world; in Myanmar, where SLORC is creating an 'addictive political economy;' in Mexico's narco-democracy; in Singapore, where small-time users suffer draconian sentences, while the powerful invest with their suppliers;[133] in the bizarre bazaar states of the former USSR; in Italy's clientist state; and in the neo-plutocratic American state, with its corrupt agencies of repression.[134]

Is it an exaggeration to imagine a postmodern, fragmented and decentered geopolitics in which the nation state becomes obsolete?[135] In many cases, nation state boundaries are already little more than markers of various narco-territories. In a world where a wild capitalism, organized crime, and corrupt politicians collaborate to carve up global markets, the nation state may dissolve into one more residual modernist institution that history is passing by. It will remain in place only so long as it can ensure territorial integrity in a segemented global marketplace.

This construction of a postmodern global politics may not yet be fully demonstrable in the real world. However, it is undoubtedly upon us. It is seen in the decentered, multipolar, postcolonial world; in the tattered legitimacy of the nation state; and in the collapse of the Cold War. But let me stress once again that modernism is not yet dead. I am not predicting the overnight demise of the institutions of global politics or of the nation state. However, there can be little doubt that the

Figure 14.2 Postborder metaphysics (Gustavo Leclerc)
About his sketch book, 'Stories about Buildings,' Gustavo Leclerc comments: Since 1990, I have been recording spatial stories of buildings and places, real and imagined, based on my own sense of displacement as an immigrant from Mexico, where I left to practice architecture here in Los Angeles. There are two constant themes which run through the sketchbook. They are ideas of the *post-border condition* and *hybrid spaces*. The post-border condition relates to notions of bridging past and present, home and dislocation and focusing on the in-between space. Hybrid spaces are those which result from the juxtaposition between the first and third worlds, between rich and poor, between North and South, and between modernity and postmodernity.

ground-rules of geopolitics are altering, in ways that are consistent with the premises of postmodernity.

A postmodern, postcolonial geopolitical dynamic takes the form of a dialectic between the external and the internal relations of the state. The external dynamic is powered by a wild capitalism within a globalizing context that is very suddenly without the stabilizing ethos of two superpowers and a Cold War. The internal dynamic is centered on the rise of gangster nations, i.e. corrupt nation states increasingly compromised in their ability to appeal for social cohesion by their links to organized crime and by overtly partisan selfishness affecting supranational, national and local government.[136] Public disgust is deflected by a new mercantalism decked out in the glitzy, belligerent rhetoric of protectionism and pandemic consumerism. The principal material consequences of these dynamics are

(1)   an acute socio-economic polarization within the nation (based on every conceivable kind of personal difference – age, gender, race, ethnicity, (dis)ability, nationality, sexual preference, education, class, geographical location, etc.); and

(2) a related legitimacy crisis of the nation state, which is no longer able to sustain a credible internal discourse on social integration or nationalism, or to interact with states beyond its borders using anything other than a crude market-oriented metric.

If democracy is principally a matter of delegated public trust,[137]then we may indeed have reached the end of democracy. The entire system spirals to another level of complication when the delegitimized nation state enters a viability crisis, i.e. it is unable to guarantee even its own survival. Buffeted by globalizing external forces, the internal difficulties of the nation-state are aggravated, and so on in a cumulative spiral of destabilization that threatens the social contract.[138]

Notes

1.   Sassen, S., 1998: *Globalization and its Discontents*, New York: The Free Press, p. xx.
2.   Hall, P., 1998: *Cities in Civilization*, New York: Pantheon Books, Chapters 5 and 6.
3.   Sassen, S., *Globalization and its Discontents*, p. xxxii.
4.   Ibid., p. xxvii.
5.   Ibid., p. xxxiii.
6.   Wolch, J. and Dear, M., 1993: *Malign Neglect: Homelessness in an American City*, San Francisco: Jossey-Bass.
7.   Cohen, Roger, 1995: "In Sarajevo, Victims of a Postmodern War," *New York Times*, May 21, A-1, 1995.
8.   Huntington, S., 1996: *The Clash of Civilizations and the Remaking of World Order*, New York: Simon & Schuster.
9.   Kennedy, P. 1989: *The Rise and Fall of Great Nations: Economic Change and Military Conflict from 1500 to 2000*, New York: Vintage Books.
10. Jowitt, K., 1995: "Our Republic of Fear: Chomsky's Denunciation of America's Foreign Policy," *Times Literary Supplement*, February 10, p.3.
11. Ibid.
12. Ibid.
13. Walker, M.,1995: "New Global Markets? Think Medieval Papacy," *Los Angeles Times*, June 18, p. M-2.
14. Ibid.
15. Risen, J., 1995: "Clinton Reportedly Orders CIA to Focus on Trade Espionage," *Los Angeles Times*, July 23, p. A-1.
16. Ibid., p. A-14.
17. Cohen, Roger, "In Sarajevo," p. 1.
18. Ibid., p. 1, p.8.
19. Dannen, F. and Silverman, I., 1995: "The Supernote," *The New Yorker*, October 23, p. 52.
20. Ibid., p. 55.
21. Ibid., p. 53.
22. Perhaps the most dramatic examples are the contemporary transformations of African States. See Bayart, J-F., Ellis, S., and Hibou, B., 1999: *The Criminalization of the State In Africa*, Indianapolis: Indiana University Press; and Gourevitch, P., 1998: *We Wish to Inform You That Tomorrow We Will Be Killed With Our Families: Stories from Rwanda*, New York: Farrar Straus and Giroux.
23. Weiner, T., 1997: "Transcripts of Nixon Tapes Show the Path to Watergate," *New York Times*, October 31, A-1 passim.
24. *Newsweek*, 1989: July 10, p. 16.

25. *New York Times*, 1989: July 31, p. A-5.
26. *Newsweek*, 1989: July 10, p. 16.
27. *Los Angeles Times*, 1989: August 3, p. I-19.
28. *Los Angeles Times*, 1989: July 30, p. I-1.
29. *New York Times*, 1989: July 25, p. A-1.
30. *New York Times*, 1989: July 29, p. A-1.
31. *New York Times*, 1989: July 2, p. E-5.
32. *New York Times*, 1989: July 31, p. A-5.
33. *New York Times*, 1989: July 23, p. A-1.
34. *New York Times*, 1989: August 5, p. A-1; *New York Times*, 1989: September 2, p. A-1.
35. *Los Angeles Times*, 1989: July 23, p. V-3.
36. *New York Times*, 1989: July 28, p. A-1.
37. *Los Angeles Times*, 1989: July 30, p. I-8.
38. *Los Angeles Times*, 1989: August 5, p. 6.
39. *New York Times*, 1990: June 12, p. C-4.
40. *New York Times*, 1990: June 12, p. A-1.
41. *New York Times*, 1990: June 28, p. A-23.
42. *New York Times*, 1990: June 25, p. A-1
43. *New York Times*, 1990: June 21, p. A-1.
44. *New York Times*, 1990: June 21, p. C-15.
45. *New York Times*, 1990: June 21, p. A-1.
46. *New York Times*, 1990: June 21, p. C-15.
47. *New York Times*, 1990: July 8, p. A-1.
48. *New York Times*, 1990: July 9, p. A-19.
49. Finnegan, W., 1997: "The Unwanted," *The New Yorker*, December 1, p. 61–78.
50. Wills, G., 1995: "The New Revolutionaries," *New York Times Book Review*, August 10, p. 50–52.
51. Ibid., p. 50
52. Ibid., p. 54.
53. Ibid., p. 54.
54. Ibid., p. 55.
55. Richards, J. R., 1999: *Transnational Criminal Organizations, Cybercrime, and Money Laundering: A Handbook for Law Enforcement Officers, Auditors, and Financial Investigators*, Boca Raton, Florida: CRC Press, p. 3
56. Ibid., p. 3
57. Ibid., pp. 31–32.
58. Castells, Manuel, 1998: *End of Millennium*, Malden, Mass: Blackwell, p. 167.
59. Richards, James R., *Transnational Criminal Organizations, Cybercrime, and Money Laundering*, p. 4–5.
60. Ibid., p. 9
61. Chossudovsky, M., 1996: "The Business of Crime and the Crimes of Business," *Covert Action Quarterly* 58, p. 24 passim.
62. Specter, M., 1998: "Traffickers New Cargo: Naive Slavic Women," *New York Times*, January 11, A-1 passim. According to Rotella, S., 1995: "Mexico's Cartels Sow Seeds of Corruption, Destruction," *Los Angeles Times*, June 16, A-1, p. 33, "the smuggling of humans is a growth industry, paralleled and sometimes linked to the smuggling of drugs."
63. Nelson, J., 1998: "Money Laundering Global in Scope," *Los Angeles Times*, February 1, A-22.
64. Perry, P. J., 1997: *Political Corruption and Political Geography*, Aldershot: Ashgate.
65. Clark, G. L., 1998: "The Anatomy of Corruption: The Practice of Pension Fund Trustee Decision Making," *Environment and Planning A*, p. 2. See, for example, Logan, J. R.

and Molotch, H. L., 1987: *Urban Fortunes: The Political Economy of Place*, Berkeley: University of California Press. Clark, G. L. and Dear, M., 1984: *State Apparatus: Structures and Language of Legitimacy*, Unwin Hyman, Boston, discusses the state as mafia.

66. Clark, G. L. "The Anatomy of Corruption", p. 2.
67. Ibid., p. 4
68. Ibid. See also Clark, G. L., 1997: "Pension Funds and Urban Investment: Four Models of Financial Intermediation," *Environment and Planning A* 29, p. 1297–316; Clark, G. L., 1997: "Rogues and Regulation in Global Finance: Maxwell, Leeson and the City of London," *Regional Studies*, 31 (3), p. 221–36.
69. Clark, G. L., *Accountability and Corruption,* p. 11; also see the essay by Mathews, R. 1997, "Public Trust and Public Deception" in Clark, G. L., Jonson, E. P., and Caldow, W. (eds), *Accountability and Corruption*, Sydney: Allen & Unwin, pp. 100–118, in the same volume.
70. Judt, T., 1997: "The Longest Road to Hell," *New York Times*, December 22, A-21.
71. Koss, M., 1996: "Gangster Nations," *Los Angeles Weekly*, December 6–12, p. 27.
72. Ibid., p. 32.
73. Holley, D., 1996: "Japanese Banks Mired in Yakuza Debt Crisis," *San Francisco Examiner*, February 26, p.A-8.
74. Kristof, N. D., 1995: "The Quake That Hurt Kobe Helps Its Gangs Get Richer," *New York Times*, June 6, A-1, p. 1.
75. Lewis, P., 1996: "A World Fed Up With Bribes," *New York Times*, November 28, C-1 passim.
76. Walsh, J., 1998: "A World War on Bribery," *Time*, June 22, pp. 25–31.
77. Bernstein, D. and Kean, L., 1996: "People of the Opiate: Burma's Dictatorship of Drugs," *The Nation*, December 16, p. 11.
78. Ibid., p. 12.
79. Ibid., p. 14.
80. Ibid., p. 16.
81. Ibid.
82. Ibid., p. 18.
83. Fineman, M. and Rotella, S., 1995: "The Drug Web That Entangles Mexico," *Los Angeles Times* June 15, p. A-1 passim; Rotella, S., 1998: *Twilight on the Line*, New York: W. W. Norton.
84. Fineman, M. and Rotella, S., "The Drug Web," p. A-16.
85. For a general treatment of the Latin American drug trade, see Castells, Manuel, *End of Millennium*, Malden, Mass: Blackwell, Chapter 3.
86. Fineman, M. and Rotella, S. 1995: "The Drug Web That Entangles Mexico" *Los Angeles Times*, June 15, A-1 passim.
87. Rotella, S. 1995: "Mexico's Cartels Sow Seeds of Corruption, Destruction," *Los Angeles Times*, June 16, A-1 passim.; see also Guillermoprieto, A., 1994: *The Heart Bleeds: Latin America Now*, New York: Knopf, p. 330.
88. Rotella, S., *Twilight on the Line*, p. 48.
89. Stille, Alexander, 1995: "The Fall of Caesar," *The New Yorker*, September 11, p. 68–83.
90. Rotella, S., "Mexico's Cartels," p. A-21.
91. Ibid., p. 236.
92. Ibid., p. 306.
93. Guillermoprieto, A., 1995: "Whodunnit?," *The New Yorker*, September 25, p. 44.
94. Ibid., p. 46.
95. Ibid., p. 49.
96. Guillermoprieto, A., 1996: "The Riddle of Raul," *The New Yorker*, October 3.

97. Castells, Manuel, *End of Millennium*, Chapter 3.

98. Kaplan, Robert, D., 1996: *The Ends of the Earth*. New York: Random House.

99. Koss, M., 1995: "It's Midnight. Do You Know Where Russia's Nukes Are?," *Los Angeles Weekly*, June 9–15, p. 20. Handelman, S., 1995: *Comrade Criminal: Russia's New Mafia*, New Haven: Yale University Press. This book is a good general study, as is Remnick, D., 1996: *Resurrection: The Struggle for a New Russia*, New York: Random House .

100. Analagous developments have been observed in the People's Republic of China. For the case of Shanghai, see Schell, O., 1995: "Shangai Daze," *Los Angeles Times Magazine*, June 18, 12 passim; Matlock, J., 1995: "Russia: The Power of the Mob," *New York Review of Books*, July 13, p. 13.

101. Matlock, J., "Russia," p. 14.

102. Ibid.

103. Quoted in Erlanger, S., 1995: "A Corrupt Tide in Russia from State–Business Ties," *New York Times*, July 2, p. A-1, p. A-5.

104. Ibid., p. A-1.

105. Schmemann, S., 1995: "Russian Wise Guys," *New York Times Book Review*, June 4, p. 18; Matlock, J., Russia, p. 12.

106. Carney, T., 1999: "Moscow 90210," *Los Angeles Magazine*, March, 112 passim.

107. Matlock, J., Russia, p. 12.

108. Ibid., p. 12.

109. Ibid., p. 14.

110. Holmes, S., 1997: "What Russia Teaches Us Now," *The American Prospect*, July-August, p. 32.

111. Ibid., p. 15. Erlanger suggests that immoral and illegal ties are "openly displayed, even brandished as a sign of power."

112. Ibid., p. 37.

113. Ibid., p. 38.

114. McCarthy, P., 1997: *The Crisis of the Italian State: From the Origins of the Cold War to the Fall of Berlusconi*, New York: St. Martin's Press.

115. McCarthy claims that the Vatican was "the prime cause of the new [Italian] state's weakness". Matt Frei writes that the Vatican is "responsible for some of the worst aspects of modern Italy." Frei, M., 1995: *Getting the Boot: Italy's Unfinished Revolution*, New York: Times Books.

116. Smith, D. M., 1995: "Italy's Dirty Linen," *New York Review of Books*, November 30, p. 10.

117. Frei, M., *Getting the Boot*, p. 12.

119. Salvati, M., 1995: "The Crisis of Government in Italy," *New Left Review*, 213, p. 76–95.

120. Frei notes that in a country of 55 million people, no less than 4 million were disability pensioners, "about whom the most invalid thing was their ailment." Denis Mack Smith adds that in 1993, the ranks of disability pensioners included 150 members of parliament, one of them because of his "obesity." Frei, M. *Getting the Boot*, p. 12; Smith, D.M. 1995. "Italy's Dirty Linen," p. 10.

121. Smith, D. M., "Italy's Dirty Linen," p. 10.

122. Ibid., p. 12.

123. McCarthy, P., 1997: *The Crisis of the Italian State: From the Origins of the Cold War to the Fall of Berlusconi*, New York: St. Martin's Press; Harris, W. V., 1996: "Italy in the Balance," *Times Literary Supplement*, July 19, p. 6; Salvati, M., "The Crisis of Government in Italy," pp. 76–95; Stille, Alexander, The Fall of Caesar, pp. 68–83.

124. Smith, D. M. "Italy's Dirty Linen," p. 15.

125. Guillermoprieto, A., 1995: "Whodunnit?," *The New Yorker*, September 25, p. 44.

126.   Johns, G., "Divided Loyalties; bureaucrats and ministries," in Clark, G. L., Johnson, E. P. and Caldon, W., 1997: *Accountability and Corruption: Public Sector Ethics*, pp. 73–92.

127.   Little, W. and Posada-Carlo, E. (eds), 1997: *Political Corruption in Latin America and Europe* (Institute of Latin American Studies Series). New York: Saint Martin's Press; See also Perry, P. J., *Political Corruption and Political Geography*, Aldershot: Ashgate for a discussion of the "prerequisites" and "proximates" (roughly, contextual factors, and causes) of corruption.

128.   Bayart, J-F., Ellis, S., and Hibou, B., 1999: *The Criminalization of the State In Africa*, Indianapolis: Indiana University Press.

129.   Gourevitch, 1998, *We Wish to Inform You*, provides a chilling account of the Rwandan genocide of 1994, when the Hutu majority murdered 800,000 Tutsi (plus Hutu sympathizers) in less than 100 days.

130.   Phillips, K., 1990: *The Politics of Rich and Poor: Wealth and the American Electorate in the Reagan Aftermath*, New York: Random House.

131.   See, for example, Donahue, J. D., 1989: *The Privatization Decision*, New York: Basic Books; Ehrenreich, B., 1997: "Spinning the Poor into Gold," *Harper's Magazine*, August, pp. 44–52; Bates, E., 1998: "Prisons For Profit," *The Nation*, January 5, pp. 11–18.

132.   Ginsberg, B. and Schefter, M., 1990: *Politics By Other Means: The Declining Importance of Elections in America*, New York: Basic Books.

133.   Bernstein, D. and Kean, L., 1997: "Singapore's Blood Money," *The Nation*, August 20, pp. 11–16.

134.   Burnham, D., 1997: The FBI, *The Nation*, August 11–18, pp. 11–26.

135.   There is a large literature on contemporary mutations of political space. I have found intriguing some recent studies of Finland, Israel, and the Spanish Basque Country (see respectively, Häkli, Jouni, 1998: "Discourse in the Production of Political Space: Decolonizing the Symbolism of Provinces in Finland," in *Political Geography*, Vol. 17, No. 3. pp. 331–63; Yiftachel, Oren, 1997: "Israel: Metropolitan Integration or 'Fractured Regions'? An Alternative Perspective," in *Cities*, Vol. 14, No. 6. pp. 371–80; and Raento, Pauliina, 1997: "Political Mobilisation and Place-specificity: Radical Nationalist Street Campaigning in the Spanish Basque Country," in *Space & Polity*, Vol. 1, No.2. pp. 191–204).

136.   On corruption of the local state, see Janhiainen (1995), and Little, W. and Posada-Carbo, E. (eds.), 1997: *Political Corruption in Latin America and Europe* (Institute of Latin American Studies Series), New York: Saint Martin's Press.

137.   Bakker, Heleen E. and Nordholt, Nico G. (eds), 1997: *Corruption & Legitimacy*, Amsterdam: SISWO, pg. 11.

138.   Phillips, K., 1997: "Who's Looking Out for Nation's Social Contract?," *Los Angeles Times*, July 27, M-1 passim.

15

Epistemological Politics

[T]he great lesson of the twentieth century is that all the great truths are false.[1]

Bernard-Henri Levy

In my professional life, I have been branded a Marxist, a liberal, and a postmodernist – all terms used pejoratively, as insults. And, from experience, I know that many teachers still refuse to discuss postmodernism with their students. So let me now speak frankly. It is clear that some people detest postmodernism. It is also evident that the suppression of postmodernism (for whatever reasons) will have consequences. In this chapter, I shall examine some of the dissidents' complaints, and show what has happened in human geography (a discipline that has been relatively open to postmodernism) and urban planning (which has not). This is not a chapter for the squeamish. Academic politics is as messy and petty as any other kind of political shenanigans. There is a saying that academic politics is so vicious because so little is at stake; this is not true in the epistemological wars that surround postmodernism. Make no mistake about this: Postmodernism Matters.

Against Postmodernism

"And in the Right corner..."

Post-modernism entices us with the siren call of liberation and creativity, but it may be an invitation to intellectual and moral suicide.

Gertrude Himmelfarb

Gertrude Himmelfarb, an eminent and conservative historian, attacked postmodernism in a long article in the *Times Literary Supplement* in 1992. It is a classic of its kind. First she claims that postmodernists tell "good historians" nothing that they do not already know:

Modernist history is not positivist in the sense of aspiring to a fixed, total, or absolute truth about the past. Like post-modernist history, it is relativistic, but with a difference, for its relativism is firmly rooted in reality. It is sceptical of absolute truth but not of partial, contingent, incremental truths. More important, it does not deny the reality of the past itself.... [The] modernist historian reads and writes history...with a scrupulous regard for the historicity, the integrity, the actuality of the past. He makes a strenuous effort to enter into the minds and experiences of people in the past, to try to understand them as they understood themselves, to rely upon contemporary evidence as

Figure 15.1 In search of the postmodern authentic (Jesse Lerner)
Jesse Lerner's *Ruins: a fake documentary* (1999) is a brilliant interrogation of how we (re)construct authenticity. In it, he tells the story of Mexican artist Brigido Lara, whose imitations of Mayan artifacts led to his arrest by the Mexican government on the grounds that he was illegally selling/exporting authentic art objects. Lara proved his innocence by manufacturing several new pieces while in custody. After his release, Lara was employed by Mexican museums to oversee restorations and to establish the authenticity of artifacts in their collections. He continues to fabricate his own art works, and claims that many of his pieces are in major international collections – under the mistaken presumption that they are of ancient Mayan origin.

much as possible, to intrude his own views and assumptions as little as possible, to reconstruct to the best of his ability the past as it "actually was"...[2]

Himmelfarb recognizes the impossibility of this ideal, conceding that historians have known all along that their work is vulnerable on three counts: "the fallibility and deficiency of the historical record on which it is based; the fallibility and selectivity inherent in the writing of history; and the fallibility and subjectivity of the historian."[3] The strength of good history relies on a tried and tested historical method that favors objectivity, but is contemptuous of a postmodernism that engages with the contingency of historical explanation:

> Critical history put a premium on archival research and primary sources, the authenticity of documents and reliability of witnesses, the need for substantiating and countervailing evidence; and, at a more mundane level, on the accuracy of quotations and citations, prescribed forms of documentation in footnotes and bibliography, and all the rest of the "methodology" that went into the "canon of evidence." The purpose of this methodology was twofold: to bring to the surface the infrastructure, as it were, of the historical work, thus making it accessible to the reader and exposing it to criticism; and to encourage the historian to a maximum exertion of objectivity in spite of all the temptations to the contrary. Post-modernists scoff at this as the antiquated remnants of nineteenth-century positivism. But is has been the norm of the profession until recently.[4]

The fallibility and relativity of history are not, in Himmelfarb's eyes, a discovery of the postmodernists. The difference between the old and the new lies in the presumptions of postmodernism: that "because there is no absolute, total truth, there can be no partial, contingent truths...[and] that because it is impossible to attain such truths, it is not only futile but positively baneful to aspire to them."[5]

In postmodernism's repudiation of Enlightenment principles, Himmelfarb identifies a political agenda that is subversive of the social order:

> Post-modernism is...far more radical than either Marxism or [other] new "isms"...all of which are implicitly committed to the Enlightenment principles of reason, truth, justice, morality, reality. Post-modernism repudiates both the values and the rhetoric of the Enlightenment. In rejecting the "discipline" of knowledge and rationality, postmodernism also rejects the "discipline" of society and authority. And in denying any reality apart from language, it aims to subvert the structure of society together with the structure of language.[6]

Even in its celebration of difference, postmodernism threatens the intellectual order: "The modernist accuses the post-modernist of bringing mankind to the abyss of nihilism. The post-modernist proudly, happily accepts that charge."[7]

Paradoxically, while she concedes the political posture implicit in any historical account, Himmelfarb decries our descent into a politics of recognition which, she claims, has removed all meaning from history

> Multiculturalism has the obvious effect of politicizing history. But its more pernicious effect is to demean and dehumanize the people who are the subjects of history. To

pluralize and particularize history to the point where people share no history in common ... is to deny the common (generic) humanity of all people, whatever their sex,
race, class, religion, and the like. It is also to trivialize history by so fragmenting it that it
lacks all coherence and focus, all sense of continuity, indeed, *all meaning*.[8](emphasis
added)

Needless to say, Himmelfarb judges that young people are particularly at risk of
contamination from postmodernism, but she is hopeful at the first signs of disaffec-
tion with postmodernism, because the appeal of novelty will surely recede:

The "herd of independent minds" ... will find some other brave, new cause to rally
around. Out of boredom, careerism (the search for new ways to make a mark in the
profession), and sheer bloody-mindedness (the desire to *épater* [skewer] one's elders),
the young will rebel, and the vanguard of today will find itself an aging rearguard ...[9]

While unclear about whether or not the era after postmodernity will restore the old,
or usher in some even more despicable fad, Himmelfarb concedes that the traditional
verities of the history profession will unlikely be recovered intact.

What Himmelfarb appears to fear most is the loss of the historical method that lies
at the heart of her vision of the discipline. It is noteworthy that she equates methodological weakness with moral failing:

One can foresee a desire to return to a more objective and integrated, less divisive and
self-interested history. What will be more difficult to restore is the methodology that is at
the heart of that history. A generation of historians ... lack any training in that methodology. They may even lack the discipline, *moral as well as professional*, required for
it.[10](emphasis added)

The traditional history now being discarded is hard and exciting, according to
Himmelfarb, involving truth, objectivity, coherence, accuracy, and good footnotes:

the old history, traditional history is hard. Hard – but exciting precisely because it is
hard. And that excitement may prove a challenge and inspiration for a new generation
of historians. It is more exciting to write true history (or as true as we can make it) than
fictional history, else historians would choose to be novelists rather than historians;
more exciting to try to rise above our interests and prejudices than to indulge them; more
exciting to try to enter the imagination of those remote from us in time and place than to
impose our imagination upon them; more exciting to write a coherent narrative while
respecting the complexity of historical events than to fragmentize history into discon-
nected units; more exciting to try to get the facts (without benefit of quotation marks) as
right as we can than to deny the very idea of facts; even more exciting to get the
footnotes right, if only to show others the visible proof of our labours.[11]

It remains unclear exactly how Himmelfarb proposes to achieve her true history, rise
above her own prejudices, excise her own imagination, prevent herself from imposing narrative coherence where none may exist, decide what 'facts' matter, and ensure
that her footnotes sufficiently attest to her serious commitment to a hard history.

John M. Ellis, in *Against Deconstruction*, arrives at broadly similar conclusions. In
his case, it is deconstructionists who offer nothing new to literary critics:

The only sense in which deconstruction can be said to represent change in the critical context lies in its giving new shape and a renewed force and virulence to pre-existing ideas and attitudes: it has given an appearance of theoretical sophistication to what had previously been the more or less incoherent attitudes and prejudices of majority practice.[12]

I am a little leery about reading this too literally. Ellis appears to be saying that the incoherent practices of the majority of his peers have been normalized by deconstructionism, a situation he laments. But what is clear to Ellis is that some people want to reject "standards of intelligent criticism" with consequences "well-nigh everyone" (presumably a different majority than the one just identified?) deplores:

> The point of good criticism cannot lie in its discovering the meaning of a text; to use that criterion would be to return to the unitary truths of science.[13] ... The prevailing critical consensus, then, has long insisted on pluralism, on the value of different viewpoints[14] ... If no one cares to talk about standards of intelligent criticism, then the content of published criticism will vary enormously – and it does; well-nigh everyone, including the most ardent advocates of theoretically unrestrained pluralism, is unhappy with at least some aspects of this situation.[15]

Ellis recognizes a yet deeper problem in "that deconstruction's major themes are themselves inherently antitheoretical in nature."[16] The process by which he reaches this conclusion is revealing.[17] First, he asks us to understand that theory is, axiomatically, disruptive:

> Theory exerts its pressure on the status quo by continual examination of the basis and rationale for the accepted activities of a field of study. Inevitably, the results will in principle be quite unlike the usual deconstructive attitudes: they should not leave us with issues and activities more undefined than ever but instead introduce a clarification and differentiation of fundamentally different kinds of activities. The consequence of this kind of activity will generally be a pressure to rearrange priorities; *by its very nature, then, theory is indeed disturbing.*[18](emphasis added)

But the kind of theory that Ellis sanctions has little room for unfettered freedom of thought, even as it appears to encompasses many of the practices which would meet the approval of those who practice, say, "hard" history:

> But theoretical argument must ... proceed with great care. It must be above all a careful, patient, analytical process: its strengths must lie in precision of formulation, in well-drawn distinctions, in carefully delineated concepts. In theoretical discourse, argument is met by argument; one careful attempt to analyze and elucidate the basis of a critical concept or position is met by an equally exacting and penetrating scrutiny of its own inner logic. That makes theoretical argument very much a communal process: there is *no room in it for individual license*, for claims of exemption from logical scrutiny, for appeals to an undefined unique logical status, for appeals to allow obscurity to stand unanalyzed, or for *freedom to do as one wishes.*[19](emphases added)

The "most enduring fault" of deconstructionist literary criticism is exposed in Ellis's own credo:

A shared inquiry means a commitment to argument and dialogue, while a criticism that insists on the value of each individual critic's perspective, in effect, refuses to make that commitment. Before deconstruction, theory of criticism worked against the laissez-faire tendencies of criticism; but now deconstruction, an intensified expression of those tendencies, has attempted to seize the mantle of theory in order to pursue this antitheoretical program. The result is an apparent novelty that, looked at more closely, consists in resistance to change and, more particularly, to that change that is most urgently needed: the development of some check on and control of the indigestible, chaotic flow of critical writing through reflection on what is and what is not in principle worthwhile – that is, through genuine, rather than illusory, theoretical reflection.[20]

Ellis is unclear about who gets to decide what is "worthwhile," or what are the standards of "genuine" theoretical reflection. I suspect it will be those same people who decided which standards were important before postmodernism came along.

"And in the Left corner..."

Postmodernity is merely a theoretical construct of interest primarily as a symptom of the current mood of the Western intelligentsia.[21]

One of the more plain-spoken attacks lobbed from the Left comes from Alex Callincos in his unambiguously titled volume: *Against Postmodernism: A Marxist Critique*. His opening sentences reveal that he, too, has contracted the virus that seems endemic among anti-postmodernists: irritation.

Yet another book on postmodernism? What earthly justification could there be for contributing to the destruction of the world's dwindling forests in order to engage in debates which should surely have exhausted themselves long ago? My embarrassment in the face of this challenge is made all the more acute by the fact that at the origins of the present book lies that unworthy emotion, irritation.[22]

I suppose this is meant to be engaging; certainly it's intended to trivialize. In any event, it does not hold out much hope for a tolerant appraisal on the part of the Irritated Intellectual. And sure enough, Callinicos promptly and unambiguously denies any merit in postmodernism as philosophy, style, or epoch. Letting the boundaries between poststructuralism and postmodernism slither through his finger-tips, he loudly declares:

I deny the main theses of poststructuralism, which seem to be in substance false. I doubt very much that Postmodern art represents a qualitative break from the Modernism of the early twentieth century. Moreover, much of what is written in support of the idea that we live in a postmodern epoch seems to me to be of small caliber intellectually, usually superficial, often ignorant, sometimes incoherent.[23]

Callinicos could have stopped there, and himself have saved a few trees from clear-cutting. After that tirade, there can be little doubt about where he stands, can there? Well, but then he adopts what turns out to be a fairly common strategy among opinionated critics: an immediate qualification that, actually, there are some good ideas in postmodernism after all. Callinicos squirms:

> I should, however, make a qualification to the judgement just passed. I do not believe that the work of the philosophers now known as poststructualist can be dismissed in this way: wrong on fundamentals Deleuze, Derrida, and Foucault may be, but they develop their ideas with considerable skill and sophistication, and offer partial insights of great value.[24]

I am sure that Deleuze, Derrida and Foucault will be relieved. But Callinicos never really engages with which of these post-structuralist theses are "false" and which of "great value."

Callinicos' main gripe is the way in which postmodernism deflects attention from a "revolutionary socialist tradition."[25] His own intellectual project

> rather uneasily occupies a space defined by the convergence of philosophy, social theory and historical writing. Fortunately, there is an intellectual tradition which is characterized precisely by the synthesis it effects of these genres, namely the classical historical materialism of Marx himself, Engels, Lenin, Trotsky, Luxemburg and Gramsci.[26]

The fact that there may be other intellectual traditions which address this synthesis is of no consequence to Callinicos:

> Only, I contend, classical historical materialism, reinforced by an account of language and thought that is naturalistic as well as communicative, can provide a secure basis for the defence of the 'radicalized Enlightenment' to which Habermas is committed.[27]

This is an odd world toward which Callinicos entices us. There is no need for an alternative epistemology; assume Marxism, and everything will fall into place. It reminds me of the bumper sticker that says: "God said it; I believe it; and there's an end to it."

Callinicos on the Left, like Himmelfarb from the Right, warns of the dire, politically-disastrous consequences of pursuing the pied pipers of postmodernism. As before, he offers us a stark (crudely oversimplified) vision of politics, showing few signs of empathy with the changing world about him :

> Unless we work toward the kind of revolutionary change which would allow the realization of this potential in a transformed world, there is little left for us to do, except, like Lyotard and Baudrillard, to fiddle while Rome burns.[28]

Terry Eagleton's *The Illusions of Postmodernism* offers another Marxist-inspired attack, although it is curiously adumbrated in its scope. Eagleton concedes that, while he finds the distinction between postmodernism and postmodernity useful, "it is not one which I have particularly respected in this book."[29] In addition to lethargy on this key topic, he also betrays advanced symptoms of the 'straw man' syndrome, confessing that he is less concerned with "the higher philosophical flights" of postmodernism, but more with what a particular kind of student today is likely to believe; and though I consider quite a lot of what they believe to be false, I have tried to say it in a way that might persuade them they never believed it in the first place.[30]

Quite what this indigestible mouthful is meant to convey remains a mystery to me. Eagleton seems willing to deal only with bastardized caricatures of popularized arguments that may be invented by impressionable young minds – hardly an invitation to a sophisticated, sustained engagement!

In the event, as one might expect from him, Eagleton's critique is wily and witty, betraying the author's weakness for wanton word-play. He wends a now-familiar way through a blistering criticism to another of those contrite confessions that postmodernism does after all have some merit, some of the time. At the end of the book, a kind of balance sheet appears:[31]

> [The] rich body of [postmodern] work on racism and identity, on the paranoia of identity-thinking, on the perils of totality and the fear of otherness: all this, along with its deepened insights into the cunning of power, would no doubt be of considerable value. But its cultural relativism and moral conventionalism, its scepticism, pragmatism, and localism, its distaste for ideas of solidarity and disciplined organization, its lack of any adequate theory of political agency: all these would tell heavily against it.

In a review of Eagleton's book, Ian Pindar laments the fact that philosophers are now being blamed for the failure of politics. Pindar claims that Eagleton and others are simply shooting the messenger: "there can be few who seriously believe that this [failure] is because our politicians have read too much Baudrillard."[32]

Not all Left critics use the apocalyptic tones of Callinicos and Eagleton. In *What's Wrong with Postmodernism* Christopher Norris invokes the usual mantra that postmodernism offers nothing new. He even traces a proto-postmodernism in Marx's writings, endorses the opinion that a postmodern pluralism offers little beyond a politics of the status quo.[33] He concludes that the main lesson to be learnt from (for instance) Baudrillard's texts is:

> that any politics which goes along with the current postmodern drift will end up by effectively endorsing and promoting the work of ideological mystification.[34]

And in his rather suspiciously-titled *The Truth about Postmodernism* Norris elaborates upon the political paralysis that accompanies postmodern's indeterminacy:

> Postmodernism can do nothing to challenge these forms of injustice and oppression since it offers no arguments, no critical resources or validating grounds for perceiving them as inherently unjust and oppressive.[35]

Kevin Robins provided a beautiful thumb-nail sketch of Norris' position that I cannot better. Writing with reference to the aftermath of the Gulf War, Robins says this of Norris:

> Against the 'intellectual fad' of postmodernity, Norris wants to vindicate, and to re-ground, what he calls 'enlightenment truth-seeking discourse.' It is [Norris claims] 'the

issues of real-world truth and falsehood that provide the only basis for reasoned opposition on the part of conscientious objectors.' Postmodernism is presented as a kind of propaganda and misinformation campaign within the intellectual world. It is as if the perversion of communication and the confusion of reason could be laid at the door of this thing called postmodernism. And Baudrillard is the Great Satan.[36]

Robins makes clear that Baudrillard's sin is "to distance himself from the cause of Reason."[37] Once again, critics are opting to eviscerate the messenger.

Cartographies of complaint

The case against postmodernism may be mapped into six basic complaints.

There is nothing new about postmodernism.   Critics revel in the claim that all the positions staked out in postmodernism have been present for indefinite periods of time in their respective disciplines. But his can be true only at an extraordinarily high level of generality. And in any event, should we therefore rest content with the familiar? Is there nothing new in the present concatenation of events and ideas? If not, why are critics so, as they put it, irritated?

No new era is presaged by postmodernity.   The epochal dimension of postmodern thought primarily exercises those on the Left who, presumably, have most to gain by identifying historical progress toward some revolutionary millennium. Their assessment is invariable: that capitalism is alive and well, and postmodernity merely a blip on the evolutionary horizon. But this is entirely the wrong question. Epochal change need not imply the end of capitalism (think of the shift from an agricultural to an industrial capitalism). The advent of a postcolonial era is already a prominent political and epistemological feature of the late twentieth century; so is the shift to an "information age." A revived political economy could help us visualize shifts that the classical model hides from view.

Old traditions and standards are best.   Those who defend old traditions and existing canons, or seek to reconstruct the project of Modernity, point witheringly to postmodernism's notorious fadishness, its proliferation of meanings, and evidence of poor scholarship. Then they steer us cantankerously back to former headings and steadfast moorings, to canons that keep us in line and them in control. Their favorite word is discipline (of the old ways). Yet because something is fashionable, i.e. of its time, does not mean it is wrong. If we multiply meanings and confusions, it's the fault of our minds. (We are like aging gymnasts pulling on the stretched spandex of modernism, watching as its meaning becomes more threadbare with each application.) And, let's face it, poor scholarship is everywhere; it is certainly not the prerogative of postmodernists.

Postmodernism's relativism has produced a cacophony of competing voices that are difficult to distinguish.   This is the complaint of a lazy and hostile critic. Relativism is OK, so say the keepers of the keys, as long as it stays in its place. But as soon as existing authority is threatened, relativism becomes an issue (just as it is now), and counter-attacks are launched. The person of Comfortable Authority has no incentive to seek an accommodation with other voices; the easier option is to dismiss them, even as the volume of contemporary voices testifies to the depth of silence imposed by earlier hegemonies. These voices are also proof-positive of the plurality of interpretive possibilities, none of which can claim to be authoritative or self-evident.

Postmodernism is antitheoretical/atheoretical.   The pejorative terms anti- or a-theoretical are usually invoked when the critic's own dearly-held beliefs are being questioned. For instance, Ellis insisted on well-drawn distinctions, exacting and penetrating scrutiny of internal logic, and a communal process; Himmelfarb required coherence, consistency, factuality; and so on. Such critics seem constitutionally incapable of conceding that alternative criteria are possible for judging scholarship. Paul Feyerabend among others has demonstrated that antitheoretical and atheoretical stances have an important and honorable status in scientific inquiry.

Postmodernism is bad politics.   This complaint has two parts: first, plain revulsion because postmodernism undermines all ideologues (rabid Republicans and dismal Democrats of all stripes); and second, impatience because a postmodern political agenda is slow in evolving. But while it may be difficult to envisage a postmodern politics, this in no way denies the relevance of the postmodern condition to contemporary politics. Postmodernists cannot be blamed for the failures of the body politic, whose wounds have been largely self-inflicted (see Chapters 10 and 11).

In my terminology, these cartographies of complaint can be summed up as follows:

- postmodernism as style is simply an ephemeral fad of no lasting value;
- postmodernism as method cannot undermine centuries of Enlightenment wisdom; and
- postmodernism as epoch has no purchase since capitalism still exists.

All three positions are easily refuted. Postmodern style was once a new fashion, but it has survived for several decades; indeed it has itself been canonized, and it cannot be ignored by those who profess to learn from the contemporary. Second, I have no doubt that the conventions of 'science' will lead us to important, life-saving and life-threatening discoveries; but I am equally convinced that the way we know things has been irrevocably altered by a postmodern consciousness. (Can anyone countenance cloning with equanimity, or have faith in the benign reassurances of scientists?) And thirdly, capitalism may be alive and well, or it may be dying. No-one can tell. But the accumulated weight of change in the latter part of the twentieth century suggests to me that epochal change is in the making. I wish a long life to those who deny this. May we all live long enough to see clearly what is already plain on the face of the earth.

Transformations in Geography and Planning

A very revealing difference is observable between the disciplines of geography and urban planning; the former has clearly absorbed many postmodern traditions and been altered by them; the latter has all but ignored postmodernism. What has caused this difference? And with what consequences? These are questions of professional and academic politics, as much as they reflect intellectual differences. My explanation must inevitably be preliminary, because we remain perforce caught up in the postmodern turn; it will focus less on detailed contributions than on broad intellectual trends; and (at the risk of causing offense) I shall be naming many scholars who probably would not label themselves as postmodernists, because their works are (to me) clearly implicated in the advent of postmodernism.

Postmodern geographies

The tidal wave of postmodernity hit human geography with predictable consequences. As in many other disciplines, it engendered intense excitement in a handful of scholars inspired by its provocations. But more generally, it met with active hostility from those who perceived their intellectual authority being threatened; incomprehension on the part of those who (for whatever reason) failed to negotiate its arcane jargon; and the indifference of the majority, who ignored what they presumably perceived as simply the latest fad. Despite the combined armies of antipathy and inertia, postmodernism has flourished.

The year 1984 is significant because it was then that Fredric Jameson published what many regard as the pivotal English-language article focusing geographers' attention on spatiality and postmodernity (see Chapters 2 and 3). Ten years later, Jameson's essay retained its vitality, and human geography had undergone a revolution of sorts. Two of the earliest geographical articles that took up Jameson's challenge were by Dear and Soja.[38] The former dealt with urban planning; the latter was an exuberant deconstruction of Los Angeles by an avowed postmodernist. Both articles appeared in a special issue of the journal *Society and Space* devoted to Los Angeles.[39] Between 1986 and 1994, over fifty major articles and an equivalent number of critical commentaries have appeared in prominent geography journals including especially *Society and Space*, but also the *Annals of the Association of American Geographers*, the *Canadian Geographer*, and the *Transactions of the Institute of British Geographers*.[40]

Traces. With the benefit of hindsight, traces of a postmodern consciousness can, of course, be uncovered in geographical writings prior to 1986.[41] The principal historical reasons for the absorption of postmodern thought into geography are properly to be found in the resurgence of Marxist social theory in the late 1960s and 1970s.[42] It was out of a broadly-based post-structuralist response to the perceived obsolescences of Marxism that impetus was imparted to the postmodern turn. In geography, this trend was instrumental in the renaissance of interest in social theory more generally, thus reconnecting the discipline with a broad spectrum of socio-economic and political debates. Of particular consequence were the substantive emphases on the urban question,[43] and the role of space in economic development and socio-spatial relations.[44] The relatively high levels of scholarly productivity and output in these areas rendered them particularly susceptible to innovation and rapid evolution.

It was not long before the neo-Marxist revival fell under scrutiny, and something like a 'golden age' of theoretical/philosophical efflorescence occurred in human geographical thought.[45] For instance, in 1978 Derek Gregory published his influential *Science, Ideology and Human Geography*, drawing attention in particular to the work of critical theorists such as Jürgen Habermas. In that same year, Gordon Clark and I began our reappraisal of the theory of the state, with a post-structural emphasis on the languages of legitimacy.[46] A humanist geography also developed to counter the Marxian emphasis,[47] and during this period very deliberate attempts were launched to investigate the ontological and epistemological bases of geographical knowledge. This was manifest in, for instance, Ed Soja's determined efforts to reposition space in the realm of social theory;[48] in Gunnar Olsson's (much-malign'd) confrontation with language;[49] and in Andrew Sayer's clear-sighted inquiry on method in the social sciences.[50]

The burgeoning connections between geography and social theory were given concrete expression in 1983, with the appearance of the journal *Society and Space* as part of the *Environment and Planning* series. The first issue included Nigel Thrift's wide-ranging reformulation of the problematic of time and space (which reflected his earlier work with Allan Pred on time geography),[51] and Linda McDowell's fundamental paper on the gender division of urban space.[52] Subsequent issues have maintained a steady flow of increasingly self-conscious attempts to link social theory and human geography. The ubiquity of this problematic may be gauged from the title of an influential 1985 collection of essays: *Social Relations and Spatial Structures.*[53] The 1986 papers by Soja and Dear may thus have crystallized a pervasive turbulence in geography's theoretical discourse and provided a platform for the next stages in the conversation. Yet these essays were not so much theoretical departures, but more a culmination of a decade's re-engagement with the central issues of social theory.

Consciousness. Jameson's identification of architecture as the privileged aesthetic of a postmodern culture made it easy for geographers to adapt his insights to their spatial agendas. Early studies by Ted Relph and David Ley drew attention to the semantics of the built environment in the landscapes of postmodernity.[54] These and other studies were instrumental in provoking an uninterrupted sequence of research on postmodern culture, emphasizing place and place-making, spectacle and carnival, and consumption. It was also inevitable that cultural geographers would be drawn to postmodernism. An early appraisal of the 'new' cultural geography is provided by Peter Jackson.[55] An independent line of geographical inquiry in the late 1980s centered on the processes of contemporary economic restructuring, particularly the move toward flexible specialization (what some call flexible accumulation). Economic geographers were attempting to analyze the emergent dynamics of post-Fordist, flexible industrial systems and their concomitant spatial organization. Although few if any of these inquiries were explicitly postmodern in nature, they inevitably intersected with the problematic of periodization, i.e. whether or not a radical break had occurred to signal the arrival of a postmodern society.[56] A third source of fertile intellectual discord concerned the emergent status of social theory in human geography. The validity of a social theoretical approach was rarely at issue; more usually, the debate took the form of sometimes vitriolic exchanges among competing orthodoxies, the details of which need not detain us here.[57] A temporary truce established two broad positions: one coalition favored maintaining the hegemony of their preferred theory (whatever that happened to be); a second advocated a theoretical pluralism that may properly be viewed as a precursor of postmodern sensibilities.

The point that these trends establish is that a postmodern consciousness emerged in human geography not from some orchestrated plot, but instead from a diversity of independent perspectives – including cultural studies, emergent economic geographies, and stand-offs in social theory.[58] Each trend had a life of its own before it intersected with postmodernism, but each (I believe) was irrevocably altered as a consequence of this engagement. By 1988, the climate was such that I was able to argue for what I styled the 'postmodern challenge' in human geography.[59] My plea was premised on the significance of space in postmodern thought and the potential of geography's contribution to a rapidly evolving field of social inquiry.

The wave. The year 1989 saw the publication of two books with postmodern geography as a central theme. Soja's *Postmodern Geographies* was a celebration of postmodernism and its challenges; Harvey's *The Condition of Postmodernity* was a hostile critique of postmodernism that attempted to subsume it within the explanatory rubric of Marxism. A year later, Phil Cooke's *Back to the Future: modernity, postmodernity and locality* appeared – a perspective on the 'localities' project in Great Britain which was sympathetic to the claims of postmodernism. Whatever their respective merits, these books and their authors concentrated a discipline's attention on the postmodern question.[60] But in truth, the wave had already gathered an unstoppable momentum. The roster of publications in 1989 and subsequent years reveals a burgeoning postmodern consciousness in the three topical areas I previously identified:

(1) *cultural landscapes and place-making*, with an increasing emphasis on the urban;[61]
(2) *economic landscapes of post-Fordism and flexible specialization*, with particular interest in global–local connections and the spatial division of labor;[62] and
(3) continuing *philosophical and theoretical disputes*, especially those relating to space and the problems of *language*.[63]

There was also an explosion of interest in the application of postmodernism to other areas, representing a deepening appreciation of the extent of postmodernism's reach and relevance.[64] The many themes that became manifest during the period 1989--93 may be grouped under four broad rubrics:

(4) *problems of representation in geographical/ethnographic writing*,[65] in *cartography*[66] and in *art and film*;[67]
(5) the historical and contemporary *politics of postmodernity*,[68] *feminist geography's discontentment with postmodernism*,[69] *orientalism and postcolonialism*,[70] and the *law* and critical legal studies;[71]
(6) an emphasis on the *construction of the individual and the boundaries of self*, including *human psychology and sexuality*;[72] and
(7) a reassertion of *nature and the environmental question*[73] which has taken many forms, including a fresh look at the relationships between place and health.[74]

By 1991, postmodernism had received an extended treatment in a textbook on geographical thought,[75] and became part of the standard fare in others.[76] Matters

were further helped by the publication of some important works in English translation. The availability of Lefebvre's *La Production de l'Espace* was especially important.[77]

In pedagogic terms, postmodernism's emphases on difference and diversity have
penetrated the academy, but its impact is difficult to document.[78] I have no idea how
much postmodernism is actually being taught in geography departments, but
attempts to reconcile cultural and social geography may be regarded as a step in
this direction.[79] A number of institutional responses in the late 1980s and early
1990s reflected a growing awareness of the need to dissolve disciplinary barriers in
teaching and research. For instance, a Center for Critical Analysis of Contemporary
Culture was set up in 1986 at Rutgers University, since when Neil Smith and
other geographers have played an important role in a broadly-based social science
and humanities research program. In 1989, at the University of Kentucky, a
Committee on Social Theory was founded in order to encourage campus-wide
collaboration, again with a strong organizational base in geography (including
John-Paul Jones and John Pickles). And an interdisciplinary master's degree in
Society and Space admitted its first students in 1992 at the University of Bristol in
England, based in the Department of Geography and the School of Advanced Urban
Studies.

Contentions.   The introduction of postmodernism into human geography was not
without dissent. The most common complaints echoed those already current in the
intellectual marketplace: that postmodernism's extreme relativism rendered it politically incoherent, and hence useless as a guide for social action; that it was itself just
one more metanarrative; and that the project of modernity remained relevant even
though there was little agreement about exactly which pieces were worth salvaging. I
have also already noted feminism's divergent path.

At a superficial though certainly not trivial level, many geographer critics simply
lost patience with the promiscuous way in which the term had been bandied about; if
it could be applied to everything, then it probably meant nothing. Others were upset
that they and their work were invoked to support a movement for which they had
no sympathy.[80] In one such case, Allan Pred angrily distanced himself with these
words:

> I have never chosen to label myself as "postmodern"....I regard "postmodern" as an
> inccurate, uncritical, deceptive, and thereby politically dangerous "epochal" labeling of
> the contemporary world...[which is] best depicted as modernity magnified, as modern-
> ity accentuated and sped up, as *hyper*modern, not *post*modern.[81]

This is an unequivocal rejection of the postmodern, even though Pred's work is
clearly implicated in the rise of postmodern geography. The most sustained rejection
of the postmodern turn in geography was undoubtedly that of Harvey (see Chapter
4).[82] Given Harvey's unassailable reputation within and beyond the discipline, it was
to be expected that the book would be widely read and the repudiation it contained
would deal a mortal blow. But, while broadly acknowledged, the book did little to
stall the production of postmodern geographical scholarship. The fact that the
book met with some stinging rebuttals may have muted its influence within the

discipline.[83] In addition, Harvey's orthodoxy might have posed problems for fellow Marxists who had begun the long and arduous task of rewriting their theory to account for the altered conditions of postmodernity.[84]

A different literature was less concerned with outright rejection of postmodernism and more with a critical engagement with its problematic. Most commonly, this work explored the genealogy of postmodern thought, its broad links with the modern era, and the persistence of modernist themes in the present discourse.[85] Postmodern thought invigorated an effort to define the parameters of modernity itself.[86] Julie Graham perceptively examined the consequences of postmodernism for a progressive politics.[87] Finally, some geographers joined the push to go beyond the terms of the current debates.[88]

Postmodern Planning

[W]e can be sure that theories of modernity and postmodernity do not help us much here; indeed, they represent a rather huge red herring in our trawl through the theoretical waters. Even if they were clearer and more coherent and more consistent, which they quintessentially are not, they deal only with a very small slice of historical reality… And they are deliberately, rather infuriatingly, aspatial: they are entirely uninterested in the question of what happens where, and why.

Peter Hall[89]

By the mid-1990s, the impact of postmodern thought on the theory and practice of city planning was almost negligible. In some respects this is unsurprising since the precepts of postmodernism seem exactly antithetical to the rationalist foundations of urban interventionism. Moreover, it is unlikely that any clients in public or private sectors would want to see undermined the rationality/ expertise bulwarks of planning, nor have their own power position exposed. On both counts, one can perhaps forgive planners their quiescence when confronted with the counter-narratives of postmodernism. But I still want to know why there is this apathy.

In 1986 I published "Postmodernism and Planning," which was, I believe, the first article to link the two subjects. In the years since then, I have counted about a dozen articles in major journals that directly address at least some aspect of postmodernism. Some of them have been written by the same authors, so the actual number of contributors to the debate is even less. The earliest of these contributions were essentially enthusiastic acceptances and extensions of the original arguments.[90] Most notable were several pieces by Beth Moore Milroy, who intelligently pursued the implications of a changing social context for emergent practices of planning. By the early 1990s, the discourse was still limited. Dennis Crow made an intriguing connection between postmodernism and the earlier modernisms of Le Corbusier's *The City of Tomorrow and its Planning*[91] His was an important reminder of the contingent, continuing relevance of the project of modernity.

About the same time, Bob Beauregard began a series of insightful essays looking beyond obsolete modernist codifications of planning. He left no doubt that postmodernism had undermined the intellectual authority of the modernist planning project, which was consequently suspended between a modernism whose validity is decaying and reconfiguring, and, a postmodernism whose arguments are convincing yet discomfiting. As planning theorists we have failed to formulate a response and failed to work with practitioners to move the planning project from its ambivalent position.[92]

Through an evocative critique of Peter Marris' novel *The Dreams of General Jerusalem* (a story of urban planning in an African post-colonial regime), Beauregard elaborates on this perceived failure:

first, modernist planners have lost touch with the prevailing political–economic forces that are restructuring cities and regions in a global context, and second, have failed to keep pace with concomitant intellectual currents and cultural forms.[93]

From this condemnation, Beauregard goes on to take some important steps toward a postmodern ethos: that knowledge is not necessarily a reliable guide to action, and that increased understanding is likely to reveal more differences rather than set directions. But yet, he asserts, "Action can he unequivocal, knowledge can be helpful, and people can struggle successfully to improve their lives."[94] And, in a later study, he argues in favor of an ideal city which is "democratic, egalitarian, multi-racial and non-sexist."[95] Complaining about the demise of utopian thinking in planning, and the cooptation of the profession by private capital, Beauregard urges planners to engage in public debates about the 'good society' and its attendant physical form. The normative core of such discourse should be "social and spatial justice and empowerment" for "fair procedures and...more just distributions."[96] But, he warns, in discussing alternative urban futures, "we must avoid lapsing into utopian fantasy or stifling multiple voices."[97] This is where Beauregard falters, in my judgement. He seems to be issuing a contradictory mandate here, specifying the need for dialogue about social justice in a good society, but warning that such dialogue should avoid too much utopianism or too much polyvocality. But how much is enough? If this is an attempt to envision a way out of the postmodern impasse, then Beauregard has bought his way out at a high price – viz., the silencing of visionaries and minorities. This can hardly be what he intended, but this is the paradoxical drift of his advice.

Beauregard is alert to the issues and manages a sustained involvement with them; others have been less successful. For instance, in 1992 Charles Hoch used insights from postmodern and critical theory to argue that practicing planners have hidden behind a cloak of professional competence, and they lack the capacity to identify or acknowledge their use of power. He shows how the "postmodern critique leaves no place for planning to hide from its attachment to power."[98] And he calls for the establishment of open "moral communities" that cut across established lines of bureaucracy and community affiliation.[99] So far so good. Two years later, however, Hoch published a book entitled *What Planners Do: Power, Politics, and Persuasion.*[100] It is undoubtedly the most authoritative text to date on this topic. Yet in it, Hoch makes not one mention of postmodernism, nor the ramifications of his conclusions of two years previously. Instead, he calls on the planner to use "craft" and "character" to build a "reform community."[101]

No such ambivalence is present in Harper and Stein, who in the mid-1990s presented what was then the most sustained engagement with the challenge of postmodern thought in planning.[102] The title of their article makes their position clear: "Out of the Postmodern Abyss: Preserving the Rationale for Liberal Planning." And, lest there be any doubt about where they stand, they write in their introduction:

> Our intent is practical. Our concern is not that planning theory might be flawed by some technical philosophical error, but rather that the uncritical adoption of postmodernist assumptions would bring us to the brink of an abyss of indeterminacy, impairing our ability to maintain social continuity through change, to treat each other in a fair and just and fully human way, and to justify public planning.[103]

These are serious charges (but where does this paranoia about uncertainty come from?) though Harper and Stein never truly demonstrate what it is about postmodernism that would lead to a revolutionary, unjust, inhuman, and planning-less society. Instead, they advocate a form of neopragmatism as a "coherent and reasonable basis for justifying planning."[104] Placing dialogue as the heart of any model of postmodern planning, Harper and Stein concede the positive implications of postmodernism: the "rejection of metanarrative," the "distrust of rigid methodology," the "celebration of plurality," and the recognition that "all voices have the right to be heard."[105] But they warn:

> full-blown [sic] postmodernism cannot provide an adequate basis for planning.... Our concern is that, taken to its extreme, full-blown postmodernism would inevitably reduce planning to the impotent state... the full-blown postmodernist alternative seemingly leaves no room for planning.[106]

They're probably right. It explains why planners tiptoe gingerly around postmodernism as if it is some form of deadly disease (full-blown, at that) which shouldn't be discussed in polite company. The more extreme form of postmodernism would certainly imply the end of all disciplines and professions.

To save planning from the apocalypse, Harper and Stein urge upon us a neopragmatism that is (in their words) nonfoundational, antiessentialist, neither absolutist nor relativistic, fallibilistic, nonretractive and nonscientific. They claim it will produce a more powerful "understanding and critique of planning practice,"[107] an assertion based on the following slogans (among others):

- "Persuasion through rational argument is the only alternative to power."[108]
- "A neopragmatic perspective allows for... objective critique."[109]
- "... we can have a planning that is truly rational."[110]
- "neopragmatism frees us to do what we know we *should do*."[111]

By adopting a neopragmatic planning, Harper and Stein conclude:

> Planners can get what they want from postmodernism (a broader notion of rationality, recognition of multiple voices and discourses, inclusivity, encouragement of many voices, empowerment) and retain significant aspects of modernism (emancipation, accountability, hope for the future).[112]

It is easy to raise an eyebrow at Harper and Stein's outrageously starry-eyed elisions over the palpable contradictions of their reconstructive vision. But they do not lack courage or conviction, and they have dealt seriously with postmodernism.

It was left to Bob Beauregard to sustain the discipline's interest in things post-modern during the mid-nineties. In his highly original 1993 study of the rhetoric of decline in the history of US cities (including the discourse of planners), Beauregard's intent is to "convey the discourse as it was heard and read by people who lived during those times."[113] In a direct assault on the tension between interpretive strategies and 'objective' analyses, he mixes methodologies lasciviously and confronts head on the question of representation:

> My intent is to subvert the authority of the discourse and compel the reader to confront its indeterminacy.[114]

Beauregard maintains this stance until the very last chapter of the book when he at last allows himself to enter directly into the analysis in order to probe "the ideolo-gical core of the discourse in order to reveal its foundational dynamics."[115] He concludes:

> There will never be one true story of urban decline, but that should not discourage us from attempting to pin down its meanings or from pursuing coherent and compelling interpretations.[116]

This is very compelling. More than anyone else in the profession, Beauregard was/is, I think, actually practicing a version of postmodern planning.

I thought Beauregard was alone until an important new collection of essays was published in 1996 under the title *Explorations in Planning Theory* (edited by Man-delbaum, Mazza and Burchell). In one of the essays, our old nemeses Harper and Stein continue their 'scorched earth' policy, this time attacking the incommensur-ability premise in comparative theoretical analysis. They begin their essay with what seems an indefensible statement: "The influence of postmodernism on planning theory seems to be increasing."[117] As before, they concede the merit of some of postmodernism's charges; but once again they rally round reason and the liberal paradigm to save the day. The most interesting thing about this book is that several contributors are actually talking about postmodernism, if only indirectly. (It may be significant that many of these voices are those of non-Americans, and many are female.) For instance, here is Jean Hillier taking a "postmodern and feminist" sensibility to the discourse of planning; Judith Allen conjoining with Foucault to examine knowledge-based politics in London; and Bent Flyvbjerg on the dark side of modernity.[118] Now, the revolution has not yet arrived; there are about a score more essays in the publication that do not broach the P word.

Just about the time when I had completed the manuscript for this book, Leonie Sandercock published her *Toward Cosmopolis: Planning for Multicultural Cities*.[119] I was then, and remain now, energized by this book's appearance, because Sander-cock's vision of a 'postmodern utopia' is a brilliant demonstration of what happens when planning truly engages postmodernism, postcolonialism and feminist thought. While her book and mine proceed from similar concerns, her emphasis is much more on urban planning practice per se. As such, it could be read alongside this present volume. In it, she is highly critical of the conventional, modernist pillars of planning wisdom, instead favoring an inclusive, people-centered style of planning that emphasizes practical wisdom, multiculturalism, and community empowerment.[120] She unabashedly aims for a "postmodern Utopia," which can never be realized, but always be in the making.[121] It deals with "social justice, a politics of difference, new concepts of citizenship and community, and a civic culture formed out of multiple publics."[122] An essential ingredient of Sandercock's postmodern planning paradigm is:

> A reinstatement of inquiry about and recognition of the importance of memory, desire, and the spirit (or the sacred) as vital dimensions of healthy human settlements and a sensitivity to cultural differences in the expressions of each.[123]

Sandercock has the courage to dream about a postmodern utopia.[124] The very existence of her book is sufficient proof, for me, of the value of the encounter with postmodernism.

The War of the Words

Give me a fruitful error any time, full of seeds, bursting with its own corrections. You can keep your sterile truth for yourself.

Vilfredo Pareto (1848-1923)

Whether we approve or are even aware of it, the postmodern wave has already broken over geography. Some chose to ride the wave; others ducked under, hoping that this too would pass. I believe that we have witnessed a revolution of sorts in human geographical thinking since 1984. In general terms, there has been:

(a) a reassertion of the role and significance of space in social theory and social process;
(b) an unprecedented rise in scholarship devoted to the relationship between space and society;
(c) a reintegration of human geography with mainstream social science and philosophy;
(d) a totally new appreciation of diversity and difference, and a consequent diversification of theoretical and empirical work;
(e) a self-conscious questioning of the relationship between geographical knowledge and social action; and
(f) an enormous efflorescence of research topics and publications.

Some or all of these events may have occurred without the advent of postmodernism; but I doubt it, at least not with the same intensity and consequences.

In contrast, the impact of postmodernism in urban planning theory and practice has been minuscule. The most obvious reason for the screaming silence on postmodernism is clientism. Consumers of planning in public and private sectors do not want uncertainty and ambiguity; nor will they pay for therapy for professionals with theoretical angst or identity crises. Instead, they reward competence and expertise, and the manly ability to see a deal through. They don't want anyone exposing (still less questioning) the powerful who dwell behind the planning dialogue. Clientism in architecture turned postmodernism into a marketing device; practising planners instead chose the 'new urbanism' as the warmed-over marketing concept *du jour.*

Clientism does not explain the lack of academic curiosity in postmodernism, although if we call students 'clients' of planning education, their insistence (for the moment, at least) on a practice-relevant and development-oriented curriculum may play a part. Despite John Friedman's marvelous maps of the intellectual terrain occupied by planners, the fact is that planners have only ever colonized tiny pieces of that terrain, apparently suspicious of the traditions of social theory. Thus, there have been no efforts to parallel John Forester's sustained engagement with Habermas, for instance. Indeed, the prominence afforded hermeneutics in planning theory is partly a consequence of the absence of alternative theories in the impoverished dialectical universe of planners (cf. Chapter 6). Even when alternative visions have surfaced, as in the case of feminist theory, there seems to have been enormous difficulties in keeping them alive. Where, for example, is the contemporary legacy of Dolores Hayden's pathbreaking work? Leonie Sandercock is, it seems, being obliged to reinvent the wheel of feminist planning. Where is Paul Davidoff when we need him? And do any of those planners obsessed with that 'abyss' of uncertainty ever read Peter Marris?

In fairness, these are difficult times of retrenchment and recession in the academy and profession, and survival in a Darwinistic universe may be more pressing than intellectual refinement. But I also understand that planners, like everyone else, cling tenaciously to their beliefs and status. Knowledge is, after all, power and we are loath to relinquish the basis for our claims to legitimacy. But is a critical openness too much to ask for? Since comparison, analogy, and metaphor are some of the principal means by which human knowledge is advanced, it would indeed be an unusual science that refused to look tolerantly beyond the horizons of tradition, or be discomfited if others cast a critical eye in its direction.

Looking ahead in present and future, I am both optimistic and pessimistic. In one respect, John Ellis was correct in his critique of deconstructionism: that it appealed not because it was a radical departure from entrenched attitudes, but because it fitted the already prevailing climate of intellectual pluralism and lent that climate a new legitimacy.[125] This is not a particularly surprising insight, given what we know about the situatedness of theory. What is more interesting is how Ellis declares himself unable to live with the consequent "chaotic flow" of critical writing, how he pleads for a return to "standards" of intelligent criticism (ignoring the fact that exactly analogous sentiments led to the original Enlightenment exclusivities). Postmodernism is about standards, choices, and the exercise of power – in real life and the academic world. It places the construction of meaning at the core of any social theory (though this is not the only concern in such theory). The key issue is authority. And postmodernism has served notice on all those who seek to assert or preserve their hegemonic position in academic and everyday worlds. These are not trivial or esoteric concerns. In individual lives, in disciplinary fortunes, in academic privilege and power, in culture wars, postmodernism matters.

"ALEX"
IDENTITY DESTROYED
BY POSTMODERNISM

Jesse Gordon/Click

Geraldo, Eat Your Avant-Pop Heart Out

By Mark Leyner

HOBOKEN, N. J.

JENNY JONES: Boy, we have a show for you today!

Recently, the University of Virginia philosopher Richard Rorty made the stunning declaration that nobody has "the foggiest idea" what postmodernism means. "It would be nice to get rid of it," he said. "It isn't exactly an idea; it's a word that pretends to stand for an idea."

This shocking admission that there is no such thing as postmodernism has produced a firestorm of protest around the country. Thousands of authors, critics and graduate students who'd considered themselves postmodernists are outraged at the betrayal.

Today we have with us a writer – a recovering postmodernist – who believes that his literary career and personal life have been irreparably damaged by the theory, and who feels defrauded by the academics who promulgated it. He wishes to remain anonymous, so we'll call him "Alex."

Alex, as an adolescent, before you began experimenting with postmodernism, you considered yourself – what?

Close shot of ALEX.

An electronic blob obscures his face. Words appear at bottom of screen: "Says he was traumatized by postmodernism and blames academics."

ALEX (*his voice electronically altered*): A high modernist. Y'know, Pound, Eliot, Georges Braque, Wallace Stevens, Arnold Schönberg,

At 14, he was ruined by reading Gilles Deleuze and Felix Guattari.

Mies van der Rohe. I had all of Schönberg's 78's.

JENNY JONES: And then you started reading people like Jean-François Lyotard and Jean Baudrillard – how did that change your feelings about your modernist heroes?

ALEX: I suddenly felt that they were, like, stifling and canonical.

JENNY JONES: Stifling and canonical? That is so sad, such a waste. How old were you when you first read Fredric Jameson?

ALEX: Nine, I think.

The AUDIENCE gasps.

JENNY JONES: We have some pictures of young Alex....

We see snapshots of 14-year-old ALEX reading Gilles Deleuze and Felix Guattari's "Anti-Oedipus: Capitalism and Schizophrenia." The AUDIENCE oohs and ahs.

ALEX: We used to go to a friend's house after school – y'know, his parents were never home – and we'd read, like, Paul Virilio and Julia Kristeva.

JENNY JONES: So you're only 14, and you're already skeptical toward the "grand narratives" of modernity, you're questioning any belief system that claims universality or transcendence. Why?

Mark Leyner is the author, most recently, of "The Tetherballs of Bougainville."

ALEX: I guess – to be cool.

JENNY JONES: So, peer pressure?

ALEX: I guess.

JENNY JONES: And do you remember how you felt the very first time you entertained the notion that you and your universe are constituted by language – that reality is a cultural construct, a "text" whose meaning is determined by infinite

Hi, my name is Alex, and I am a postmodernist.

associations with other "texts"?

ALEX: Uh, it felt, like, good. I wanted to do it again.

The AUDIENCE groans.

JENNY JONES: You were arrested at about this time?

ALEX: For spray-painting "The Hermeneutics of Indeterminacy" on an overpass.

JENNY JONES: You're the child of a mixed marriage – is that right?

ALEX: My father was a de Stijl Wittgensteinian and my mom was a neo-pre-Raphaelite.

JENNY JONES: Do you think that growing up in a mixed marriage made you more vulnerable to the siren song of postmodernism?

ALEX: Absolutely. It's hard when you're a little kid not to be able to just come right out and say (*sniffles*), y'know, I'm an Imagist or I'm a phenomenologist or I'm a postpainterly abstractionist. It's really hard – especially around the holidays. (*He cries.*)

JENNY JONES: I hear you. Was your wife a postmodernist?

ALEX: Yes. She was raised avantpop, which is a fundamentalist off-shoot of post-modernism.

JENNY JONES: How did she react to Rorty's admission that postmodernism was essentially a hoax?

ALEX: She was devastated. I mean, she's got all the John Zorn albums and the entire Semiotext(e) series. She was crushed.

We see ALEX'S WIFE in the audience, weeping softly, her hands covering her face.

JENNY JONES: And you were raising your daughter as a postmodernist?

ALEX: Of course. That's what makes this particularly tragic. I mean, how do you explain to a 5-year-old that self-consciously recycling cultural detritus is suddenly no longer a valid art form when, for her entire life, she's been taught that it is?

JENNY JONES: Tell us how you think postmodernism affected your career as a novelist.

ALEX: I disavowed writing that contained real ideas or any real passion. My work became disjunctive, facetious and nihilistic. It was all blank parody, irony enveloped in more irony.

It merely recapitulated the pernicious banality of television and advertising. I found myself indiscriminately incorporating any and all kinds of pop kitsch and shlock. *(He begins to weep again.)*

JENNY JONES: And this spilled over into your personal life?

ALEX: It was impossible for me to experience life with any emotional intensity. I couldn't control the irony anymore. I perceived my own feelings as if they were in quotes.

I italicized everything and everyone. It became impossible for me to appraise the quality of anything. To me everything was equivalent – the Brandenburg Concertos and the Lysol jingle had the same value.... *(He breaks down, sobbing.)*

JENNY JONES: Now, you're involved in a lawsuit, aren't you?

ALEX: Yes. I'm suing the Modern Language Association.

JENNY JONES: How confident are you about winning?

ALEX: We need to prove that, while they were actively propounding it, academics knew all along that postmodernism was a specious theory.

If we can unearth some intradepartmental memos – y'know, a paper trail – any corroboration that they knew postmodernism was worthless cant at the same time they were teaching it, then I think we have an excellent shot at establishing liability.

JENNY JONES wades into audience and proffers microphone to a woman.

WOMAN *(with lateral head-bobbing)*: It's ironic that Barry Scheck is representing the M.L.A. in this litigation because Scheck is the postmodern attorney par excellence. This is the guy who's made a career of volatilizing truth in the simulacrum of exculpation!

VOICE FROM AUDIENCE: You go, girl!

WOMAN: Scheck is the guy who came up with the quintessentially postmodern re-bleed defense for O. J., which claims that O. J. merely vigorously shook Ron and Nicole, thereby re-aggravating pre-existing knife wounds. I'd just like to say to any client of Barry Scheck – lose that zero and get a hero!

The AUDIENCE cheers wildly.

WOMAN: Uh, I forgot my question.

D*issolve to message on screen:*
If you believe that mathematician Andrew Wiles' proof of Fermat's last theorem has caused you or a member of your family to

dress too provocatively, call (800) 555-9455.

Dissolve back to studio. In the audience, JENNY JONES extends the microphone to a man in his mid-30's with a scruffy beard and a bandana around his head.

MAN WITH BANDANA: I'd like to say that this "Alex" is the single worst example of pointless irony in American literature, and this whole heartfelt renunciation of postmodernism is a ploy – it's just more irony.

The AUDIENCE whistles and hoots.

ALEX: You think this is a ploy?! (*He tears futilely at the electronic blob.*) This is my face!

The AUDIENCE recoils in horror.

ALEX: This is what can happen to people who naïvely embrace postmodernism, to people who believe that the individual – the autonomous, individualist subject – is dead. They become a palimpsest of media pastiche – a mask of metastatic irony.

> **Note to Readers**
> *The Op-Ed page welcomes unsolicited manuscripts. Because of the volume of submissions, however, we regret that we cannot acknowledge an article or return it. If manuscripts are accepted for publication, authors will be notified within two weeks. For further information, call (212) 556–1831.*

JENNY JONES: (*biting lip and shaking her head*): That is so sad. Alex – final words?

ALEX: I'd just like to say that self-consciousness and irony seem like fun at first, but they can destroy your life. I know. You gotta be earnest, be real. Real feelings are important. Objective reality does exist.

AUDIENCE members whoop, stomp and pump fists in the air.

JENNY JONES: I'd like to thank Alex for having the courage to come on today and share his experience with us.

Join us for tomorrow's show, "The End of Manichean, Bipolar Geopolitics Turned My Boyfriend Into an Insatiable Sex Freak (and I Love It!)."

Figure 15.2 "Alex" – Identity destroyed by Postmodernism ("Alex," New York Times 12 / 21 / 97, article copyright © 1997 The New York Times co., reprinted by permission. Photograph: Jesse Gordon/Click)

Notes

1. Bernard-Henri Levy, 1992: quoted in the *New York Times*, December 13, p. E-9.
2. Himmelfarb, G., 1992: "Telling It as You Like It: Post-Modernist History and the Flight from Fact," *Times Literary Supplement*, October 16, p. 12.
3. Ibid.
4. Ibid.
5. Ibid.
6. Ibid., p. 14.
7. Ibid., p. 15.
8. Ibid., p. 14.
9. Ibid., p. 15
10. Ibid.
11. Ibid.
12. Ellis, J. M., 1989: *Against Deconstruction*, Princeton: Princeton University Press, p. 153.
13. Ibid., p. 154.
14. Ibid., p. 155.
15. Ibid., p. 156.
16. Ibid., p. 158.
17. Ibid., pp. 158–9.
18. Ibid., p. 158.
19. Ibid., pp. 158–9.
20. Ibid., p. 159.
21. Callincos, A., 1990: *Against Postmodernism: A Marxist Critique*, New York: St. Martin's Press, p. 9.
22. Ibid., p. 1.
23. Ibid., pp. 4–5.
24. Ibid., p. 5.
25. Ibid., p. 7.
26. Ibid., pp. 5–6.
27. Ibid., p. 7.
28. Ibid., p. 174.
29. Eagleton, T., 1996: *The Illusions of Postmodernism*, Cambridge, Mass: Blackwell, p. viii.
30. Ibid.
31. Ibid., p. 143.
32. Pindar, I. 1997: "Tickling the Starving," *Times Literary Supplement*. March 28, p. 25.
33. Norris, C., 1990: *What's Wrong with Postmodernism*, Baltimore: Johns Hopkins University Press, p. 33.
34. Ibid., p. 191.
35. Norris. C., 1993: *The Truth about Postmodernism*, Cambridge, Mass: Blackwell, p. 287.
36. Robins, K., 1996: *Into the Image: Culture and Politics in the Field of Vision*, London; New York: Routledge, p. 323.
37. Ibid.
38. Dear, M., 1986: "Postmodernism and Planning," *Environment and Planning D: Society and Space* 4, pp. 367–84; Soja, E., 1986: "Taking Los Angeles Apart," *Environment and Planning D: Society and Space* 4, pp. 255–72.
39. It was no accident that much of the initial impetus to a postmodern human geography derived from Southern California. This was, after all, the site of one of Jameson's most provocative postmodern encounters (with the Bonaventure Hotel). In addition, Charles Jencks, the principal chronicler of the postmodern movement in architecture, was on the faculty of the University of California at Los Angeles; the humanities program at the

University of California at Irvine (in Orange County) played frequent host to Derrida, Lyotard, and other luminaries; and a deliberate attempt was underway to reconceptualize late-twentieth century urbanism under the auspices of the LA School.

40. These papers are not identified here, but most are listed in the Endnotes to these chapters. My survey of the literature since 1984 has been confined to English-language sources; I have also deliberately excluded from consideration the vast outpouring of postmodern literature in disciplines other than geography since that date. Both strategies were adopted to contain this review within manageable proportions. One other methodological point is pertinent: I am acutely aware that, in dealing with essays and books according to their dates of publication, I am ignoring the true chronology of conception and writing. Some may regard this as a minor problem because a work must appear in print to achieve its widest impact. On the other hand, this logic skirts the undoubted influence of precirculated drafts, conference presentations, etc. Unfortunately, I know of no straightforward way to overcome this bias.

41. Gregory, D., "Areal Differentiation and Post-Modern Human Geography," in Gregory, D. and Wolford, R. (eds) 1989: *Horizons in Human Geography*, Basingstoke: Macmillan, pp. 67–96 provides a succinct and authoritative overview of geography's external connections with political economy, sociology, and anthropology during this period.

42. This is not to suggest that there was no relevant history before the Marxist renaissance; quite the contrary. See, for example, King, L. J., 1976: Alternatives to Positive Economic Geography, *Annals of the Association of American Geographers* 66, pp. 293–308, a remarkably prescient and perceptive essay assessing the way ahead in post-quantitative economic geography; and Gould, P., 1979: Geography 1957–1977: The Augean Period, *Annals of the Association of American Geographers* 69(1), pp. 139–51, a caustic retrospective on the decades between 1957 and 1977. Here, I shall focus on postmodernism's principal genealogy rather than an exhaustive disciplinary history.

43. Castells, M., 1977: *The Urban Question*, Oxford: Blackwell.

44. Harvey, D., 1982: *The Limits to Capital*, Chicago: University of Chicago Press; Massey, D., 1984: *Spatial Divisions of Labour*, London: Methuen.

45. A detailed historiography of the truly exceptional period between 1965 (the year in which Haggett's *Locational Analysis in Human Geography* was published by Edward Arnold, London) and 1986 (the explicit appearance of the postmodern in geography) remains to be written.

46. Gregory, D., 1978: *Science, Ideology and Human Geography*, London: Hutchinson.

46. Dear, M. and Clark, G., 1978: "The State and Geographic Process," *Environment and Planning A* 10, pp. 173–83.

47. Ley, D. and Samuels, M., 1978: *Humanistic Geography: Prospects and Problems*, Chicago: Maaroufa Press.

48. Soja, E., 1980: "The Socio-spatial Dialectic," *Annals of the Association of American Geographers* 70, pp. 207–25.

49. Olsson, G., 1980: *Birds in Egg/Eggs in Bird*, London: Pion.

50. Sayer, A. 1984: *Method in Social Science: A Realist Approach*, London: Hutchinson.

51. Thrift, N. J., 1983: "On the Determination of Social Action in Space and Time," *Environment and Planning D: Society and Space* 1, pp. 23–58.

52. McDowell, L., 1983: Toward an Understanding of the Gender Division of Urban Space, *Environment and Planning D: Society and Space* 1, pp. 59–72.

53. Gregory, D. and Urry, J. (eds), 1985: *Social Relations and Spatial Structure*, Basingstoke: Macmillan.

54. Relph, E., 1987: *The Modern Urban Landscape*, Baltimore: Johns Hopkins University Press and Ley, D., 1987: "Styles of the Times: Liberal and Neo-Conservative

Landscapes in Inner Vancouver, 1968–1986," *Journal of Historical Geography* 13, pp. 40–56.

55. Jackson, P., 1989: *Maps of Meaning*, London: Unwin Hyman. But see also Agnew, J. and Duncan, J. (eds), 1989: *The Power of Place: Bringing Together the Geographical and Sociological Imaginations*, Boston: Unwin Hyman; Cooke, P., 1988: "Modernity, Post-modernity and the City," *Theory, Culture and Society* 5, pp. 475–92; Cosgrove, D. and Daniels, S. (eds), 1988: *The Iconography of Landscape*, Cambridge: Cambridge University Press; Freeman, M., 1988: "Developers, architects and building styles: post-war redevelopment in two town centers," *Transactions of the Institute of British Geographers N.S.* 13, pp. 131–47; Larkham, P. J., 1988: "Agents and Types of Change in the Conserved Townscape," *Transactions of the Institute of British Geographers N.S.* 13, pp. 148–64; Mills, C.A., 1988: "Life on the Upslope: The Postmodern Landscape of Gentri-fication," *Environment and Planning D: Society and Space* 6, pp. 169–89; Sack, R. D., 1988: "The Consumer's World: Place as Context," *Annals of the Association of American Geographers* 78(4), pp. 642–64; Shields, R., 1989: "Social Specialization and the Built Environment: The West Edmonton Mall," *Environment and Planning D: Society and Space* 7, pp. 147–164.

56. Cooke, P., 1988: "Flexible Integration, Scope Economies, and Strategic Alliances," *Environment and Planning D: Society and Space* 6, pp. 281–300; Gertler, M., 1988: "The Limits to Flexibility," *Transactions of the Institute of British Geographers* N.S. 13, pp. 419–32; Schoenberger, E., 1988: "From Fordism to Flexible Accumulation," *Environment and Planning D: Society and Space* 6, pp. 245–62; Scott, A. J., 1988: *Metropolis: From the Division of Labor to Urban Form*, Berkeley: University of California Press; Storper, M. and Walker, R., 1989: *The Capitalist Imperative: Territory, Technology, and Industrial Growth*, Cambridge, Mass: Blackwell.

57. See Saunders, P. and Williams, P., 1986: "The New Conservatism: Some Thoughts on Recent and Future Developments in Urban Studies," *Environment and Planning D: Society and Space* 4, pp. 393–99, and the subsequent can(n)on fire in volume 5/4 of *Society and Space*.

58. There undoubtedly were other important trends besides the three I have identified (e.g. the localities research initiative in Great Britain). I have not attempted an exhaustive review of all the threads in the postmodern web, merely to establish their critical contributory presence prior to postmodernism's appearance.

59. Dear, M., 1988: "The Postmodern Challenge: Reconstructing Human Geography," *Transactions of the Institute of British Geographers N.S.* 13, pp. 262–74.

60. Cooke, P., 1990: *Back to the Future: modernity, postmodernity and locality*, London: Unwin Hyman. My own critical assessments of Soja and Harvey are to be found in Chapter 9 of this book. Other extended commentaries are to be found in Deutsche, R., 1991: "Boys town," *Environment and Planning D: Society and Space* 9, pp. 5–30; Massey, D., 1991: "Flexible Sexism," *Environment and Planning D: Society and Space* 9, pp. 31–57 and Relph, E., 1991: "Review Essay: Post-modern Geography," *The Canadian Geographer* 35(1), pp. 98–106.

61. Anderson, K. and Gale, F. (eds), 1992: *Inventing Places: Studies in Cultural Geography*, New York: Wiley, Halstead Press; Beauregard, R. A., 1989: "Between Modernity and Postmodernity: The Ambiguous Position of U.S. Planning," *Society and Space*, 7, pp. 381–95; Dear, M., 1989: "Privatization and the Rhetoric of Planning Practice," *Environment and Planning D: Society and Space* 7, pp. 449–62; Duncan, J. S., 1990: *The City as Text: The Politics of Landscape Interpretation in the Kandyan Kingdom*. Cambridge: Cambridge University Press; Glennie, P. D., and Thrift, N. J., 1992: "Modernity, Urbanism, and Modern Consumption," *Environment and Planning D: Society and Space* 10, pp. 423–33; Hopkins, J.S.P., 1990: "West Edmonton Mall:

Landscape of Myths and Elsewhereness," *The Canadian Geographer* 34(1), pp. 2–17; Robins, K., 1991: "Prisoners of the City: Whatever Could a Postmodern City Be?" *New Formations* 15, pp. 1–22; Shields, R., 1989: "Social Specialization and the Built Environment: The West Edmonton Mall," *Environment and Planning D: Society and Space* 7, pp. 147–64; Short, J. R., 1989: "Yuppies, Yuffies and the New Urban Order," *Transactions of the Institute of British Geographers N.S.* 14, pp. 173–88; Zukin, S., 1991: *Landscapes of Power*, Berkeley: University of California Press; and the essays in Barnes, T. J. and Duncan, J. (eds), 1992: *Writing Worlds: Discourse, Text and Metaphor in the Representation of Landscape*, New York: Routledge; Sorkin, M. (ed.), 1992: *Variations on a Theme Park*, New York: Hill and Wang; and Wolch, J. and Dear, M. (eds), 1989: *The Power of Geography: How Territory Shapes Social Life*, Boston: Unwin Hyman.

62. Barnes, T. J. and M. R. Curry, 1992: "Postmodernism in Economic Geography: Metaphor and the Construction of Alterity," *Environment and Planning D: Society and Space* 10, pp. 57–68; Dunford, M., 1990: "Theories of Regulation," *Environment and Planning D: Society and Space* 8, pp. 297–321; Gertler, M., 1988: "The Limits to Flexibility," *Transactions of the Institute of British Geographers N.S.* 13, pp. 419–32; Leborgne, D. and Lipietz, A., 1988: "New Technologies, New Modes of Regulation," *Environment and Planning D: Society and Space* 6, pp. 263–280; Sayer, A. and Walker, R., 1992: *The New Social Economy: Reworking the Division of Labor*, Cambridge, Mass: Blackwell; Schoenberger, E., 1988: "From Fordism to Flexible Accumulation," *Environment and Planning D: Society and Space* 6, pp. 245–62; Scott, A. J., 1988: *Metropolis: From the Division of Labor to Urban Form*, Berkeley; Slater, D., 1992: "On the Borders of Social Theory: Learning From Other Regions," *Environment and Planning D: Society and Space* 10, pp. 307–27; Slater, D., 1992: "Theories of Development and Politics of the Postmodern," *Development and Change* 23, pp. 283–319; Storper, M. and Walker, R., 1989: *The Capitalist Imperative: Territory, Technology, and Industrial Growth*, Cambridge, Mass: Blackwell; Webber, M., 1991: "The Contemporary Transition," *Environment and Planning D: Society and Space* 9, pp. 165–82.

63. Curry, M. R., 1991: "Postmodernism, Language, and the Strains of Modernism," *Annals of the Association of American Geographers* 81(2), pp. 210–28; Doel, M. A., 1992: "In Stalling Deconstruction: Striking Out the Postmodern," *Environment and Planning D: Society and Space* 10, pp. 163–79; Folch-Serra, M., 1989: "Geography and Post-modernism: Linking Humanism and Development Studies," *The Canadian Geographer* 33(1), pp. 66–75, Hannah, M. and Strohmayer, U., 1991: "Ornamentalism: geography and the labor of language in structuration theory," *Environment and Planning D: Society and Space* 9, pp. 309–27; Harris, C., 1991: "Power, Modernity, and Historical Geography," *Annals of the Association of American Geographers* 81(4), pp. 671–83; Jones, J. P., Natter, W. and Schatzki, T., 1993: *Postmodern Contentions: Epochs, Politics, Space*, New York: Guilford Press; Milroy, B. M., 1989: "Constructing and Deconstructing Plausibility," *Environment and Planning D: Society and Space* 7(3), pp. 313–26; Peet, R. and Thrift, N. (eds), 1988: *The New Models in Geography* (2 volumes) Boston: Unwin Hyman; Philo, C., 1992: "Foucault's Geography," *Environment and Planning D: Society and Space* 10, pp. 137–61; Pile, S., 1990: "Depth Hermeneutics and Critical Human Geography," *Environment and Planning D: Society and Space* 8, pp. 211–32; Schatzki, T. R., 1991: "Spatial Ontology and Explanation," *Annals of the Association of American Geographers* 81(4), pp. 650–70; Scott, J. S. and Simpson-Housley, P., 1989: "Relativizing the Relativizers: On the Postmodern Challenge to Human Geography," *Transactions of the Institute of British Geographers N. S.* 14, pp. 231–36; Smith, S. J., 1989: "Society, Space and Citizenship: a Human Geography for the 'New Times'?" *Transactions of the Institute of British Geographers N. S.* 14, pp. 144–56.

64. The rush of publications in 1992 was partly due to Marcus Doel and David Matless who assembled two remarkable issues of *Society and Space* (volumes 10/1 and 10/2) devoted entirely to the postmodern question.

65. Barnes, T. J. and Duncan, J. (eds), 1992: *Writing Worlds: Discourse, Text and Metaphor in the Representation of Landscape*, New York: Routledge; Crang, P., 1992: "The Politics of Polyphony," *Environment and Planning D: Society and Space* 19, pp. 527–50; Jackson, P., 1991: "The Crisis of Representation and the Politics of Position," *Environment and Planning A: Society and Space* 9, pp. 131–34; Marcus, G., 1992: "More Critically Reflexive than Thou: The Current Identity Politics of Representation," *Environment and Planning D: Society and Space* 19, pp. 489–94; Matless, D., 1992: "An Occasion for Geography: Landscape, Representation, and Foucault's Corpus," *Environment and Planning D: Society and Space* 10, pp. 41–56; Katz. C., 1992: "All the World is Staged: Intellectuals and the Projects of Ethnography," *Environment and Planning D: Society and Space* 19, pp. 495–510; Keith, M., 1992: "Angry Writing," *Environment and Planning D: Society and Space* 19, pp. 551–68; Reichert, D., 1992: "On Boundaries," *Environment and Planning D: Society and Space* 10, pp. 87–98.

66. Harley, B., 1989: "Deconstructing the Map," *Cartographica* 26, pp. 1–20; Pickles, J., "Texts, Hermeneutics and Propaganda Maps," in Barnes, T. J. and Duncan, J. (eds), 1992: *Writing Worlds*, London, pp. 193–230; Wood, D., 1992: *The Power of Maps*, New York.

67. Bonnett, A., 1992: "Art, Ideology, and Everyday Space: Subversive Tendencies from Dada to Postmodernism." *Environment and Planning D: Society and Space* 10, pp. 69–86; Daniels, S., "The Implications of Industry," in Barnes, T . J. and Duncan, J. (eds), 1992: *Writing Worlds*, London: Routledge, pp. 38–49; Aiken, S. C. and Zonn, L. E., 1994: *Place, Power, Situation and Spectacle: A Geography of Film*, Lanham: Rowman and Littlefield.

68. Dalby, S., 1991: "Critical Geopolitics: Discourse, Difference, and Dissent," *Environment and Planning D: Society and Space* 9, pp. 261–83; Driver, F., 1992: "Geography's Empire: Histories of Geographical Knowledge," *Environment and Planning D: Society and Space* 10, pp. 23–40; Graham, J., 1992: "Post-Fordism as politics: the political consequences of narratives on the left," *Environment and Planning D: Society and Space* 10, pp. 393–420; Hepple L. W., Metaphor, "Geopolitical Discourse and the Military in South America," in Barnes T. J. and Duncan J. (eds), 1992: *Writing Worlds*, New York; O'Tuathail, G., 1992: "Foreign Policy and the Hyperreal," in Barnes T. J. and Duncan J. (eds), 1992: *Writing Worlds*, New York; Pile, S. and Rose, G., 1992: "All or Nothing? Politics and Critique in the Modernism–Postmodernism Debate," *Environment and Planning D: Society and Space* 10, pp. 123–36.

69. Bondi, L. and M. Domosh, 1992: "Other Figures in Other Places: On Feminism, Postmodernism and Geography," *Environment and Planning D: Society and Space* 10, pp. 199–213; Christopherson, S., 1989: "On Being outside 'The Project'," *Antipode* 21, pp. 83–9; Domosh, M., 1991: "Toward a Feminist Historiography of Geography," *Transactions of the Institute of British Geographers N. S.* 16, pp. 95–104; Pratt, G., 1992: "Spatial Metaphors and Speaking Positions," *Environment and Planning D: Society and Space* 10, pp. 241–4.

70. Driver, F., 1992: "Geography's Empire: Histories of *Geographical Knowledge*," *Environment and Planning D: Society and Space* 10, pp. 23–40; Gregory, D., 1991: "Interventions in the Historical Geography of Modernity," *Geografiska Annaler* 73B, pp. 17–44.

71. See Blomley, N. and Clark, G., 1990: "Law, Theory and Geography," *Urban Geography* 11, pp. 433–46.

72. Respectively Bishop, P., 1992: "Rhetoric, Memory, and Power: Depth Psychology and Postmodern Geography," *Environment and Planning D: Society and Space* 10, pp. 5–22;

Hoggett P., 1992: "A Place for Experience," *Environment and Planning D: Society and Space* 10, pp. 345–56; and Geltmaker, T., 1992: "The Queer Nation Acts Up," *Environment and Planning D: Society and Space* 10, pp. 609–50; Moos, A., "The Grassroots in Action: Gays and Seniors Capture the Local State in West Hollywood, California," in Wolch, J. and Dear, M. (eds) 1989: *The Power of Geography*, Boston: Unwin Hyman; Knopp, L., 1992: "Sexuality and the Spatial Dynamics of Capitalism," *Environment and Planning D: Society and Space* 10, pp. 651–670; Valentine, G., 1993: "Negotiating and Managing Mutiple Sexual Identities: Lesbian Time–Space Strategies," *Transactions of the Institute of British Geographers*, 18, pp. 237–48.

73. Bordessa, R., 1993: "Geography, Postmodernism, and Environmental Concern," *Canadian Geographer* 37, pp. 147–55; Emel, J.,1991: "Ecological Crisis and Provocative Pragmatism," *Environment and Planning D: Society and Space* 9, pp. 384–90; Fitzsimmons, M., 1989: "The Matter of Nature," *Antipode* 21, pp. 106–20; Matless, D., 1992: "A Modern Stream: Water, Landscape, Modernism, and Geography," *Environment and Planning D: Society and Space* 10, pp. 569–88; Matless, D., 1992: "An Occasion for Geography: Landscape, Representation, and Foucault's Corpus," *Environment and Planning D: Society and Space* 10, pp. 41–56; and Matless, D., 1991: "Nature, the Modern and the Mystic: Tales from Early Twentieth Century Geography," *Transactions of the Institute of British Geographers N. S.* 16, pp. 272–86.

74. Gesler, W., 1993: "Therapeutic Landscapes," *Environment and Planning D: Society and Space* 11, pp. 171–90; Kearns, R., 1993: "Place and Health: Toward a Reformed Medical Geography," *Professional Geographer* 45, pp. 139–47.

75. Cloke, P., Philo, C. and Sadler, D., 1991: *Approaching Human Geography*, New York: Guilford Press.

76. See, for example, Johnston, R. J., 1991: *Geography and Geographers: Anglo-American Human Geography since 1945*, (4th edition), London: Arnold; Livingstone, D. N., 1992: *The Geographical Tradition*, Cambridge, Mass: Blackwell; Unwin, T., 1992: *The Place of Geography*, Harlow.

77. Lefebvre, H., 1991: *The Production of Space*, Cambridge, Mass: Blackwell; Werlen, B., 1993: *Society, Action and Space*, New York.

78. My argument in this paragraph closely follows that in Graff, G., 1987: *Professing Literature: An Institutional History*, Chicago: Chicago Press.

79. Philo, C., 1991: *New Words, New Worlds: Reconceptualizing Social and Cultural Geography*, Aberystwyth.

80. This is likely to be true of some of the authors I have cited in this chapter. So let me repeat my earlier caveat: not all authors referred to in my discussion will see themselves or their work as implicated in the postmodern turn. However, while I have no desire to foist an unwanted label on anyone, I will insist on a connection between their works and the historiography of this essay.

81. Pred, A., 1992: "Commentary on 'Postmodernism, Language and the Strains of Postmodernism' by [M.R.] Curry," *Annals of the Association of American Geographers* 82(2), p. 305.

82. Harvey, D., 1989: *The Condition of Postmodernity: An Inquiry into the Origins of Cultural Change*, Oxford: Blackwell.

83. For example, Dear, M., 1991: "Review of The Condition of Postmodernity," *Annals of the Association of American Geographers* 81; Massey, D., 1991: "Flexible Sexism," *Environment and Planning D: Society and Space* 9, pp. 31–57.

84. See, for example, the special issue of *Antipode* 21, 1989: special issue on "What's Left to do?," pp. 81–165, especially the essays by Clark and Walker.

85. Curry, M. R., 1991: "Postmodernism, Language, and the Strains of Modernism," *Annals of the Association of American Geographers* 81(2), pp. 210–28;

Strohmayer, U. and Hannah, M., 1992: "Domesticating Postmodernism," *Antipode* 24, pp. 29–55.

86. For example, Ward, D. and Zunz, O. (eds), 1992: *The Landscape of Modernity*, New York; see also Giddens, A., 1990: *The Consequences of Modernity*, Stanford: Stanford University Press.

87. Graham, J., 1992: "Post-Fordism as politics: the political consequences of narratives on the left," *Environment and Planning D: Society and Space* 10, pp. 393–420.

88. Pile, S. and Rose, G., 1992: "All or Nothing? Politics and Critique in the Modernism–Postmodernism Debate," *Environment and Planning D: Society and Space* 10, pp. 123–36; and especially Thrift, N. J., 1991: "For a New Regional Geography 2," *Progress in Human Geography*, 15(4), pp. 456–65; Thrift, N. J., 1993: "For a New Regional Geography 3," *Progress in Human Geography*, 17(1), pp. 92–100; see also Borgmann, A., 1992: *Crossing the Postmodern Divide*, Chicago: University of Chicago Press.

89. Hall, P., 1988: *Cities in Civilization*, New York: Pantheon, p. 14.

90. See Simonsen, K., 1990: "Planning on 'Postmodern' Conditions," *Acta Sociologica* 33, pp. 51–62; Punter, J., 1988: "Postmodernism," *Planning Practice and Research*, 4, pp. 22–8; Milroy, B. M., 1989: "Constructing and Deconstructing Plausibility," *Environment & Planning D: Society & Space* 7(3), pp. 313–26; Milroy, B. M., 1990: "Critical Capacity and Planning Theory," *Planning Theory Newsletter* 4: pp. 12–18; Milroy, B. M., 1991: "Into postmodern weightlessness," *Journal of Planning Education and Research* 10, pp. 181–7.

91. Crow, D., "Le Corbusier's Post-Modern Plan," in Crow, D. (ed.) 1990: *Philosophical Streets: New Approaches to Urbanism*, Washington DC: Maisonneuve Press, pp. 71–92.

92. Beauregard, R. A., 1991: "Without a Net: Modernist Planning and the Postmodern Abyss," *Journal of Planning Education and Research*, 10, p. 193; see also Beauregard, R. A., 1989: "Between Modernity and Postmodernity: The Ambiguous Position of U.S. Planning," *Society and Space*, 7.

93. Beauregard, R. A. "Without a Net," p. 192.

94. Ibid., p. 193.

95. Beauregard, R. A., 1994: *Distracted Cities*, Los Angeles: UCLA Graduate School of Architecture & Urban Planning, p. 6.

96. Ibid., p. 12.

97. Ibid.

98. Hoch, C. J., 1992: "The Paradox of Power in Planning Practice," *Journal of Planning Education and Research* 11, p. 207.

99. The phrase is due to Mandelbaum, S., 1988: "Open Moral Communities: Theorizing about Planning within Myths about Community," *Society* 26(1), pp. 20–7.

100. Hoch, C., 1994: *What Planners Do: Power, Politics & Persuasion*, Chicago: Planners Press.

101. Ibid., Chapter 12.

102. Harper, T. L. and Stein, S. M., 1995: "Out of the Postmodern Abyss: Preserving the Rationale for Liberal Planning," *Journal of Planning Education & Research* 14, pp. 233–44.

103. Ibid., p. 233.

104. Ibid.

105. Ibid., p. 240.

106. Ibid. I think the terminology of *full-blown* postmodernism is ill advised, since the only other context where this term is in current use is in the case of AIDS/HIV (as in: full-blown AIDS).

107. Ibid., p. 241.

108. Ibid.
109. Ibid., p. 242.
110. Ibid.
111. Ibid., emphasis is original.
112. Ibid.
113. Beauregard, R. A., 1993: *Voices of Decline: The Postwar Fate of U.S. Cities*, Oxford: Blackwell, p. x.
114. Ibid., p. 49.
115. Ibid., p. 280.
116. Ibid., p. 281.
117. Harper, T. L. and Stein, S. M., "Postmodernist Planning Theory: The Incommensurability Premise," in Mandelbaum, S. J., Mazza, L. and Burchell, R. W. (eds) 1996: *Explorations in Planning Theory*, New Brunswick: Center for Urban Policy Research, pp. 414–29.
118. Hillier, J. 1996: "Deconstructing the Discourse of Planning," pp. 289–98; Allen, J. 1996. "Our Town: Foucault and Knowledge-Based Politics in London," pp. 328–44; Flyvbjerg, B. 1996: "The Dark Side of Planning: Rationality and 'Realrationalität'," pp. 383–94. All these essays appear in Mandelbaum, S. J., Mazza, L., and Burchell, R.W. (eds), *Explorations in Planning Theory*.
119. Sandercock, L. 1998: *Toward Cosmopolis: Planning for Multicultural Cities*, New York: Wiley.
120. Ibid. pp. 27–30.
121. Ibid. pp. 163.
122. Ibid. pp. 199.
123. Ibid. p. 214.
124. Ibid. pp. 218–9.
125. Ellis, J. M., 1989: *Against Deconstruction*, Princeton: Princeton University Press, Chapter 7.

Epilogue: Beyond Postmodernism

There is no room for caution in these closing paragraphs, so let me be clear about my assertions. We live in a postmodern age, characterized by a 'radical break' in the way we know things, and in the way cities are created. These ruptures in epistemology and material life may be distinguished as (respectively) *postmodernism* and *postmodernity*.

Postmodernism is an ontological stance that incorporates the conditions of knowing as an integral part of the problematic of social theory. Truth, morality, fact – all are conditional, contextual, and contested. Postmodernism foregrounds what was already evident, but often buried: that radical incommensurabilities separate many views about things worth knowing about the world. Our knowledge lacks firm reference points; indeed, it is the absence of such mental moorings that defines the real. The postmodern challenge is to locate ways of dealing with this, particularly to determine the diverse degrees of veracity, and the contingencies of morality and social choice. A key piece in the postmodern puzzle has been the resurrection of space in social theory. In retrospect, this is easy to understand, since postmodernism's relativism has emphasized the need for groundedness in social analysis (sometimes literally). Despite talk of placelessness, time–space compression, and the like, the postmodern hyperspace is resolutely place-bound.

Postmodernity refers to a radical break in the material conditions of human existence. In Western thought, its earliest obsession with culture is best understood as a post-structural correction to structuralism's regard of the cultural as epiphenomenal. My inquiry has extended postmodernity's interrogation of the material to incorporate the urban condition. The signature difference in postmodern urbanism is that the urban hinterland is now organizing what is left of the center, whereas in previous eras it was the center that structured the hinterlands. The processual dynamics causing this shift, plus the consequent mutations in urban morphology, include flexism, hybridity, globalization, and a privatized civic will.

Taken together, postmodernity and postmodernism have highlighted the issue of representation, including the difficulties of theorizing contemporaneity, as well as the authoritarian ambiguities uncovered by deconstructionism. In the relationship between architecture and film, I excavated another key trope of the postmodern turn: the shift from the logocentric to the virtual/visual now dominates the interpretive gaze; and the screen becomes the cultural dominant of the postmodern. In postmodernism/postmodernity, cybercities and virtual realities dominate emerging utopian discourse; yet human life, as I have stressed, perforce remains in place. In this way, postmodern urbanism is axiomatically an environmental issue. Nanotechnic biocentrism is a way of positioning the virtual/real urban against the finiteness of Nature's resources; it merges ontological consciousness with vital material questions of planetary and species survival.

Intentionality in postmodern urbanism is about politics. How could it be otherwise? Our ability to choose, to act, even to speak about the future depends on how we adjust to the altered intentionalities of a postmodern age. Politics begins with the personal, but quickly proceeds to local as well as global place-making. A radical de-centeredness has impacted both identity politics and geopolitics. Multiculturalism, minoritization, and hybridization define the postmodern urban condition, as do the belligerent local autonomies and viability crises that undermine the nation state. Endemic to all level of politics is the evacuation of traditional alliances and frameworks of meaning. In the politics of the culture wars, including academic life, we encounter analogous de-centerings. These are met this time by the exterminating gestures of people unwilling to relinquish their power and authority. Postmodernism has exposed the sham of scholarship – its pretense of objectivity, its false accuracies, its vacuous authority. In postmodernism/postmodernity, a higher degree of scholarly integrity is possible.

I am loath to end this book. It is only a preliminary statement on the postmodern urban condition; and despite its length, a great deal has been left out. My greatest hope is that others will now take up its challenges. My principal fear is that critics will sigh: "It's all been said before; there's nothing new here!" But the capitalism of the information age is radically different from what preceded it; and those reassuring historical–geographical equivalences (between, say, the morphologies of medieval and contemporary suburbs) entirely miss the crucial differences in the present. The reductionism inherent in these crass oversimplifications is essentially conservative in outlook, with dangerous tendencies toward erasure, the silencing of alternative voices.

In the final analysis, I speak only for myself. I do not pretend to be a 'pure' postmodernist; my scholarly, personal and professional lives are too committed to social activism to be comfortable with extremes of relativism. But my youthful commitments to scientific and Marxian epistemologies (both characterized by a naked search for order and causality!) have been radically undermined. After postmodernism, I understand why I can never have the same knowledge. This is a personal discovery that I heartily commend to others, for the task now is to embrace postmodernity even as we reach beyond postmodernism.

A Beginners' Guide to Postmodernism

There are more than enough references in this book's bibliography to satisfy even the most avid consumer of postmodernism. This Guide is addressed to those less familiar with the field, and who need a beginner's map to enable them to gain a rapid understanding of postmodernism's frames of reference.

Absolute neophytes could do a lot worse than open up Jim Powell's *Postmodernism for Beginners* for a cartoon-infested orientation. Just as quirky is Joseph Natoli's *A Primer to Postmodernity.*

To understand why postmodernism is on the intellectual horizon at this time, works by Charlene Spretnak and Stephen Toulmin provide a long view of the evolution of Western thought. Ian Craib gives a short, witty introduction to what's at stake in "modern social theory."

Sooner or later, the beginner will need to confront some of the classics in the field. Fredric Jameson's 1984 essay is an essential point of departure; and Hal Foster's edited collection (originally published 1983) is still read by many seeking to grasp the outlines of the post-modern turn.

I think that Best and Kellner's *Postmodern Theory* remains the best single account of the origins and consequences of postmodern thought. Pauline Rosenau provides another good introduction targeted specifically toward social scientists. Charles Jencks' *The Postmodern Reader* is unusually broad in its overview, encompassing culture, architecture, urbanism, feminism, science and religion.

The best collection of essays summarizing feminism's intersection with postmodernism is Linda Nicholson's *Feminism/Postmodernism.*

Needless to say, culture plays a big role in the postmodern oeuvre. Steven Connor's is an excellent introduction. Those interested in art, literature, and poetry should consult Risatti, Geyh et al., and Hoover, respectively. An excellent critical perspective on the architecture of postmodernism is that by Nan Ellin.

Less well covered is the field of political economy. Perhaps Krishan Kumar's *From Post-Industrial to Post-Modern Society* is the most accessible and convincing. Anne Friedberg's *Window Shopping* is, for me, the most engaging and illuminating treatment of the cinema and postmodernism.

In the specific fields of geography and planning, as they have encountered the postmodern turn, I recommend the collection by Benko and Strohmayer, and Leone Sandercock's *Cosmopolis.* Bob Beauregard's *Voices of Decline* is a good introduction to the work of a sensitive, sensible urbanist. Derek Gregory's *Geographical Imaginations* is not a book for beginners, but it is by far the best explanation of space in a wide range of contemporary social theories.

Those who are against postmodernism tend to produce somewhat arcane and self-referential texts (a complaint that could also be leveled at much postmodern writing!). Terry Eagleton's *The Illusions of Postmodernism* may be the best place to begin.

Since I have relied so much on Los Angeles and Southern California as my inspiration in this book, let me conclude by suggesting three books that, taken together, form the most comprehensible available history of this unbelievable city: McWilliams takes a long view of Southern California; Fogelson surveys LA's urban history up to 1930; and Mike Davis bring that history up to date. For a flavor of what is happening as LA encounters the postmodern, see the collections by Scott and Soja (*The City*), and Dear, Schockman and Hise (*Rethinking Los Angeles*).

Beauregard, R.A. 1993: *Voices of Decline: the postwar fate of U.S. cities*, Oxford: Blackwell.

Benko, G. and Strohmayer, U. (eds), 1997: *Space and Social Theory: Interpreting Modernity and Postmodernity*, Oxford: Blackwell.

Best, S. and Kellner, D. 1991: *Postmodern Theory: Critical Interrogations*, New York: Guilford.

Connor, S. 1989: *Postmodernist Culture*, Oxford: Blackwell.

Craib, I. 1992: *Modern Social Theory: From Parsons to Habermas* (2nd edition), New York: Harvester Wheatsheaf.

Davis, M. 1990: *City of Quartz: Excavating the Future in Los Angeles*, New York: Verso.

Dear, M., Schockman, H.E., and Hise, G. (eds), 1996: *Rethinking Los Angeles*, Thousand Oaks: Sage Publications.

Eagleton, T. 1996: *The Illusions of Postmodernism*, Oxford: Blackwell.

Ellin: N. 1996: *Postmodern Urbanism*, Oxford: Blackwell.

Fogelson, R. 1967: *The Fragmented Metropolis: Los Angeles 1850–1930*, Berkeley: University of California Press.

Foster, H. (ed.) 1985: *Postmodern Culture*, London: Pluto Press. First published as *The Anti-Aesthetic*, 1983. Port Townsend: Bay Press.

Friedberg, A. 1993: *Window Shopping: Cinema and the Postmodern*, Berkeley: University of California Press.

Geyh, P., Leebrou, F.G., and Levy, A. (eds), 1998: *Postmodern American Fiction: A Norton Anthology*, New York: Norton.

Gregory, D. 1993: *Geographical Imaginations*, Oxford: Blackwell.

Hoover, P. (ed.) 1994: *Postmodern American Poetry: A Norton Anthology*, New York: Norton.

Jameson, F. 1992: *Postmodernism, or the Cultural Logic of Late Capitalism*, Durham: Duke University Press. Chapter 1 was originally published in *New Left Review*, 146, 1984.

Jencks, C. (ed.) 1992: *The Postmodern Reader*, London: Academy Editions.

Kumar, K. 1995: *From Post-Industrial to Post-Modern Society*, Oxford: Blackwell.

McWilliams, C. 1946: *Southern California: An Island on the Land*, Salt Lake City: Peregrine Smith Books.

Natoli, J. 1997: *A Primer to Postmodernity*, Oxford: Blackwell.

Nicholson, L.J. (ed.) 1990: *Feminism/Postmodernism*, New York: Routledge.

Powell, J. 1998: *Postmodernism for Beginners*, New York: Writers and Readers.

Risatti, H. 1990: *Postmodern Perspectives: Issues in Contemporary Art*, Englewood Cliffs: Prentice-Hall.

Rosenau, P. M. 1992: *Postmodernism and the Social Sciences*, Princeton: Princeton University Press.

Sandercock, L. 1998: *Towards Cosmopolis: Planning for Multi-cultural cities*, Chichester: John Wiley.

Scott, A. J. and Soja, E. (eds), 1996: *The City: Los Angeles and Urban Theory at the End of the Twentieth Century*, Berkeley: University of California Press.

Spretnak, C. 1997: *The Resurgence of the Real: Body, Nature, and Place in a Hypermodern World*, Reading: Addison-Wesley.

Toulmin, S. 1990: *Cosmopolis: The Hidden Agenda of Modernity*, New York: The Free Press.

Index